WITHDRAWN

Humor in
British Literature,
From the Middle Ages
to the Restoration

Humor in British Literature, From the Middle Ages to the Restoration

A Reference Guide

DON L. F. NILSEN

GREENWOOD PRESS
Westport, Connecticut • London

Library of Congress Cataloging-in-Publication Data

Nilsen, Don Lee Fred.
    Humor in British literature, from the Middle Ages to the
Restoration : a reference guide / Don L. F. Nilsen.
        p. cm.
    Includes bibliographical references (p.) and index.
    ISBN 0-313-29706-1 (alk. paper)
    1. English wit and humor—History and criticism—Bibliography.
2. English literature—Middle English, 1100–1500—History and
criticism—Bibliography.   3. English literature—Early modern.
1500–1700—History and criticism—Bibliography.   4. English drama
(Comedy)—History and criticism—Bibliography.   5. Civilization,
Medieval, in literature—Bibliography.
    Z2014.W57N55   1997
    [PR931.N]
    016.827009—dc20   96–26190

British Library Cataloguing in Publication Data is available.

Library of Congress Catalog Card Number: 96–26190
ISBN: 0–313–29706–1

First published in 1997

Greenwood Press, 88 Post Road West, Westport, CT 06881
An imprint of Greenwood Publishing Group, Inc.

Printed in the United States of America

The paper used in this book complies with the
Permanent Paper Standard issued by the National
Information Standards Organization (Z39.48–1984).

10 9 8 7 6 5 4 3 2

Copyright Acknowledgements

The author and publisher are grateful for permission to reprint the following material:

Raymond MacDonald Alden. *The Rise of Formal Satire in England under Classical Influence* (1961). Permission granted by University of Pennsylvania Press.

A. G. L'Estrange. *History of English Humour* (1878). Permission was requested from Franklin Press, but this press is no longer in operation. Note that *History of English Humour* was published more than 100 years ago.

Marylynn Layman. "A Language Best Conceived," a 1944 M.A. Thesis at Arizona State University. Permission granted by Marylynn Layman.

John Peter. *Complaint and Satire in Early English Literature* (1956). Permission granted by Oxford University Press, and from the Clarendon Press.

Alice Rayner. *Comic Persuasion: Moral Structure in British Comedy from Shakespeare to Stoppard* (1987). Permission granted by University of California Press.

Hugh Walker. *English Satire and Satirists* (1925). Permission granted from J. M. Dent.

Robert N. Watson. *Ben Jonson's Parodic Strategy: Literary Imperialism in the Comedies* (1987). Permission granted by Harvard University Press, and the President and Fellows of Harvard College.

Trevor Woodford. "Shakespeare's Comic Characters." Unpublished Paper at Arizona State University, 1994. Permission granted by Trevor Woodford.

Every reasonable effort has been made to trace the owners of copyright materials in this book, but in some instances this has proven impossible. The author and publisher will be glad to receive information leading to more complete acknowledgments in subsequent printings of the book and in the meantime extend their apologies for any omissions.

Dedicated to Robert E. Bjork, Daniel T. Brink, and Jean R. Brink, who have played such an active roll in the development of the Arizona State University Branch of the Arizona Center for Medieval and Renaissance Studies

Contents

Preface

This book is arranged chronologically according to the birth year of the author being discussed. Note that for ease of reference the birth and death dates of the various authors are given both in the text and in the index. The main body of the book is divided into four centuries, Fourteenth, Fifteenth, Sixteenth, and Seventeenth; however these chapters are preceded by a "foregrounding" chapter on "Humor in Medieval British Literature.

Such terms as "humour," "wit," and "comedy" have changed drastically between the time of the Middle Ages and the Restoration. This book documents that change. It also documents the love that England has for eccentrics, and the reputation that England has for appreciating and encouraging a sense of humor. England has a very long tradition of joke telling. Throughout English history, it is Joe Miller's name that it most associated with the joking tradition. W. Carew Hazlitt says, "He is the jocular laureate of the new Hanoverian time and of all time to come.... He will endure as long as the earth's crust--as long as Shakespeare, and longer, perhaps, than Milton" (Jerrold 58). Joe Miller wrote during a time when lengthy titles were in vogue, and the title of one of his books is as follows:

> Joe Miller's Jests; or, the Wit's Vade-Mecum; being a collection of the most brilliant Jests; the politest Repartees; the most elegant Bon Mots and most pleasant Short Stories in the English language. First carefully collected in the company, and many of them transcribed from the mouth of the Facetious Gentleman whose name they bear; and now set forth and published by his lamentable friend and former companion, Elijah Jenkins, Esq. Most humbly inscribed to those Choice Spirits of the Age, Captain Bodens, Mr. Alexander Pope, Mr. Professor Lacy, Mr. Orator Henley, and Job Baker, the Kettle-Drummer. London: Printed and sold by T. Read, in Dogwell Court, White's Fryars. Fleet Street. MDCCXXXIX. (Jerrold 59)

Although significant bodies of humorous literature written by British authors can be found in almost any library in the world, and although there is much criticism of this humorous literature around the world, it is at present very difficult to find and use the appropriate criticism of humorous literature. As a result many critics write criticisms of humorous literature without a full appreciation of the criticism that has already been written, and which would probably influence their treatment if they had access to it. This book is written, therefore, in hopes of acquainting critics of humorous literature with the appropriate criticism that has already been written. Rather than starting from scratch, they can then start by standing on the shoulders of previous critics.

Acknowledgments

I would like to express my appreciation to members of the Arizona State University Humanities Computing Facility--Dan Brink, Mike Hopper, Lorna Hughes, and Peter Lafford--for managing the facility in such a way as to make it convenient to provide high quality camera ready copy to the publisher. I would also like to express my appreciation to Karen Adams, Dawn Bates, Willis Buckingham, Lee Croft, Barbara Lafford, Roy Major, Elly van Gelderen, and Wendy Wilkins, for their encouragement and support of scholarly research.

Special thanks goes to Robert E. Bjork, O. M. (Skip) Brack, Dan Brink, Jean R. Brink, Arthur L. Colby, Taylor Corse, Bruce Davis, Bettie Anne Doebler, John W. Doebler, John X. Evans, James L. Green, Nancy Gutierrez, Kathryn M. Harris, Marjorie J. Lightfoot, Dhira B. Mahoney, Sandra Nagy, Anita Obermeier, Curtis Perry, Sean Pollack, John D. Ramage, David Schwalm, Thelma J. Shinn, Scott Stevens, Gene Valentine and Michael Vanden Heuvel for their constant input on Medieval, Renaissance, and Restoration Humor, and also for reading large sections of the manuscript and offering many important suggestions for expansion and revision. Special thanks goes to Nicolette (Nilsen) Wickman for reading the manuscript and offering many important suggestions for revision. Extra special thanks goes to my wife, Alleen, who has seen or heard the manuscript in many forms and has offered tons of constructive criticism.

Without the above support, and without a sabbatical leave from Arizona State University, there is little hope that this project would ever have been completed.

Introduction

Tragedy vs. Comedy:

In discussing the relationship between tragedy and comedy, Walter Sorell made the following statement: "Tragedy preceded comedy by about fifty years, and every human being has cried before he learned to laugh. Our first reaction to life is a cry, while the pleasurable feelings leading to a smile come later" (Sorell 319). But even though tragedy precedes comedy, both for the individual and for the development of mankind in general, it is comedy, not tragedy that tends to survive the test of time:

> Who, in his right theatrical mind, would produce George Lillo's Merchant of London nowadays? Yet John Gay's Beggar's Opera--a satire by Lillo's contemporary--has triumphed in its Brechtian version in our time. How often do we see a tragedy by Dryden? How often a comedy by Congreve, Wycherley, Goldsmith, or Sheridan? How contemporary is Molière! How faded the writers of tragedies, Racine and Corneille, with whom he shared the stage! (Sorell 322)

British Comedy:

In a book entitled Comic Persuasion: Moral Structure in British Comedy from Shakespeare to Stoppard, Alice Rayner presents a rather good definition of comedy:

> Virtue and appetite, sobriety and revelry, respectability and knavery, constancy and mutability: the opposition of moral conditions like these defines the fundamental moral tension in many comedies. Comedy often operates out of the collision of desires and restrictions. (Rayner 24)

Almost all of the humor discussed in this book has universal qualities, qualities which transcend the time and the place of its original appearance. However one of the reasons for writing a book of this nature is to go back in time and go across the ocean in space and find out about how people in other times and places think. This book is therefore very concerned with trends in literature, and how these trends reflect the spirit of the times (Zeitgeist) in which they were written.

Vernacular Humor and the Oral Tradition in British Literature:

Humor and comedy were firmly established in English literature during the fourteenth century, and the single most important author in doing this was, of course, Geoffrey Chaucer (1340-1400). Chaucer's writing was significantly influenced by the Roman literary tradition. Anne Payne suggests that Chaucer's Troilus and Criseyde, his The Nun's Priest's Tale, and his The Knight's Tale were all influenced by the tradition of Menippean satire, especially such writers as Seneca, Petronius, Apuleius, and especially Lucian and Boethius. Payne feels that Chaucer read these authors not only as philosophers, but as satirists as well (x). Based on Earle Birney's work, Beryl Rowland distinguishes seven distinct types of irony that are to be found in Chaucer's writing, and suggests that Chaucer himself was very aware of the distinctions. They were 1) verbal irony, 2) narrator vs. poet irony, 3) dramatic irony, 4) cosmic irony, 5) irony of values and beliefs, 6) thematic irony, and 7) structural irony (Rowland xviii-xxvi)

The Complaint as Forerunner of Satire in British Literature:

One of the earliest forms of humor was the "complaint," which was later to develop into the "satire." This genre was already well developed by William Langland's time (c1332-c1400), and with Langland, as with many other authors, the language of the complaint was often "nothing more than a tissue of Latin and English puns" (Peter 290). The complaint travelled from the fourteenth century into the later centuries in the writings of William Langland (c1332-c1400), Geoffrey Chaucer (1340-1400, John Lydgate (1370-c1451), Alexander Barclay (c1475-1552), John Harington (1561-1612), John Marston (c1575-1634), and Cyril Tourneur (c1575-1626). Langland describes the erratic gait of a drunken glutton stumbling in all directions, like a man setting his lines to snare birds. Similarly, Chaucer satirically compares an "old man lechur" to a dog lifting its leg and making "a countenaunce" to empty its bladder. Lydgate used "antiphrasis" in the complex alliteration of his Treatise of a Galaunt, in which each of seven stanzas alliterates on a new letter, eventually spelling out the word "galawnt." Barclay's complaints contain vivid and accurate observations, and are written in the vernacular. Harington laments that "fauorites increase the Churches rents." Marston and Tourner use a great deal of imagery in their complaints (Peter 290). Typically, the "complaint" was written in verse form, and it was racy, vivid, colloquial, and used a great deal of language play (punning, etc.). John Peter believes that the "satyrist" of the seventeenth century inherited the earlier tradition of the "complaint" and refined it in the form of satiric dramatic plays (Peter 291).

Satire in British Literature:

Edward Rosenheim indicates that satire is an ancient genre, but compared with tragedy, or lyric poetry, it has received very little systematic discussion, because "The works which, at one time or another, have been called satiric represent an enormous diversity in substance, structure, style, and motive." In one age satire is marked by certain identifiable conventions; however in a later age these conventions disappear or altered (Rosenheim 2). Because it is so topical, satire resists our attempts to establish principles which can be used to identify the satirist over the ages. We can, however, assume that the satirist is a hard-boiled individualist,

> ...whose talent for derision can be employed to advantage upon those who strive to reduce his art to rules and who plod in his wake with solemn explanations of what it is that he has done. When the satirist discusses his own art, he is seldom very thorough or convincing: Swift's statements about satire are oblique and fragmentary, Dryden's pedantic and sanctimonious, Pope's of doubtful applicability to his own work. (Rosenheim 3)

William Anderson sees satire as shapeless, but also as capable of assuming many shapes. It is a highly unstable genre because it has an inconsistent points of view, and elusive themes. The satirist like the satire he creates is also unstable. "We consider the satirist himself unstable, inconsistent, an unsettling fellow who mixes laughter with anger." Both the satirist and the satire are chameleon-like. They are multiformed and multi-toned, because "satire keeps turning towards its audience and playing up to its sense of humor, its delight with wit and literary finesse as well as to its moral perceptions" (Anderson 211).

Throughout the centuries writers with a strong commitment to religion have written satires that criticize religion. The literary talents of these churchmen have seldom been challenged even by the harshest critics. Such authors as Chaucer, Dante, Erasmus, Jerome, Langland, More, Lucian, Luther, Pope, and Swift have written strong satires against certain church practices even though the Christian commitment of these men could hardly be questioned. These writers have been considered by some in the church to be "humanistic harbingers, and therefore dangerous to the imperfectly literate multitudes" (Kantra). However, the greatness of these authors is due partly to their allegiance to their faith, and due partly to their commitment to literary values (Kantra 44).

In 1566, Thomas Harman published his Caveat or Warning for Common Cursetors. According to Hugh Walker there were three satires written around this time which dealt with vagabonds, and he feels that of the three, Walker's piece is the best, even though the satire in Harman's piece is largely incidental (Walker 91-92). William Roy and Jerome Barlow, two Franciscan friars who also flourished during the sixteenth century, wrote one of the earliest satires written England. It was entitled Rede Me and be nott Wrothe, and Hugh Walker considers it remarkable and deserving of close attention not because of its literary merit, but rather because of its significant place in history. The piece was written in response to the persecution of the Lutherans, and in fact was written by two friars who had been driven out of England and had to settle in Strasburg--where they wrote the satire (Walker 41).

Walker contrasts the contribution made to sixteenth century satire made by Joseph Hall with that made by Sir Thomas Wyatt. Walker points out that in the critical literature the space devoted to Hall is immense, while that devoted to Wyatt is paltry by comparison. Walker then continues:

> It is true that Wyatt has left only three satires, while to Hall we owe six books. It is true also that Hall's satires are in heroic couplets, which became the orthodox measure for the satire, while Wyatt's are not. But on the other hand, there is nothing in Hall more effective than Wyatt's pieces, and nothing comparable to them in charm. (Walker 59)

Walker points out that during the last few years of the reign of James I, and throughout the reign of William III, satire in England became incidental. This eclipse of satire in England occurred both in prose and in verse, and lasted about twenty years (Walker 120). Walker suggested the reason for the eclipse: "The carelessness, real or affected, of the Cavaliers was inconsistent with the seriousness of the sustained satire; and the seriousness of the Puritan, though more than sufficient, was the sort which finds expression rather in the pulpit. It is the final clash of the two which starts satire anew." (Walker 121)

Burlesque and Parody in British Literature:

Henryk Markiewicz distinguishes five kinds of parody, as follows:
PARODY SENSU LARGO: Comical recast or imitation of literary model
PARODY SENSU STRICTO: Comical Exaggeration and Condensation of the Features of the Literary Model

> LOW BURLESQUE: Comicality of discrepancy between serious subject and
>   low style
> HIGH BURLESQUE: Comicality of discrepancy between common or
>   trifling subject and high style
> TRAVESTY: Close imitation of the plot with details and style changed, or
>   close imitation of the pattern of style and composition of the model,
>   with change in content. (Petro 13)

In a book entitled Survey of Burlesque and Parody in English, George Kitchin notes
that parody and satire become especially for realistic authors either at the beginnings of
their careers, or at the ends. Fielding's first two novels are parodies. Jane Austen, Charles
Dickens, and William Makepeace Thackeray also wrote early parodies and burlesques
(Kitchin 247). Kitchin notes that burlesque is a serious art, and for a long time it has been
an established mode of criticism (Kitchin ix). Chaucer's Sir Thopas, a satire targeting
outworn literary conventions, is one of the first English examples of satiric parody, and
there has been a steady stream of such satiric parodies of medieval codes of love and
chivalry from Chaucer's time straight through to the Seventeenth Century. The most witty
of these satiric parodies were the result of schooling in the classics. In fact, parody exposes
this relationship more clearly than other forms of satire. Most of the parodies after Sir
Thopas were of mediocre quality, until the age of dramatic burlesque in the rule of King
James I. Apart from "burlesque drama" there is little more in the Tudor and Elizabethan
ages than the artless parodies of the poem-and-answer type which are sprinkled throughout
Tottel's Miscellany. There was later a genre which Kitchin calls "direct parody." This is
of the crude type of Marston's Pygmalion, which is probably a travesty of the school of
poetry to which Shakespeare's Venus and Adonis belongs. Many of these direct parodies
were amusing replies which "remind us that we are still living in the atmosphere of the late
medieval Querelle des Dames." Similarly, the songs of the Caroline lyricists were the
object of numerous witty or nasty rejoinders which found their way into political pieces in
the Seventeenth Century such as Mock Songs, Wit's Recreation, Wit Restored, Westminster
Drollery, etc. (Kitchin 8). The type of parody which was most prevalent during this time
would turn a Caroline lyric into something caustic and nasty (Kitchin 9).

Of equal coarseness were some of the political parodies, such as the Rump
collection of songs. At this time nearly every form of satiric parody could be found--the
mock epitaph, the mock elegy, the mock will and testament, as well as direct parodies.
Because of his superior wit, John Suckling stands out as a notable exception to this
"universal squalor." Suckling was "the experienced mocker, the complete atheist to love,"
but his indecencies identify his work with that of the coarser miscellanies. Hudibras was
to come later, as were imitations of Cervantes's Don Quixote, which had a certain vogue
in prose fiction. "But, on the whole, direct satire held the field in the age of Dryden and
Pope." Later there were the innumerable parodies of Alexander's Feast, and still later, of
Gray's Elegy. The parodies were evidences of the popularity of these poems, and no
criticism was involved in most of the parodies. More critical was The Rolliad, and in fact
the later Anti-Jacobins established parody as an increasingly successful rival of satire
(Kitchin xi).

Comedy, Theatre, and Drama in British Literature:

Lorraine Stock indicates that the ubiquity of humor in the English Mystery Play
Cycles has only recently been accepted by critics. Earlier critics had staunchly maintained
that these plays served a strictly religious purpose, and that any comic or secular aspects
were to be regarded as infringements upon and deterrents from the basic religious purpose
of the play. Stock believes, however that underneath the surface of formal seriousness

there can always be found "funny, bumptious, coarse, or improvisatory comic actions," and she feels that such actions "have their roots in serious earth" (Stock 211-212). For Stock, the slapstick, farce, parody, comic anachronism, and grotesque or cruel humor represented in the Chester Plays are not ornaments, but are an integral part of the dramatic structure. As she says, "the comedy is the foundation for the dramatic structure rather than a gay frieze applied to the already existing dramatic edifice" (Stock 226).

Irony and Wit in British Literature:

Irony was an important method that British authors used to achieve wit in their writing. Through irony, there was a discrepancy between what was said and what was meant (Hunt 16). Peter Pindar, for example, compared his dinner companions to beasts. Some were calves; others were hogs, bears, monkeys, cats, dogs, elephants, and even tigers (23). Burlesque is still another method a writer uses to achieve wit. The word "burlesque" comes from the Italian "burlare" meaning "to jest or jeer," and is associated with "burrasca" and "burberia" (storm and swelling). The term was originally used to describe the puffing and blowing of the cheeks of the old comedians, and is the caricature of the comic, or the mock-heroic style as opposed to the serious and pretentious style of the day (Hunt 25). One Cromwellite is said to have stated "Put your trust in God," but then he added, "and keep your powder dry" (Hunt 27). Still another way of achieving wit is through exaggeration. Shakespeare's Falstaff, for example, is an exaggeration both of praise and of blame (Hunt 33). And Hunt's final rhetorical device for achieving wit is wordplay. He lists puns, macaronic poetry, half-jargon burdens of songs and nonsense verses. In this device there is the juxtaposition of ideas having pleasant effects; but there is also the more superficial juxtaposition or association of comical sounds. In England the important distinction between wit and humor appears to have developed as the result of a hard-hitting verbal battle between John Dryden (1631-1700) and Thomas Shadwell (c1642-1692), one of Ben Jonson's disciples. Shadwell was trying to revive the older Jonson concept of "comedy of humors," while Dryden was trying to move on to the newer, more elegant and sophisticated, French-inspired, comedy of manners (Levin Veins 11).

Meanwhile in Ireland, Jonathan Swift (1667-1745) was avoiding the controversy altogether, for he felt that humor should not be analyzed. As Swift stated the matter, "What humor is, not all the tribe of logick-mongers can describe" (Levin Veins 2). Joseph Addison (1672-1719) was not convinced by Swift's pronouncement, for he thought he knew how to spot, and even evaluate true wit. For Addison, the test of true wit was its ability to be translated. He felt that genuine humor was transcendent, and should not, therefore, be bounded by frontiers of any kind. Harry Levin, however, points out that there is much to be learned from a foreign perspective, even when this foreign perspective is untranslatable. In fact, Levin believes that the development of humor in England was a direct result of the translation of humor from the continent. As he states it,

> Mr. Punch may embody the typically English figure of fun, yet he was born in Naples, and acquired his beak and hump in France.... The particularity of English humor seems, at all events, to have been universally acknowledged. Locally it was a matter of self-recognition--and of self-congratulation, too.... (Levin Veins 5)

Humorous British Poetry:

In a chapter entitled "Chaucer to Skelton," of Notes on English Verse Satire, Humbert Wolfe metaphorically tells the difference between prose and poetry: "Verse rings the gong. Prose lays (and even eats) the dinner." He continues that "verse has the hammer-note. It should therefore be, and is, the principal working-tool of the satirist (Wolfe 27). Since ridicule is an important aspect of satire, it is like a joke, and is best developed when the point is quickly made (Wolfe 33). Wolfe considers Chaucer to have been the most effective English writer of satiric verse (Wolfe 34). In Chaucer's Parlement of Foules, "he gave Occleve occasion for The Horse, Sheep, and the Goose, and encouraged Henryson in the tradition of Æsop. The same poem points the allegorical path to the rebuke of wickedness that is followed equally in Dunbar's The Dance of the Seven Deidle Synnes, and Skelton's The Bowge of Court." The satiric poets that followed Chaucer and preceded Skelton. "They are, let it be admitted, interesting rather as monuments than as living poetry. Lydgate and Occleve are noticeable primarily as showing the triumph of Chaucer and not in themselves" (Wolfe 39-40). Dunbar and Burns are both harsh satirists as they target their native lands. There is a great deal of sting in Dunbar's To the Merchantes of Edinburgh, which reads in part as follows:

> My nane pas throw your principall Gaittis
> For stink of haddockis and of scaittis;
> For cryes of carlinges and dibaittis;
>   For fensum flyttingis of defame;
>   Think ye nocht schame,
> Befoir strangeris of all estaittis
>   That sic dishonour hurt your Name!" (Wolfe 41)

There is also much sting in Dunbar's Tydingis fra the Sessioun, and his Testament of Mr. Andro Kennedy (Wolfe 42). J. D. Browning considers the focus of Morris Brownell's "Poetical Villas: English Verse Satire of the Country House 1700-1750" to be "ridicule, complaint, and the deft traducing of an ideal" (Browning 3).

Feminist Issues in British Humorous Literature:

In a book entitled Comic Women, Tragic Men, Linda Bamber suggests that in Shakespeare's plays the natural order is for men to rule women, and that it is an exceptional situation whenever they fail to do so. But Bamber further suggests that in comedy the pattern is reversed, for it is common here for women to rule men (Bamber 27). In comedy, women are given holiday from social constraints. They are allowed to rebel against the rules of everyday life. In comedy, Shakespeare endorses both sides. "Holiday is, of course, the subject and the analogue of each play; but the plays always end in a return to everyday life" (Bamber 30).

When he is writing comedies, Shakespeare is almost a feminist, or if not that, he is at least "a man who takes the woman's part." "Often the women in the comedies are more brilliant than the men, more aware of themselves and their world, saner, livelier, more gay. In the tragedies, however, Shakespeare creates such nightmare female figures as Goneril, Regan, Lady Macbeth, and Volumnia" (Bamber 2).

Bamber relies on C. L. Barber's distinction between satirical and saturnalian comedy to help support her claim. According to this distinction, satirical comedy deals with the relationships between social classes and the aberrations in dealings between them. Saturnalian comedy, on the other hand, is only incidentally satiric. It derives from the movement between the antithetical poles of restraint and release. The shrew is the figure of satire and the comic heroine is the figure of saturnalia, because the shrew is an aberration in the social order, while the comic heroine is proof that the social order can expand to meet new conditions.

> Satirical comedy has a kind of righting moment: disorder is introduced into
> a society that rights itself like a balance toy that has been pulled over.... But
> in saturnalian comedy the pleasure comes from the temporary release, as it

were, from the laws of gravity altogether. The return to normalcy is implicit, but it does not provide the energy that drives the play. (Bamber 36)

Margaret McDonald considers the comic heroines of English restoration drama to be saucy, and independent. She compares Millamant in William Congreve's The Way of the World (1700) to Shakespeare's Beatrice and to Shaw's Vivi Warren as three of the most delightful heroines in all of English drama.

> She represents...the flowering of a long tradition of young, intelligent, articulate women who rebel against a male-dominated society. That tradition must include the heroines of Dryden, Etherege, Wycherly and Crowne, as well as the young women who dominate the comedies of Southerne, Vanbrugh and Cibber in Congreve's own decade. (McDonald 1)

McDonald suggests that one of the most important contributions to English Restoration drama was the use of actresses on the English stage. In 1642 there had been an edict of English Parliament that all London theatres were to be closed, and prior to this time, all roles were played by men, with young boys assuming the female roles. But in 1660, Charles II reopened the theaters and granted licenses to the King's Company and the Duke's Company, and from this time on, women graced the London stage. McDonald feels that what made this drastic change possible was the exile of Charles II to France when his father Charles I was executed in 1649. While in France, Charles II frequented the court of the French King Louis IV. By the time he arrived in Dover, England, in May of 1660 to restore the English monarchy, "he brought with him a coterie of Royalist cavaliers who had left England during Cromwell's Commonwealth and had, like Charles himself, absorbed many of the French mannerisms and an interest in French drama"--a drama which had women playing many of the major roles (McDonald 2).

In an article entitled "Dwindling into Wifehood: The Romantic Power of the Witty Heroine in Shakespeare, Dryden, Congreve, and Austen," Donald Bloom looked at the witty dialogue of five comic heroines: Rosalind from Shakespeare's As You Like It, Florimell from Dryden's Secret Love and Doralice from his Marriage à la Mode, Millamant from Congreve's The Way of the World, and Elizabeth Bennet from Austen's Pride and Prejudice, the first four of these being plays, and the last containing many scenes that exhibit "superb comic drama" form (Bloom 53). These witty heroines use verbal power games with the romantic heroes in a way that demonstrates both their power and their strong personalities (Bloom 54).

Introduction Bibliography

Alden, Raymond MacDonald. The Rise of Formal Satire in England under Classical Influence. New York, NY: Archon, 1961.

Anderson, William. "The Mock-Heroic Mode in Roman Satire and Alexander Pope." Satire in the 18th Century. Ed. J. D. Browning. New York, NY: Garland 1983. 198-213.

Bloom, Donald A. "Dwindling into Wifehood: The Romantic Power of the Witty Heroine in Shakespeare, Dryden, Congreve, and Austen." Look Who's Laughing: Gender and Comedy. Ed. Gail Finney. Amsterdam, Netherlands: Gordon and Breach, 1994. 53-80.

Bloom, Edward A., and Lillian D. Bloom. Satire's Persuasive Voice. Ithaca, NY: Cornell University Press, 1979.

Blyth, Reginald H. Humor in English Literature: A Chronological Anthology. Tokyo, Japan: The Folcroft Press, 1970.

Carlson, Richard S. "Benign Humorists of Children's Literature: Milne, Potter, and Wodehouse." The Benign Humorists. New York: Archon, 1975.

Carlson, Susan. Women and Comedy: Rewriting the British Theatrical Tradition. Ann

Arbor, MI: University of Michigan Press, 1991.

Cazamian, Louis. The Development of English Humor Durham, NC: Duke University Press, 1952.

Elkin, P. K. The Augustan Defence of Satire. Oxford, England: Oxford University Press, 1973.

Evans, James E. "English Comic Literature." Comedy: An Annotated Bibliography of Theory and Criticism. Metuchen, NJ: Scarecrow Press, 1987, 105-176.

Feinberg, Leonard. The Satirist: His Temperament, Motivation, and Influence. New York, NY: Citadel Press, 1965.

Guilhamet, Leon. Satire and the Transformation of Genre. Philadelphia, PA: University of Pennsylvania Press, 1987.

Hammer, Stephanie Barbé. Satirizing the Satirist: Critical Dynamics in Swift, Diderot, and Jean Paul. New York, NY: Garland, 1990.

Hannay, James. Satire and Satirists. Folcroft, PA: Folcroft Press, 1854.

Harrop, John. "The Last Laugh: Comedy as a Political Touchstone in Britain from The Entertainer to Comedians. Theatre Journal 32 (1980): 5-16.

Harvey, William. Scottish Chapbook Literature. New York, NY: Burt Franklin, 1903.

Heath-Stubbs, John. The Verse Satire. London, England: Oxford University Press, 1969.

Hunt, Leigh. Wit and Humour Selected from the English Poets. London, England: Smith, Elder and Co. 1882.

Jerrold, Walter. A Book of Famous Wits. London, England: Methuen, 1913.

Kantra, Robert A. All Things Vain: Religious Satirists and Their Art. University Park: Penna State University Press, 1984.

King, William, and John Arbuthnot, eds. A Miscellany of the Wits. London, England: Philip Allan, 1920.

Kitchin, George. Survey of Burlesque and Parody in English. New Haven, CT: Yale University Press, 1959.

Kirk, Eugene P. Menippean Satire: An Annotated Catalogue of Texts and Criticism. New York, NY: Garland, 1980.

L'Estrange, A. G. History of English Humour. New York, NY: Burt Franklin, 1878.

Levin, Harry. Playboys and Killjoys: An Essay on the Theory and Practice of Comedy. New York: Oxford Univ Press, 1987.

Levin, Harry, ed. Veins of Humor. Cambridge, MA: Harvard Univ Press, 1972.

Lockwood, Thomas. "The Augustan Author-Audience Relationship: Satiric vs. Comic Forms." Journal of English Literary History 36 (1969): 648-658.

Mathewson, Louise. Bergson's Theory of the Comic in the Light of English Comedy. New York, NY: Oxford University Press, 1987.

Moore, John B. The Comic and the Realistic in English Drama. New York, NY: Russell, 1965.

Parnell, Michael, ed. Meadow Prospect Revisited. Bridgend, Wales: Seren Books, 1992.

Payne, F. Anne. Chaucer and Menippean Satire. Madison, WI: University of Wisconsin Press, 1981.

Pearson, Hesketh. Lives of the Wits New York, NY: Harper and Row, 1962.

Peter, John. Complaint and Satire in Early English Literature. Oxford, England: The Clarendon Press, 1956.

Petro, Peter. Modern Satire: Four Studies. Berlin, Germany: Mouton, 1982.

Pollard, Arthur. Satire. New York, NY: Methuen, 1970.

Previté-Orton, C. W. Political Satire in English Poetry. New York, NY: Henry Holt, 1954, 133-150.

Priestly, J. B. The English Comic Characters. New York, NY: Phaeton, 1972.

Priestley, J. B. English Humour. New York: Stein and Day, 1976.

Rayner, Alice. Comic Persuasion: Moral Structure in British Comedy from Shakespeare to Stoppard. Berkeley, CA: University of California Press, 1987.

Richards, Alun. Dai Country. New York, NY: Michael Joseph, 1973.

Richards, Alun. The Former Miss Merlthyr Tydfil. New York, NY: Penguin, 1979.

Rodway, Allan. English Comedy: Its Role and Nature from Chaucer to the Present Day. Berkeley, CA: University of California Press, 1975.

Rogers, Pat. Grub Street: Studies in a Subculture. London, England: Methuen, 1972.

Rosenheim, Edward W., Jr. Swift and the Satirist's Art. Chicago, IL: University of Chicago Press, 1963.

Rowland, Beryl, ed. Essays on Chaucerian Irony. Toronto, Canada: Univ of Toronto Press, 1985.

Russell, Leonard, ed. English Wits. London, England: Hutchinson, 1940.

Sampson, H. Grant. "The Phormio Syndrome: The Tricky Slave in English Comedy." From Pen to Performance: Drama as Conceived and Performed. Ed. Karelisa V. Hartigan. Lanham, MD: University Press of America, 1983. 91-101.

Sewell, Elizabeth. The Field of Nonsense. London, England: Chatto and Windus, 1952.

Simpson, Harold. Excursions in Comedy. London, England: Besant, 1930.

Sitter, John. Arguments of Augustan Wit. New York, NY: Cambridge University Press, 1991.

Sorell, Walter Facets of Comedy New York, NY: Grosset and Dunlap, 1972.

Stock, Lorraine Kochanske. "Comedy in the English Mystery Cycles: Three Comic Scenes in the Chester Shepherd's Play." Versions of Medieval Comedy Ed. Paul G. Ruggiers. Norman, OK: Univ of Oklahoma Press, 1977, 211-226.

Stubbs, John Heath. The Verse Satire London, England: Oxford University Press, 1969.

Sutherland, James. English Satire. Cambridge, England: University Press, 1958.

Swinfen, Ann. In Defence of Fantasy: A Study of the Genre in English and American Literature since 1945. London, England: Routledge and Kegan Paul, 1984.

Tave, Stuart M. Lovers, Clowns, and Fairies: An Essay on Comedies. Chicago, IL: University of Chicago Press, 1993.

Test, George A. Satire: Spirit and Art. Tampa, FL: University of South Florida Press, 1991.

Thackeray, W. M. The English Humorists: Charity and Humour: The Four Georges. New York, NY: Dutton, 1912.

Thomas, Dylan. Collected Stories London, England: Dent, 1983.

Thorndike, Ashley H. English Comedy. New York, NY: Macmillan, 1929.

Traugott, John. "The Rake's Progress from Court to Comedy: A Study in Comic Form." Studies in English Literature, 1500-1900 6 (1966): 381-407.

Turner, F. McD. C. The Element of Irony in English Literature. Cambridge, England: University Press, 1926.

Walker, Hugh. English Satire and Satirists. London, England: J. M. Dent, 1925.

Weiss, Wolfgang. Die Englische Satire. Darmstadt, Germany: Wissenschaftliche Buchgesellschaft, 1982.

Wimsatt, W. K. Jr. English Stage Comedy. New York, NY: Columbia University Press, 1955.

Wolfe, Humbert. Notes on English Verse Satire. London, England: Leonard and Virginia Woolf, 1929.

Worcester, David The Art of Satire. New York: NY: Russell and Russell, 1960.

Humor in
British Literature,
From the Middle Ages
to the Restoration

1

Humor in Medieval British Literature

EARLIEST MONARCHS OF ENGLAND:

Egbert (Ecgberht)	Saxon	828-839
Ethelwulf	Saxon	839-858
Ethelbald	Saxon	858-860
Ethelbert	Saxon	860-866
Ethelred I	Saxon	866-871
Alfred the Great	Saxon	871-899
Edward the Elder	Saxon	899-924
Athelstan	Saxon	924-940
Edmund	Saxon	940-946
Edred	Saxon	946-955
Edwy	Saxon	955-959
Edgar	Saxon	959-975
Edward the Martyr	Saxon	975-978
Ethelred II (the Unready)	Saxon	970-1016
Edmund Ironside	Saxon	1016-1016
Canute (Cnut)	Danish	1016-1035
Harold I (Harefoot)	Danish	1035-1040
Hardecanute	Danish	1040-1042
Edward the Confessor	Saxon	1042-1066
Harold II	Saxon	1066-1066
William I (the Conqueror)	Norman	1066-1087
William II (Rufus)	Norman	1087-1100
Henry I (Beauclerc)	Norman	1100-1135
Stephen	Norman	1135-1154
Henry II (Curtmantle)	Plantagenet	1154-1189
Richard I (Coeur de Lion)	Plantagenet	1189-1199
John Lackland	Plantagenet	1199-1216

| Henry III | Plantagenet | 1216-1272 |
| Edward I (Longshanks) | Plantagenet | 1272-1307 |

During the ninth, century King Alfred charmed the Danes with his minstrelsy, and in the Arthurian legends, Sir Kaye is portrayed as a constantly amusing knight (L'Estrange 218). In Anglo Saxon England there were "gleemen," who were of humble origin, and who performed music and tricks, and later among the Normans there were the barons who amused each other with "gabs." These gabs were boastful and exaggerated accounts of their achievements. At this time there were also "jougleurs." The word derives from the Latin "joculator," and was often mistakenly written as "jongleur" (L'Estrange 219).

The first satires in England were in the form of songs, called Sirventois and written against Arnould, who was Robert Courthose's chaplain at the time of William Rufus (eleventh century). The humor of these satires depended mainly on visual imagery and hostility (L'Estrange 182).

The evolution of the devil during the English Middle Ages is interesting to note from the standpoint of humor. Before the tenth century, the devil was thought to be too powerful to portray at all. But later, as the Church was exhibiting the torments of hell, the idea occurred that potential sinners might be deterred if they were presented with the devil and other evil spirits depicted in as frightful form as possible. However, as time progressed, people began to fear the devil less and less, and began to be amused at these strange and grotesque carvings. Instead of viewing them with fear, they viewed them as ludicrous, and it was only a step beyond this to start humorously caricaturing the devil on purpose. This is why imps and demons are frequently brought in to perform comic aspects of the Church mysteries, and the ludicrous did not take long in becoming the humorous. Thus, we have the devil portrayed as a merry fellow, playing all kinds of practical jokes on mankind, and the devil as trickster archetype was soon to develop (L'Estrange 209-210).

During the tenth century the clergy searched for stories that could be used to amuse the post-prandial hour. These stories tended to be extravagant, indelicate, or profane, for this is how the people talked at these times, but they also provided a period of sophisticated and active thought. One tenth century English humorous piece often retold was "Supper." The reader is invited to a grave assembly of scriptural figures from Adam and Eve onwards.

> Cain sits on a plough, Abel on a milk-pail etc. Two, Paul and Esau, are obliged to stand for want of room, and Job complains of having nothing to sit on but a dunghill. Jonah is here the butler. Samson brings honey to the dessert, and Adam apples. (L'Estrange 223)

We sometimes have the impression that during the Middle Ages in England there was not a great deal of intellectual stimulation. This is not a correct impression, however. William Fitzstephen, the biographer of Thomas Becket, describes a scene in a London church yard about the year 1170 among a group of boys ranging in age from twelve to fourteen:

> The scholars dispute, some in demonstrative rhetoric, others in dialectic. Some "hurtle enthymemes," others with greater skill employ perfect syllogisms. Boys of different schools strive against one another in verse, or contend concerning the principles of grammar, or the rules concerning past and future. There are others who employ the old art of crossroads in epigrams, rhymes, and metre. (Murphy, 202)

Louis Cazamian feels that English during the Middle Ages stressed discipline and repression, and mirth was then the outbreak of pent-up forces that allowed for the natural man to come forth. "The various authorities of religion, chivalry, the feudal system, courtly love were rejected in a mood of rebellion" (Cazamian 27).

Saint Hilary, who lived in the fourth century and probably died in the year 367, was the first person known by humor scholars to have left a written humor legacy. Hilary started playing with words and introducing rhymes into church hymns, and some of these verses have survived till today (L'Estrange 180). Leofric, Earl of Mercia and first Bishop of Exeter, lived in the eleventh century, and probably died in 1057. He published the first religious meditations and legends of Saints, or "gnomic verses" in English. These verses contained allegorical descriptions by means of animals, and there were riddles as well (L'Estrange 181).

During Anglo Saxon times there was no clear distinction between the ludicrous and the humorous. The "fool" was a strange mixture of both. In intelligence the fool varied from a mere idiot who was the butt of everyone else's jokes to the man of genius whose intelligence was far superior to that of his master. Often the fool exhibited mental weakness, or eccentricity, and he was often dwarfish or deformed in some way. He wore "motley" clothing of discordant colors to make him look as ridiculous as possible, and the incongruities of his clothing corresponded to similar incongruities in his mind and actions. Sometimes he wore a petticoat or calf-skin to resemble an idiot. He often had his head shaved and wore a cowl to make him look like a monk; on this point L'Estrange indicates that the nobles had no great affection for the church (L'Estrange 220-221). The Roman mime is the source of the medieval English fool. After the fall of Rome, it was the mime who pleased the Italian country people with his coarse and debased burlesque parodies. Some scholars even trace the present-day pantomime to classical Roman times, considering harlequin to be "Mercury, the clown Momus, pantaloon Charon, and columbine Psyche" (L'Estrange 217).

As early as the twelfth century, the clergy in England were developing a reputation for having a sense of humor. Nigellus Wireker was a monk in Canterbury who died in 1169. Wireker wrote an amusing attack on his brethren in Latin elegiac verse. It was directed against ambition, and discontent, and L'Estrange considers it to be similar to Horace's first satire. In this satire, the discourse is developed through talking animals, especially Brunellus, an ass who provides the name for the title of the poem. The main vices attacked in the poem are passion and avarice (L'Estrange 184).

In a book entitled The Scandal of the Fabliaux, R. Howard Block explains the importance of this genre in the early development of entertainment literature.

> What I am suggesting is that the fabliaux constitute a limited case of what has characterized to a lesser or greater degree the discourse of medievalism for at least two centuries. As a privileged ground of realism, the comic tale, more than any other literary type, has fostered certain mystifications that are part and parcel of what we have come to think of as the Middle Ages. (Block 8)

Robert Goldsmith points out that in Medieval England, the natural fool was tolerated and allowed certain freedoms to engage in wanton talk and parody. And this was incentive for many perfectly sane men to enlist as counterfeit fools, giving rise to the court jester. Welsford states that as early as the twelfth century a distinction was being made between "natural fools" and "fools artificial" (Goldsmith 6-7).

A. G. L'Estrange considers John of Salisbury (who died in 1180) to have had remarkable judgment in humor and insight into its nature for his time. His Polycraticus, for example, is an amusing religious character. John of Salisbury also talks of "Court Trifles" such as dice, music, dreams, and many of his statements are pithy and insightful. "Our age," he says, "has fallen back into fables" (L'Estrange 186). John of Salisbury noticed a particular literary genre whereby an author jests about a category he himself falls under, as when a pauper laughs at poverty. John of Salisbury warns that convivial jesting can be dangerous, and suggests that personal defects should not be the targets of humor.

He also says that all jokes should be told without bitterness (L'Estrange 186).

The Harleian Manuscript was written during the reign of Edward I (1272-1307), and in this manuscript there is a French poem pretending to eulogize a new order of the convent in which men and women live together in great luxury and are bound to "perpetual idleness." Several specific monasteries in England are mentioned as providing these types of living accommodations for the clergy (L'Estrange 183). It is interesting to note that in very early English humor the clergy also attacked and ridiculed each other, but this activity is not quite so strange if it is remembered that at this time there was virtually no reading public, and the few copies of books that were in existence were mostly kept in the monasteries and read almost exclusively by the clergy. Thus, a common subject of the writers of these books would be such things as the letters of St. Jerome, and the writings were not meant to disgrace the Church, but were rather meant to improve its discipline. And the humor was not confined to literature. Many parish priests and monks would caricature each other in making grotesque heads of corbels and gargoyles, and Luther himself portrayed the Pope to the public in the form of a jackass (L'Estrange 205). In fact many monks during this time amused themselves with "cloister humor" which consisted mainly of logical paradoxes and verbal curiosities like those of Tryphiodorus, the lipogrammatist, who wrote an Odyssey in twenty-four books without using the letter A (L'Estrange 209).

Much of the earliest English religious art used figures of animals to caricature important people or important stereotypes. There are two geese hanging a fox at Sherborne and Wellingborough Minsters. At St. Mary's in Beverley, there are two foxes in religious vestments each holding a pastoral staff, with a goose peeping out of one of the hoods (L'Estrange 205-206). In the old church of Budleigh, in Devonshire (which Sir Walter Ralegh regularly attended, and where his head is still buried) it is possible to find all kinds of devices hewn into the pews--a scissors, a man-of-war, a cook holding a sheep by the tail, etc. In Beverley Minster there is a monkey riding on a hare, and a bedridden goat with a monkey as a doctor. At Winchester a boar is playing on a fiddle, and a young pig is dancing. And probably the most famous incongruity of all is the imp in the rafters of the Lincoln Cathedral (L'Estrange 207). L'Estrange points out that it was a short step from such incongruous visual art to the literary humor which was to follow (L'Estrange 207).

The rationale for such art was popularity. It got people's attentions and got them to the church. The attitude was that those who had come to laugh, might remain to pray, so a strange assortment of incongruities made their way onto sacred soil (L'Estrange 207). There was, of course, precedence for this type of thinking. As early as the tenth century, Theophylact of Constantinople had introduced the licentious "Feast of Fools" into the Church in order to wean the people from the revels of their old religions. This tradition is continued in the games, frolics, gluttony, drunkenness, and riotous proceedings (including mistletoe) accompanying the "Nativity of Our Lord," and continuing as Mardi Gras and other religio-secular celebrations. So the injunction (made in 680) of the British Church that no bishop was allowed tricks or jocosities to be exhibited before him seems not to have been retained for long (L'Estrange 206-208). It must be remembered that at this time people were highly emotional and demanded very little complexity or truth in their humor, so such people were much amused to see such things as a boar playing on the bagpipes (L'Estrange 208).

In a book entitled Literature as Recreation in the Later Middle Ages, Glending Olson notes that medieval prose contained a number of nondidactic genres written mainly for entertainment, among them, the Goliardic verse, the fabliaux, the trivial court lyrics, and even some of the work written by Boccaccio and Chaucer (Olson 9). During the Middle Ages, not only did light verse and amusing stories exist, but many people in the Middle Ages had coherent ideas and a high degree of acceptability for these kinds of discourse

(Olson 12).

Derek Brewer notes that there were few popular comic tales written in English prior to 1400. The first example of such a tale was <u>Dame Sirith</u>.

> It recounts, in tail-rhyme verse, the seduction of a young wife by a young clerk. He invokes the aid of an old woman, who makes the eyes of her bitch stream by feeding her with pepper and mustard. The old woman then tells the young wife that the bitch is the old woman's daughter, magically transformed to a bitch because she resisted the advances of a young clerk, and now weeps with regret. The young wife tells the old woman to hurry away and find the clerk, whom she then enthusiastically receives. (Brewer 131)

Brewer notes that there is generally a lack of sympathy in medieval popular comic literature for the innocent victims of bad luck, for elderly cuckolds, for outraged parents, or for unmarried pregnant girls. The acceptance of the norms of medieval society, of hierarchy, of conventional standards, and of common sense were also remarkable. "It is those who are in some way outside the norms, or who abuse them, who are mercilessly mocked." Thus, these social norms are implicitly supported in the popular medieval comic tales, supported not only by the dominant official ecclesiastical culture, but by the lower classes as well (Brewer 144). Derek Brewer states that the "medieval popular comic tales are precious evidence of a vigorous <u>secular</u> culture whose norms were not ecclesiastical, or not entirely so." The medieval popular comic tale is therefore not subversive, since it reinforces, though in jest, "the dominant, secular this-worldly culture of which it is so important and entertaining a witness" (Brewer 145).

During the reign of Edward I (1272-1307), there were Christmas games in England which contained much pageantry and humor. On one Christmas the royal court made use of eighty tunics of buckram of various colors, forty-two vizors, fourteen faces of women, fourteen faces of men, fourteen faces of angels, and in addition there were costumes of dragons, peacocks, and swans. But there were opposing attitudes in thirteenth century England on the value of festivals, and Robert Grosseteste, Bishop of Lincoln, submitted a proclamation that forbade the celebration of the "Feast of Fools" in English churches because during this ceremony the clergy wore masks and anonymously danced and gesticulated in the streets, and Grosseteste thought this was unseemly (L'Estrange 215).

The most significant piece of humorous writing of twelfth-century England was a poem entitled "The Owl and the Nightingale." The poem is attributed to Nicholas of Guildford, whose name is mentioned at the beginning of the poem, and was probably written about 1180 (Cazamian 59). It is a beast fable in which an Owl argues with a Nightingale about the possible coexistence of both spiritual and sensual love. The Owl represents virtue, and the old religious point of view, and a strict mood of moral restraint; the Nightingale represents pleasure, the new love poetry, an early humanism, a softened ideal of conduct (Cazamian 59), but their arguments are very similar since "the Nightingale insists that pleasure causes virtue, and the Owl that virtue brings pleasure" (O'Hearn 62). Carolyn O'Hearn points out that this poem is in the dialogue tradition, and that in this tradition, there are two major types--the vertical dialogue and the horizontal dialogue. The vertical dialogue represents an unequal status of speakers like a teacher and a student or an adult and a child, or some other imbalance where one speaker is informed and the other is ignorant. The vertical dialogue tends to be didactic and instructional, with one member of the dialogue considered to be an authority and therefore always given the last word. "The Owl and the Nightingale," however, is written in the tradition of the horizontal dialogue, in which both speakers are equally well informed and have equal authority, and which therefore does not end with one speaker winning the debate. The horizontal dialogue exposes truth, but it does not result in a single unambiguous conclusion. Guildford's poem does not resolve the paradox or the contradictions of life so much as it sheds light on them. John Peter suggests that The Owl and the Nightingale is a special kind of complaint. For Peter, the Owl symbolizes the diatribes and jeremiads of religious writers and their spirit of brooding and reproach. The Nightingale accuses the Owl of being "hateful to men," and the Owl must begrudgingly admit that there is some truth to the charge. Peter points out The Owl and the Nightingale thus falls into a special genre of thirteenth century literature: "The survival of even a few burlesques from this period indicates that a surreptitious literature existed in which the earnestness of the preachers and poets was mocked at" (Peter 56-57).

Louis Cazamian feels that The Owl and the Nightingale is a synthesis of the French and English cultures. He feels that it is in the tradition of the French "trouvères" that were an early form of debate. But it is also associated with the fable or animal theme whose special home is England. The Owl and the Nightingale is a synthesized work, like the works of Chaucer who wrote two centuries later. This work significantly testifies to the cosmopolitanism of the twelfth century. Furthermore, it embodies a general stimulation of thought and art, the source of which can be traced to France. This work also blends the more refined and conscious spirit into an original whole with a solidly English inspiration. (Cazamian 61)

Kathryn Hume claims that the poem presents a "burlesque satire on human contentiousness" (Hume 128); however, Brian Stone considers it simply as an allegory debating the possibilities of coexistence of spiritual and sensual love (Risden 48). All critics admit that the poem is filled with the fun of abusive wit in which the poet is safely distanced from the argument by the use of beast characters. In this way, the arguments cannot be taken to relate either to particular people, or to particular classes of people. The fable stance also allows the moral lessons to have a more general applicability. If the fable stance provides distance for the poet, the humorous tone and abusive wit provide even more distance. But one effect of achieving this distance is that the poet is no longer able to arrive at specific and unambiguous moral conclusions, and this is why Risden considers the poem to be a "postmodernist play," or a "medieval stand-up comedy." Like postmodernist literature, and like stand-up comedy, the poem brings up and strongly debates significant moral dilemmas. But like these other two genres, the poem also fails to arrive at a fixed solution. In post-modernist fashion, the poem uses ironic probing to shed light on the contemporary issues of the power of the church, and the spreading of courtly love, without resolving the issues (Risden 48).

An important genre which developed during the twelfth and thirteenth centuries is the "complaint." This is the genre which would later become the satire. In a book entitled Complaint and Satire in Early English Literature, John Peter notes how often references to the Seven Deadly Sins are encountered in twelfth- and thirteenth- century literature. For example, Robert of Brunne refers to them in his Confessio Amantis; John Gower used them as a backdrop for his poems; William Langland devotes quite a bit of space to them; Geoffrey Chaucer also writes about them in his "Parson's Tale;" and "they are mentioned with varying degrees of particularity in a great number of the early poems, from the "poema Morale" to Dunbar's 'Dance of the Sevin Deidly Synnis'" (Peter 47).

Peter feels that in terms of subject, the medieval "complaint" can be divided into four categories. First, there were the direct attacks upon various corrupt professions or businesses such as lawyers, and usurers. Second, there were the attacks on people with particularly disturbing characteristics like backbiters, atheists, or misers. Third, there were attacks directed at certain actions like swearing or the use of cosmetics. Finally, there were the attacks on the fundamental ideas or beliefs or attitudes which were responsible for the "complaints" (Peter 60).

The "complaint" took on a particularly negative and pessimistic point of view, as

can be seen from a particular passage from <u>Roman de la Rose</u>:
> Man is a murderer, proud and base,
> A thief, a felon void of grace,
> A hateful, despitous self-seeker,
> A gluttonous wretch, an evil-speaker,
> A forger, a disloyal traitor,
> A recreant vile, a false delator. (Peter 63)

And the basic notion behind all of the "complaints" is that man will be doubly punished for his sins--once here on earth, and again later in heaven. Thus when Gower is talking about panderers and prostitutes he says that they will receive not only venereal disease, but eternal damnation as well. Another writer of complaints suggested that gluttony (another of the deadly sins) would lead to "dropesie, and many other siknes" and would also lead to "euerlastynge deth" (Peter 78).

Humor in the Earliest of English Literature Bibliography

Bestul, Thomas H. <u>Satire and Allegory in "Wynnere and Wastoure</u>. Lincoln, NE: University of Nebraska Press, 1974.

Bloch, R. Howard. "The Fabliaux, Fetishism, and the Joke." <u>The Scandal of the Fabliaux</u>. Chicago, IL: University of Chicago Press, 1986, 101-128.

Brewer, Derek. "The International Medieval Popular Comic Tale in England." <u>The Popular Literature of Medieval England</u>. Ed. Thomas J. Heffernan, 1985, 131-147.

Campbell, K. S. "Irony Medieval and Modern and the Allegory of Rhetoric." <u>Allegorica</u> 4 (1979): 291-300.

Cazamian, Louis. <u>The Development of English Humor</u>. Durham, NC: Duke University Press, 1952.

Duncan, Robert L. "Comedy in the English Mysteries: Three Versions of the Noah Story." <u>Illinois Quarterly</u> 35 (April, 1973): 5-14.

Eckhardt, Caroline D. "Arthurian Comedy: The Simpleton-Hero in <u>Sir Perceval of Galles</u>." <u>Chaucer Review</u> 8 (1984): 205-220.

Elliott, John R., Jr. "The Sacrifice of Isaac as Comedy and Tragedy." <u>Studies in Philology</u> 66 (1969): 36-59.

Falke, Anne. "The Comic Function of the Narrator in <u>Troilus and Cryseyde</u>." <u>Neophilologus</u> 68 (1984): 134-141.

Gardner, John. <u>The Construction of the Wakefield Cycle</u>. Carbondale, IL: Southern Illinois Univ Press, 1974.

Gibson, Gail McMurray. " 'Porta haec clausa erit': Comedy, Conception, and Ezekiel's Closed Door in the <u>Ludus Coventriae</u> Play of 'Joseph's Return.' " <u>Journal of Medieval and Renaissance Studies</u> 8 (1978): 137-156.

Goldsmith, Robert H. <u>Wise Fools in Shakespeare</u>. East Lansing, MI: Michigan State University Press, 1955.

Green, D. H. <u>Irony in the Medieval Romance</u>. Cambridge, England: Cambridge University Press, 1979.

Haidu, Peter. <u>Aesthetic Distance in Crétien de Troyes; Irony and Comedy in Cliges and Perceval</u>." Geneva, Switzerland: Librarie Droz, 1968.

Helterman, Jeffrey. "Satan as Everyshepeterd: Comic Metamorphosis in <u>The Second Shepherd's Play</u>." <u>Symbolic Action in the Plays of the Wakefield Master</u>. Athens, GA: Univ of Georgia Press, 1981, 95-114.

Hume, Kathryn. <u>The Owl and the Nightingale: The Poem and Its Critics</u>. Toronto, Canada: Univ of Toronto Press, 1975.

Hunt, Tony. "Irony and Ambiguity in 'Sir Gawain and the Green Knight.' " <u>Forum for</u>

Modern Language Studies 12.1 (1976): 2-16.

Janicka, Irena. The Comic Elements in the English Mystery Plays against the Cultural Background (Particularly Art). Poznan, Poland: Praca Wydana Z Zasitku Polskiej Akademii Namk, 1962.

Jones, Edward T. "The Sound of Laughter in Sir Gawain and the Green Knight." Mediaeval Studies 31 (1969): 343-345.

Kitchin, George. "Medieval Burlesque." Survey of Burlesque and Parody in English. London, England: Oliver and Boyd, 1931, 1-37.

L'Estrange, A. G. History of English Humour with an Introduction upon Ancient Humour. New York, NY: Burt Franklin, 1878.

Levey, D. " 'Nowe is Fulfillid all my For-thought': A Study of Comedy, Satire and Didacticism in the York Cycle." English Studies in Africa 24 (1981): 83-94.

Lowers, James K. "High Comedy Elements in Medwall's Fulgens and Lucres." Journal of English Literary History 8 (1941): 103-106.

McAlindon, T. "Comedy and Teror in Middle English Literature: The Diabolical Game." Modern Language Review 60 (1965): 323-332.

McNight, George H., ed. Middle English Humorous Tales in Verse. Boston, MA: D. C. Heath, 1913.

Martin, Leslie Howard. "Comic Eschatology in the Chester Coming of Antichrist." Comparative Drama 5 (1971): 163-176.

Mathewson, Jeanne T. "Sir Gawain and the Medieval School of Comedy." Interpretations 15.2 (1984): 42-52.

Morgan, Margery M. " 'High Fraud': Paradox and Double-Plot in the English Shepherd's Play." Speculum 39 (1964): 679-689.

Munson, William F. "Audience and Meaning in Two Medieval Dramatic Realisms." Comparative Drama 9 (1975): 44-67.

Murphy, James J., ed. Medieval Eloquence: Studies in the Theory and Practice of Medieval Rhetoric. Berkeley, CA: Univ of California Press, 1978.

Myers, Robert Manson. From Beowulf to Virginia Woolf: An Astounding and Wholly Unauthorized History of English Literature. Urbana, IL: University of Illinois Press, 1984.

Nilsen, Don L. F. "Humor in the Earliest English Literature." Kansas English 79.1 (1993): 36-45.

O'Hearn, Carolyn. "The Virtues of Pleasure, the Pleasures of Virtue: The "Beastification" of Paradox in The Owl and the Nightingale. WHIMSY 4 (1986): 61-62.

Olson, Glending. Literature as Recreation in the Later Middle Ages. Ithaca, NY: Cornell University Press. 1982.

Peter, John. Complaint and Satire in Early English Literature. Oxford, England: Clarendon Press, 1956.

Previté-Orton, C. W. "Introduction: Political Satire in the Middle Ages." Political Satire in English Poetry. New York, NY: Russell and Russell, 1968, 1-30.

Reiss, Edmond. "Medieval Irony." Journal of the History of Ideas. 42.2 (1981): 209-226.

Risden, E. L. "The Owl and the Nightingale: Postmodernism Play and Medieval Stand-up Comedy." WHIMSY 7 (1989): 48-49.

Rossiter, A. P. English Drama from Early Times to the Elizabethans: Its Background Origins and Developments. New York, NY: Barnes, 1950.

Ruggiers, Paul G., ed. Versions of Medieval Comedy. Norman, OK: University of Oklahoma Press, 1977.

Schless, Howard H. "The Comic Element in the Wakefield Noah." Studies in Medieval Literature: In Honor of Professor Albert Croll Baugh. Ed. MacEdward Leach. Philadelphia, PA: Univ of Pennsylvania Press, 1961, 229-241.

Speyser, Suzanne. "Dramatic Illusion and Sacred Reality in the Towneley Prima Pastorum."
  Studies in Philology 78 (1981): 1-19.
Staines, David. "To Out-Herod Herod: The Development of a Dramatic Character."
  Comparative Drama 10 (1976): 29-53.
Stock, Lorraine Kochanske. "Comedy in the English Mystery Cycles: Three Comic Scenes
  in the Chester Shepherd's Play. Versions of Medieval Comedy. Ed. Paul G.
  Ruggiers. Norman, OK: University of Oklahoma Press, 1977, 211-226.
Swain, Barbara. Fools and Folly during the Middle Ages and the Renaissance. New York,
  NY: Columbia University Press, 1932.
Taylor, P. B. "Commerce and Comedy in Sir Gawain." Philological Quarterly 50 (1971):
  1-15.
Thorndike, Ashley H. "Medieval and Classical Influences." English Comedy. New York,
  NY: Macmillan, 1929. 18-34.
Travis, Peter W. "The Comic Structures of Communal Celebration, Paginae VI-XI."
  Dramatic Design in the Chester Cycle. Chicago, IL: Univ of Chicago Press, 1982,
  108-141.
Wickham, Glynne. "English Comedy from its Origins to 1576." Early English Stages 1300-
  1600. London, England: Routledge, 1981. 173-218.
Williams, Arnold. "The Comic in the Cycles." Medieval Drama. Ed. Neville Denny. New
  York, NY: Crane, 1973, 109-123.
Winslow, Ola Elisabeth. Low Comedy as a Structural Element in English Drama from the
  Beginnings to 1642. Folcroft, PA: Folcroft, 1969.
Wood, Frederick T. "The Comic Elements in the English Mystery Plays." Neophilologus
  25 (1939-40): 39-48, 194-206.
Wright, M. J. "Comic Perspective in Two Middle English Poems." Parergon 18 (1977): 3-
  15.

Aldhelm, Bishop of Shirburn (c640-709)

Anglo Saxon "humor" was rooted in fun, romping around, practical jokes, and boisterous games. English amusement during this period was connected with the senses. The Anglo-Saxons were also fond of giving people nicknames that related to their personal peculiarities. The only sophisticated humor that was available to the Anglo Saxons came from translations of the Latin riddles of the Symposius by Aldhelm, Bishop of Shirburn, who was a relative of Ina, King of the West Saxons. Aldhelm was a harper, a poet, a theologian, and England's first literary humorist (L'Estrange 179).

Aldhelm, Bishop of Shirburn, Bibliography

L'Estrange, A. G. History of English Humour with an Introduction upon Ancient Humour.
  New York, NY: Burt Franklin, 1878.

Walter Mapes (c1140-c1209)

Walter Mapes, also known as Walter Map, was a Norman-Welshman whose writing was considered by Louis Cazamian to be impudent and irresponsible in its humorous intent, "quietly chuckling over the contrast between manner and matter, language and theme" (Cazamian 50). Most of Mapes's humor is at the word level or the sentence level. He frequently commends his favorite saints as being jocund and pleasant men, however, A. G.

L'Estrange feels that Mapes's own wit and humor are disappointing by comparison (L'Estrange 187).

L'Estrange considers Mapes to have been the first writer of note in England who was able to reconcile divinity and wit. Mapes had a reputation of being a man of humor, a man of pleasure; however, L'Estrange finds the humor of his writings to be weak, and the expression of religious feelings to be much stronger. Mapes loved to recount the miracles of the saints. When the devil is exorcised from the body of Peter of Tarentaise, for example, Peter proved his cure by exclaiming, "Mother of God, have mercy upon me!" On hearing this, John the bishop said of Peter, "This is the only bishop--the rest of us are dogs unable to bark" (L'Estrange 186-187). Mapes also enjoyed telling extraordinary stories about infidels who walked around after death calling people by name. These people always died shortly afterwards. Mapes also enjoyed composing epigrams like "May God omnipotent grant you not to be deceived by woman omnipotent. (L'Estrange 187-188). Such is the humor of Walter Mapes.   There is an interesting story told about Walter Mapes. It is said that Mapes went to see a Cistercian Abbot who was dangerously ill, and gave the Abbot the advice that his illness was caused by his avarice and rapacity, which he should thenceforth give up. The Abbot not only refused Mapes's advice, but is said to have retorted with the words, "Get thee behind me, Satan." A short time later, Mapes became ill, and the Abbot went to visit Mapes, strongly recommending Mapes to renounce his light jesting habits, to give up his liberal thinking, and to become a member of the Cistercian order. At this point, the Abbot is said to have handed Mapes a gown and cowl with which he was ready to invest him. Mapes, who was in his characteristic good humor at the time, called his servants and told them that if he ever became so ill that he desired to become a monk they were to consider it a sign that he had lost his senses and keep him locked up and unable to do anything foolish (L'Estrange 188-189).

Walter Mapes Bibliography

Cazamian, Louis. The Development of English Humor. Durham, NC: Duke University
      Press, 1952.
L'Estrange, A. G. "Anglo Saxon Humor: Mapes, Goliardi, Erasmus, Skelton, et. al."
      History of English Humour. New York, NY: Burt Franklin, 1878, 179-210.

2

Humor in Fourteenth-Century British Literature

FOURTEENTH-CENTURY MONARCHS OF ENGLAND:

Edward I (Longshanks)	**Plantagenet**	**1272-1307**
Edward II	**Plantagenet**	**1307-1327**
Edward III	**Plantagenet**	**1327-1377**
Richard II	**Plantagenet**	**1377-1399**
Henry IV (Bolingbroke)	**Lancaster**	**1399-1413**

In a chapter entitled "From Plague to Pleasure," Glending Olson suggests that to a large extent the plague was responsible not only for increased attention to hygiene, but for increased attention to pleasurable reading as well, both of the fictional and of the nonfictional types.

> This material appears in the years following the Black Death, and it involves a relationship between plague and mental pleasure, usually in the form of a structural movement from a world riddled by pestilence to a happier, healthier environment dominated by repose and recreational enjoyment. (Olson 164)

The name "Black Death" was not applied to the plague which swept over Europe during the fourteenth century; it was a name given centuries later. Glending Olson suggests that in our minds this plague has become more devastating over time. While Boccaccio's and Machaut's real purpose in writing about the horrors of the plague, were to transcend these horrors. But the Black Death did not promote only increased morbidity in literature. "Amidst all the work that reflects the fear of death and that looks to last things, there is some, at least, that reflects the value of secular life and that looks to proximate things. For the living, singing songs and telling pleasant tales are important means of coping with the plague" (Olson 204). By the end of the fourteenth century, a large number of entertaining stories were making their way around Europe, and many of these stories were not in any way didactic or religious in aim or tone. The two most significant examples of this trend were Boccaccio's <u>Decameron</u>, and Chaucer's <u>Canterbury Tales</u>, each of which contained a number of comic and entertaining tales. During the fifteenth and sixteenth centuries this trend increased because of the increasing literacy of these periods (Brewer 133).

In an article entitled, "A Vocabulary for Chaucerian Comedy: A Preliminary sketch," Paul Ruggiers says the following about the fourteenth century: "Clearly no system can do justice to any of the great geniuses of comic writing, their wit and irony, the special flavor of license, their power to challenge staid opinion, that peculiar innocence that allows them to escape defilement even in the relating of the obscene" (Ruggiers 194). James Winny says that in Medieval literature the low-life characters are treated much as they are in Shakespeare--"to embody laughable or disreputable aspects of human nature." It is the function of the knights and gentlefolk to demonstrate the serious aspects of life, as can be seen in Chaucer's courtly tales. "When ordinary people are admitted--artisans, tradesmen, churls and servants--they usually perform a limited function, often farcical" (Winny 21).

Louis Cazamian considers Robert of Brunne's Handlyng Synne (written in the first years of the fourteenth century) to be one of the earliest good pieces of humor in fourteenth-century England. Despite its moralizing and didactic tone, the piece demonstrates a homely native spirit and realism (Cazamian 52). In this piece, a witch has hoodwinked a bishop and persuaded him that when she says some magical words a bag will fly out of the room and milk all of his cows. When the magic doesn't work, the bishop becomes suspicious, but the witch responds that the problem is that the bishop lacks faith. If he will only believe in her words, and pronounce them in the right spirit, the miracle will happen. Cazamian considers this to be "one of the first authentic notes of exquisite humor in English. The paradox of the situation, the mute eloquence of the inverted parts of teacher and taught, the fine essence of relativity and irony are set off by the economy and subdued tenor of the style (Cazamian 53).

Brunne's Handlyng Synne is a very good example of what John Peter would call "Complaint." The fourteenth-century genre of "complaint" had its roots in the twelfth and thirteenth centuries, and would later become the "moralized tragedy," and still later the "satire." John Gower wrote a poem about a proud atheist which can be classed as a "complaint." The atheist received his just reward in Gower's poem, and ended up being smitten to powder (Peter 80).

Fourteenth-century scholars do not know who the author of Wynnere and Wastoure was, but they do know that it is significant as one of the earliest poems of the alliterative revival of the fourteenth century and it has generally been regarded as a piece of high quality. It is a topical satire directed against Edward III (which is probably why we don't now know the author) in the same tradition as Sir Gawain and the Green Knight, and Piers Plowman (Bestul ix). The local detail in the piece helps to date it as having been written in 1352 or 1353 (Bestul 1). There are basically two allegorical figures in the poem, which is about two opposing armies about to do battle. In Winner's army the reader finds the pope, friars, lawyers, and merchants. Winner stands for the wealthy and increasingly powerful middle class. In Waster's army the reader finds "sadde men of armes," "bolde sqwyeres of blode," and "boweman many." Thus Waster represents basically the military and the landed gentry (Bestul 4). According to Thomas Bestul, "Winner stands for thrift, good husbandry, and acquisitiveness, while Waster represents extravagance and high living" (Bestul 5).

Sir Gawain and the Green Knight was written late in the fourteenth century to expose the apparent contradictions of the chivalric tradition. Gwendolyn Morgan sees this piece as displaying a sympathetic humor in which the author "treats the plights of his various protagonists and, by extension, the human condition itself." The author is making no attempt to expose King Arthur's nephew (Sir Gawain) as a rake, but instead, he is "reducing him to human status in this imperfect and foolish world." The poet "has not diminished Gawain's heroic status but merely accorded him some human failings," and according to Morgan, it is only Sir Gawain who has missed the point (Morgan 432). There were three aspects of the chivalric code, true knighthood, Christian virtue, and courtly love, but these virtues often came into conflict with each other, and they certainly came into conflict in Sir Gawain and the Green Knight. As an ideal courtly lover, Gawain would have to show courtesy and hospitality to Lady Bertilak, and he would have to honor her wishes to make love to her, but this would violate his Christian virtue. As a true knight, he had to be a proud, courageous and skilled fighter, but this would violate his Christian humility. Lady Bertilak gives him a magical girdle to protect him, but believing in this girdle violates his Christian faith. As Gwendolyn Morgan states, "Courtly love, with its sensual basis and often illicit consummation, runs counter to a number of Christian virtues. Certainly , too, making love to a friend's wife is a breach of honor and etiquette on all counts." Morgan concludes, "In the final analysis, no one aspect of the chivalric ideal has been upheld at the expense of another; all are equally betrayed." But even though this is true, it is also true that "the chivalric ideology remains an admirable standard for human behavior, and although even the most perfect of knights cannot fulfill it, his greatest honor lies in the attempt" (Morgan 431).

According to John Peter, all professions were attacked by the "complaint;" however, it was the clergy that received special recognition. They were "pilloried in almost every complaint of the period" (Peter 80), and the reason is that many of the clergy entered their profession not as a result of dedication, but rather as a result of convenience. "A high percentage of them, like Fra Lippo Lippi, had turned to the Church more out of desperation than a sense of vocation" (Peter 80), and once in the priesthood such men were soon looking for ways to manipulate the rules to their own advantage and personal comfort. Because of this there was a proverb in fourteenth-century England that read, "The nearer to church, the farther from God" (Peter 81).

A great irony of the fourteenth century was that the preachers who wrote "homilies," and the poets who wrote "complaints" were actually very much like each other. One reason for this is that the preachers accumulated and elaborated on poets' themes in order to make their sermons more interesting. John Peter states it well,

> it is rather as though the preachers, dissatisfied with the inattention during service--the flirting which, according to Gower, went on in church and, if we can believe a fifteenth-century carol, even the card-games there--had pursued their parishioners out of doors and beyond the range of the pulpit itself, railing against them from every bush and hedge along the road home. (Peter 50-51)

It is easy to see why the preachers were a favorite target for the poets in their "complaints" (Peter 50).

Fourteenth-Century England Bibliography

Alden, Raymond MacDonald. "Medieval and Early English Satire." The Rise of Formal Satire in England under Classical Influence. New York, NY: Archon, 1961, 4-31.

Allen, Judson B. "The Ironic Fruyt: Chauntecleer as Figura." Studies in Philology 66 (1969): 25-35.

Bestul, Thomas H. Satire and Allegory in "Wynnere and Wastoure." Lincoln, NE: Univ of Nebraska Press, 1974.

Birney, Earle. "English Irony Before Chaucer." University of Toronto Quarterly 6 (1937): 538-557.

Bloomfield, Morton W. "The Man of Law's Tale: A Tragedy." Publications of the Modern Language Association 87 (1972): 384-390.

Brewer, Derek. "The International Medieval Popular Comic Tale in England." The Popular Literature of Medieval England. Ed. Thomas J. Heffernan. Knoxville, TN: University of Tennessee Press, 1985, 131-147.

Brockman, Bennett A. "Comic and Tragic Counterpoint in the Medieval Drama: The Wakefield Mactacio Abel." Mediaeval Studies 39 (1977): 331-349.

Broes, Arthur T. "Sir Gawain and the Green Knight: Romance as Comedy." Xavier Review 4 (1965): 35-54.

Bronsted, P. O. "The Medieval 'Comedia': Choice of Form." Classica et Mediaevalia 31 (1970): 258-268.

Campbell, K. S. "Irony Medeival and Modern and the Allegory of Rhetoric." Allegorica 4 (1979): 291-300.

Cazamian, Louis. The Development of English Humor. Durham, NC: Duke University Press, 1952.

David, Alfred. "Sentimental Comedy in The Franklin's Tale." Annuale Mediaevale 6 (1965): 19-27.

Davis, Bruce J. "The Development of Sustained Narrative Irony in Fourteenth-Century Europe." Unpublished Paper MA Thesis. Tempe, AZ: Arizona State University, 1991.

Dean, William. "The Towneley Cycle as Religious Comedy." Journal of the Australasian Universities Language and Literature Association. 45 (1965): 19-27.

Farnham, Willard. "The Medieval Comic Spirit in the English Renaissance." Joseph Quincy Adams Memorial Studies. Eds. James G. McManaway, Giles E. Dawson, Edwin E. Willoughby. Washington, DC: Folger Shakespeare Library, 1948, 429-437.

Green, D. H. Irony in the Medieval Romance. Cambridge, England: Cambridge University Press, 1979.

Haidu, Peter. Aesthetic Distance in Chrétien de Troyes: Irony and Comedy in Cliges and Perceval. Geneva, Switzerland: Librarie Droz, 1968.

Hunt, Tony. "Irony and Ambiguity in 'Sir Gawain and the Green Knight'." Forum for Modern Language Studies 12.1 (1976): 2-16.

Kern, Edith. The Absolute Comic. New York, NY: Columbia University Press, 1980.

Kernan, Alvin. The Cankered Muse: Satire of the English Renaissance. New Haven, CT: Yale University Press, 1959.

Lambdin, Robert T. "Master Wakefield." Encyclopedia of British Humorists: Geoffrey Chaucer to John Cleese: Volume II. Ed. Steven H. Gale, 1966, 1165-1168.

McCollom, William. "From Dissonance to Harmony: The Evolution of Early English Comedy." Theatre Annual 21 (1964): 69-96.

Morgan, Gwendolyn. "The Gawain/Pearl Poet." Encyclopedia of British Humorists: Geoffrey Chaucer to John Cleese: Volume I. Ed. Steven H. Gale, 1966, 429-434.

Olson, Glending. Literature as Recreation in the Later Middle Ages. Ithaca, NY: Cornell University Press, 1982.

Owen, D. D. R. "Burlesque Tradition in Sir Gawain and the Green Knight." Forum for Modern Language Studies 4 (1968): 125-145.

Peter, John. Complaint and Satire in Early English Literature. Oxford, England: Clarendon Press, 1956.

Pittock, Malcolm. The Prioress's Tale: The Wife of Bath's Tale. Oxford, England: Basil Blackwell, 1973.

Reiss, Edmond. "Medieval Irony." Journal of the History of Ideas. 42.2 (1981): 209-226.

Ross, Thomas W. The Colorado College Studies: A Satire of Edward II's England: A critical Edition. Colorado Springs, CO: Colorado College, 1966.

Rossiter, A. P. English Drama from Early Times to the Elizabethans: Its Background, Origins and Developments. New York, NY: Barnes, 1950.

Ruggiers, Paul G., ed. Versions of Medieval Comedy. Norman, OK: University of Oklahoma Press, 1977, 211-226.

Ruggiers, Paul G. "A Vocabulary for Chaucerian Comedy: A Preliminary Sketch." Medieval Studies in Honor of Lillian Herlands Hornstein. Ed. J. B. Bessinger and R. Raymo. New York, NY: New York University Press, 1977, 193-225.

Steadman, John M. Disembodied Laughter: Troilis and the Apotheosis Tradition: A Re-Examination of Narrative and Thematic Contexts. Berkeley, CA: University of California Press, 1972.

Swain, Barbara. Fools and Folly during the Middle Ages and the Renaissance. New York, NY: Columbia University Press, 1932.

Winny, James, ed. The Wife of Bath's Prologue and Tale: From the Canterbury Tales by Geoffrey Chaucer. Cambridge, England: Cambridge University Press, 1965.

John Gower (c1325-1408)

Even though Gower was Chaucer's contemporary, he died a few years after him, and may therefore be regarded as Chaucer's first successor. There is no fourteenth-century writer who was more influenced by French literature than was John Gower; nevertheless, whatever humor he had was not of the type that French literature would have inspired (Cazamian 85). Louis Cazamian does not consider Gower to be a humorist, but he doesn't consider him to be a pedant or a preacher either. "There is in him a fund of observation and shrewdness, and he can see the other side of a subject; more than that, he can hint at it" (Cazamian 86). Gower realized that things are diverse, and that they are relative (Cazamian 87).

Raymond Alden considers Gower to be Chaucer's most distinguished literary contemporary, and a satirist of significance. Although Gower had almost no sense of humor, he was skilled in what Alden calls "direct rebuke" (Alden 12). Gower wrote two important satiric poems, both with long Latin titles that are characteristic of the two important methods of construction of early English satire. The first method was that of classifying material by vices, and this method was a tradition all the way back to the medieval sermon books. The second method was that based on social classes. This method is again found in early medieval religious literature, and according to Alden is more than the first method a "product of the satirical spirit" (Alden 12).

Gower wrote a satirical poem entitled "On the Times" during the reign of Richard II. This poem alternates English and Latin lines, and is a condemnation of fourteenth-century life. It deals with the fact that there were better days in the past, and with the fact that wars oppress people. It also deals with flatterers, and how the rich exploit the poor, and that there is no relief in the law, and that fashions in dress are absurd, and that lechery is everywhere, and that the church is corrupt, and so on (Alden 13).

In Gower's Confessio each book (except for Book 7) deals with a cardinal sin in its personal, social, historical, and religious context. Confessio starts with the sin of pride and concludes with the sin of lechery, and each sin contains many exampla ranging in length from short allusions to well developed tales that extend over forty pages of text. The effect of many of these tales is curious or unsettling, since the tale very often expresses the opposite to the moral point being made (Leonard 67-68). Gower's allegories of individual and universal love range from flat and non-evocative images to richly suggestive passages which invite multiple interpretations. By presenting each poem in the form of a confession, Gower imposes a general structure which is capable of being interpreted on a number of different levels. The confessions center on a variety of human personalities, and they also investigate the ethical nature of man as they analyze and correct the relationships between men and God (Leonard 66).

John Gower Bibliography

Alden, Raymond MacDonald. "Gower." The Rise of Formal Satire in England under

Classical Influence. New York, NY: Archon, 1961, 12-14.

Cazamian, Louis. "Gower, Hoccleve, Lydgate." The Development of English Humor. Durham, NC: Duke University Press, 1952, 85-89.

Leonard, Frances McNeely. Laughter in the Courts of Love: Comedy in Allegory, from Chaucer to Spenser. Norman, OK: Pilgrim, 1981.

Peter, John. Complaint and Satire in Early English Literature. Oxford, England: Clarendon Press, 1956.

William Langland (c1332-c1400)

For centuries it has been assumed that William Langland is the author of Piers Plowman, and Hugh Walker goes along with this assumption. Walker considers Piers Plowman to be "the first satirical composition in English which has any claim to be called great" (10). He also said that this poem "at once raised satire to a height it had never before reached in England" (9). Langland chose the dream as the framework for this poem, and he developed his dream as an allegory. The poem is basically a satire on fourteenth-century England, but to an important extent it is also a satire on human nature in general, and therefore survives quite well to the present day (10). In this poem, there is no class of people who escape being Langland's targets, but there are three targets which he especially enjoys satirizing--the Church, the Law, and Trade. "Langland's satire of ecclesiastical corruptions is so unsparing that there is danger of forgetting that all the while he is a faithful son of the Church" (11). John Peter feels that Langland's Piers Plowman is a special sort of complaint in that it adds the sniping of poets to the constant preaching of the churchmen in presenting their didactic messages. Peter proposes that many fourteenth-century individuals found the atmosphere of the Complaint to be oppressive (Peter 56).

Louis Cazamian characterizes the ironic passages of Piers Plowman as having "a shrewd sense of the other side of things," although he further feels that the tense seriousness of the piece stands in the way of its full humor potential (Cazamian 54). Cazamian gives some examples of the humor of Langland's piece, as he tells about the holy men who turned themselves into hermits, "in order to have their ease," and about the term "restitution" which is described as "another name for stealing," and about the pilgrims who went on their way full of many wise tales that would allow them to "lie all their lives after," and about the palmer who had been to all the shrines of the holy world, but had never yet met a person called Truth (Cazamian 54).

William Langland Bibliography

Cazamian, Louis. The Development of English Humor. Durham, NC: Duke University Press, 1952.

Peter, John. Complaint and Satire in Early English Literature. Oxford, England: Clarendon Press, 1956.

Walker, Hugh. "Langland and Chaucer." English Satire and Satirists. New York: J. M. Dent, 1925, 9-23.

Geoffrey Chaucer (c1340-1400)

Jean Jost says that the humorous and the comedic are both generously infused into Chaucer's writing style. His humorous elements tend to be "local," and they are furthermore, "funny, clever, surprising (in reversals and unmaskings), appealingly deceptive, lighthearted, and jovial" (Jost 230). Chaucer's writing was significantly influenced by the Roman literary tradition. Anne Payne suggests that Chaucer's Troilus and Criseyde (1382-1385), his The Nun's Priest's Tale (1377), and his The Knight's Tale (1386-1394) were all influenced by the tradition of Menippean satire, including such writers as Seneca, Petronius, Apuleius, and especially Lucian and Boethius. Payne feels that Chaucer read these authors not only as philosophers, but as satirists as well. After reading Boethius's The Consolation of Philosophy, Chaucer wrote a freewheeling parody of the piece. Payne notes the paradox that resulted from Chaucer's attempt to parody an author he had so much respect for (Payne x). In her Chaucer and Menippean Satire, Payne explains that she focused on Lucian and Boethius as Chaucer's influences rather than dealing in detail with all of the Menippean satirists who influenced Chaucer in a major way. It was "because Lucian is the first Menippean satirist from whom we have complete works--he acts, therefore, as a kind of touchstone for the genre--and because Boethius's Consolation is the Menippean satire that Chaucer cites most frequently." (Payne xi)

Louis Cazamian suggests that the broad and full effect of Chaucer's writing emerges "with the suddenness of a miracle" (Cazamian 63). Before Chaucer, humor was just "a momentary gleam, a lucky accident, or at best an incipient disposition, gathering strength into some distinct flashes" (Cazamian 63); however, Chaucer's humor became the soul and essence of an artist and his art for the first time in the history of English literature, and perhaps for the first time in the history of literature in general (Cazamian 63). Chaucer's humor was a way of thinking, an attitude toward life. It had a spirit of relativity, of diversity, of unreasonableness. It was the natural outcome of a new kind of tolerance, a readiness to understand and sympathize. It represented a broad genial view of humanity, and could even be said to illustrate a kind of tenderness and love (Cazamian 64). Chaucer had the ability to view everyday happenings with a sense of novelty and freshness, an intellectual amusement, a "pleasure of satisfied curiosity" (Cazamian 65). Chaucer's stories were constituted in a Gallic vein of frankness with a touch of cynicism; they also were rich in native racy realism as viewed from a playfully shrewd mind (Cazamian 80).

Paul Ruggiers suggests that Chaucer derived a nice balance between the hard and objective world and an inner allegorical tendency from the Roman literary tradition. This resulted in the subordination of the literal and the realistic in favor of the symbolic and allegorical (Ruggiers Versions 12).

Chaucer's writing was also significantly influenced by the writings of Italy's Giovanni Boccaccio (1313-1375). In fact, Chaucer's defence of the use of the comic form mirrored Boccaccio's earlier pronouncements. Like Boccaccio, Chaucer told the reader never to attribute the words or attitudes of characters to the author. Chaucer said that he was merely being faithful to tales that he had been told, and that he was being as faithful as possible in the retelling. Chaucer said that he was attempting to be like Christ, or like Plato in making words truly represent the things being described. If there is coarseness, therefore, in Chaucer's writing, this is not because of Chaucer's embellishments, but is rather because the actions he describes are themselves coarse (Ruggiers Versions 15). Chaucer distanced himself not only from his texts, but from the characters of his texts as well. As Chaucer said, "You cannot expect very much from rascals like the Miller and the Reeve. In any event, do not take the game so seriously" (Ruggiers Versions 16).

Humbert Wolfe proposes that Chaucer was the first English author to develop "characters," a form of literature that culminated in the writings of Ben Jonson and Sir Thomas Overbury. Chaucer's art in this mode has a wide range--from ironic indulgence to plain satire (Wolfe 34-35). A. G. L'Estrange suggests that hardly any part of Chaucer's writing would raise a laugh today, though it might raise a blush. Nevertheless, L'Estrange feels that Chaucer was not a man of indelicacy. In fact, he feels that what Chaucer wrote was moderate for the time in which he lived. Furthermore, when Chaucer makes an offensive allusion, he usually adds some excuse for it (L'Estrange 224-225). Chaucer was considered very witty during his day, and in fact his Romaunt of the Rose (1370) greatly praises the idea of mirth (L'Estrange 225). Chaucer also speaks of "Dame Gladnesse" in the highest terms. Chaucer was fond of allegory, as can be seen in "Romaunt of the Rose," and "House of Fame." In "Assembly of Fowls" Chaucer explores the genre of fable (L'Estrange 226).

Jean Jost says that one aspect of the comic dimension of The Canterbury Tales (1386-1389) results from the appropriate juxtaposition with contrary or opposing tales, and Jost further suggests that this juxtaposition results more in a "comic satisfaction" than the "uproarious jocularity" that results from other aspects of the tales. T. W. Craik, for example, notices that The Miller's Tale follows The Knight's Tale as a sort of unintentional parody of antimasque, and for this same reason, it also precedes The Reeve's Tale (Jost 232).

Jost also notes that the wife in Chaucer's Wife of Bath Tale (1390-1394) to be "humorous in its excess" since she is a hyperbolic wife. She has five husbands "at the Church door" and still welcomes the sixth when he arrives. "The circumstances of her life with each of them are equally jocose in their vivid, even bombastic, quest for life" (Jost 232). Hugh Walker says that many critics consider the Wife of Bath tale to be a warning against matrimony, but Walker feels that it is a satire on lascivious women. "But in this instance Chaucer is so mastered by his humour, so carried away by his realization of the character, that the satire becomes a minor thing, and the picture is enjoyed just for what it is, irrespective of the vices of her who is delineated" (Walker 23). Walker considers the Wife of Bath to be one of the most amusing female figures in all of literature (Walker 23). The Wife of Bath is portrayed with gaudy stockings and a flamboyant hat that is "as broad as a buckler or a shield" (Chaucer 39), and her "incongruous obsession with husbands and pilgrimages" identifies her as audacious and forthright (Winny 2). She is filled with pent-up energy and physical stamina, and her outfit is very much overstated. At the beginning of the pilgrimage, the Wife of Bath doesn't wait to be invited, but launches into what James Winny describes as "a shameless autobiographical confession that holds the pilgrims fascinated, and with one exception speechless, to the end" (Winny 1). The Wife of Bath has "gap-teeth, set widely, truth to say" (Chaucer 38), and Malcolm Pittock notes that during the Middle Ages physical characteristics were often interpreted to be reflections of moral character, often taken as a sign of lasciviousness (Pittock 45). When it is noted that the Husband of the Wife of Bath is constantly grumbling about their married life, the Wife of Bath responds:

> Then you compared a woman's love to Hell
> To barren land where water will not dwell,
> And you compared it to a quenchless fire,
> The more it burns the more is its desire.
>
> To burn up everything that burnt can be.
> You say that just as worms destroy a tree
> A wife destroys her husband and contrives,
> As husbands know, the ruin of their lives (Chaucer 292; 371-377).

The irony of this situation lies in the Wife's repeating this complaint as evidence of the exasperation that she has to bear. The comparison with wild fire applies aptly to a woman who has consumed five husbands and is looking for a sixth.

In The Monk's Tale (1376-1377), W. T. Craik says that Chaunticleer provides a comic visual image in The Nun's Priest's Tale (1377) by falling into the mouth of the teasing fox. "The cock shuts his eyes when he should keep them open, the fox opens his mouth when he should keep it shut" (Craik, 71). Donald MacDonald says that in The Nun's Priest's Tale,

> The comic effect of a fable of even the most primitive kind derives from the basic incongruity in the spectacle of animals behaving like humans and, in particular, using human speech; this incongruity is increased in proportion to the degree in which animals not only use the language of humans but, in so doing, display impressive erudition and a mastery of rhetorical forms (MacDonald 464)

Francis J. Smith says that the manner and the spirit of Chaucer's Parliament of Fowles is light and gay, and adds that,

> such a mirthful approach is immediately delivered by the title itself, which is essentially mock serious, as well as the opening line "The lyf so short, the craft so long to lerne," which is, with deliberate comedy, distorted to fit a context of love matters. In other words, Chaucer did not save his fun for the chatter of birds in the last fourth of the poem but only allowed the comedy to rise gradually to the full climax in that part of it. (Smith 16-17).

Of course the humorous verbosity of the birds at the end of Parliament of Fowles as they argue among themselves, is Chaucer's attempt at comic resolution (Smith 17).

In many of Chaucer's tales there are inappropriate places for particular activities, and misplaced objects, which are funny either because of their incongruity or because of their unexpected and ironically apt congruity. Furthermore, the ribald humor in the fabliaux "often plays on misplaced or well-placed obscenity." Laura Kendrick goes so far as to suggest that the three washtubs hanging from the rafters in The Miller's Tale (1389), two of them round, and the other one long, represent God's giant "privitee" (Jost 231). In The Miller's Tale, Chaucer foregrounds the "fart" by introducing the first part of the rhyme as follows, "Speek, sweete bird, I noot nought wher thou art," and this delicate line sets up the ensuing "fart" that he considers to have been "as grete as it hadde been a thonder-dent" (Campbell 147). The fart was so powerful that it almost struck Absalom blind (Campbell 148). The Miller's Tale is preceded by The Knight's Tale which had grandly elaborated the courtly love situation. The Miller's Tale contrasts with The Knight's Tale by making the courtly love situation into a farce (Snipes 151). In The Miller's Tale, Young Absolom, wily Nicholas, and the asinine husband all play fools in a "three-ring carnival of desire" (Snipes 151). The three men represent the full sweep of a man's life. Nicholas and the husband represent different stages of physical (though not mental) maturity. Absolom is the naive youngster, or more specifically in terms of fourteenth-century mentality, he is the comic version of the young squire learning the tradition of courtly love. In the reversal of expectation that is the climax to the tail, it is Absolom who jumps to the incredible "logical" conclusion that the lady he is trying to seduce must have a beard (Snipes 152).

Much of the humor of The Knight's Tale (1386-1394) results from its being told in a "serious" tone. Edward Foster says "We cannot avoid the comic irony of the newly victorious Arcite falling off his charger.... Even Arcite's funeral pyre is made of wood whose cutting comically disposes the woodland gods" (Foster 92). The appearance of the knight is comic, as he appears in his rusted and spattered armor. "The comedy is the most generous possible, always in a tone of admiring sympathy" (Jost 233). Edward Foster says that the straight narration or monologue is "broken with witty, clever, ironic, or incongruously funny language." He says that the word play in The Knight's Tale contains

> ambiguous possibilities of the repetition of "queynte" four times in five lines...especially apparent since the scene is the shrine of the virgin goddess and Emily is asking that her virginity be preserved.... With these puns in mind it does not take an especially dirty mind to notice the frequency of the word "harnys," which does mean armour but is also a curiously appropriate

complement to the puns on the female organs. Such a pun adds a realistic
dimension to the courtly combat Palamon and Arcite plan. (Foster 89-90)
Foster recounts the humorous episodes of The Knight's Tale as follows: 1. the Knight's
delicate refusal to discuss Emily's ritual, 2. the mixture of catastrophe and trivia in the
temple of Mars, 3. Saturn's speech about his qualifications to restore order, 4. the
displacement of the woodland gods for Arcite's pyre, and 5. the Homeric comedy in the
behavior of the gods (Foster 89). The Reeve's Tale (1389) contains the shocking visual
imagery of Allen crawling into bed next to the snoring Miller Symkin to gloat about his
rollicking love-making with the miller's daughter (Jost 231).

According to Leigh Hunt, Chaucer's humor is entertaining, profound, and good-
natured. His comic genius is so perfect that it influenced much of the comic writing which
followed. Chaucer's liberal-thinking joviality can be found in the writings of Rabelais. His
moral portraitures can be found in Cervantes. His comic poetry can be found in
Shakespeare. His knowledge and learning is seen in Jonson, his manners and wit in
Charles the Second, his "bonhomie" in Sterne, and his insidiousness without malice in
Voltaire. One of the significant contributions of Chaucer was his tranquil detection of
particulars after the stating of a more general situation. He said that the Prioress speaks
French, but then adds that her French is "after the school of Stratford at Bow." Chaucer's
Lawyer was the busiest man in the world, but Chaucer then adds that he "seemed busier
than he was" (Hunt, 68-69).

Geoffrey Chaucer had a great eye for irony, though he may not have realized the
irony of his warning about the Middle English spelling system that "Ther is so great
diversite in English, and in wryting of oure tonge, So prey I god that non myswrite thee"
(Fromkin and Rodman 154). Irony is found throughout Chaucer's writings, from his
earliest lyrics on (Rowland viii). Earle Birney distinguished seven distinct types of irony
that are to be found in Chaucer's writing, and suggests that Chaucer himself was very
aware of the distinctions. Chaucer's verbal irony results from his frequent use of word
play, as in the Shipman's Tale (1386-1394) where the word "taille" is associated with
money and sex, being an indirect allusion to a woman's "tail" and the "tally" of a person's
worth (Rowland xviii). For Chaucer there was also the irony caused by the discrepancy
between the narrator telling the tale, and the poet (Chaucer himself) (Rowland xix).
Dramatic irony is the type of irony that allows the audience to have an advantage over the
protagonist and the other characters in the play (Rowland xx). Dramatic irony becomes
cosmic irony when it leaves the stage to take on the dimensions of the world or the
universe and heavens. Cosmic irony is sometimes called "irony of fate," "tragic irony,"
"irony of life or chance or events." It is also called philosophical irony." In cosmic irony
there is usually a grim reversal of circumstances that is in direct contradiction to what is
anticipated (Rowland xxi-xxii). The fifth type of irony is sometimes called the irony of
beliefs, values, or perceptions. This is the irony which highlights the contradictions,
incongruities, and disparities that exist between the ideals and the expectations of culture
on the one hand, and the actualities on the other (Rowland xxiii). Thematic irony is
Chaucer's sixth type. In the Canterbury Tales, for example, the group embarks on a
spiritual pilgrimage; yet the thoughts and the stories of the group are almost totally
committed to the world of the flesh (Rowland xxv). Chaucer's seventh type of irony is
described by Rowland as "structural irony," and is considered by Rowland to be "the most
innovative and striking characteristic of Chaucer's narrative style" (Rowland xxv). The
structural irony contrasts the discrepancies that occur within the discourse itself. This is
the type of irony that occurs, for example, between the Merchant and the Clerk. In subject-
matter, these two tales are classed with some other tales in forming the "marriage group."
However, in point of view, the tales contrast, for the Clerk, who tells a tale about a young
marquis and his marriage to an impossibly devoted wife concludes that "wives should be

as gay as a leaf on a linden tree and let their husbands 'care, and wepe, and wrynge, and waille' " (Rowland xxvi). However, the Merchant responds by telling a tale about his own caring and weeping and wringing and wailing because he has married a wife who is a match for the devil. By so doing he inverts the message of the Clerk's tale that women should be allowed to follow their own paths of liberation (Rowland xxvi).

> Chaucer placed the greatest emphasis on two principal modes: "dramatic irony," which, in his words "characterized passages in drama or dramatic narrative where a speaker's words convey more to the alert and informed reader or spectator than they convey either to the speaker or to some other character or characters listening to him within the world of the story itself"; and "verbal irony," which superimposed on dramatic irony, is one of the most pervasive and familiar kinds. (Rowland vii)

Many critics have faulted Chaucer for not being serious enough, and it is true that Chaucer enjoys telling stories about "hot coulters, bare bottoms, and swyved wives" (Garbáty 173). But it is also true that Chaucer's perspective was perfectly serious--though it was not a tragic perspective. Chaucer just could not remain in the tragic mindset for any extended period of time. "If we look at the whole corpus of his work, we see his tragic poems all interrupted, unfinished, or transfigured into celestial comedy" (Garbáty 173).

In an article entitled "The Gloomy Chaucer," Morton Bloomfield investigates the serious aspects of Chaucer's humor. Chaucer was a devoted Catholic, and his writing tended to be grave, moralistic, and didactic in tone. Bloomfield feels that Chaucer uses the tragicomic stance to preach the vanity of human desires (Bloomfield 58-59). Chaucer felt that there should be a balance in the universe between the religious tradition and the imperfection of all human endeavor (Bloomfield 61). Bloomfield summarizes Chaucer's stance in the following way:

> If we can comprehend this tragic perspectivism, we may grasp something of the Chaucerian humor, which hates human meanness and cruelty and which at the same time pities human weakness and affectation and even at times sin. Even though we may condemn it, we should also acknowledge that this attitude comes from a love for life. (Bloomfield 68)

Erich Segal has made a study of comic Schadenfreude (gallows humor) throughout literary history, and he feels that Chaucer's Canterbury tales can certainly be studied from this perspective. For example, Oswald, the Reeve, tells a lusty tale that involves aggressive sexuality. In this tale, two scholars "swyve" the wife and daughter of a miller in revenge for his having shortchanged them. At the end of the tale there is a great deal of physical violence:

> And on the nose he smoot hym with his fest
> Doun ran the blody streem upon his brest. (4275-4276) (Segal 74).

In a chapter entitled "Chaucer's Comic Visions," Frances McNeely Leonard points out that Chaucer's first poetry was in the form of allegory that contained comedy, and his last poetry was comedy that contained allegory. These contributions have affected the history of humor in two important ways. One is that Chaucer developed not only allegorical models in particular but the poetic tradition in general in a way that was to influence late medieval poets like Lydgate, Henryson, Hawes, Dunbar, Douglas, and Skelton, and the poets of the English Renaissance like Spenser as well. The history of humor in England was also influenced by the fact that both Dryden and Pope chose The Canterbury Tales for their "translations" and imitations, thus further enhancing Chaucer's reputation as the greatest comic poet in English literature (Leonard 27).

Louis Cazamian feels that Chaucer's intellectual detachment and his ability to play with shades of characterization signal a new style of maturity of reflection. The clearness of his artistic purpose, and the subtlety of his humor, though not entirely foreign, did not represent any stylistic development that, outside of Chaucer, was happening in England at the time. Chaucer's style embodied all of the heritage of the French finesse, and Cazamian feels that Chaucer's style was as French as would be possible without ceasing to be English (Cazamian 84).

In 1892, Thomas Lounsbury found only two puns in Chaucer; and as late as 1933, F. N. Robinson found only nine puns in Chaucer, but this was before readers had become aware of Chaucer's indebtedness to the precepts of medieval rhetoric. In his "Rhetorical Word-Play in Chaucer," Helge Kökeritz found a large number of puns in Chaucer, both of the innocent and of the bawdy varieties (Kökeritz 937-952). In his "More Puns in Chaucer," Norman Hinton says that Chaucer's puns are not merely the result of a superabundant sense of humor, nor the result of a "low mind," nor even the results of a mixed style.

> Most of the puns tend to complicate the thing which is being said. I do not want to claim that this makes Chaucer a more "ironic" writer, or a composer of verse with levels of meaning.... It does suggest, however, that Chaucerian verse is more intricate than many critics have been willing to admit--that Chaucer is saying more than one thing at a time in more places than were previously suspected. (Hinton 145)

In Chaucer's Bawdy, Thomas Ross says that Chaucer viewed copulation with "healthy and effervescent good humor."

> The "swyvynge" that goes on in the "Miller's" or the "Reeve's" Tales is supremely good fun for those involved directly. In the latter narrative, the daughter and the wife enjoy immensely their (respective) fornication and adultery. We readers, the indirect participants, enjoy the comic ribaldry too. (Ross 16)

Ross suggests that Chaucer's sexual puns are a "rich lode in his mine of comedy." He further suggests that these puns are both hilarious and hazardous. "We must be cautious, or we will begin to see covert sexual allusions in almost every line" (Ross 19).

Chaucer tends to think and write in clusters of ambiguity. His use of "pleye" in conjunction with "pryvetee" and "queynte," and with "jouste" and "daunce" reinforces the sexual innuendoes. "Pryve" seems to suggest to Chaucer "place" and "grace", and "serve" (or "service," "servant" etc.) goes with "grace," "holly," and "plesaunce."

> If one is uncertain whether a word has a palimpsest or secondary sexual meaning in a particular passage, the sudden surge of clusters of associated words will often provide mutual reinforcement and heightened probability.... Kökeritz saw that the congruence of 'mayden' and 'hede' was suggestive. But no one has observed that 'acqueyntaunce' often suggests the 'queynte' referred to so shamelessly and directly by Alison of Bath. (Ross 21)

Interpreting the puns in Chaucer is a tricky business. Ross says that "queynte" (quaint) and "luxurie" have now mainly lost the sexual connotations they once had. Similarly, during the Middle Ages, "corage" could mean valor, but it also could mean the capability to achieve and maintain an erection. Other words are sexual to modern ears but were not sexual in Chaucer's day. These words include "bawdy," "harlot," "lewde," ravysshed," and "sluttish," all of which had relatively innocent meanings in Chaucer's day (Ross 22).

Geoffrey Chaucer Bibliography

Abraham, David H. "Cosyn and Cosynage: Pun and Structure in the Shipman's Tale." Chaucer Review 11 (1977): 319-327.

Adams, John F. "The Structure of Irony in The Summoner's Tale." Essays in Criticism 12 (1962): 126-132.

Allen, Judson B. "The Old Way and the Parson's Way: An Ironic Reading of the Parson's Tale." Journal of Medieval and Renaissance Studies 3 (1973): 255-271.

Ames, Ruth M. "Prototype and Parody in Chaucer's Exegesis." The Fourteenth Century. Ed. P. E. Szarmach and B. S. Levy. Binghampton, NY: SUNY, 1977, 87-105.

Andreas, James R. "Festive Liminality in Chaucerian Comedy." Chaucer Newsletter 1 (1977): 3-6.

Andreas, James R. "The Rhetoric of Chaucerian Comedy: The Aristotelian Legacy." Comparist 8 (1984): 56-66.

Baum, Paul F. "Chaucer's Puns." Publications of the Modern Language Association 71 (1956): 225-246.

Baum, Paull F. "Chaucer's Puns: A Supplementary List." Publications of the Modern Language Association 73 (1958): 167-170.

Besserman, Lawrence L. "Chaucerian Wordplay: The Nun's Priest and his Woman Divyne." Chaucer Review 12 (1979): 68-73.

Birney, Earle. "The Beginnings of Chaucer's Irony." Publications of the Modern Language Association 54 (1939): 637-655.

Birney, Earle. Essays on Chaucerian Irony. Toronto, Canada: Univ of Toronto Press, 1985.

Birney, Earle. "Is Chaucer's Irony a Modern Discovery?" Journal of English and Germanic Philology 41 (1942): 303-319.

Blanch, Robert J. "Irony in Chaucer's Merchant's Tale." Langston Hughes Review 8 (1966): 8-15.

Block, R. Howard. The Scandal of the Fabliaux. Chicago, IL: University of Chicago Press, 1986.

Bloomfield, Morton W. "The Gloomy Chaucer." Veins of Humor Ed. Harry Levin. Cambridge, MA: Harvard Univ Press, 1972, 57-68.

Bloomfield, Morton W. "The Man of Law's Tale: A Tragedy of Victimization and a Christian Comedy." PMLA 87 (1972): 384-390.

Bonjour, Adrien. "Aspects of Chaucer's Irony in The Friar's Tale." Essays in Criticism 11 (1961): 121-127.

Bowker, Alvin W. "Comic Illusion and Dark Reality in The Miller's Tale." Modern Language Studies 4.2 (1974): 27-34.

Brewer, Derek S. "The International Medieval Popular Comic Tale in England." The Popular Literature of Medieval England. Ed. Thomas J. Heffernan. Knoxville, TN: University of Tennessee Press, 1985, 131-147.

Brewer, Derek S. "Structures and Character-Types of Chaucer's Popular Comic Tales." Estudios Sobre los Géneros Literarios, I (Grecia clásica et Inglaterra). Salamanca, Spain: Univ de Salamanca, 1975, 107-118.

Brodie, Alexander H. "Hodge of Ware and Geber's Cook: Wordplay in the 'Manciple's Prologue.' " Neuphilologische Mitteilungen 72 ((1971): 62-68.

Brown, Emerson, Jr. "Word Play in the Prologue to the Manciple's Tale, 98." Chaucer Newsletter 2.2 (1980): 11-12.

Burkhart, Robert E. "Chaucer's Absolom: A Sinful Parody of the Miller." Cithara 8.2 (1969): 47-54.

Burrow, J. A. "Irony in the Merchant's Tale." Anglia 75 (1957): 199-208.

Campbell, Dowling G. "Flatulence from Chaucer to Salinger." WHIMSY 1 (1983): 147-150.

Cazamian, Louis. The Development of English Humor. Durham, NC: Duke University Press, 1952.

Chaucer, Geoffrey. The Canterbury Tales. Trans. Nevell Coghill. Baltimore, MD: Penguin, 1952.

Clark, Roy Peter. "Wit and Whitsunday in Chaucer's Summoner's Tale." Annuale

Mediaevale 17 (1976): 48-57.

Coffman, George R. "The Miller's Tale: 3187-215: Chaucer and the Seven Liberal Arts in Burlesque Vein." Modern Language Notes 67 (1952): 329-331.

Cook, Thomas D. The Old French and Chaucerian Fabliaux: A Study of Their Comic Climax. Columbia, MO: Univ of Missouri Press, 1978.

Corsa, Helen Storm. Chaucer, Poet of Mirth and Morality. Notre Dame, IN: Univ of Notre Dame Press, 1964.

Craik, T. W. The Comic Tales of Chaucer. London, England: Methuen, 1964.

Dane, Joseph A. "The Mechanics of Comedy in Chaucer's Miller's Tale." The Chaucer Review 14 (1980): 215-224.

David, Alfred. "Chaucerian Comedy and Criseyde." Essays on Troilus and Criseyde." Totowa, NJ: Rowman, 1979, 90-104.

David, Alfred. "Sentimental Comedy in the Franklin's Tale." Annuale Mediaevale 6 (1965): 19-27.

DeNeef, A. Leigh. "Chaucer's Pardoner's Tale and the Irony of Misinterpretation." Journal of Narrative Technique. 3 (1973): 85-96.

Dempster, Germaine. Dramatic Irony in Chaucer. New York, NY: The Humanities Press, 1959.

Eliason, Norman E. "Some Word-Play in Chaucer's Reeve's Tale." Modern Language Notes 71 (1956): 162-164.

Falke, Anne. "The Comic Function of the Narrator in Troilus and Criseyde." Neophilologus 68 (1984): 134-141.

Finlayson, John. "The Satiric Mode and the Parson's Tale." Chaucer Review 6 (1971): 94-116.

Foster, Edward E. "Humor in the Knight's Tale." Chaucer Review 3 (1968): 88-94.

Frank, Robert W., Jr. "The Reeve's Tale and the Comedy of Limitation." Directions in Literary Criticism: Contemporary Approaches to Literature. Ed. Stanley Weintraub and Philip Young. University Park, :PA: Pennsylvania State University Press, 1973, 53-69.

Fromkin, Victoria, and Robert Rodman. An Introduction to Language 3rd edition. New York, NY: Holt, Rinehart and Winston, 1983.

Garbaty, Thomas J. "Chaucer and Comedy." Versions of Medieval Comedy. Ed. Paul Ruggiers. Norman, OK: University of Oklahoma Press, 1977, 173-190.

Garbaty, Thomas J. "Satire and Regionalism: The Reeve and His Tale." Chaucer Review 8 (1973): 1-8.

Gellrich, Jesse M. "The Parody of Medieval Music in the Miller's Tale." Journal of English and Germanic Philology 73 (1974(: 176-188.

Goddall, Peter. "An Outline History of the English Fabliau after Chaucer." Journal of the Australasian Universities Language and Literature Association 57 (1982): 5-23.

Grennen, Joseph E. "Makying in Comedy: 'Troilus and Criseyde,' V, 1788." Neuphilologische Mitteilungen 86 (1985): 489-493.

Harrington, David V. "Dramatic Irony in the Canon's Yeoman's Tale." Neuphilologische Mitteilungen 66 (1965): 160-166.

Hinton, Norman D. "More Puns in Chaucer." American Notes and Queries 2 (1964): 145-155.

Hunt, Leigh. "Selections from Chaucer, with Critical Notice." Wit and Humour Selected from the English Poets. New York, NY: Folcroft Library, 1972, 66-110.

Jennings, Margaret. "Ironic Dancing Absolom in the Miller's Tale." Florilegium 5 (1983): 178-188.

Jost, Jean E. Chaucer's Humor: Critical Essays. New York: Garland, 1994.

Jost, Jean E. "Geoffrey Chaucer." Encyclopedia of British Humorists, Volume I. Ed. Steven

H. Gale, New York, NY: Garland, 1996, 228-243.

Kendrick, Laura. Chaucerian Play: Comedy and Control in the Canterbury Tales. Berkeley, CA: University of California Press, 1988.

Kirk, Eugene P. Menippean Satire: An Annotated Catalogue of Texts and Criticism. New York, NY: Garland, 1980.

Knapp, Robert S. "Penance, Irony and Chaucer's Retraction." Assays 2 (1982): 45-67.

Knox, Norman. "The Satiric Pattern of The Canterbury Tales." Six Satirists. Ed. Austin Wright. Pittsburgh, PA: Carnegie Institute of Technology, 1965, 17-34.

Kökeritz, Helge. "Rhetorical Word-play in Chaucer." Publications of the Modern Language Association. 69 (1954): 937-952.

L'Estrange, A. G. "Origin of Modern Comedy: Chaucer, Heywood, et. al." History of English Humour. New York: Burt Franklin, 1878, 211-230.

Lancashire, Ian. "Moses, Elija and the Back Parts of God: Satiric Scatology in Chaucer's Summoner's Tale." Mosaic 14 (1980): 17-30.

Lanham, Richard A. "Game Play and High Seriousness in Chaucer's Poetry." English Studies 48 (1967): 1-24.

Lenaghan, R. T. "The Irony of the Friar's Tale." Chaucer Review 7 (1973): 281-294.

Leonard, Frances McNeely. "Chaucer's Comic Visions." Laughter in the Courts of Love: Comedy in Allegory, from Chaucer to Spenser. Norman, OK: Pilgrim, 1981, 27-56.

Leonard, Frances McNeely. "The School for Transformation: A Theory of Middle English Comedy." Genre 9 (1976): 179-191.

Levitan, Alan. "The Parody of Pentecost in Chaucer's Summoner's Tale." University of Toronto Quarterly 40 (1971): 236-246.

Levy, Bernard S. "Biblical Parody in the Summoner's Tale." Texas Studies in Literature and Language 11 (1966): 45-60.

MacDonald, Donald. "Proverbs, Sententiae, and Exempla in Chaucer's Comic Tales: The Function of Comic Misapplication." Speculum 41 (1966): 453-465.

MacDonald, Dwight, ed. Parodies: An Anthology from Chaucer to Beerbohm--And After. New York, NY: Random House, 1960.

McGalliard, John C. "Chaucerian Comedy: The Merchant's Tale, Jonson, and Molière." Philological Quarterly 25 (1946): 343-370.

Mann, Jill. Chaucer and Medieval Estates Satire: The Literature of Social Classes and the General Prologue to the Canterbury Tales. New York, NY: Cambridge Univ Press, 1973.

Martin, B. K. "The Miller's Tale as a Critical Problem and Dirty Joke." Studies in the Age of Chaucer 5 (1983): 86-120.

Marzec, Marcia Smith. "The Man of Law's Tale as Christian Comedy; Or, the Best-laid Schemes." Proceedings of the Patristic, Medieval and Renaissance Conference 12-13 (1987-1988): 197-208.

Mehl, Dieter. "Chaucerian Comedy and Shakespearean Tragedy." Shakespeare-Jahrbuch 81 (1984): 111-127.

Neuse, Richard. "The Knight: The First Mover in Chaucer's Human Comedy." University of Toronto Quarterly 31 (1962): 299-315.

Neuss, Paula. "Double Entendre in The Miller's Tale." Essays in Criticism 24 (1974): 325-340.

O'Hearn, Carolyn. "The Virtues of Pleasure, the Pleasures of Virtue: The 'Beastification" of Paradox in The Owl and the Nightingale." WHIMSY 4 (1986): 61-62.

O'Reilly, William M., Jr. "Irony in the Canon's Yeoman's Tale." Greyfriar 10 (1968): 23-39.

Olson, Glending. Literature as Recreation in the Later Middle Ages. Ithaca, NY: Cornell University Press, 1982.

Owen, Charles A., Jr. "Morality as a Comic Motif in The Canterbury Tales." College
    English 16 (1955): 226-232.
Owen, Charles A., Jr. "A Study in Irony and Symbol." Journal of English and Germanic
    Philology 52 (1953): 294-311.
Payne, F. Anne. Chaucer and Menippean Satire. Madison, WI: University of Wisconsin
    Press, 1981.
Pearsall, Derek. "The Canterbury Tales II: Comedy." The Cambridge Chaucer Companion.
    Ed. Piero Boitani and Jill Mann. Cambridge, England: Cambridge University Press,
    1986, 125-142.
Peter, John. Complaint and Satire in Early English Literature. Oxford, England: Clarendon
    Press, 1956.
Pittock, Malcolm. The Prioress's Tale: The Wife of Bath's Tale. Oxford, England: Basil
    Blackwell, 1973.
Ramsey, Vance. "Modes of Irony in the Canterbury Tales." Companion to Chaucer Studies
    Second Edition. Ed. Beryl Roland. New York, NY: Oxford Univ Press, 1979, 352-
    379.
Reid, David S. "Crocodilian Humor: A Discussion of Chaucer's Wife of Bath." Chaucer
    Review 14 (1979): 73-89.
Reiss, Edmund. "The Final Irony of the Pardoner's Tale." College English 25 (1964): 260-
    266.
Rodway, Allan. English Comedy: Its Role and Nature from Chaucer to the Present Day.
    Berkeley, CA: Univ of California Press, 1975.
Ross, Thomas W. Chaucer's Bawdy. New York, NY: Dutton, 1972.
Rothman, Irving N. "Humility and Obedience in the Clerk's Tale with the Envoy
    Considered as an Ironic Affirmation." Papers on Language and Literature 9 (1973):
    115-127.
Rowland, Beryl, ed. Essays on Chaucerian Irony. Toronto, Canada: University of Toronto
    Press, 1985.
Rowland, Beryl. "The Play of the Miller's Tale: A Game within a Game." Chaucer Review
    5 (1970): 140-146.
Rowland, Beryl. "Seven Kinds of Irony." Essays on Chaucerian Irony. Ed. Earle Birney.
    Toronto, Canada: University of Toronto Press, 1985.
Rudat, Wolfgang E. H. "Chaucer's Spring of Comedy: The Merchant's Tale and other
    'Games' with Augustinian Theology." Annuale Mediaevale 21 (1981): 111-120.
Ruggiers, Paul G. ed. Versions of Medieval Comedy. Norman, OK: Univ of Oklahoma
    Press, 1977.
Ruggiers, Paul G. "A Vocabulary for Chaucerian Comedy: A Preliminary Sketch."
    Medieval Studies in Honor of Lillian Herlands Hornstein. Eds. Jess B. Bessinger,
    Jr., and Robert R. Raymo. New York, NY: New York Univ Press, 1977, 193-225.
Sands, Donald B. "The Non-Comic, Non-Tragic Wife: Chaucer's Dame Alys as Sociopath."
    Chaucer Review 12 (1978): 171-182.
Sarno, Ronald A. "Chaucer and the Satirical Tradition." Classical Folia 21 (1967): 41-61.
Scheps, Walter. "The Goldyn Targe: Dunbar's Comic Psychomachia." Papers on Language
    and Literature 11 (1975): 339-356.
Segal, Erich. "Marlowe's Schadenfreude: Barabas as Comic Hero." Veins of Humor. Ed.
    Harry Levin. Cambridge, MA: Harvard Univ Press, 1972, 69-92.
Siegel, Paul N. "Comic Irony in the Miller's Tale." Boston University Studies in English
    4 (1960): 114-120.
Slade, Tony. "Irony in the Wife of Bath's Tale." Modern Language Review 64 (1969):
    241-247.
Smith, Francis J. "Mirth and Marriage in The Parliament of Foules." Ball State University

Forum 14 (1973): 15-22.

Snipes, Katherine W. "The Miller's Tale, Jack Falstaff, and the Ambiguous Fall of Man." WHIMSY 1 (1983): 150-153.

Stevens, Martin. "'And Venus Laughneth': An Interpretation of the Merchant's Tale." Chaucer Review 7 (1972): 118-131.

Stillwell, Gardiner. "Unity and Comedy in Chaucer's Parlement of Fowles." Journal of English and Germanic Philology 49 (1950): 470-495.

Szittya, Penn R. "The Green Yeoman as Loathly Lady: The Friar's Parody of the Wife of Bath's Tale." Publications of the Modern Language Association 90 (1975): 386-394.

Taylor, Willene P. "Chaucer's Technique in Handling Anti-Feminist Material in 'The Merchant's Tale': An Ironic Portrayal of the Senex-Amans and Jealous Husband." College Language Association Journal 13 (1969): 153-162.

Thro, A. Booker. "Chaucer's Creative Comedy: A Study of the Miller's Tale and the Shipman's Tale." Chaucer Review 5 (1970): 97-111.

Toole, William B., III. "Chaucer's Christian Irony: The Relationship of Character and Action in the Pardoner's Tale." Chaucer Review 3 (1968): 37-43.

Veldhoen, N. H. G. E. "Which Was the Mooste Fre: Chaucer's Realistic Humour and Insight into Human Nature, As Shown in The Frankelyens Tale." In Other Words Ed. J. Lachlan Mackenzie and Richard Todd. Dordrecht, Netherlands, Foris, 1989, 107-116.

Walker, Hugh. "Langland and Chaucer." English Satire and Satirists. New York, NY: J. M. Dent, 1925, 9-23.

Winny, James, ed. The Wife of Bath's Prologue and Tale: From the Canterbury Tales by Geoffrey Chaucer. Cambridge, England: Cambridge University Press, 1965.

Wolfe, Humbert. "Chaucer to Skelton." Notes on English Verse Satire. London, England: Leonard and Virginia Woolf, 1929, 27-48.

Wood, Chauncey. "Chaucer and Sir Thopas: Irony and Concupiscence." Texas Studies in Literature and Language 14 (1972): 389-403.

Woolf, Rosemary. "Chaucer as Satirist in the General Prologue to the Canterbury Tales." Critical Quarterly 1 (1959): 150-157.

Wurtele, Douglas. "Ironical Resonance in the Merchant's Tale." Chaucer Review 13 (1978): 66-79.

Henry Heywood (1340-1400)

A. G. L'Estrange considers Henry Heywood (basically an epigrammist) to be the "Father of English Comedy." All of his writing appeared before 1550, and each of his pieces was short and simple and seem to the modern eye to be deficient in both delicacy and humour (L'Estrange 227).

Henry Heywood Bibliography

L'Estrange, A. G. History of English Humour. New York, NY: Burt Franklin, 1878.

3

Humor in Fifteenth-Century British Literature

FIFTEENTH-CENTURY MONARCHS OF ENGLAND:

Henry IV (Bolingbroke)	Lancaster	1399-1413
Henry V	Lancaster	1413-1422
Henry VI	Lancaster	1422-1461
Edward IV	York	1461-1483
Edward V	York	1483-1483
Richard III	York	1483-1485
Henry VII (Tudor)	Tudor	1485-1509

Louis Cazamian feels that humor is like other literary fields in that it stagnated and decayed during the hundred years that followed Chaucer's death (119). Raymond Alden believes that during the fifteenth century all English literature, especially satirical poetry, languished. The one exception to this rule was political ballads (13-14). Hugh Walker believes that John Lydgate and Thomas Hoccleve may have been the two best satirical poets in the very barren century to which they belonged; however, he also believes that James I of Scotland was an excellent satirist, and even goes so far as to say that "James I, and not either Lydgate or Hoccleve, was the earliest writer who deserves to be called a successor of Chaucer" (Cazamian 26-27). Walker's praise of James I goes even further: "If he was the author of Peblis to the Play and Christ's Kirk on the Green, he would have to be regarded as the earliest Scottish satirist" (Walker 27).

In contrasting the English satire of the fifteenth century with that of the sixteenth century, Hugh Walker suggests that there is no real history of satire in prose prior to the Elizabethan age; there are only a few scattered pieces of satirical prose. However, in the sixteenth century, English prose emerged from its infancy and became significant, and this statement is true of both the satires and the other prose pieces. It was works like Epistolae Obscurorum Virorum, and Erasmus's Moriae Encomium that set the stage for the sophisticated satires of the sixteenth century (Walker 91).

Gavin Douglas's The Palice of Honour is modeled on Chaucer's The House of Fame. Even though this is a brilliant and busy poem, it doesn't wear well over a series of close readings. It is something of a virtuoso piece, filled with flourishes and poetic devices, but it lacks subtlety. Furthermore, the themes and images are presented too forcefully, almost violently, until the reader becomes weary of the prolonged excitement and longs for a quieter tone. But even though the poem is tedious, it is never dull, and there are many surprises in this allegory of love (Leonard 107-108).

During the fifteenth and the sixteenth centuries, broadsides were distributed which turned the world upside down, and were extremely popular. In these broadsides, one could see, for example, a child feeding the mother, or fish nesting in a tree, or an ox slaughtering a man, or a child beating a father, or an army of women attacking a fortress, or an armed woman standing beside her unarmed husband, who is spinning. David Kunzle argues that such broadsides made an important contribution to Lutheran propaganda against the pope, and may have been associated with the peasant revolt of 1525 as well (Little 5).

Fifteenth-Century England Bibliography

Alden, Raymond MacDonald. The Rise of Formal Satire in England under Classical Influence. New York, NY: Archon, 1961.

Beck, Ervin. "Terence Improved: The Paradigm of the Prodigal Son in English Renaissance Comedy." Renaissance Drama NS6 (1973): 107-122.

Bennett, Josephine W., Oscar Cargill, and Vernon Hall, Jr., eds. Studies in the English Renaissance Drama: In Memory of Karl Julius Holzknecht. New York, NY: New York Univ Press, 1959.

Bowen, Barbara C., ed. One Hundred Renaissance Jokes: An Anthology. Birmingham, AL: Summa Publications, 1988.

Cazamian, Louis. The Development of English Humor. Durham, NC: Duke University Press, 1952.

Davenport, W. A. "Mankind and Medieval Comedy." Fifteenth-Century English Drama: The Early Moral Plays and their Literary Relations. Totowa, NJ: Rowman, 1982, 36-78.

Hannaford, Stephen. " 'My Money Is My Daughter': Sexual and Financial Possessions in English Renaissance Comedy." Shakespeare-Jahrbuch 81 (1984): 93-110.

Jensen, Ejner J. "The Changing Faces of Love in English Renaissance Comedy." Comparative Drama 6 (1972-73): 294-309.

Kantra, Robert A. "Jerome and Erasmus in Renaissance Art." All Things Vain: Religious Satirists and Their Art. University Park, PA: Penn State University Press, 1984, 35-53.

Kernan, Alvin B. The Cankered Muse: Satire of the English Renaissance. New Haven, CT: Yale University Press, 1962.

Leonard, Frances McNeely. Laughter in the Courts of Love: Comedy in Allegory, from Chaucer to Spenser. Norman, OK: Pilgrim Books, 1981.

Little, Judith. Comedy and the Woman Writer: Woolf, Spark, and Feminism Lincoln, NE: 1983.

Peter, John. "Renaissance Satire." Complaint and Satire in Early English Literature. Oxford, England: Clarendon Press, 1956, 104-156.

Randolph, Mary Claire. "The Medical Concept in English Renaissance Satiric Theory." Studies in Philology 38 (1941): 125-157.

Robinson, Fred Norris. "Satirists and Enchanters in Early Irish Literature." Studies in the History of Religions Presented to Crawford Howell Toy. Eds. David Lyon and George Moore. New York, NY: Macmillan, 1912, 95-130.

Swain, Barbara. Fools and Folly during the Middle Ages and the Renaissance. New York, NY: Columbia University Press, 1932.

Walker, Hugh. English Satire and Satirists. London, England: J. M. Dent, 1925.

Thomas Hoccleve (c1370-c1450)

John Peter feels that Hoccleve was like earlier poets in crying out against the evils of money and such practices as coin clipping or shaving. But he feels that for Hoccleve, and for Lydgate as well, the outcry is taken from the stance of an "impoverished grumbler" rather than from that of a genuine moralist. In fact, Hoccleve admits that he would probably be happier if he himself were more deeply involved in the search for mammon (Peter 48).

Hugh Walker feels that Hoccleve has a wider range of satire than Lydgate, but he feels that he does not have greater skill as a satirist. Hoccleve's La Male Règle "has points of contact with [Lydgate's] London Lickpenny" (Walker 26). Hoccleve's A Dialogue with a Friend is a harsh verse satire on women. Walker feels Hoccleve is ineffective in this piece which depends mainly on the "vice of inversion" (26). The satire of Hoccleve's A Letter of Cupid to Lovers, his Subjects is written as a defence, and Walker considers this satire to be a great deal more effective (Walker 26).

Louis Cazamian believes that Hoccleve appears to be naive but is not. He asks if there might not be a touch of slyness when Hoccleve, as he is praising Chastity, mentions an episode of the Roman lady whose husband had bad breath, but she didn't realize it because "she lacked the necessary standards for comparison" (Cazamian 88). Cazamian suggests that Hoccleve's humor is understated: "He is not the dull ass he pretends to be" (Cazamian 88). He exhibits what Cazamian calls "virtual humor, made up of a pithy knowledge of things, just enough alive and conscious to be half actualized at times, but too much repressed by a heavy didacticism to become fully actual" (Cazamian 88).

Thomas Hoccleve Bibliography

Cazamian, Louis. "Gower, Hoccleve, Lydgate." The Development of English Humor. Durham, NC: Duke University Press, 1952, 85-89.
Peter, John. Complaint and Satire in Early English Literature. Oxford, England: Clarendon Press, 1956.
Walker, Hugh. English Satire and Satirists. London, England: J. M. Dent, 1925.

John Lydgate (c1370-c1451)

In Lydgate's earlier works, The Temple of Glass, and Reason and Sensuality, there is a certain liveliness in the free play and spontaneous fancy of the style. This can be seen in the dialogue between the author and Diana concerning the "chaste goddess's vivacious, realistic faultfinding with Venus" (Cazamian 89). Lydgate's Fall of Princes also has a kind of "virtual humor." Fall of Princes deals with the great catastrophes of history, beginning with Adam and ending with King John's being taken prisoner in France by Prince Edward (Cazamian 88).

Lydgate's A Tale of Threescore Folys and Thre is sometimes called The Order of Fools, and is similar to Barclay's Ship of Fools. In this satire, Lydgate indicates that the order of fools is longstanding, and consists of sixty-three members (Alden 14). He enumerates these sixty-three fool categories, concluding each enumeration with the phrase that they "shall never thrive" (Alden 14-15). In his various satires, Lydgate exposes many types of fools and folly, but like most other satirists of his day, his special target is the vice of hypocrisy or deceit (Alden 15).

Hugh Walker points out that some of Lydgate's minor poems are satirical, but unlike the satire of Chaucer's <u>Canterbury Tales</u>, Lydgate's satire is crude and unsophisticated. Lydgate's <u>So as the Crabbe goeth Forwarde</u>, and his <u>As Straight as a Ram's Horn</u> are what Walker terms "contraries." The titles of these two pieces provide the first clues that the meanings of the poems are ironic and are therefore the opposite of what is explicitly stated (Walker 24).

Raymond Alden points out that Lydgate's <u>Satirical Ballad on the Times</u> is ironic. In each stanza, things are first declared as they should be, but this is always followed by the modification "So as the crabbe goeth forwarde," at which point Lydgate sketches out the problems of changing fortune, or hypocrisy, or unrighteous princes, or unjust lawyers, or the discontented poor, or the worldly grounding of religion, or newfangled women, or dishonest merchants, and so on. "The times, like the crab, are clearly going the wrong way" (Alden 14).

It is generally assumed that Lydgate is the author of <u>London Lickpenny</u>, and if this is indeed the case, Walker feels that Lydgate deserves higher recognition as a quality satirist than would otherwise be warranted. <u>London Lickpenny</u> may be rude, but it shows a great deal of spirit, and effectively uses humor to depict Lydgate's era (Walker 25).

John Lydgate Bibliography

Alden, Raymond MacDonald. "Lydgate." <u>The Rise of Formal Satire in England under Classical Influence</u>. New York, NY: Archon, 1961, 14-15.
Cazamian, Louis. "Gower, Hoccleve, Lydgate." <u>The Development of English Humor</u>. Durham, NC: Duke University Press, 1952, 85-89.
Walker, Hugh. <u>English Satire and Satirists</u>. London, England: J. M. Dent, 1925.

Robert Henryson (c1430-1506) SCOTLAND

Louis Cazamian considers Robert Henryson and William Dunbar to be Chaucer's most worthy successors, as "the <u>Kingis Quair</u> is unmatched in the south for its lyrical fervor and charm" (Cazamian 89). Cazamian also points out that the English and Scottish views of each other are not always totally accurate. "The English have it that Scottish humor is of the broadest kind..., but can anything be more broad than the popular English tales and fabliaux of the fifteenth century?" (Cazamian 90). Cazamian feels that the conscious art and dramatic management of such Scottish authors as Robert Henryson, William Dunbar, Gavin Douglas, and David Lindsay were influenced greatly by the writings of Chaucer. But Cazamian suggests that they are <u>not</u> indebted to Chaucer for their humor. "This [humor] is a native growth, racy of the soil, and the vein of which, with them, answers to the more popular tone of their inspiration (Cazamian 91).

Hugh Walker considers much of Robert Henryson's writing to contain "an element of satire," though he considers this satire not to be significant. A couple of Henryson's <u>Fables of Aesop</u> are satirical, and the moral at the end of <u>The Tail of the Dog, the Scheip, and the Wolf</u> satirizes the fact that the law of Henryson's time tended to oppress the poor in favor of the rich (Walker 27). Walker considers <u>Sum Practysis of Medicine</u> to be obscure and difficult, but clearly satirical in purpose. Walker compares this satire of medical practices to Chaucer's <u>Prologue</u>, and <u>The Nun's Priest's Tale</u> which also have medical practices as a target, but he concludes that except for the medical target, there is little in common between Chaucer and Henryson (Walker 28).

Louis Cazamian considers Robert Henryson to be the "only writer of the age who can be mentioned in the same breath with Chaucer" (91). Although Henryson owes a large debt to Chaucer, he owes an even larger debt to Scotland and to his own individuality. His writing may be inferior in delicacy, subtlety, suppleness, and range of humorous expression, but it is superior in its sense of tragic irony that uses philosophical bitterness to instill a sense of romantic or modern flavor into his greatest poem (91).

Henryson's Testament of Cresseid uses thoughtful pessimism to sustain a vigorous tone in a firm and sophisticated style (Cazamian 91). His Sum Practysis of Medecyne is a Rabelaisian outburst, as it develops in rough merrymaking and irrepressible fun. His The Garment of Good Ladies, his The Reasoning between Age and Youth, his Robyn and Makyne, and his Fables exhibit writing of a finer and gentler kind. In these pieces, "the neat, nimble cleverness of Chaucer's manner is often caught" (Cazamian 91), as in the couplet about tide and opportunity: "The man that will not when he may / Shall have not when he would" (Cazamian 91-92).

Robert Henryson Bibliography

Cazamian, Louis. "Scottish Writers; Skelton." The Development of English Humor. Durham, NC: Duke University Press, 1952, 89-99.
Walker, Hugh. English Satire and Satirists. London, England: J. M. Dent, 1925.

4

Humor in Sixteenth-Century British Literature

SIXTEENTH-CENTURY MONARCHS OF ENGLAND:

Henry VII (Tudor)	Tudor	1485-1509
Henry VIII	Tudor	1509-1547
Edward VI	Tudor	1547-1553
Mary I (Bloody Mary)	Tudor	1553-1558
Elizabeth I	Tudor	1558-1603

John Scogan was a jester in the court of Edward VII, and his practical jokes were still popular during Queen Elizabeth's time. Scogan is said to have been "of pleasant wit and bent to merrie devices." His practical jokes often attacked the clergy. (L'Estrange 279).

At the beginning of his reign, Henry VIII was a great patron of men of wit and learning, and it was probably Sir Thomas More's humor and virtue which made him a favorite of the king. Cardinal Morton, who was a boy during the reign of Henry VIII was also a humorous figure. During Christmas company, Morton, then a boy, would climb onto the stage and extemporize with so much wit and talent that he surpassed all of the professional players. During his university course, and shortly thereafter, he wrote a number of Latin epigrams, one of which can be translated as follows:

> Once in the loving cup, a guest saw flies,
>
> Removed them, drank, and then put back a few.
>
> And being questioned, sagely thus replies,
>
> "I like them not--but cannot speak for you."

> (L'Estrange 276-277)

Louis Cazamian believes that the period that followed Chaucer's death was not a period of decay in the domain of humor. At this time, there were two basic tendencies of humor in England. One of these was the publication of humorous pieces, and the singing of ballads. The other was the carvings, with their grotesque fantasy that are to be found in the cathedrals and churches of the time (Cazamian 97).

Ernst Cassirer suggests that our modern notion of humor was not only present during the English Renaissance, but in fact it was invented during that time. This type of humor is a strange mixture of "gentleness and energy, of cautious skepticism and of fiery reforming enthusiasm." It is much more than mere wit and wordplay. It has a plastic power which interrelates language with thought (Cassirer 177). Charles Ross uses a script-based theory of humor to investigate Renaissance allegoresis, since both script theory and allegory are concerned with symbolic readings in which we are made to think about things we already know. Allegory provides for a number of levels--the psychological level, the cosmological level, the philosophical level, and so forth. Script-theory allows for the appropriate interpretation of these levels. When there is allegory, there is the requirement that the reader must ask the appropriate questions of the text or must recognize the underlying scripts, some of which are essentially humorous. Ross suggests that this is why successful discussions of romantic epics like Spenser's are always funny, never serious (Ross 154).

King Hart tells of a lifelong journey through the Court of Love. It is anonymously written, and is neither Chaucerian in quality, nor a pilgrimage on the narrative level, but Frances McNeely Leonard nevertheless feels that it needs to be mentioned in his Laughter in the Courts of Love (Leonard 107). King Hart is a metaphorical, allegorical pilgrimage which establishes a special relationship between the poem and the reader. As with literal pilgrimages, there is the going out on a mission, the hero's adventures, and the return of the hero. But the pilgrimage of the poem involves not one, but rather two journeys, as it takes the protagonist through youth to age with the resultant development of the mind and atrophy of the body. At the end, the hero has a corrected moral vision that allows him to evaluate his squandered youth and manhood (Leonard 126). As the hero moves from the lusty riotousness of youth to the lamentations of age, the poem modulates from bright comedy to somber irony. King Hart's testimony is that the natural shape of such a pilgrimage begins with the fires of passion, and ends with the ashes of regret. "The comedy of youth becomes the tragedy of loss. Only through the grace of God can the pilgrimage be redeemed and redirected; then the comedy of error becomes a song of joy" (Leonard 131).

Queen Elizabeth had an incredible love of humor, and according to the custom of her day, she exhibited this not only in what she said, but also by receiving comedians into the "great houses" (L'Estrange 277). Queen Elizabeth had a natural gift for humor, and many of her witty sayings have come down to us through history. On one occasion a particular archbishop found fault with some of her actions, and quoted Scripture to prove that she had acted more as a politician than as a Christian. "I see, my lord," she replied, "that you have read the scriptures, but not the book of Kings" (L'Estrange 279). On another occasion, she agreed to knight seven men whom Lord Burleigh had recommended. The seven men to be knighted were placed in a line of descending order so that the Queen would give precedence to the men which Lord Burleigh liked the most. But the men he liked the most were the least worthy. The Queen, therefore, passed down the row and took no notice of the men to be honored. Then when she had reached the end of the line she turned around and said, "I had almost forgotten my promise," and proceeded to knight the men from the lower end up. When she had finished, she turned to Lord Burleigh, and said, "I have but followed the scripture--'the first shall be last and the last first' " (L'Estrange 280).

In 1583 Queen Elizabeth ordered that twelve humorous men should be made grooms of her chamber, be sworn to her as Queen's servants, and be clothed in the Queen's livery. The most remarkable of these was Richard Tarlton (L'Estrange 277). Tarlton's humor was that of the common fool. It depended mainly on how he acted, looked, and spoke; his face was therefore his fortune, for he had a flat nose and squinting eyes. On one occasion he peeped out from behind a curtain at his audience, probably with a grimace on his face, and this caused such a burst of laughter that one of the justices, who didn't understand what had happened, beat the people on their heads because, they, "being farmers and hinds, had dared to laugh at the Queen's men." Tarlton was celebrated for his extemporaneous songs, called jigs, which were accompanied with tabor and pipe, and sometimes also included dancing (L'Estrange 278). In Elizabethan theatre the players often interacted with the audience in this carnivalesque way. The clown improvised within the play and improvised much repartee with the audience.

> Such improvisation was both politically dangerous, because uncensored, and aesthetically unsettling, because it refused any strict divorce between representation and audience. The compromise was the jig--if the clown was downgraded in the course of the play and limited to the lines written for him by the playwright, after the dramatic finale he issued forth to conduct a jig which established a more direct rapport with the audience. (MacCabe 9)

As her reign went on, and Queen Elizabeth was surrounded by the details of sovereignty, and opposition from her Roman Catholic subjects, the Queen's humor became more severe in complexion, and her thoughts became more earnest, and her jests more cynical (L'Estrange 280). Nevertheless, Elizabethans loved words and they loved word play. They delighted in puns, and they liked to use and interpret words in as many different senses as possible. The art of retort, both courteous and discourteous, was considered an important skill (Rose 62). Elizabethan puns occurred not only in everyday speech, but in educated elegant speech as well. They liked to repeat sounds, to balance clauses, to embellish their witty writing with earthy quips about sex, priests, or cuckolds. Elizabethan writing is filled with the lilt of language, the rhythm of speech, the wonder of words, the humor of language that mocks the base and the high born as well. England was an island and its isolation from the mainland resulted in a kind of provinciality that loved to make fun of foreigners. In the sixteenth century there may not have been a growing sense of English power, but there was a growing sense of the power of the English language.

In a chapter entitled "Jerome and Erasmus in Renaissance Art," Robert Kantra points out that during the early Renaissance two countervailing forces were in effect. One of these was the distrust of the classics. The other was the constant use of the classics. And one of the most important ways that English sixteenth-century authors were indebted to the classical authors was for the sense of humor, or more specifically, for the feeling that "humor is characteristic of the spiritual man" (Kantra 38). Nevertheless, during the sixteenth century, there was a separation in English humor of humanism and puritanism, but despite this separation there were many cross-currents or oscillations between the two positions, and Kantra feels that no discussion of Renaissance religious satire can avoid a discussion of these cross-currents (Kantra 39).

Louis Cazamian suggests that the humor of Nicholas Udall, the schoolmaster, and Sir Philip Sidney, the nobleman and knight, and the "University Wits," and most other sixteenth-century humorists is colored by an intimate knowledge of pre-existing literary patterns (Cazamian 120). It should be remembered that during the sixteenth century the Renaissance was awakening in France and Spain with its spirit of critical reflection. François Rabelais (1490-c1553), Michel Eyquem de Montaigne (1553-1592), and Miguel de Cervantes Saavedra (1547-1616) all "wrote in the light of a bolder reason that did not fear to take itself as the test and measure of all things," and of course the works of these three writers, which were pervaded by an atmosphere of humor, had a significant influence on English literature during the late sixteenth and early seventeenth centuries (Cazamian 120). Cazamian feels that from that time until now, England has been ruled by "the spirit of Sancho." "The trusty squire has found there in many respects his real, not imaginary, island kingdom" (Cazamian 148). As evidence of Sancho Panza's influence, Cazamian points out that England's Sir Roger de Coverley, Parson Adams, Uncle Toby, the Vicar of Wakefield, Mr. Pickwick and many others are spiritual brothers or cousins of the Spanish squire (Cazamian 148-149). Cazamian continues that the respective authors created these characters in order to allow their creative fancy to play. In fact, Cazamian feels that the influence of Don Quixote on English literature is central to the development of modern English humor (Cazamian 149).

Humbert Wolfe feels that Geoffrey Chaucer should not be called a satirist just because he has written satires. For Wolfe, Chaucer's influence on later deliberate satirists such as John Lydgate in London Lackpenny, and on Robert Henryson in The Moral Fabelles of Esop, and especially on John Skelton is as important as his own satires, for without an understanding of this influence, Wolfe feels that Lydgate, Henryson, and Skelton cannot be fully understood (Wolfe 37).

Stephen Hawes's The Pastime of Pleasure followed Lydgate, who followed Chaucer; however there is little that is Chaucerian in Hawes's piece in either spirit or structure. Chaucer wrote with exuberance, while Hawes merely plods along. Hawes seems to feel, however, that comedy is a requisite part of the journey he is describing, for he includes a clown in the poem. The clown, named Godfrey Gobylyve, is there mainly for comic relief (Leonard 107).

Hugh Walker suggests that the establishment of the five-beat iambic line, and ultimately the heroic couplet was important not only to the development of sixteenth-century drama in particular but to the development of satire in general. Walker points out that Sir Thomas Wyatt helped to establish the normal metre for satire, but that a few years after Wyatt, Robert Crowley was writing satire in his "pleasant free doggerel verse," and still later, Edward Hake used a kind of a ballad metre in his News Out of Paul's Churchyard (Walker 57).

Walker notes that Hake's News Out of Paul's Churchyard is a flat and prosaic collection of eight satires directed at the Church, the law, and medicine. Hake sides strongly with the Puritans and against the Papists, whom he calls "bloody beasts and foul infected swine" (Walker 59). Raymond Alden notes that Hake is often considered to be one of the very earliest English satirists, since his News preceded Gascoigne's Steele Glas (Alden 62). The style of the satire in News is characteristic of early English satire, with its rugged and sometimes violent language and themes, and its abundant alliteration. Hake's style was vigorous, and fluent, and filled with the vernacular, but it was also monotonous at times. Hake's satires are preceded by a dedication to the Earl of Leicester, and the Earl's coat-of-arms is also reproduced in the piece (Alden 63). Alden notes that a major rhetorical device in Hake's satire is direct rebuke (Alden 64); he also notes that the style and local color of these satires are typically English (Alden 65).

Alfred Gu L'Estrange suggests that "Doctor Double Ale," written about the time of the Reformation, is a good satire, showing a great deal of humor in subject, in language, and in versification. Many humorous poems which had been written earlier against the church were republished during the Reformation, and this illustrates that for centuries the follies of the clergy had been a source of comment. For example, The Sak Full of Nuez, written before 1575, contains a collection of humorous pieces of rough and rude character, and there are a number of hits which target the church (L'Estrange 202-203).

In a chapter entitled "The Renaissance, the Reformation, and Humor," Louis Cazamian points out that these two countervailing forces of the sixteenth century both helped to establish humor as part of the national character of England. For Cazamian, the Renaissance is the logical period for the development of English humor, as it is the period for the development of learning in general. During this period, humor and pleasantry not only showed an increasing vitality, but it also reached a degree of self-realization (Cazamian 103). During the English Renaissance, humor developed mainly along two lines. The humor of humanism was concentrated to a few exceptional minds, mainly writers, thinkers, and the more highly cultivated and refined. It was a prevalent aspect of the aristocracy, of the inner circles of the court, the nobility, people of leisure, and the inner circles of the universities. This line of humor was in close contact not only with the classics, but also with foreign literatures, especially those of Italy and France (Cazamian 104-105). Hugh Walker states that the sixteenth century literature was inspired by the literature of classical antiquity, and in the case of satire, especially in the writings of Persius, Horace, and Juvenal (Walker 57). Cazamian suggests that sixteenth century English parody was especially associated with the literature of refinement and scholarship, and George Kitchin says, "Nothing is clearer than that the best products of our wit were the result of schooling in the classics" (Kitchin x).

The other line that was developing during the sixteenth century was popular humor. This humor was much more widely diffused, and was in fact common to all ranks and classes, and it consisted of shrewdness, raciness, rough patterns of speech and thought, and a down-to-earth reaction to life (Cazamian 105).

But Cazamian feels that English humor owes as much to the Reformation as it does to the Renaissance. He elaborates by saying that the spiritual decision by means of which sixteenth-century England chose her religious traditions and established for herself an ideal of "sober earnestness" did not inhibit the development of her humorous gifts. In fact, it decidedly furthered the process (Cazamian 118).

Nevertheless, even though the concept of "humor" developed greatly during the sixteenth century, the word itself still retained its archaic meanings, and would continue to do so until the time of Ben Jonson. Even at the end of the sixteenth century all the nations of Europe were alike in that they possessed the term "humor" but used this term in its primal medical sense as one of the four cardinal elements constituting make-up of mankind, and it was only by a natural extension of the sense that the word came to be used throughout Europe for disposition or temperament in general (Cazamian 328).

The fluids that were at this time considered to be the "cardinal humors" were blood, phlegm, choler, and melancholy, and each of these related to a particular color, and particular physical and mental temperament. The notions of oddity and eccentricity became closely related to the word "humor" and by the latter half of the sixteenth century, the word was in constant use and the idea of the "humors" grew to be almost an obsession (Cazamian 310). There was at this time, however, also the development of a new literary kind of humor, the "Theophrastian portrait or 'character' " (Cazamian 310).

It was during the Renaissance that tragedy and comedy started to be mixed into a new genre called "mongrel tragicomedy" by Bernard Dukore, and this genre continued on, and was greatly strengthened in the twentieth century. During the Renaissance "tragicomedy" meant the blending of a serious action (as in tragedy) with a happy ending (as in comedy), or the scenes of a major tragic plot were alternated with those of a comic subplot, or there was a mixture of aristocratic characters (appropriate to tragedy) with humble characters (appropriate to comedy)(Dukore 1).

At the end of the sixteenth century, an important humorous event occurred. During Lent of 1599, William Kempe did a jig all the way from London to Norwich. He later wrote up this event in his Kempes Nine Daies Wonder. Before this event, Kempe had been a Shakespearian actor at the Globe theatre, and one of the things he enjoyed doing most was to leave the script and address the audience in an aside (also called a "jig"). But unlike the northern theatres of England, the Globe was "consciously turning its back on what they saw as an outdated dramatic form and, most importantly, the relation it implied with the audience." Kempe had enjoyed this informal relationship with his audience, and thus at the same time that he resigned as an actor, he did his jig all the way to Norwich. Later, in his book, he indicates that the best way of understanding his journey is that he was dancing himself "out of the world." MacCabe feels that this is a clear allusion to the theatre he was leaving--the Globe (11-12).

Sixteenth-Century England Bibliography

Alden, Raymond MacDonald. The Rise of Formal Satire in England under Classical Influence. New York, NY: Archon Books, 1961.

Baskervill, C. J. The Elizabethan Jig. Chicago, IL: University of Chicago Press, 1929.

Bradbrook, M. C. The Growth and Structure of Elizabethan Comedy. Berkeley, CA: Univ of California Press, 1956.

Bristol, Michael D. "Carnival and the Institutions of Theatre in Elizabethan England." Journal of English Literary History 50 (1983): 637-654.

Cassirer, Ernst. The Platonic Renaissance in England. Austin, TX: University of Texas Press, 1953.

Cazamian, Louis. The Development of English Humor. Durham, NC: Duke University Press, 1952.

Cole, Douglas. "The Comic Accomplice in Elizabethan Tragedy." Renaissance Drama 9 (1966): 125-139.

Coolidge, John S. "Martin Marprelate, Marvell, and Decorum Personae as a Satirical Theme." Publications of the Modern Language Association 74 (1959): 526-532).

Curry, John V. Deception in Elizabethan Comedy. Chicago, IL: Loyola Univ Press, 1955.

Doran, Madeleine. Endeavors of Art: A Study of Form in Elizabethan Drama. Madison, WI: Univ of Wisconsin Press, 1954.

Dukore, Bernard F. Where Laughter Stops: Pinter's Tragicomedy. Columbia, MO: University of Missouri Press, 1976.

Farnham, Willard. "The Medieval Comic Spirit in the English Renaissance." Joseph Quincy Adams Memorial Studies. Eds. James G. McManaway, Giles E. Dawson, and Edwin E. Willoughby. Washington, DC: Folger Shakespeare Library, 1948, 429-437.

Feldman, Sylvia D. The Morality-Patterned Comedy of the Renaissance. The Hague, Netherlands: Mouton, 1970.

Freeburg, Victor Oscar. Disguise Plots in Elizabethan Drama: A Study in Stage Tradition. New York, NY: Bloom, 1965.

Gransden, K. W., ed. Tudor Verse Satire. London, England: Athlone, 1970.

Haselkorn, Anne M. Prostitution in Elizabethan and Jacobean Comedy. Troy, NY: Whitston, 1983.

Holden, William P. Anti-Puritan Satire 1572-1642. New Haven, CT: Yale University Press, 1954.

Ingram, R. W. "Gammar Gurton's Needle: Comedy Not Quite of the Lowest Order?" Studies in English Literature, 1500-1900 7 (1967): 257-268; NOTE: Attributed to William Stevenson (-1575).

Ingram, William. "Minstrels in Elizabethan London: Who Were They, What Did They Do?" English Literary Renaissance 14.1: 29-54.

Jensen, Ejner J. "The Changing Faces of Love in English Renaissance Comedy." Comparative Drama 6 (1972): 294-309.

Kantra, Robert A. All Things Vain: Religious Satirists and Their Art. University Park, PA: Pennsylvania State University Press, 1984.

Kernodle, George R. "The Mannerist Stage of Comic Detachment." The Elizabethan Theatre III. Ed. David Galloway. Hamden, CT: Shoe String, 1973, 119-134.

Kitchin, George. "Elizabethan Dramatic Burlesque." Survey of Burlesque and Parody in English. London, England: Oliver and Boyd, 1931, 38-67.

L'Estrange, Alfred Gu. History of English Humour. New York, NY: Burt Franklin, 1878.

Leonard, Frances McNeely. Laughter in the Courts of Love: Comedy in Allegory, from Chaucer to Spenser. Norman, OK: Pilgrim, 1981.

MacCabe, Colin. "Abusing Self and Others: Puritan Accounts of the Shakespearian Stage."

Critical Quarterly 30.3 (1988): 3-17.

McCollom, William. "From Dissonance to Harmony: The Evolution of Early English Comedy." Theatre Annual 21 (1964): 69-96.

Priestley, J. B. "Some Elizabethans and Jacobeans." English Humour. New York, NY: Stein and Day, 1976, 13-17.

Rose, Sandra Priest. "Lyly and Tudor Humor." WHIMSY 4 (1986): 62-64.

Ross, Charles. The Grim Humor of Spenser's "Faerie Queene": Women and Laughter in a Renaissance Epic. Humor: International Journal of Humor Research 2.2 (1989): 153-164.

Schäfer, Jürgen. Wort und Begriff Humour in der Elisabethanischen Komödie. Münster, Germany: Verlag Aschendorff, 1966.

Somerset, J. A. B. " 'Fair is foul and foul is fair': Vice-Comedy's Development and Theatrical Effects." The Elizabethan Theatre V. Ed. G. R. Hibbard. Hamden, CT: Shoe String, 1975, 54-75.

Staton, Shirley F. "Female Transvestism in Renaissance Comedy: 'A Natural Perspective, That Is and Is Not.' " Iowa State Journal of Research 56 (1981): 79-81.

Stevenson, David Lloyd. The Love-Game Comedy. New York, NY: Columbia Univ Press, 1946.

Stubbs, John Heath. "Tudor Satire." The Verse Satire. London, England: Oxford University Press, 1969, 8-21.

Thorndike, Ashley H. "Conclusion to Elizabethan Comedy." English Comedy. New York, NY: Macmillan, 1929, 252-268.

Thorndike, Ashley H. "Elizabethan Beginnings." English Comedy. New York, NY: Macmillan, 1929, 47-73.

Thorndike, Ashley H. "Elizabethan Varieties." English Comedy. New York, NY: Macmillan, 1929, 140-166.

Thorndike, Ashley H. "The Later Elizabethans." English Comedy. New York, NY: Macmillan, 1929. 218-251.

Walker, Hugh. English Satire and Satirists. New York, NY: J. M. Dent, 1925.

Weiss, T. The Breadth of Clowns and Kings. New York: Atheneum, 1971.

Weld, John S. Meaning in Comedy: Studies in Elizabethan Romantic Comedy. Albany, NY: State University of New York Press, 1975.

Welsford, Enid. The Fool: His Social and Literary History. New York, NY: Farrar and Rinehart, 1936.

White, R. S. " 'Comedy' in Elizabethan Prose Romances." Yearbook of English Studies 5 (1975): 46-51.

Wolfe, Humbert. Notes on English Verse Satire. London, England: Leonard and Virginia Woolf, 1929.

William Dunbar (c1460-c1520) SCOTLAND

Pamela Shaffer says that Dunbar delighted in the play of sounds as he wrote his poetry (Shaffer 343). She furthermore says that the satiric mode is one of the most distinctive traits of Dunbar's poetry. "The poetic modes that he uses include allegory and dream vision, panegyric, moralizing, comic narrative, and satire." Dunbar writes poetry in three distinct and contrasting styles that can be classified as "high," "middle," and "low." "It is with poems in the low style that Dunbar exhibits the wild, satiric humor which is one of his most distinctive qualities. These poems often illustrate Dunbar's play with the conventions of courtly love and the romance tradition." In this "low" style, Dunbar's diction is often coarse and contains a number of linguistic elements found in the Scots

Gaelic tongue (Shaffer 341).

Hugh Walker contrasts Scottish and English satire in the following way:

> It is remarkable that the same instinct [concreteness] shows itself in all the other Scottish satirists from Dunbar to Burns; while the English satirists, from Piers Plowman to the close of the Elizabethan age, are, with few exceptions, far more abstract. The difference is all the more striking in view of the reputation of the northern people for metaphysical speculation, and that of the southern, one for practicality and a belief in that which can be seen and handled, and, it seems to be thought, in that alone. (56)

Hugh Walker indicates that the effectiveness of Dunbar's satire is the result of his powerful imagination, and his mastery of poetic technique. Nevertheless, he feels that Dunbar is deficient as a satirist, because he lacked moral earnestness. Walker says, "there is seldom behind his satire that force of conviction of which we are sensible in Piers Plowman. Neither has he any prevailing theme" (28-29). Dunbar was a Franciscan who believed in his order, but who nevertheless satirized religious men and even satirized his own Franciscan order. Some critics have suggested that Dunbar could not have been the author of The Freiris of Berwik because it is critical of the Franciscan order; however, Walker feels that he is the author, and points out that Dunbar satirizes the Franciscans in his The Visitation of St. Francis, and it is certain that Dunbar was the author of this later piece. Walker feels that The Freiris of Berwik is an admirable satiric tale that almost equals Chaucer's writing in its effective five-foot iambic line (28). The satire of Dunbar's The Fenzeit Freir of Tungland is directed at a single individual. According to Walker, it is as spirited as is Burns's Death and Dr. Hornbook, though Walker considers the humor of Dunbar's piece to be far inferior to that of Burns's piece (Walker 29).

Dunbar's The Thrissill and the Rois, and his Dance of the Sevin Deidly Synnis are imaginative and allegorical satirical poems. Dunbar's The Twa Mariit Wemen and the Wedo is coarse but powerful satire written in alliterative metre that parodies a number of different genres (Shaffer 342). Its strong satire and alliterative metre are similar to Piers Plowman. Walker compares this piece to Chaucer's The Wife of Bath, though he considers it to be a great deal less human than is Chaucer's work (Walker 29). Dunbar's The Devil's Inquest indiscriminately satirizes almost every class of tradesman, and his To the Merchants of Edinburgh he makes an unsavory presentation on the dirt and stench of this Scottish city (Walker 30).

"Ana Ballat of the Fenyeit Freir of Tungland" (1507) is a dream allegory written in a popular medieval poetic form to burlesque John Damian's attempt to fly off from the heights of Spring Castle. Here Dunbar uses heavy alliteration in order to ridicule Damian, as he describes Damian being attacked by birds during his fall which ends up with Damian's disgrace at the foot of the castle" (Shaffer 341).

Fasternis Evin in Hell is another poem which burlesques the genre of the dream vision, and also the genre of the chivalric romance. This is especially true of the first part, entitled "The Dance of the Sevin Deadly Sins," and the second part "The Turnament." In Dance, Dunbar targets, among other things, the jealousy that exists between the people of the Scottish Highlands and the Lowlands" (Walker 30). In "The Dance of the Sevin Deadly Sins" there is a procession of sins in Hell, each of these sins personified as a figure that behaves in a way that embodies that particular sin. These dancers "writhe and twitch in a scene that is lurid and painfully comic," as they exhibit a quality called "eldritch." This "eldritch" is exuberant, is frightful, is weird, and is a common quality in Dunbar's comic and satiric poetry, and "eldritch" can be seen when the followers of Avarice vomit hot molten golden on each other, while the devils pour more hot gold down their throats (Shaffer 342).

"The Turnament" is a parody of chivalric romance, and is therefore filled with excretory jokes (Shaffer 342). "In secreit Place" contains a dialogue between a foul-mouthed man and a foolish kitchen maid. Although it begins in the courtly manner, it is not long until the true nature of the participants is revealed, as their conversation degenerates into animal metaphors and reduplicative baby talk (Shaffer 342). "Schir Thomas Norny" is also a parody of courtly romance, and uses tail-rhyme stanzas and conventional romance diction specifically to ridicule a particular character in the court of James IV. Some critics believe that the target of the ridicule is the court fool (Shaffer 342). "The Dregy of Dunbar Maid to King James The Fowrth being in Strivilling" is a parody of the "Office of the Dead," and "The Tesment of Maister Andro Kennedy" is a comic satire which employs Dunbar's use of alternating lines in Scots Gaelic and Latin (Shaffer 342).

John Peter sees a great deal of ribaldry in William Dunbar's works, but he disagrees with those critics who consider Dunbar to be only ribald. Peter agrees with J. Small who said, "beneath the humourist in Dunbar there was the moralist always, and at times the preacher" (Peter 51). Louis Cazamian feels that Dunbar was important in establishing the broad vein of humor that characterized older Scottish humor. Talking about Dunbar's comic verve, Cazamian said, "Nothing can exceed the Rabelaisian gusto with which the 'Two Married Women and the Widow' converse on the theme of their conjugal experiences." Their conversation is impudently realistic and fun, with its tone of popular raciness (Cazamian 92). Although Dunbar has clear judgment and keeps a clear head, his writing is filled with fiery invectives.

Cazamian feels that Dunbar is one of the best poets ever to come out of Scotland. Dunbar's is the poetry of exaggeration, the poetry that mixes humor with farce, fantasy, and the author's pretended unawareness of the wild improbability of the tale he is telling. Dunbar's poetry is filled with an amusing assortment of vivid picturesque words that shock the reader with their grotesque impudence and indecency (Cazamian 92). But in Cazamian's view, Dunbar sometimes goes too far. Cazamian considers Dunbar's writing to be too explicit when he tells the reader, "Such comfort to my heart it wrought / With laughter near I burst." Here is a writer who is too impressed with his own humor (Cazamian 93).

There has been a great deal of argument among Dunbar critics as to whether the allegory in The Golden Targe is there for decoration or for revelation. C. S. Lewis says, "The trappings of allegory are retained, but the true interest of the poet lies elsewhere, sometimes in satire, sometimes in amorous dialectic, and often in mere rhetoric and style" (Leonard 81-82). It is interesting to note that the same critics who believe that Dunbar is not an allegorist nevertheless agree that the most distinctive aspect of his writing is his "wild comic fantasy," of the type that permeates The Dance of the Sevin Deidly Synnis, The Justis Betwix the Telyour and the Sowtar, and The Tretis of the Tua Mariit Wemen and the Wedo, this last being now considered as Dunbar's best poem (Leonard 85). In The Tretis, Dunbar contrasts the differences between appearance and reality by plotting the lovely appearance of the women as contrasted with their base natures (Shaffer 343).

William Dunbar Bibliography

Cazamian, Louis. The Development of English Humor. Durham, NC: Duke University Press, 1952.

Leonard, Frances McNeely. Laughter in the Courts of Love: Comedy in Allegory, from Chaucer to Spenser. Norman, OK: Pilgrim, 1981.

Peter, John. Complaint and Satire in Early English Literature. Oxford, England: Clarendon Press, 1956.

Shaffer, Pamela K. "William Dunbar." Encyclopedia of British Humorists, Volume I. Ed.

Steven H. Gale, New York, NY: Garland, 1996, 340-344.
Walker, Hugh. English Satire and Satirists. London, England: J. M. Dent, 1925.
Wolfe, Humbert. Notes on English Verse Satire. London, England: Hogarth Press, 1929.

John Skelton (c1460-1529) SCOTLAND

John Skelton is the protagonist of one of the most popular jestbooks in the sixteenth century, and according to John Timpane, Skelton is the first great poet of the English Renaissance and one of its greatest humorists (Timpane 1013). Skelton's two most characteristic genres were satire, and low humor. Skelton's satire "combined his zest for invective with his moral sense." Skelton was especially adept when it came to the sharp and biting insult. Skelton developed a poetic form known as "Skeltonic" whereby the poet keeps rhyming the same sound for as long as possible. "The effect is uncannily like watching someone make up a rhyme on the spot. It is this impression of improvisation--our sense that we are watching a witty, trenchant mind spew forth ideas right in front of us--that makes Skeltonics so forceful and so much fun." In addition to having this bombarding rhyme pattern, Skelton's poetry is a mixture of the sacred and the profane, of sobriety and mirth. There is an element of fun even in Skelton's most serious writing, and there is an element of seriousness even in his lowest humor (Timpane 1015).

According to James Hannay, John Skelton's satire tended to be written in short flowing rhymes; he further described it as "helter-skelter doggerel (Hannay 113). In a satiric poem entitled Why Come Ye Not to Court? Skelton attacks Wolsey. "Here is rattling, galloping, fiery doggerel--the fire smoky enough--for Skelton is like those ecclesiastics who burned their victims with green wood" (Hannay 114).

John Skelton was Poet Laureate of England, and Hugh Walker feels that his poetry can still be read with pleasure, for although the rhymes are rude, they are also vigorous. Humbert Wolfe concludes his discussion of Skelton's contribution by saying that Skelton's satire, like the rest of his work, is " 'peculiar' in the sense that he was the first Englishman to write so" (Walker 46). Hugh Walker feels that Skelton's characteristic virtue is his energy. "He is rude, boisterous, uncouth, but sincere and strong" (Walker 34). Walker feels that Skelton is the only satirist of his time who remains more than the shadow of a name (Walker 34).

Louis Cazamian considers Skelton's poetry to have been written with verve, animation, and a sense of fun. Skelton delights in a wide range of amusements "from pure farce to jolly satire and self-mockery." The rhythm of his mirth is filled with a "nimbleness of quick, flashing, prancing thoughts" and "invested with the ironical jingle of sonorous, almost macaronic rhymes." For Cazamian, "the soul of burlesque is diffused through all his work--as the free paganism of the jolly priest was the triumphant humor of his life" (Cazamian 95).

In Why Come Ye Nat to Courte? the target of satire is a single individual--Cardinal Wolsey; however, Skelton's invective on Wolsey can appropriately be read as having a broader target--"the corrupt, voluptuous Church, and the oppressors of England (Alden 27), for Alden is probably correct in suggesting that Cardinal Wolsey is merely a prototypical symbol of the larger target (Alden 27). Even though Skelton satirized the clergy, Walker does not consider him to be a reformer. Skelton's Replycacion is "a piece of scurrilous abuse of the six Oxford readers of Tyndale who were made to join in the burning of translation" (Walker 34).

In The Tunning of Elynour Rummynge, Skelton paints a coarse but realistic picture of English low life (Walker 34). This is Skelton's most famous poem, and it is about a some frowzy women who are the dregs of society who make a mock pilgrimage to the

"Running Horse," a tavern in Leatherhead, Surrey. The tavern is run by a woman named
Alianora Romyng, and the poem goes as follows:

>Some wenches come unlased,
>Some huswyves come unbrased,
>With theyr naked pappes,
>That flyppes and flappes,
>It wygges and wagges
>Lyke tawny saffron bagges--. (Timpane 1016)

In a book entitled The English Poets, Churton Collins evaluates Skelton's poetry
ambivalently. Collins concludes his discussion of Elinore Rummynge by saying that, "in
this sordid and disgusting delineation of humble life he may fairly challenge the supremacy
of Swift and Hogarth" (Wolfe 42-43). Humbert Wolfe suggests that as a poet, Skelton was
a sturdy innovator. Wolfe challenges Collins's suggestion that Skelton writes "headlong
doggerel" by saying, "not only had nobody before Skelton used the form he so brilliantly
applied in such poems as those against Garnesche, but no one has been able completely to
master it since" (Wolfe 45). Consider Skelton's lament on Philip Sparrowe:

>Sometyme he wolde gaspe
>When he saw a waspe;
>A fly or a gnat
>He wolde fly at that;
>And prettily he wolde pant
>When he saw an ant;
>Lord! how he would pry
>After the butterfly!
>Lord! how he wolde hoppe
>After the gressop! (Wolfe 45)

Wolfe says that this is not a poem about a sparrow. It is the sparrow, "in a verse that jerks
it as neat as his two strutting feet" (Wolfe 45). Alfred Gu L'Estrange considers Skelton's
most entertaining pieces to be "Speke Parrot," "Phyllyt Sparrowe," and "Elynour
Rummynge." In "Speke Parrot" a fair lady mourns the death of her bird which had been
killed by "those vylanous false cattes" (L'Estrange 199). As noted above, she reminisces
about how her sparrow used to pant when it saw an ant, how it would pry after a butterfly,
and how it would hop "After the gressop" (L'Estrange 199).

Raymond Alden and Hugh Walker both believe that John Skelton was the first
English writer to have the reputation of being primarily a satirist (Alden 25, Walker 33).
His Boke of Three Fooles is based on Brandt's Narrenschiff. Skelton selected as his three
categories of fools, the person who marries for money, the person who is envious, and the
person who is voluptuous or gluttonous (Alden 25). Skelton's The Bowge of Courte,
which Hugh Walker feels is quite polished, is a satirical allegory that relies heavily on
French methods of development (Alden 27). The Bowge of Courte is expected to evoke
the same sensations as a nightmare. Skelton prepares the way for the nightmare by saying
that he is a perturbed poet who in incapacitated by his own uncertainty. He wants to write
a poem about vice or morality, but Ignorance discourages him with the assurance that his
cunning is not equal to his ambition (Leonard 88). All of the subjects and situations of the
poem are changeable. As in a nightmare, they flow from their original non-threatening
forms into menacing shapes that create a nagging sense of uneasiness. The structure of the
poem is also fluid, as it changes its course and reshapes its form until it develops in the
Dreamer a feeling of terror. The allegory of the poem is not made up of traditional images
and accepted truths, but rather of new images that resemble the old ones, but only
momentarily before they undergo change. The "Courte" in the title is seen as a ship, which
is steered by Fortune, and all of the passengers are there because they want to profit from

trade. Skelton's dreamer is named Drede, and he also boards the ship in order to make a profit (Leonard 88). The poem is written in the form of a nightmare crescendo that starts off as guilelessness, goes to suspicion, then to acute nervousness, and finally to panic and awakening. Unlike most other dream visions, however, there is no resolution in The Bowge of Courte, since there is no clear distinction between the dream world and the real world, and the Dreamer can therefore not wake up. The energy of the poem, the busy-ness of the eight passengers, and the swiftness and directness of incident following incident intensify the nightmare effect, and so does Drede's uneasiness, jumping, turning and trying to discover additional perils. The Bowge of Courte introduces such characters as Sauncepere, Favore, Daunger, Drede, Favell, Dysdayne (Alden 27).

The target of the satire in Bowge of Courte is courtly life in general. In contrast, the target of the satire of Colyn Cloute is the ignorance and sensuality of the clergy, though there are suggestions that the targeted characteristics of the clergy can be found in all other classes as well (Alden 27). Colyn Cloute considers the clergy to be idle and greedy; their sheep remain unfed, but the wool is plucked from them nevertheless. Skelton specializes in severe personal vituperation. In his Colyn Cloute he assailed the clergy in general, but he also wrote personal attacks on Garnesche (a courtier), and on Cardinal Wolsey. Wolsey had been Skelton's patron at one time, and Skelton had dedicated such poems to him as "A Replycacion," which was written to denounce the followers of Wickliffe and Luther. Alfred Gu L'Estrange points out that many of Skelton's humorous writings, such as "The Balade of the Mastarde Tarte" have become lost (L'Estrange 197). In the poems that have survived, it is seen that Skelton had a quick, short metre, sometimes compared with the "swift iambics" of the Greek humorists. Skelton sometimes alternated Latin with English in a conceit, a common practice towards the end of the fourteenth century and into the fifteenth and sixteenth centuries as well (L'Estrange 200).

John Timpane considers Skelton's A Hundred Merry Tales (1925) to be "the first fully native English jestbook," and it contains an important story about two capons by the names of "Alpha" and "Omega" (Timpane 1016). In this tale, the Bishop of Norwich calles the Skelton character on the carpet, and Skelton brings two capons with him. The Bishop assumes that the two capons are being brought as tribute, but Skelton informs him that his two capons have names: "This capon is named Alpha, this is the fyrst capon that I dyd ever geve to you; and this capon is named Omega, and this is the last capon that ever I will give you; & so fare you well" (Timpane 1017). Skelton's Merie Tales, Newly Imprinted, Made by Master Skelton Poet Laureate was evidently not published until 1567. These stories were written down while Skelton was still alive, and Skelton may be the author, but critics do not know this for sure (Timpane 1016).

Some of Skelton's best satire depicts the irony inherent in the haughtiness of a statesman named Thomas Wolsey in contrast to his humble beginnings (Walker 33). Alfred Gu L'Estrange feels that the bulk of Skelton's humor appears in several personal vituperations. In "Colyn Cloute" he attacked the clergy in general, but also attacked a courtier named Garnesche, and Wolsey. L'Estrange was not able to explain how the quarrel between Skelton and Wolsey first developed; however, he was able to shed some light on the nature and intensity of Skelton's attack of Wolsey by quoting from "Why Come Ye not to Courte?" Skelton says that God should grant Wolsey a place, "Endlesse to dwell, / With the Deuyll of hell," and "He wolde so brage and crake, / That he wolde then make / The deuyls to quake, / To shudder and to shake" (L'Estrange 199). Because of the intensity of such attacks, Skelton had to flee and take sanctuary at Westminster. It was there that he died (L'Estrange 199).

John Skelton Bibliography

Alden, Raymond MacDonald. "Skelton." The Rise of Formal Satire in England under Classical Influence. New York, NY: Archon, 1961, 25-29.

Cazamian, Louis. "Scottish Writers; Skelton." The Development of English Humor. Durham, NC: Duke University Press, 1952, 89-96.

Hannay, James. Satire and Satirists. Folcroft, PA: Folcroft Press, 1969; originally published in 1854.

L'Estrange, Alfred Gu. "Anglo Saxon Humor: Mapes, Goliardi, Erasmus, Skelton, et. al." History of English Humour. New York, NY: Burt Franklin, 1878, 179-210.

Leonard, Frances McNeely. Laughter in the Courts of Love: Comedy in Allegory, from Chaucer to Spenser. Norman, OK: Pilgrim, 1981.

Timpane, John. "John Skelton." Encyclopedia of British Humorists, Volume II. Ed. Steven H. Gale, New York, NY: Garland, 1996, 1013-1017.

Walker, Hugh. "The English and Scottish Chaucerians; and Skelton." English Satire and Satirists. New York, NY: J. M. Dent, 1925, 24-38.

Wolfe, Humbert. "Chaucer to Skelton." Notes on English Verse Satire. London, England: Leonard and Virginia Woolf, 1929, 27-48.

Desiderius Gerhards Erasmus (c1466-1563)

At the beginning of the sixteenth century, Erasmus's "Letters of Obscure Men" was published in Germany. In this piece Erasmus tells of a great calamity. A thief has stolen three hundred florins, which the preachers had obtained by the sale of indulgences. Now the people who paid the money don't know whether or not they still have absolution. Erasmus calms the sinners by saying that they need not be alarmed, for they have as much absolution as they had before giving their money to the friars. Erasmus plays with religion in this way. He asks whether or not it is a sin to play at dice in order to buy indulgences (L'Estrange 193-194). Erasmus's "Letters of Obscure Men" were evidently based on real letters containing real questions about real concerns. But Erasmus found these letters to be hilarious. It is said that at one time he started laughing so hard that he almost burst an abscess that could have killed him. Erasmus was a rare man who was able to combine both humor and learning in a nice balance (L'Estrange 194). Erasmus was so in love with amusement that he was able to laugh at both sides of a question--with the Reformers and against them. When Erasmus heard that Luther had married a nun, and that the offspring of such an unholy alliance would be the Antichrist, Erasmus merely said, "Already are there many Antichrists!" (L'Estrange 195).

Although Erasmus was basically a Dutch author and scholar, he is included here because he spent some time in England from 1498 to 1499 when he met Grocyn, Linacre, and More at Oxford, and again from 1510-1514 when he taught Greek at Cambridge (Kantra 41, Neilson 484). Robert Kantra says that many critics have wondered how it is possible for religious leaders like Jerome and Erasmus to ridicule religion, but Kantra sees no contradiction of values here, and in fact suggests that Jerome and Erasmus are part of a tradition in literature, art, and sculpture which see an affinity between religion and ironic humor (Kantra 36). The subjects of Erasmus's satire were wide ranging. He targeted grammarians, scholars, philosophers, divines, monks, preachers, begging friars, princes, popes, cardinals, bishops, and common priests. It is no surprise to Robert Kantra that much of Erasmus's satire is strong and biting (Kantra 50).

Louis Cazamian notes that the mind of Erasmus, like the mind of Sir Thomas More, was filled with the classical literature, and that "their subtle handling of suggestive understatement can be traced in particular to the lessons of Lucian, the Greek master of irony" (Cazamian 119). Erasmus's Moriae Encomium was written in the home of Sir Thomas More, in England, and the title contains a pun on Sir Thomas More's name (Walker 91).

Erasmus's The Praise of Folly is written in the form of a paradox which sets forth the values and advantages of folly. With many humorous illustrations, he develops a number of conceits and jests, but his main point is that youth is the most delightful period in a person's existence, and youth is also the time of the most folly. In maturity and old age we lose our folly, and our pleasure, unless there is a second childhood, in which case both the pleasure and the folly are returned (L'Estrange 195-196). According to Erasmus, it was at the suggestion of folly that woman was introduced into the world. Erasmus considers woman to be "a foolish, silly creature, no doubt, but amusing, agreeable, and well adapted to mitigate the gloom of man's temper" (L'Estrange 197).

Northrop Frye would call The Praise of Folly Menippean satire. Robert Kantra points out that this was a favorite form of satire for Erasmus. He further suggests that this piece is more deliberately stylized than colloquial, and deals less with particular people than with people's attitudes (Kantra 50-51). In Erasmus's The Praise of Folly, and his Colloquies the fine, discreet humor is more prevalent than is the open, pungent satire; however, both can be found (Cazamian 121). Nevertheless, Raymond Alden says that The Praise of Folly is "neither an early popular satire nor a formal satire on classical models. Erasmus was too original to follow any form" (Alden 25). Still, Erasmus derived a great deal from the classics, and his method of heaping up quotations from the classics and from the Scriptures was totally consistent with medieval practices (Alden 25). Robert Kantra feels that the "medieval satire of estates" and the "Renaissance paradox" of Erasmus's The Praise of Folly have not quite coalesced, though this lack of coalescence does not bother most critics (Kantra 36-37). On this point, Kantra suggests that a person might "argue that structural dualities are more customary than useful in reading the satires of Jerome and Erasmus, that temperamental and cognitive perspectives are not necessarily exclusive of each other, and that the religious satires of Jerome and Erasmus are generically and not emotively ambivalent" (Kantra 44).

According to Robert Polhemus, Erasmus sanctifies folly and unifies it with the spirit of Christianity by the end of The Praise of Folly. Erasmus, like Rabelais, Swift, and Sterne, was an ordained cleric and a professional churchmen, and like these other authors, Erasmus tried to reconcile his comic and satirical impulses with his Christian vocation. The sense of humor that was an important aspect of all of these minister-authors gave them a way of rationalizing their faith. "Erasmus shows that comic folly can be rehabilitated and used to put life in proper perspective. He uses folly, for example, to criticize and ridicule the sinful pride of the Church" (Polhemus 13).

Robert Kantra is certain that Erasmus considers his Colloquies satiric, and in these Colloquies, the satire is neither entirely active nor entirely contemplative, neither entirely talking about this world, or the next. Erasmus was both a literary ridiculer and an intellectual revolutionary, and like Thomas More, he remained all of his life a believing Roman Catholic (Kantra 49).

Alden considers Erasmus to be a humanist and reformer, and suggests that like many other sixteenth-century English satirists, he was greatly influenced by Barclay's The Ship of Fools (Alden 22). Like Barclay and other medieval satirists, Erasmus's primary method of satire was personification of folly; however Erasmus's satire was much better than that of his contemporaries because it was "thoroughly concrete and self-conscious," and was "marked by a keenness and a fine irony" (Alden 23). Like other medieval satirists, Erasmus's favorite target was hypocrisy, but this trait showed up in many guises. Like other satirists of his day, Erasmus targeted such follies as vanity, old people pretending to be young, the insanity of passion, various excesses (such as hunting and building), the subjectivity of alchemy and astrology, gambling, the telling of lies, false titles, pompous funerals, flattery, jealousy, gluttony, and all of the follies associated with kings, courtiers, merchants, and the clergy (Alden 23). But Erasmus had more targets than did the other satirists of his day, for he also targeted scholarship and the whimsy of "formal logic," and grammarians and teachers, and philologists (Alden 23).

Robert Kantra suggests that at least in the English speaking world, Erasmus's reputation results more from his academic and scholarly prowess than from his religious reputation. Kantra notes that when Erasmus was in England he spent much more of his time at Oxford and Cambridge Universities than he spent at the monastery (Kantra 47).

Desiderius Erasmus Bibliography

Alden, Raymond MacDonald. "Erasmus." The Rise of Formal Satire in England under Classical Influence. New York, NY: Archon, 1961, 22-25.

Cazamian, Louis. The Development of English Humor. Durham, NC: Duke University Press, 1952.

Kantra, Robert A. "Jerome and Erasmus in Renaissance Art." All Things Vain: Religious Satirists and Their Art. University Park, PA: Penn State University Press, 1984, 35-53.

L'Estrange, Alfred Gu. "Anglo Saxon Humor: Mapes, Goliardi, Erasmus, Skelton, et al." History of English Humour. New York, NY: Burt Franklin, 1878, 179-210.

Neilson, William Allan. Webster's Biographical Dictionary Springfield, MA: G. & C. Merriam, 1971.

Polhemus, Robert M. Comic Faith: The Great Tradition from Austen to Joyce. Chicago, IL: University of Chicago Press, 1980.

Walker, Hugh. English Satire and Satirists. London, England: J. M. Dent, 1925.

Watson, Donald Gwynn. "Erasmus's Praise of Folly and the Spirit of Carnival." Renaissance Quarterly 32 (1979): 333-353.

Bishop Gavin Douglas (c1474-1522) SCOTLAND

In his The Development of English Humor, Louis Cazamian says that the poetry of Bishop Gavin Douglas is much lower in quality than is that of William Dunbar. It is less vigorous, since it is driven by a more gentle spirit. Humor for Douglas is often "a pleasant gleam that lights up the moralizing and the allegory of his verse" (94). Douglas's King Hart is an interesting enough poem written in the tone of reflective detachment. There are touches of mild playfulness that Cazamian considers closely akin to the essence of much modern humor (94).

Bishop Gavin Douglas Bibliography

Cazamian, Louis. The Development of English Humor. Durham, NC: Duke University Press, 1952.

Alexander Barclay (c1475-1552)

Raymond Alden considers Alexander Barclay's translation of Sebastian Brandt's Narrenschiff to be "the most important work in the history of English satire before the

Elizabethan period" (Alden 15); Alden further suggests that The Ship of Fools can be considered as "the starting point of classical influence in English satire (Alden 17). However, G. R. Owst has suggested that "the only original part of Barclay's translation was its woodcuts" (Peter 51). Alfred Gu L'Estrange would disagree, saying that "Alexander Barclay altered it so considerably in the rendering as almost to make a new work, especially applicable to the state of things in this country" (L'Estrange 201).

Since Brandt's original book had dealt with the general field of folly, Barclay's translation was entitled The Ship of Fools, and was published in 1508. Barclay's chapter headings indicate his preoccupation with the traditional themes of preachers of the day, and did a good job of listing not only the fools of his day, but the fools of almost any day. According to Raymond Alden, there were basically six types of fools: 1) those who offend religion (such as the blasphemers), 2) those who offend the law (such as the shysters), 3) those who are insolent or quarrelsome, 4) those who dance, gamble, use bad language, or eat and drink too much in public, 5) those who neglect their children or other responsibilities, (especially those who neglect their own duties in order to meddle in other people's affairs), and 6) the simpletons (Alden 19-20). And Hugh Walker notes that as the fools are paraded by the reader, "every phase of satire is inevitably touched" (Walker 31).

All of the fools in Barclay's The Ship of Fools are types, not individuals, and some of them reach allegorical proportions (Alden 21). Like other satirists of his day, Barclay was very careful to show that his satiric lance was not pointed at the people to whom he owed allegiance. In fact, in the chapter on "the great myght and power of folys" he categorizes King Henry as a man of clean conscience, a man "from whom may be learned all meekness and godly wysdome" (Alden 17).

Hugh Walker considers The Ship of Fools to be exceedingly dull and tedious, though it may deserve a place in history for three reasons. In the first place, it is comprehensive. In the second place it gives a detailed depiction of sixteenth century England. And in the third place it has little competition, for it was written at a time when there was not very much good literature in England (Walker 30). In addition, Barclay himself does not allow his work to be criticized, for one of the latest categories of fools he considers is "the backbiters of good men, and against them that shall disprayse this work" (Walker 30). Despite this admonition, however, Walker states that Barclay doesn't show even a spark of genius, and says that his work is ponderous and not even original, since it relies on a free translation of Sebastian Brandt's Narrenschiff, "and Barclay's additions are of no great importance" (Walker 31).

It is difficult to know whether Barclay's The Ship of Fools should be considered a satire or not. It is certainly a pessimistic piece, as it talks about the fools who are "banysshed in doctryne" who "wander in derknes" (Alden 17). Even Barclay himself is uncertain about what genre his book represents: "This present Boke myght have ben callyd nat inconvenyently the Satyr...the reprehencion of foulysshnes, but the neweltye of the name was more plesant unto the fyrst actour to call it the Shyp of foles" (Alden 19). Brandt's original book had influenced England greatly, but Barclay's translation influenced England just as greatly (Alden 21).

Alexander Barclay Bibliography

Alden, Raymond MacDonald. The Rise of Formal Satire in England under Classical Influence. New York, NY: Archon, 1961.

Peter, John. Complaint and Satire in Early English Literature. Oxford, England: Clarendon Press, 1956.

Walker, Hugh. English Satire and Satirists. London, England: J. M. Dent, 1925.

Sir Thomas More (1478-1535)

More's Utopia was first published in Latin in 1516 and was translated into English in 1551, where it became an English classic. Utopia belongs to the early part of the reign of Henry VIII and is a comprehensive and penetrating satire of England which helped to start the vagabondage satire tradition. More had an observant eye and a biting pen. His passages of pungent satire deal with breaches of faith, with inhuman punishments, with mercenary soldiers, and other controversial issues of sixteenth-century England (Walker 36). More especially targets the devastation of wars (both civil and foreign) in his satire, but he also targets the abuses of the court and its nobility (Walker 37). Yet More did not target the Queen nor any of her ministers or her representatives. Political controversy was clearly not a legitimate subject for satire at a time in England when heads rolled so easily (Rose 64).

Sir Thomas More Bibliography

Rose, Sandra Priest. "Tudor Humor." WHIMSY 4 (1986): 62-64.
Walker, Hugh. English Satire and Satirists. London, England: J. M. Dent, 1925.

Sir David Lindsay (1490-1555) SCOTLAND

Sir David Lindsay's poetry is described by Louis Cazamian as earnest, heavy, and filled with vigorous irony. Cazamian considers Lindsay's character of John the Common Weal in The Satire of the Thrie Estaitis to be a Scottish counterpart to William Langland's Piers Plowman. Lindsay's satire well represents the spirit of the Reformation, a new age in satire.

Sir David Lindsay Bibliography

Cazamian, Louis. The Development of English Humor. Durham, NC: Duke University Press, 1952.

John Heywood (c1497-1580)

Alfred Gu L'Estrange points out that Heywood, who was the first English author to write original dramas, has been called the "Father of English Comedy." Heywood's dramas represented ordinary social life in England. All of his writings appeared before 1550, and all were short, simple, and "deficient in delicacy and humour" (L'Estrange 227). Nevertheless, in his day Heywood was considered to be a great wit. He was a court jester and provoked hearty laughter from King Hal and could even make the fanatical Mary smile occasionally. Once when Queen Mary told Heywood that priests had to forego their wives, Heywood is said to have answered, "Then your Grace must allow them lemons, for the clergy cannot live without sauce" (L'Estrange 227). Although Heywood was considered to be an epigrammatist, L'Estrange feels that most of Heywood's "jests" have "little point" (L'Estrange 227).

Louis Cazamian considers Heywood to be thoroughly English, and is therefore not surprised to find his work to be not only serious, earnest, and moralizing, but humorous as well. Although his temper might not seem to be especially compatible with comic invention, he nevertheless developed, as a playwright, comic tricks, jokes, fun, and innuendo to please the groundlings in the more than two hundred plays that he wrote (Cazamian 348).

Heywood translated Lucian's Dialogues into English verse, and from then on, Lucian's humor appears as an important influence not only on Heywood's work, but on the work of other English authors as well. In The English Traveller, there is a clown named Roger who serves Old Wincott. In the tradition of Touchstone or Feste, Roger tries to draw the best expression out of the people he comes into contact with. Cazamian considers Clem the Vintner, the clown in the romantic comedy The Fair Maid of the West, to be more successful than Roger. Clem uses racy talk and homely impudence to enliven a number of episodes of that play. Heywood's humor is sophisticated, and foreshadows much of the humor to come later. Much of Heywood's humor is refined, but he is also not averse to rollicking farce, and he wrote scenes which depicted some of the broadest humor of his time (Cazamian 349). His broad farces include The Wise Woman of Hogsdon, where the tavern scene (I,i) for example is fresh, lively, and truly amusing, and The Rape of Lucrece where the jesting and singing of Valerius is the center of a Lucian-like spirit of merriment that makes the play read to Cazamian like "a schoolboy's parody of the classics" (Cazamian 350).

John Heywood Bibliography

Cazamian, Louis. "Thomas Heywood." The Development of English Humor. Durham, NC: Duke University Press, 1952, 348-350.
L'Estrange, Alfred Gu. "Origin of Modern Comedy: Chaucer, Heywood, et. al." History of English Humour. New York, NY: Burt Franklin, 1878, 211-230.

Sir Thomas Wyatt (1503-1542)

Hugh Walker and Raymond Alden consider Wyatt to be the first polished English satirist (Walker 59). Wyatt wrote three satirical poems which were published in Totel's Miscellany in 1557. They are entitled, Of the Meane and Sure Estate, Written to John Poins, Of the Courtiers Life, Written to John Poins, and How to Use the Court and Him Selfe Therein, Written to Syr Fraunces Bryon (Alden 52). All of these satires were written during Wyatt's retirement in Allington between July of 1541 and October of 1542, and Wyatt died shortly thereafter. All of the satires were published posthumously. There are some critics who feel that Wyatt mistook his talents in becoming chiefly a sonneteer rather than a satirist (Alden 53). Hugh Walker says that a new beginning in the development in English satire can be found in Sir Thomas Wyatt, for it is Wyatt who "takes the first step in the evolution of satiric verse which culminates in Dryden and Pope" (Walker 59).

Wyatt used the "terza rima" as the metre of his satires. Italy was a source of not only of Wyatt's metre, but a source of some of his other inspiration as well. Wyatt's style is compact but smooth, and quite urbane. It is epistolary in nature, and reminds the reader of Horace in its ease and naturalness. The style is simple, idiomatic, and reflective, with the ethical aspects being presented especially vigorously (Alden 54). The narrative is secondary to the philosophy. There is direct rebuke in the satires, but it is not strong. The mildly pessimistic tone is again a reminder of Horace (Alden 55).

Wyatt's fable about two mice appeared originally in Horace's writings, but Wyatt was also indebted to Robert Henryson in terms of the mode of presentation. There are also some differences between Wyatt's mice and Horace's and Henryson's mice.

In Horace the mice are friends; in Henryson and in Wyatt they are sisters.

In Horace and Henryson the story begins with a visit of the town mouse to the country; in Wyatt it does not. In Horace there is little direct conversation recorded; in Henryson and in Wyatt there is considerable, and in each case the mice say "peep." In Horace the country mouse is frightened by dogs; in Henryson and Wyatt by the cat. In Horace the catastrophe is not recorded; in Henryson the mouse is caught but escapes; in Wyatt it is caught, and there is no intimation of escape. (Alden 55)

Wyatt's second satire is entitled Of the Courtier's Life. It is an adaptation from the Alamanni piece which was addressed to Thommaso Sertini, and it dealt with the numerous petty hypocrisies that occur in court life. Wyatt's paraphrase is quite close to the original, but with Wyatt's usual freedom of adaptation. He follows Alamanni in his criticism of France, Germany, Spain, and Italy, but differs in other important aspects (Alden 57).

Wyatt's third satire has Horace's fifth Satire of Book 2 (on legacy hunting) as a source, but the source is not followed closely. This third satire is addressed to Sir Francis Bryan (Alden 57). Lines 60-66 of Wyatt's satire have no counterpart in Horace, and suggest in fact the more bitter satiric style of Juvenal (Alden 58).

Raymond Alden suggests that Wyatt's metre is the result of Alamanni's influence. It was also from Alamanni that Wyatt developed the idea of the epistolary form of satire, as well as the idea of adapting the classical style to the local conditions of England at the time of Wyatt's writing.

There is considerable classical influence on Wyatt's satires. Like classical satires they are in an artificial form of verse and are pessimistic in tone. Like classical satires, they are also calm and ironical, without the suggestion of reform being intimated. Like classical satires, they also concentrated on private rather than public morals, and virtue is portrayed in connection with its opposite. There is a distinctly individual point of view on Wyatt's satires (Alden 58).

In the classical tradition, Wyatt's humor is subtle, and is in part based on classical motifs. Wyatt's targets involved mainly private morals such as ambition, covetousness, and especially flattery and deceit. He also targeted legacy-hunting, a common theme in both classical and Elizabethan satire. Wyatt's satires are primarily in the reflective mood, and probably their greatest merit is that they were effectively adapted to contemporary conditions and purposes. Wyatt treated his satires "in a truly poetic and idealizing spirit. It is no undue anticipation to say that in all these matters Wyatt had no successor" (Alden 59).

Sir Thomas Wyatt Bibliography

Alden, Raymond MacDonald. "Sir Thomas Wyatt." The Rise of Formal Satire in England under Classical Influence. New York, NY: Archon, 1961, 52-59.
Walker, Hugh. English Satire and Satirists. London, England: J. M. Dent, 1925.

Robert Sempill (c1505-1572)

Robert Sempill wrote an important satire entitled Legend of the Bishop of St. Androis Lyfe. Hugh Walker feels that the most remarkable feature of Sempill's satire is its concreteness. Walker also notes that in Sempill's work there is a curious resemblance to the incantations of Shakespeare's Macbeth on the one hand, and certain passages in Chaucer, Heywood, Lindsay, and other satirists on the other (Walker 56).

Robert Sempill Bibliography

Walker, Hugh. English Satire and Satirists. London, England: J. M. Dent, 1925.

Nicholas Udall (1505-1556)

Alfred Gu L'Estrange considers Udall's Royster Doister to be one of the earliest English comedies (L'Estrange 227). It was found entered in the books of the Stationers' Company in the year 1566. In the play, Royster Doister is a conceited fool who thinks that every woman is in love with him. Much of the humor is sound symbolic, and there are a great many sound repetitions, as in the following couplet, "Then to our recorder with toodle doodle poope, As the howlet out of an yvie bushe should hoope" (L'Estrange 228). Roister Doister is tricked into sending Custance a love-letter, telling her that he is after her fortune, and that he will annoy her constantly after marriage. When he discovers that he has been duped, Roister becomes determined to take revenge on the scrivner who wrote the love-letter for him. Since Custance and her friends consider Roister to be a coward, he writes them a letter saying, "Yea, they shall know, and thou knowest I have a stomacke." The ensuing dialogue shows that the scribe understands the word "stomach" in a different way from that which Roister intends it to be understood, and Roister finally says, "Nay, a man's stomacke with a weapon mean I". To this the scribe responds, "Ten men can scarce match you with a spoon in a pie" (L'Estrange 228-229).

Nicholas Udall Bibliography

L'Estrange, Alfred Gu. History of English Humour. New York, NY: Burt Franklin, 1878.
Maulsby, D. L. "The Relation between Udall's Roister Doister and the Comedies of Plautus and Terence." Englische Studien 48 \92907\0; 362-377.

George Buchanan (1506-1582)

Buchanan's Franciscanus is a satire about the Franciscan monks. It was written at the request of the English king, and was begun in 1535 and finished in 1564. It is in Latin (Alden 61).

George Buchanan Bibliography

Alden, Raymond MacDonald. "George Buchanan." The Rise of Formal Satire in England under Classical Influence. New York, NY: Archon, 1961, 61-62.

Robert Crowley (c1518-1588)

Robert Crowley's One and Thirty Epigrams was published in 1550. In the medieval fashion of "Exempla," the epigrams are arranged in alphabetical order, according to subject, beginning with Abbeys, Alehouses, Alleys, and Almshouses, and ending with Unsatiable Purchasers, Usurers, and Vain Writers. Crowley complains, for example that alehouses are placed in the country exactly in men's paths as they are on their way to church, so that "those who do not like to be told their faults drink instead" (Walker 58). Hugh Walker feels that Crowley's book needs to be better known, because even though it has only modest literary merit, "the light which it throws upon the manners and customs of the time is of considerable value" (Walker 59). Raymond Aldman feels that the Epigrams are too long to be called epigrams, and should instead be called "satires," though not satires in the classical sense of the word. Because these epigrams are satirical in nature, some critics consider Crowley to be among the earliest of English satirists. The epigrams are presented as four-stress couplets. The style is vernacular English, and the tone is Puritanical and scriptural. The epigrams deal with the evils of the day (Alden 60). There is a special emphasis on the oppression of the poor, and on the problems related to city life and those related to not being adequately religious (Alden 60).

In 1559 Crowley published Editio Princips of Piers Plowman, and Langland's influence on Crowley, both here and elsewhere, is obvious (Alden 60). Crowley was like other satirists of the sixteenth century in attacking the holding of double benefices, the giving of special attention to flatterers, and the "inventors of strange news." Like Plato, he compared these inventors of strange news to the poets and orators of his day (Alden 60). In his satires, Crowley targeted forestallers, and women's fashions. His only literary target was "vayne wryters" which he classed with "vayne talkers" and "vaine hearers" (Alden 61). In 1559 (the same year as Crowley's edition of Piers Plowman appeared), Crowley also published Voyce of the Laste Trumpet, Blowen by the Seventh Angel. This is a satiric classification of types of men--the beggar, the servant, the yeoman, the unlearned priest, the scholar, the physician, the magistrate, the gentleman, and so on (Alden 61).

Crowley's satires were basically within the genre of pure rebuke. His attitude is pessimistic, but there is hope in his writing of moral reform. All of this is typical of early English satire. So is the progressive spirit, the religious tone, the emphasis on public morals, and the slight amount of humor in his writing (Alden 61).

Robert Crowley Bibliography

Alden, Raymond MacDonald. "Robert Crowley." The Rise of Formal Satire in England under Classical Influence. New York, NY: Archon, 1961, 60-61.
Walker, Hugh. English Satire and Satirists. London, England: J. M. Dent, 1925.

George Gascoigne (c1525-1577)

In 1575 Gascoigne published Tale of Hemetes the Hermit addressed to the Queen of England and declared himself to be a satirical writer. In fact, Mr. Arber, the editor of Steele Glas, considers Gascoigne to be "the first English satirist" (Alden 68). Gascoigne's The Steele Glas and The Complainte of Phylomene were both published in 1576. Of these three satires, The Steele Glas was most widely read and admired. It is called by Gascoigne a "satyre written without rime, but I trust not without reason" (Alden 68). This piece is probably the first satire in English literature to have been written in blank verse. Alden suggests that it was possibly the last as well, and the reason is that the metre of blank verse, while it is smooth, is in addition quite monotonous. Alden points out that in the verse form of The Steele Glas the fourth syllable is followed by a persistent cesura, usually indicated by a comma whether the sense would require such punctuation or not. The tone is direct and bookish, but there are occasional glints of mild humor and some passages of vigor. Alden feels that the satire lacks the excellence of either Horace or Juvenal (Alden 69). The Steele Glas is a satirical moral poem that views the present age as degenerate as contrasted to the former, classical, age which is constantly referred to as a time of loftier virtue. The purpose of the satire is "to thunder mighty threats against vice" (Alden 70). Gascoigne was influenced by William Langland in The Steele Glas, and near the end of the poem "Peerce Plowman" is referred to as having a special kind of honesty (Alden 71).

Although Gascoigne's satire is not primarily based on classical models, there are nevertheless a number of classical elements mingled with native English elements in his satire. The religious aspect of his satire, and the interest in public affairs and official virtue, however, are strictly English in character. The point of view presented in Gascoigne's satire is a distinctly individual one, a point of view that originates not in fighting against external conditions, but rather in reflections of the mind (Alden 71). Gascoigne's satires tend to be didactic, and such subjects as morals, fashions, classes, and religion are constant targets. Gascoigne also frequently targets classes of people in a way similar to that found in Barclay's The Ship of Fools (Alden 72). Like most other satirists of his day, Gascoigne dealt very gently with royalty, though he was much harsher in his criticism of the petty cheating of London merchants (Alden 73).

George Gascoigne Bibliography

Alden, Raymond MacDonald. "George Gascoigne." The Rise of Formal Satire in England under Classical Influence. New York, NY: Archon, 1961, 67-74.

Nicholas Breton (c1545-c1626)

Breton published a series of satirical poems in 1600. They were entitled, Pasquil's Madcap, Pasquil's Foolscap, Pasquil's Mistress, and Pasquil's Passe, and Passeth Not. These poems may not be formal satires, but they are certainly satirical in content, and they were incited by the satires of Joseph Hall and John Marston. Breton indicates at the beginning of Pasquil's Madcap that it is an invective against the wicked of the world, which fall in to such categories as gentlemen, soldiers, clergy, lawyers, women, etc. (Alden 162). Pasquil's Foolscap is described by Raymond Aden as an exhaustive classification of follies. He further says that Pasquil's Passe is a procession of all kinds of undesirable people (Alden 163).

Breton's No Whippings, nor Trippinge: but a Kinde Friendly Snippinge is a protest against the bitternesses of personal satire. As usual, Breton's tone was gentle (Alden 164). In fact, the tone of all of Breton's work is milder and more amiable than is to be found in formal satire (Alden 163).

Nicholas Breton Bibliography

Alden, Raymond MacDonald. "Nicholas Breton." The Rise of Formal Satire in England under Classical Influence. New York, NY: Archon, 1961, 162-163.

Gabriel Harvey (c1545-c1630)

It was Gabriel Harvey who first introduced hexameter verse into English. George Peele would later put this type of verse into effective use. One of Peele's lines reads as follows: "Dub, dub-a-dub bounce, quoth the guns with a sulphurous huff shuff" (L'Estrange 242). Thomas Nashe, a contemporary of Gabriel Harvey and George Peele, considers this type of verse to be a drunken staggering kind of poetry that is up hill and down hill, like the way between Stamford and Beechfield. To Nashe, this verse "goes like a horse plunging through the mire in the deep of winter, now soust up to the saddle and straight aloft on his tip toes" (L'Estrange 242).

Thomas Nashe described Gabriel Harvey in rather unflattering terms. Harvey was considered by Nashe to be so thin-cheeked , gaunt, and starved that

> As he was blowing the fire with his mouth the smoke took him up like a light strawe, and carried him to the top or funnell of the chimney, wher he had flowne out God knowes whither if there had not been crosse barres overthwart that stayde him. (L'Estrange 239)

Gabriel Harvey Bibliography

L'Estrange, Alfred Gu. "Robert Greene--Friar Bacon's Demons--The "Looking Glasse"-- Nashe and Harvey." History of English Humour. New York, NY: Burt Franklin, 1878, 231-242.

Walter Ralegh (c1552-1618)

David Rosen says that humor is a central feature of Sir Walter Ralegh's poetry, and is furthermore a central feature of his sensibility generally. It was Sir Walter Ralegh who made the witty remark that "if one follows the heels of truth too closely one will get his teeth kicked in." This remark illustrates one of the pervading features of Sir Walter Ralegh's humor--his skepticism. In Sir Walter Ralegh: A Study in Elizabethan Skepticism, Ernest Strathmann discusses how Sir Walter Ralegh's wit should be described and placed into the general field of intellectual history (Rosen 903).

The earliest work we know of in Sir Walter Ralegh's canon is Ralegh's comments on George Gascoigne's satirical Stele Glasse (1576), and it should be no great surprise that Sir Walter Ralegh's poetic commentary "not only supports the unflattering likenesses drawn in Gascoigne's humorous mirror, but [it also] suggests a similarly aggressive satirical stance on Sir Walter Ralegh's part" (Rosen 902). Sir Walter Ralegh's most famous poem is a piece of wit entitled, "The Nymph's Reply to the Shepherd." It was collected in England's Helicon and was evidently written in collaboration with Christopher Marlowe. It is ironic, then that "The Nymphs Reply to the Shepherd" is actually a parody of Christopher Marlowe's own verse (Rosen 902). In his "On the Life of Man," Sir Walter Ralegh paints a humorous view of the womb as the room where "we are dressed for this short Comedy." This image points up how important comedy is to Ralegh (Rosen 902-903).

For Sir Walter Ralegh the comic aspects of life are treated in dead seriousness, and the dead serious is treated as comedy. In such poems as "The Lie," and "A Secret Murder," the humor is very dark and biting, and even borders on invective. Sir Walter Ralegh is only one of the candidates for authorship of "The Lie," which is "an elegant satire on court life." Nevertheless, "The Lie" is consistent with Sir Walter Ralegh's sensibility, style, and humor. "The Lie" also is consistent with Sir Walter Ralegh's penchant for "conceit," for his love of surprising metaphor, and for his tendency toward "a realism that gives rise to melancholy, partakes heavily of disillusionment, and leads to a skeptical stance." According to David Rosen, Sir Walter Ralegh viewed life as a comedy with a tragic ending. In a single poem, he was able to create a kind of dark humor that could move "from embracing mirth to rasping satire." His humor Beneath Sir Walter Ralegh's humor, there flowed "deep undercurrents of skepticism, melancholy, and even cynicism" (Rosen 903). Much of Ralegh's other humor is sly and contains double meanings, hints, and misdirections.

Walter Ralegh Bibliography

Rosen, David. "Walter Ralegh." Encyclopedia of British Humorists, Volume II. Ed. Steven
    H. Gale, New York, NY: Garland, 1996, 901-904.
Strathmann, Ernest Albert. Sir Walter Ralegh: A Study in Elizabethan Skepticism. New
    York, NY: Columbia University Press, 1951.

John Lyly (c1554-1606)

In the 1580s, John Lyly wrote five comedies for the entertainment of Queen
Elizabeth and her Court. These were entitled Campaspe, Sapho and Phao, Gallathea,
Endemion, and Love's Metamorphosis. Unlike the public drama of the time, all of Lyly's
plays except Campaspe had classical gods as major characters. In other Elizabethan plays
the classical gods may appear briefly, but their position in the play is not so prominent.
Even in Campaspe, Lyly develops a character named Alexander, who is based partly on
history and partly on legend to provide some of the same classical associations (Saccio 1).

Peter Saccio considers Lyly's court comedies to be relatively static, each revolving
around one or more situations rather than developing any extended plot. In these plays,
little takes place because they are so controlled by the situations (Saccio 2). Saccio also
notes that Lyly's plays rely heavily on allegory in a way that follows naturally from their
plotlessness, since the emphasis is on the events and the characters as they suggest concepts
that relate not to the world of social interactions, but to the world of ideas (Saccio 4).

One important aspect of many sixteenth-century authors was their ability to weave
familiar maxims or proverbs into their writings or conversations. Such proverbs would be
contrived to the modern eye and ear, but for the sixteenth-century audience such allusions
were expected. It should be noted that these sayings were old even in Tudor times (Rose
63). John Lyly, for example wrote that "When the fox preacheth, the geese perish," and
"The crocodile shroudeth greatest treason under most pitiful tears" (Lawlis 164).

In "Lyly and Euphuism" Louis Cazamian suggests that it is difficult to define
precisely the relationship between John Lyly and humor (Cazamian 131). Lyly was prone
to a gentle play of spontaneous wit, and a subtle "atmosphere of raillery" is pervasive in
his work. Lyly had a comic instinct which he usually demonstrated in elusive and indirect
ways. The comic flavor that can be found in most of his writings is discreet and reserved
and can be broadly assigned to the category of humor (Cazamian 132).

Cazamian stresses that euphuism is not humor, but the mood of euphuism does not
run counter to the mood of humor (Cazamian 134). Lyly was a euphuistic writer, and
Cazamian sees a number of parallels between euphuism and humor. "Both are sophisticated
tricks of expression and imply a duality of meaning." However, "the motive for the
duality, is, on the face of it, very different: humor is free, Euphuism seems to be tied, a
slave to a stubborn, desperate earnestness" (Cazamian 133). Furthermore, Cazamian
suggests that euphuism can transform into humor, even without the author's noticing it: "He
might be innocent of any irony at first, but who will assert that he was to the end?"
(Cazamian 133). Cazamian suggests that the distance from euphuism to humor is not great.
"It just took writing the same stuff in a spirit of slight self-mockery, instead of pure, stiff
pretentiousness. The disillusioned Euphuist, if a humorist, will be a competent one"
(Cazamian 136).

Lyly's Campaspe is a quaint play full of light merriment. The character of Pandora,
the protagonist of The Woman in the Moon, is ironically depicted as a woman who is ruled
by the stars, but whose patroness is fickle Cynthia. There are also delightful scenes
between Venus and Vulcan in the play Sapho and Phao. In all of these plays the

imaginative sense of the comic expresses itself in an easy flow of good lively humor (Cazamian 135). Lyly's plays breathe a spirit of discreet comedy; The humor is genuine and charming, and is as suitable to the scholar as it is to the courtier, the moralist, and the humanist. Lyly's object is to "breed soft smiling, not loud laughing" (Cazamian 135). In 1579 John Lyly wrote his Euphues: The Anatomy of Wit, where he pondered on the challenge, "I have ever thought so superstitiously of Wit, that I fear I have committed idolatry against wisdom" (Nicholls 163).

John Lyly Bibliography

Cazamian, Louis. "Lyly and Euphuism." The Development of English Humor. Durham, NC: Duke University Press, 1952, 131-136.

LaCapère, Anne. "The Dramatic Use of the Supernatural in John Lyly's Court Comedies." Caliban 11 (1974): 49-55.

Lawlis, Merritt, ed. Euphues: The Anatomy of Wit in Elizabethan Prose Fiction. New York, NY: Odyssey Press, 1967.

Nicholls, Mark. The Importance of Being Oscar: The Wit and Wisdom of Oscar Wilde Set Against His Life and Times. New York, NY: St. Martin's Press, 1980.

Powell, Jocelyn. "John Lyly and the Language of Play." Elizabethan Theatre. Eds. John Russell Brown, and Bernard Harris. New York, NY: St. Martin's, 1961, 147-167.

Rose, Sandra Priest. "Lyly and Tudor Humor." WHIMSY 4 (1986): 62-64.

Saccio, Peter. The Court Comedies of John Lyly: A Study in Allegorical Drama. Princeton, NJ: Princeton Univ Press, 1969.

Thorndike, Ashley H. "Lyly, Peele, and Greene." English Comedy. New York, NY: Macmillan, 1929. 74-94.

Sir Philip Sidney (1554-1586)

Sidney was a refined writer of exquisite culture and high principle. In his writing (as in his life) his primary goals were heroism, morality, and beauty. Although morality was important to Sidney, he was not prudish, because he was flexible, and his humor enlivened the serious, didactic eloquence of his message in such works as his Apology for Poetry. The playful spirit of Apology is evident, especially at the beginning and at the end, but even in between these two points as well humor peeks through by way of a sly, offhanded detachment. The effectiveness of Sidney's wit and humor are based on his reserve and spiced implication (Cazamian 138-139). The delightful humor of Sidney's Arcadia adds to the romantic fancy of the piece. Here there are many types of language play--conceits, repetitions, parallelisms, puns, Euphuism, "all the signs of a juvenile intoxication with words" (Saccio 138). Edmund Miller notes that in Arcadia there are princes disguised as shepherds, who are wooing princesses who are, of courses, disguised as shepherdesses (Miller 304).

Even though Sidney's humor is usually reserved and discreet, there is also sometimes broad fun that is often seen in the popular ballad of the day as well, as in the doggerel poem in praise of the beauties of Mopsa. There are also touches of deliberate farce, as, for example, when Damoetas is described as "an Ape that had newly taken a purgation" (Saccio 139). Nevertheless, the more usual tenor of Sidney's humor and wit are associated with delicate hints and light innuendoes (Saccio 139).

According to James Keller, early critics of Sydney's Astrophel and Stella have seen the grief and despair in these poems and have considered them to be autobiographical, and have therefore given them a maudlin reading. More recent critics, however, "recognize the silliness of Astrophel's predicament, the exaggerated sentiment of his complaints, the unflattering absurdity in his descriptions of Stella, and the melodrama of his mock battles with Cupid." This silliness can be seen in the visual imagery of "Sonnet 19," for example where Astrophel compares himself as a man who "Looks to the skies, and in a ditch doth fall," as he describes his admiration for Stella. "The silliness of this scene is evident in his self-pitying self-absorption." As further evidence of the humorous reading, consider also the fact that Sydney tells future writers who want originality in their writing to observe Stella and thus "to nurse at the fullest breasts of fame." Keller says that this way of contemplating Stella's beauty is "irreverent, erotic, humorous," and he goes on to suggest that the exaggeration is so extreme that it is "equivalent to milking her" in the name of creativity. In "Sonnet 50" Sydney reverses the male and the female reproductive roles by suggesting that Astrophel is made pregnant by Stella's beauty. He furthermore suggests that Astrophel's children are his poems, "all of which bear Stella's image" (Keller 981). "Sonnet 52" can also be used to support the humorous aspects of Sydney's writing. In this sonnet, there is a glaring and witty example of Astrophel's lasciviousness when Astrophel describes the conflict between "Virtue" and "Love." Astrophel argues that "Love" possesses Stella's eyes, her lips, and a number of other physical attributes, while "Virtue" is in control of her soul and her inner self. Astrophel concludes that "Virtue" can "have that Stella's self" as long as "Love" and Astrophel can have her body (Keller 982).

"Sonnet 59" is also filled with sensual humor, as Astrophel displays his jealousy of Stella's lap dog, "which enjoys more of the lady's favors than he." Astrophel argues that the lap dog might love Stella, but not with the same heated passion that he [Astrophel] has for her. "The dog will wait for her instructions, but not for as long as Astrophel has already lingered; the dog barks for her, although Astrophel's songs are much more pleasing; and finally,, the dog will fetch an article of her clothing, but Astrophel will bring her his very soul." But the coup de grace is that "Stella will allow the dog to lick her lap and her lips with its foulbreath when she will not grant the same permission to a pleasantly scented man." Astrophel concludes that if Stella is only willing to reward the services of "witless things," then he will himself sacrifice his wit, since this seems to be "an impediment to his desires" (Keller 982). In "Sonnet 59," Sydney frequent reference to the "beams" of Stella's eyes "portray her as a farcical caricature rather than a beautiful woman." In addition, his flattery is so exaggerated that it becomes unflattering, as in "Sonnet 9," where he compares Stella's face to the front of a building. James Keller feels that what Sydney is trying to do in Astrophel and Stella is not to praise Stella, but "to demonstrate wit in the execution of a clever conceit."

James Keller feels that the failure of early literary critics to recognize and applaud the humjor of Astrophel and Stella is both the effect and the cause of their over-sentimentalizing of the subject matter. "Although the end of the sequence becomes maudlin and unrelentingly melancholy, this does not subvert the occasionally playful, irreverent, and comic tone of the early sonnets" (Keller 983).

Sir Philip Sidney Bibliography

Cazamian, Louis. "Greene, Sidney, Peele." The Development of English Humor. Durham, NC: Duke University Press, 1952, 136-141.

Chalifour, Clark L. "Sir Philip Sidney's Old Arcadia as Terentian Comedy." Studies in English Literature 16 (1976): 51-63.

Keller, James. "Philip Sidney." Encyclopedia of British Humorists, Volume II. Ed. Steven H. Gale, New York, NY: Garland, 1996, 980-984.

Miller, Edmund. "Thomas Deloney." Encyclopedia of British Humorists, Volume I. Ed. Steven H. Gale, New York, NY: Garland, 1996, 302-307.

Edmund Spenser (1554-1599) IRELAND

See: Nilsen, Don L. F. Humor in Irish Literature: A Reference Guide. Westport, CT:
Greenwood Press, 1996.

Richard Tarlton (c1555-1588)

In England, Richard Tarlton was the most famous clown of his day, and he became
the semiofficial court jester in the court of Queen Elizabeth for a period of five years.
Tarlton was also the most popular comic actor on the pre-Shakespearean stage. There is
a famous woodcuut that shows Tarlton playing the pipe and tabor together with one leg
raised in the air to show that he is dancing the jig (Timpane 1103). Dick Tarlton (it is
assumed that this is probably the Richard Tarlton under discussion) wrote such well-known
pamphlets as Tarltons Toyes (1576), Tarltons Tragical Treatise (1578), Tarltons Tragical
Treatise (1578), Tarltons devise upon this unlooked for great snowe (1579), and the most
known of today, Tarltons jigge of a horse loade of fooles (1579). Tarlton's success made
him bold, and he often used his wit against some powerful men in the court. On one
occasion, he is said to have pointed toward Sir Walter Raleigh and said, "See the Knave
commands the Queen!" (Timpane 1104).

In both "The Crow Sits on the Wall," and "A Jigge of a Horse Load of Fools," the
singer satirizes the class or the profession of each member of the audience. The song is
loosely written so that it is easy for the singer to ad-lib according to the types of people
who happen to be in the audience. The refrain allows the singer time to look around and
see who is there, and fashion a verse for someone he sees in the audience.

Tarlton also wrote a drama named The Seven Deadly Sins (c1585) which is a
morality play that dramatizes the conflict of good and evil, and which personifies such
characters as Gluttony, Sloth, etc. The play is designed to leave a great deal of room for
ad-libbing and improvisation. Tarlton may also have been a co-author of The Famous
Victories of Henry the Fifth (c1584) which served as the model for Shakespeare's Henry
IV plays, and provided the model for Shakespeare's Falstaff (Timpane 1105). Richard
Tarlton was also a major inspiration for Will Kempe, Shakespeare's first clown. Kempe
was recognized as the heir to the Tarlton tradition of jigs, merriments, and knock-about
humor. It is said that Tarlton was also the personal apprentice of Robert Armin, who
played many of Shakespeare's fool roles when Kempe left the Globe Theatre Company in
1599 (Timpane 1106).

Richard Tarlton Bibliography

Timpane, John. "Richard Tarlton." Encyclopedia of British Humorists, Volume II. Ed.
Steven H. Gale, New York, NY: Garland, 1996, 1103-1106.

George Peele (1556-1596)

The Araygnement of Paris (1584) is an elaborate pastoral play which discusses the
myth of Paris and the golden apple. Here Peele is able to use the predicaments of Paris
and the gods, and the pastoral setting to create a comic tone that lightens the tone. The
opening act begins with punning references to sexual misconduct among various pastoral
deities. There are also a number of ironic understatements which occur in the play.

Although Peele first presents the goddesses as regal, their conversation quickly turns to sexual indiscretion and cuckoldry. Peele further demystifies them and turns them comic in their reaction to the golden ball. As each of them claims herself the fairest, Peele reduces them to sophisticated fishwives, each one willing to sink Paris in mortal sin for her own pride. (Free 842).

Mary Free feels that The Old Wives' Tale (1595) is Peele's most comic work. The play is very romantic, and it incorporates a number of folk tale elements, such as a conjurer, a damsel in distress, a ghost who aids the hero in rescuing the damsel in distress and then demands half of her according to the bargain they had struck earlier. In the play there are also puns, invectives, and magic, and various stereotypes can also be seen, such as the clown, and the braggart soldier. The episodic nature of the development also contributes to its humor (Free 842). The targets of the mocking tone of The Old Wives' Tale includes religion, and it also includes Gabriel Harvey's poetic style, and it also "parodies Petrarchanism in Huanebango's praise of Zantippa." The humor also results from Eumenides's innocence and from Jack's wit. Eumenides has promised Jack half of all he wins in his journeys, and this means that Eumenides must meet Jack's demand for half of Delia. It is only through humor that the reader is able Delia's patent acceptance of her death. "The moment is not only comic in its very absurdity but also in keeping with jest-book Renaissance humor. The play is a tour de force" (Free 843).

Louis Cazamian notes that there is quite a bit of humor in Peele's The Old Wive's Tale, but Cazamian chides critics for making rather excessive claims about the originality and significance of Peele as a humorist (Cazamian 139-140). Alfred Gu L'Estrange feels that Peele was a gay playwright who was fond of surprises and miraculous inventions. In the "Arraignment of Paris" a fantastic golden tree grows up, and in "The Old Wives Tale" the head of Huanebango arises from a well. L'Estrange considers "The Old Wives Tale" to be the most humorous of Peele's writings. Peele likes to deal with Latinisms, barbarisms, and sound-symbolic words. At one place he has Corebus say,

> "O falsum Latinum
> The fair maid is minum
> Cum apurtinantibus gibletis and all." (L'Estrange 241-242)

Peele was a popular writer of his day and was often asked to write pieces for the Lord Mayor and for royal occasions. He sometimes used Hexameter verse, as the following illustrates:

> Dub, dub-a-dub bounce,
> Quoth the guns with a sulphurous huff shuff. (L'Estrange 242)

George Peele Bibliography

Cazamian, Louis. "Greene, Sidney, Peele." The Development of English Humor. Durham, NC: Duke University Press, 1952, 136-141.

Free, Mary. "George Peele." Encyclopedia of British Humorists, Volume II. Ed. Steven H. Gale, New York, NY: Garland, 1996, 841-844.

L'Estrange, Alfred Gu. "Peele." History of English Humour. New York, NY: Burt Franklin, 1878, 241-242.

Thorndike, Ashley H. "Lyly, Peele, and Greene." English Comedy. New York, NY: Macmillan, 1929. 74-94.

Robert Greene (1558-1592)

Mary Free says that Robert Greene was a more prolific writer, and a more profligate individual than were any of the other "University Wits" (Free 485). Alfred Gu L'Estrange considers Robert Greene to be one of the principal humorists of his time. He primarily wrote plays and pamphlets, and his titles were as humorous as his motto, "Omne tulit punctum qui miscuit utile dulci" (L'Estrange 231). Greene says that his "Euphues" contains "mirth to purge melancholy" and that his "Quips for an Vpstart Courtier" is "a quaint dispute between velvet-breeches and cloth breeches," that his "Notable Discovery of Coosnage" has "a delightful discourse of the coosnage of Colliers," and that his "Second and Last Part of Conny-Catching" contains "new additions containing many merry tales of all lawes worth the reading, because they are worthy to be remembered" but although much humor is promised, little humor is actually contained in the pieces. L'Estrange indicates that a very small amount of humor was then thought to be considerable. In fact, L'Estrange says that in Greene's "Comicall Historie of Alphonsus, King of Arragon," the reader would not be able to find anything humorous at all, "unless the speaking of a brazen head, and letting Venus down from Heaven and drawing her up again, could have been so regarded" (L'Estrange 231-232).

Mamillia (1580) is about the faithless Pharicles who repeatedly proves that men are more fickle than women. In his preface entitled, "Gentlemen Readers," Greene mocks his fellow authors whose prefatory letters tend to be self-deprecating and tend to say that the work is of little or now value. With tongue in cheek, Greene playfully notes that these authors claim their works to be poor while he [Greene] has found their works to be highly skilled and perfectly polished. In his own preface, Greene says that he is not able to find words that are bad enough to apply to his own writing, since other writers have already preempted these words in their own prefaces. In this way, Greene "more highly praises his own work through satirizing the extremes of his predecessors."

In Mamillia the flights of alliteration enhance the humorous tone. One such example is "yea the concord of their nature was such, as no sops of suspicion, no mists of distrusts, no floods of fickleness, could once foil their faith." Another example of too-much alliteration that contributes to the comic diminution of the scene describes the couple who are "flowing in floods of felicity," and who are "by the falsehood of Pharicles soused in the seas of sorrow." This over-alliterative pattern

> sets the comic tone for exploring the question of who is more fickle--man or woman. The Italian setting allows Greene to satirize the country's citizens and by implication those "Italianate" Englishmen who ape Continental fashions. The men who seek to woo Mamillia would "correct nature" via dress to improve their narrow shoulders, thin bellies, crooked legs, small shanks, and--most importantly--their two faces. (Free 486)

L'Estrange considers Greene to be characteristic of his time in his love of introducing magic and enchantment, and in his introduction of characters from classical and scriptural history. Greene is especially fond of having devils as characters (L'Estrange 232). Greene's characters are typically amusing fellows, who like Greene himself, are free livers and fond of wine (L'Estrange 235). Nevertheless, Greene died in a most woeful state at the home of a poor shoemaker near Dowgate. Before dying, he had written his "Groat's-worth of Wit Bought with a Million of Repentance," in which he warns his former companions not to "spend their wits in making playes" (L'Estrange 237).

Pandosto (1588) is a drama that ends as a comedy in the broad sense of the word. The reconciliation happens when the shepherds and shepherdesses return to their courts and happily mary each other. Irony is a controlling trope in Pandosto. Early in the play Egistus arrives for a lengthy stay at Pandosto's court, and Pandosto greets his friend, by saying that "nothing in the world could have happened more acceptable to him than his coming." But while he is saying this he is plotting to poison Egistus within the space of a few pages. Mary Free says that there are two important ironies in Pandosto. The first irony is that Fawnie does not know anything about her royal lineage, even though her deportment loudly conveys this royal lineage. The second irony is that Pandosto incestuously lusts after Fawnia (Free 487).

The plot of Menaphon (1589) is very complex, and again irony is the primary comic device. Here the irony is that Sephestia falls in love with Milcertus, who is actually her husband, Maximus. There is a further dramatic irony in that neither of them recognizes the other, even though they are closely related--husband and wife (Free 487). Menaphon ends comically in that all of the ironies are resolved, and the company of the court is revitalized by its pastoral experience and returns to the constraining world of the court (Free 488).

Orlando Furioso (1594) could be a parody of Christopher Marlowe's Tamburlaine. Orlando Furioso is what Mary Free calls "overtly comic," in that "the comedic center of the play pits the title character against Sacraphant as they pursue the fair Angelica." Sacraphant is developed as a bombastic fool, and this character therefore satirizes the theatrical excesses of Greene's fellow playwrights (Free 488). Much of the humor of Orlando Furioso comes from Orlando's madness, as when he mistakes his servant, Orgalio for Angelica's supposed lover (Free 488).

In Robert Greene's plays there is a spirit of fun and jollity that waxes and wanes, and this is especially true in his Friar Bacon and Friar Bungay (c1589), which is both humorous and English to the core (Cazamian 136-137). Miles, who is the poor scholar, and to some extent also Ralph the King's fool in Friar Bacon can be compared to the clowns of Shakespeare. Greene's dramatic humor shows sympathy with life, and respect for the basic decencies, and these heighten its representative, national appeal (Cazamian 137). Friar Bacon and Friar Bungay (1594) is a comic play in which the clowns mock their masters in various ways. Rafe is the king's jester, and he makes bawdy but ironically appropriate puns about the "love" that Price Edward says he has for the humble Margaret. Miles is Bacon's poor scholar, and this character satirizes "learning" and the pretensions related to "learning." Miles displays physical comedy as well as verbal comedy. There is a pun in the play about the Pope's nose, and this puns actually satirizes the Roman Catholic church (Free 489).

The comic resolution of James IV (1598) occurs when James recognizes his folly and rejects his former behavior. He rues his agreement to kill his queen Dorothea, and he reconciles himself with her. Mary Free feels that the framing device which Greene uses is responsible for the "pure comedy" in the play. She also feels that Slipper is a witty servant who is "akin to Shakespeare's Launcelot Gobbo in Two Gentlemen of Verona. It is Greene's Slipper who offers to keep his master's "stable when it is empty, and his purse when it is full." James IV, and Alphonsus, King of Aragon (1599) are romantic comedies which some critics feel influenced Shakespeare's later romantic comedies (Free 489).

Mary Free says that in his final period as an author, Greene produced his cony-catching and his repentance pamphlets. This is the period that Louis Cazamian is referring to when he calls Greene's humor to be "rich" and "concrete." These adjectives characterize the humor in his "Conny-Catching" pamphlets, as well as that in A Quip for an Upstart Courtier, and The Blacke Bookes Messenger (Cazamian 137). Mary Free says that Greene's pamphlets "have their comic moments." The cony-catching pamphlets employ card tricks, diversions, and "bait and run" dodges, and the repentance pamphlets have a brittle comedy that targets various types of "gulls." "We laugh at the gulls and know that we could not possibly fall victim to such schemes." Nevertheless, Greene seems to be laughing at his readers as well as the victims of the various schemes (Free 490).

Robert Greene Bibliography

Braunmuller, A. R. "The Serious Comedy of Greene's James IV." English Literary

Renaissance. 3 (1973): 335-350.

Cazamian, Louis. "Robert Greene, Sir Philip Sidney, and George Peele." The Development
    of English Humor. Durham, NC: Duke University Press, 1952, 136-141.

Free, Mary. "Robert Greene." Encyclopedia of British Humorists, Volume I. Ed. Steven H.
    Gale, New York, NY: Garland, 1996, 485-491.

L'Estrange, Alfred Gu. History of English Humour. New York: Burt Franklin, 1878.

Sanders, Norman. "The Comedy of Greene and Shakespeare." The Early Shakespeare. Eds.
    John Russell Brown, and Bernard Harris. New York, NY: St. Martin's, 1961, 35-53.

Thorndike, Ashley H. "John Lyly, George Peele, and Robert Greene." English Comedy.
    New York, NY: Macmillan, 1929. 74-94.

Thomas Lodge (1558-1625)

Thomas Lodge was different from other satirists of his period in writing his A Fig
for Momus, Containing Pleasant Varietie, Included in Satyres, Eclogues, and Epistles near
the end of, rather than near the beginning of, his literary career. As an experimental piece,
the Fig for Momus was different from Lodge's earlier writing, and it was not widely read
during Lodge's time, because of the absence of local color in the satires, and the absence
as well of very much humor (Alden 90-91). Despite this fact, however, Thomas Lodge was
included in Meres's list of successful English satirists in his Palladis Tamia, published in
1598. As late as 1615 Thomas Lodge's satires must have been read by a large number of
people, because Anthony Nixon in that year published his Scourge of Corruption, in which
he plagiarized the opening of Lodge's first satire, changing the text from poetry to prose
in order to hide the plagiarism (Alden 91).

Lodge's decasyllabic couplet metre foreshadowed John Donne's writing which was
to follow shortly. Lodge's verse, however, is much smoother than Donne's, and
demonstrated the practiced hand of an author who had been writing not only good verse,
but admirable verse for years (Alden 91-92). Since Lodge and Donne were contemporaries,
the question has been raised as to who influenced whom, but Raymond Alden points out
that Lodge's verse preceded that of Donne by at least two years, and although Donne's
work may have been in manuscript form before the publication of the Fig for Momus it is
unlikely that Lodge saw the manuscript (Alden 92).

Lodge's monotonous style is neither bright enough or energetic enough to deserve
much praise. But the style is lucid and they may or may not be Horatian--critics disagree.
There are four or five satires in number, depending on what is counted.

> Satire I treats the tendency of all the world to love flattery and reject
> reproof. Bribes, lechery, usury, ambition, the praise of bad poetry,
> luxury, flattery, and avarice are attacked in particular.
>
> Satire II treats the examples of parents and the durability of early
> impressions, particularly in the matters of gambling, lust, profanity,
> and extravagance.
>
> Satire III is addressed to "a deere friend lately given over to covetousnesse."
> There is a picture of the miser's miserable lot: the real poverty of his
> home, life, and prospects.
>
> Satire IV treats the commonly mistaken ideas of what is truly good, and of
> the striving for what is really weariness. Ambition, conquest, and
> fraudulent dealing are rebuked; and there is in conclusion an account
> of the happiness of a lowly life, free from fear of enemies or
> calamity. (Alden 94)

Lodge's satire is grounded mostly in rebuke and admonition, though there are places of reflection as well. There is a great deal of evidence that Lodge used Juvenal as a model, with influence of the satires of Horace, and to some extent of Persius as well, also being present. Nevertheless, there is also a strong native English element in Lodge's satire, as evidenced in the hopeful, earnest tone. While the substance is mainly classical, and the moral elements mainly English, there is not the Christian coloring that is found in Gascoigne or even in Donne (Alden 95).

Louis Cazamian considers the humorous streak in Thomas Lodge to be quite pronounced. He further feels that Lodge's Rosalynde is charming, simple, and fresh, and causes the reader to smile. The lively interchanges between the heroine and her friend, Aliena, "have a quality of sprightliness, enhanced by reserve and tact that reveals the essential soul of sly, indirect pleasantry" (Cazamian 140).

Thomas Lodge Bibliography

Alden, Raymond MacDonald. "Thomas Lodge." The Rise of Formal Satire in England
    under Classical Influence. New York, NY: Archon, 1961, 90-97.
Cazamian, Louis. The Development of English Humor. Durham, NC: Duke University
    Press, 1952.

George Chapman (c1559-1634)

George Chapman was one of the first really important comic playwrights. His Blind Beggar is considered by some critics to be the first comedy of humors, a genre which would later be popularized by Ben Jonson. Chapman also helped to develop the genre of the romantic comedy. C. L. Barber would consider Chapman's plays to be "saturnalian." His comic formula involves a struggle between the forces of moderation and the forces of riot. Most often, a good-natured "intriguer" wants to expose folly and to remove any obstacles there are to mirth and romance. In doing this, he liberates the conservative and inhibiting characters from their pretensions and preoccupations Keller 224).

In Elizabethan Comic Character Conventions as Revealed in the Comedies of George Chapman, Paul Kreidler has three chapters on the use and modification of conventional comic characters. Two of these are on domestic figures, and include such archetypes as the harsh and indulgent fathers, the old man in love, the avaricious father, the elderly husband with a gay young wife, the ridiculous lover, the Pantalone's daughter, the matchmaker, the intriguers, the gallant, the faithless wife, the loyal woman, and the shrew. The other chapter on comic archetype characters deals with figures from the street like the braggart, the pedant as schoolmaster, the pedant as doctor, the pedant as lawyer, the stupid official, the parasite, the lout, and the gull. This chapter ends with a statement of how Chapman modified these stock figures (Kreidler ix-x and 51-116).

Kreidler points out that Chapman utilized the style and plot that were most in vogue during his day, and this included bombast and slapstick humor. Most critics are in agreement that Chapman was not a great dramatist. John Dryden described Chapman's Bussy D'Ambois as

> "a jelly, nothing but a cold, dull mass..., a dwarfish thought, dressed up in gigantic words, repetition in abundance, looseness of expression, and gross hyperboles; the sense of one line expanded prodigiously into ten, and, to sum up all, incorrect English, and an hideous mingle of false poetry, and true nonsense" (Kreidler 1).

Kreidler considers Dryden's criticism to be overly severe, and explains that Dryden's harshness was "the expression of seventeenth-century impatience with Renaissance exuberance," adding that any author with as little dramatic genius as Chapman had wouldn't have dreamed of writing plays in any period other than the Elizabethan period (Kreidler 2).

The protagonist in The Blind Beggar of Alexandria (1596) assumes so many different disguises that it is difficult to determine exactly who he is. He is Irus, the blind visionary, but he is also Cleanthes the banished Duke, and Leon the notorious usurer, in addition to being an ill-tempered Count. The Blind Beggar, therefore is the Lord of Misrule. He represents the spirit of riot and disorder (Keller 224). But even though Chapman had little talent as a playwright, he was a very good humorist, and the humor motif is evident in the entire range of his comedies. His earliest play is entitled The Blind Beggar of Alexandria, and on the title page of the 1598 edition it is described as "most pleasantly discoursing his variable humours in disguised shapes full of conceite and pleasure" (Kreidler 146). Furthermore, the words "humour," and "humourous" are constant and conspicuous in Chapman dialogues, and such characters as Cleanthes "have as many humours as disguises" (Kreidler 146).

Chapman's most humorous play is An Humourous Day's Mirth (1597). In this play all of the characters are stock figures defined mainly by their humors. In fact, Chapman devotes entire scenes to character development, totally neglecting the advancing of the plot, while his queer and unimportant characters parade their follies around the stage (Kreidler 147). Two of the characters of this play can be described as purely humorous--Blanuel and Dowsecer, but in the play can be found also many stock figures which Chapman presents through their humorous idiosyncrasies. There are jealous husbands and wives, foolish lovers, and ridiculous fathers, and there are also a number of other stereotypes to be found in comedies of Chapman's day. Blanuel and Dowsecer are like all of the other characters in that they do nothing significant and arrive nowhere in particular (Kreidler 151). This play can be defined, then, as a "comedy of humors," in that it employs the caricaturist's method of revealing stock figures in humorous and exaggerated ways. It is devoted almost entirely to the depiction of grotesque characters and characteristics, so that the tenuous plot collapses completely in scene after scene in order to make way for the action, which is nothing more than the exposure of folly (Kreidler 152).

In An Humorous Day's Mirth, Lemot is the comic manipulator who exposes the hypocrisy of Florila by discovering that she finds ways to reassure her husband while at the same time she plots her various acts of adultery. When her husband isn't looking, Florila agrees to a rendezvous with Lemot, but she soon discovers that Lemot is trying to strip her of her "pretensions to virtue." When they meet, Lemot courts the lady in a rough manner by biting her hand, but when she complains, he tells her to return to her husband and to quit her puritanical pose, for she has forever disgraced her religion. Ironically, when she returns to her husband, she resumes her posture of puritanism and upbraids her husband for his mistrust. (Keller 224)

The main conflict in All Fools is established by the restrictions imposed by the older generation and by the attempts of the younger generation to circumvent these restraints. Gostanzo has the foolish belief that he understands and controls his son, Valerio. He believes that Valerio is inexperienced in the arts of love, but in reality, Valerio has already married--in secret.

> The playful inter-generational conflict between fathers and sons is truly saturnalian comedy. The young men and women represent the riotous spirit of fun, while the fathers constitute the obstacles to pleasure and romance. Through his actions, Rinaldo circumvents the impediments to mirth, undermining the foolish constraints of the fathers nd promoting the progressive values of the sons. (Keller 225)

All Fools is a play based on "humor" in the older sense of the word. In All Fools, Cornelio, the jealous husband of Gazetta, is mainly a humorous character. Gazetta describes Cornelio as vainly jealous, and unreasonable in his suspicions. It is ironic that Cornelio does his best to conceal his anxiety for fear that his jealousy will become a self-fulfilling prophesy (Kreidler 152). In this confusing play, there is much talk and little action. It is a story which is "full of sound and fury, signifying nothing" (Kreidler 154). "How little Chapman cared about the plot is evident from the fact that from start to finish the position of Gazetta is ambiguous. Cornelio's jealous humour can rage equally well whether she be true or disloyal to him" (Kreidler 154).

Sir Giles and his ill-humored companions are gulled in Sir Giles Goosecap by Foulweather and Rudesby. This gulling actually constitutes a subplot, but a subplot that contains "all of the truly amusing events in the drama" (Keller 225). There are three humorous characters in Chapman's Sir Giles Goosecap, all exhibiting peculiarities of speech and mannerisms of conduct. Sometimes the humors which the characters display are self imposed. For example, Blanuel assumes a melancholy that he doesn't feel, and Cornelio wilfully displays a jealous exterior for political reasons. Sir Giles is a weak, effeminate, apish simpleton, who is not able to understand his own mother tongue, and who is constantly contradicting himself. Captain Foulweather is portrayed as a hero clothed in fantastic raiment because he has visited the continent. Captain Foulweather belittles the manners and the affectation of the English and the tastes and interests of the French. He does this by piling up adjectives, nouns, and phrases. His favorite word is "emphatical." In contrast to Captain Foulweather there is Sir Cuthbert Rudesby, who is blunt, and sullen, and whose comments are invariably gruff (Kreidler 154-155).

In Monsieur d'Olive, Chapman again satirizes folly, this time by suggesting that those people who take themselves too seriously should be considers objects of ridicule Monsieur d'Olive is a parody of the pomp and circumstance that accompanies courtly life. The most humorous aspect of the play is in the satiric subplot that parallels Vendome's actions in which Monsieur d'Olive is an upstart courtier who is a malcontent, and who is therefore very critical of others. "Upon his introduction, he attacks many of the common objects of satire, such as corrupt courtiers, lawyers, and women. However, as is predictable, this satirist becomes the object of ridicule himself." One of the great ironies of the play is that the more that Monsieur d'Olive tries to be a proper courtier, the more he becomes a dolt.

Chapman's last comedy is The Widow's Tears. Here the hero is of the humourous sort, and his foibles demand correction. Kreidler suggests that all of Chapman's comic plays depend on "humours" in the development not only of characters, but in the development of situations as well (Kreidler 155). Tharsalio's boldness in The Widow's Tears (1612) allows him to court the widowed Countess, Eudora, and this boldness is amusing. Tharsalio has arrived at the humorous conclusion that after a woman's husband dies, her vow of chastity can be easily fractured, so he vigorously courts Eudora, even though she constantly rejects and humiliates him (Keller 226).

George Chapman Bibliography

Cazamian, Louis. "Chapman." The Development of English Humor. Durham, NC: Duke
    University Press, 1952, 332-337.
Dean, William. "Chapman's May Day: A Comedy of Social Reformation." Parergon 16
    (1976): 47-55.
Grant, Thomas Mark. The Comedies of George Chapman: A Study in Development.
    Salzburg, Germany: Institut Fuer Englische Sprache und Literatur. 1972.
Holaday, Allan, ed. The Plays of George Chapman: The Comedies. Urbana, IL: University
    of Illinois Press, 1970.
Keller, James R. "George Chapman." Encyclopedia of British Humorists, Volume I. Ed.

Steven H. Gale, New York, NY: Garland, 1996, 223-228.

Kreidler, Paul. Elizabethan Comic Character Conventions as Revealed in the Comedies of George Chapman. Ann Arbor, MI: University of Michigan Press, 1935.

Preussner, Arnold W. "Chapman's Anti-Festive Comedy: Generic Subversion and Classical Allusions in The Widow's Tears." I.S.J.R. 59 (1985): 263-272.

Tricomi, Albert H. "The Focus of Satire and the Date of Monsieur D'Olive." Studies in English Literature, 1500-1900 17 (1977): 281-294.

Weidner, Henry M. "Homer and the Fallen World: Focus of Satire in George Chapman's The Widow's Tears." Journal of English and Germanic Philology 62 (1963): 518-532.

John Penry (1559-1593), WALES

Hugh Walker indicates that John Penry is known as the father of Welsh nonconformity. According to Walker, the first genre for good English satire to appear in important places was that of the political pamphlet. The most prominent political pamphleteer of this time was Martin Marprelate, though this was a penname for John Penry, who wrote the tracts with the aid of John Udall, Robert Waldegreve, Job Throckmorton and W. Pierce (Walker 92). Walker suggests that Penry was provoked into writing the Marprelate Tracts, since on one occasion when he was summoned to answer for one of his books the archbishop called him a "boy," "knave," "slanderer," "lewd boy," and "lewd slanderer" (Walker 93).

John Penry Bibliography

Walker, Hugh. English Satire and Satires. London, England: J. M. Dent, 1925.

Thomas Deloney (c1560-c1599)

Thomas Deloney was a writer who truly represented the lower middle class in England. He was in constant contact with the working people of his time, and his instincts were to a large extent fashioned by that contact. Deloney's humor was popular, realistic, and colloquial. He wrote jestbooks and collections of funny stories told in the vernacular. His Jack of Newbury, his The Gentle Craft, and his Thomas of Reading are basically just collections of anecdotes, roughly organized around the central figure of each book. Louis Cazamian considers Jack of Newbury to be merry, shrewd, ironic and pleasant. There is usually a point or a moral to Deloney's tales; the tales are didactic, but they are funny as well (Cazamian 176). Deloney had a clever and sly mind that allowed him to use indirect comedy and understatement very well. His wit can be compared to that of the French of his day, but it was modified by the English quality of concrete raciness (Cazamian 176-177).

In terms of realistic descriptions of his contemporary scene, and in terms of creating satire and humor from character and incident instead of just from wit and word play, Thomas Deloney was ahead of the other authors of his period (Miller 303). Jack of Newbery (1597) is a novel which is episodic in its construction. The novel contains eleven chapters which tell "what is essentially a self-contained humorous anecdote" (Miller 304). Deloney has a light and satiric writing style that leads Merritt E. Lawliss to say, "Surely no other English writer of prose fiction of the sixteenth and seventeenth centuries can entertain us so well, and no other before Dickens gives us so much well-conceived and fully satisfying characters." Edmund Miller says that Deloney's works are filled with "rollicking good humor," and "engaging realistic style" as it presents the "middle-class dream of success" (Miller 305).

Thomas Deloney Bibliography

Cazamian, Louis. "Deloney." The Development of English Humor. Durham, NC: Duke
     University Press, 1952, 175-179.
Miller, Edmund. "Thomas Deloney." Encyclopedia of British Humorists, Volume I. Ed.
     Steven H. Gale, New York, NY: Garland, 1996, 302-307.

Michael Drayton (1563-1631)

Michael Drayton's The Owl, published in 1604, is a poem that is satirical in content, though it is not a formal satire in the classical tradition. The Owl was written in the style of Spenser's Mother Hubbard's Tale. In Drayton's poem, the Owl tells of public and private vices in the bird kingdom, but the human analogues are apparent. Many of the contemporary allusions are lost to the modern reader, but it is clear that the Eagle represents the king. It is also clear that the Eagle (king) is never attacked, and it is in fact the Eagle who at the end of the poem summarizes the admonitions against the evils which are throughout his 'kingdom. The title page of the 1619 edition of Drayton's poems contains an engraving representing the heroic, lyrical, satiric, and pastoral aspects of writing. The pictures are of a plumed warrior minerva, a musician playing a lyre, a shaggy satyr, and a shepherd with a pipe and crook (Alden 171).

Drayton was influenced by Rabelais and Cervantes, but he was especially influenced by Chaucer and Shakespeare. His Nymphidia, or the Court of Fairies (1627) is an imitation of Chaucer's "Sir Thopas" in parody form, and it is, of course, written in the same meter as Chaucer's original. But although Drayton's Nymphidia, or the Court of Fairies parodies Chaucer in meter and style, it parodies Shakespeare's A Midsummer Night's Dream in subject and theme, for it is a fresh and picturesque description of the world of fairies (Cazamian 369). Drayton's Oberon is taken from Shakespeare, as is his Demetrius and Lysander, both of whom appear in Midsummer Night's Dream (III,ii) (Cazamian 369). But Drayton's humor looks forward as much as it looks back. "It has seeds and promises which point forward not only to Hudibras but to Peter Pan" (Cazamian 370).

Drayton's writing tone is light and graceful, and there is a faint flavor of humor associated with incongruence of the epic dignity of the occasion as contrasted with the recounting of trifling incidents. The effect is mock-heroic. There is a "sufficient measure of unruffled seriousness to invest it with a quality of reserve" (Cazamian 369).

Michael Drayton Bibliography

Alden, Raymond MacDonald. "Michael Drayton." The Rise of Formal Satire in England
     under Classical Influence. New York, NY: Archon, 1961, 171-172.
Cazamian, Louis. "Drayton." The Development of English Humor. Durham, NC: Duke
     University Press, 1952, 369-370.

Christopher Marlowe (1564-1593)

Stephen Lynch feels that all of Christopher Marlowe's plays contain humor, though he also says that the humor has a bitter and sardonic edge (Lynch 724). In an article entitled "Marlowe and the 'Comic Distance,' " J. R. Mulryne and Stephen Fender contrast Aeneas in Dido, Queen of Carthage with Ovid's Pygmalion and with Shakespeare's Leontes, the difference being that Aeneas cannot give life to his statue. "Aeneas cannot 'awake his faith' and have it rewarded by the redemption of past time. In Marlowe, the mind is at odds with the facts, while the heart oscillates baffled between two kinds of knowledge" (Mulryne and Fender 49). In this scene the hero, Aeneas, has been deflated, and "in his delusion he becomes for the moment comic" (Mulryne and Fender 50). Many critics have recognized the comic devices in Dido. Some of these critics use these comic devices as evidence that the play is funny throughout. Anthony Trollope called the play a "burlesque," adding that it parodies the story by Vergil (Mulryne and Fender 52). Clifford Leech contends that humor is the "dominant tone" in Dido and that it is "a gentle and delighting humour" in which "the affairs of men and gods are seen as a spectacle engagingly absurd" (Leech 46).

The ambivalence in Dido is characteristic of Marlowe's writing. There are
> many instances in Marlowe in which contradictory views of experience are brought together and left unresolved: the ideal and the common sense; the hint of a comprehensive order and the rejection of all order; the socially concerned and the individualist; the moral and the libertine; metaphor and fact. (Mulryne and Fender 50)

Mulryne and Fender contend that Marlowe's conjunction of such contradictions is responsible for many of the critical disputes that have been prompted by Marlowe's plays. But Marlowe is not doing this just to be provocative; rather, this is how he sees the world: "The 'structure of feeling' in Marlowe is one that requires such opposites, and involves a genuine ambivalence (not an ambiguity) of feeling" (Mulryne and Fender 50).

Mulryne and Fender consider Tamburlaine The Great, I (ca. 1587) to be more effective in its comic techniques than is Dido because it better involves the reader in an extended switching of attitudes. The polarities of the audience's responses are played out over the play's two parts. "We want to call Tamburlaine I 'comic' not because we wish to place it in a formal category..., but because the name of comedy helps us to locate, much more accurately than 'tragedy' or 'history,' what we take to be the essential nature of our response to the play" (Mulryne and Fender 52-53). Mulryne and Fender feel that the ambivalence in Tamburlaine I is so pervasive and so structured that it should instead be called "paradox," and they further point out the importance of paradox in the history of comic theory (Mulryne and Fender 53).

Stephen Lynch says that Tamburlaine I is reminiscent of the comic antics of the Vice figure of medieval morality plays. Just as the Vice figure irreverently mocks Christian morality, Tamburlaine attacks the religious and political values of Elizabethan England. "Much of the humor in the play lies in the technique of reversal which is found in Tamburlaine's outrageous assaults on orthodox values, treating the serious frivolously, the reverent irreverently, the sacred indecently--comically turning the world upside down." In Tamburlaine I, Bajazeth, the Emperor of the Turks, is captured by Tamburlaine's soldiers, and they put him in a cage and carry him around to be mocked and ridiculed. But Bajazeth takes control of the situation by committing suicide. The stage directions read, "He brains himself against the cage." About this, Zabina, his wife, says, "His skull all riven in twain! his brains dash'd out." Then she follows her husband's example. The stage directions read that she "runs against the cage, and brains herself." Lynch says that the effect of these two brainings was "probably not unlike that of a modern horror film--distasteful to some, gutbusting humor to others." This type of episode is not uncommon in Marlowe's plays, and Lynch suggests that such violence is akin to such popular forms of Elizabethan entertainment as bear-baiting, in which the bears would be chained to a stake and attacked by dogs. "Elizabethan theaters were often located in the vicinity of bear-baiting amphitheaters, were architecturally modeled on such amphitheaters, and most likely could provide an atmosphere as raucous and irreverent. In fact, fights between members of the theater audience and actors on stage were not uncommon" (Lynch 721).

Tamburlaine The Great, II (ca. 1588) is about Tamburlaine's defeating various kings, placing horse's bits into their mouths, and forcing them to draw him around in his chariot as he whips them and feeds them raw meat. "Marlowe presents a spectacle of kings made beasts by a shepherd made king." Tamburlaine defies Mohamet, and orders his soldiers to burn the Koran, but then Tamburlaine falls ill. Stephen Lynch suggests that the timing of his sickness and death implies that "if there is any moral order it must be Islamic," but adds that Tamburlaine does not indeed die as the result of divine wrath, but rather dies from purely natural causes. "Marlowe momentarily affirms Islam in order to satirize Christianity, only to then turn around and satirize Islam" (Lynch 722).

There is much black humor targeting Christianity in The Jew of Malta (ca. 1590). T. S. Eliot considers this to be a farce, since the stage actions are often wildly exaggerated and sensational. A lot of the humor comes from Marlowe's treatment of Christian hypocrisy. Barabas may be morally superior to the other characters only because "his unabashed greed is more straightforward; it is not masked by pious hypocrisies." Barabas makes many witty barbs aimed at Christian hypocrisy. "The play amuses with scene after scene of outrageous Machiavellian cunning" (Lynch 722). "Barabas provokes two friars into a heated competition for his soul and the money that would come with it. In an exquisitely cunning scheme, he strangles one friar, sets the corpse upright against a wall, and waits for the rival friar to arrive and beat the already dead corpse until "his brains drop out on's nose" (Lynch 723).

When Barabas purchases Ithamore, the slave in The Jew of Malta, they exchange anecdotes about their clever misdeeds with each other: Barabas says that at knight he walks around killing sick people who are groaning under walls. Sometimes he also goes around poisoning wells. Ithamore responds by saying that he sets Christian villages on fire, and chains eunuchs and binds galley slaves. He says that in Jerusalem he once spread grains of marble stones around where he knew that the pilgrims kneeled, so that their knees would be "rankled." Then he had a good laugh watching the cripples limping home to Christendom on crutches. Stephen Lynch points out that this is not mere comedy, it is parody as well. By wildly exaggerating Renaissance stereotypes of Jews, Marlowe is not actually parodying Jews so much as he is parodying Christian perceptions of Jews (Lynch 723).

The comedy of The Tragical History of Dr. Faustus (ca. 1592) is mostly confined to the subplot involving Wagner, Robin, and Dick, and this comic subplot functions as an ironic inversion of the tragic main plot. Faustus is a magician who plays tricks on the Pope. Dishes and cups are snatched away; the triple crown is stolen; the Pope's ears are boxed. Then Faustus throws fireworks into a group of friars, to the delight of the Protestant audience. Then Robin and Dick steal a cup from a vintner, and are turned into an ape and a dog respectively by Mephistopheles. Thus the subplot undermines the heroic dignity of Faustus (Lynch 723). "Ironically, Faustus's longing for superhuman knowledge and power debases him into a subhuman clown" (Lynch 724). Compared to The Tragical History of Dr. Faustus, The Tragedy of Edward II (ca. 1592), is more sophisticated and subtle, and the humor is darker (Lynch 724).

Clifford Leech considers Marlowe's Hero and Leander (1598) to be a "major comic poem" (Leech 81). In an article entitled "Comic Method in Marlowe's Hero and Leander, Brian Morris explains some of the ambivalence of the piece by describing Marlowe's breaking or shifting of stereotypes. "The comedy works by the deliberate inversion of all orthodox attitudes toward human dignity and human love, by the frustration of normal expectations" (Morris 115). In Hero and Leander, the description of the woman (Hero) consists of a "detailed survey of her garments, in which the main point is the triumph of Art over Nature." The only reference to Hero's body in this part of the poem is to her "naked neck," which Cupid is said to embrace (Morris 116). In contrast, the man (Leander) is "pictured naked, and the narrator dwells sensuously on his body" (Morris 116).

> Yet this grave inversion of the traditional techniques of physical description does not create comic characters. Both Hero and Leander are so far neutral, statuesque figures, and the comedy resides in the narrator's odd manipulation of his story. (Morris 117)

The detached, amused, ambivalent tone of the narrator can be seen in the following couplet which refers to Leander's sighs and tears,

> Which like sweet music enter'd Hero's ears;
> And yet at every word she turn'd aside,
> And always cut him off as he replied. (Morris 117-118)

Morris concludes that the basic theme of Hero and Leander is that young love is absurd, and that the dominant tone is comic. But he also concludes that

> The central figure is the suave, detached narrator, who asserts an unshakable comic control over narrative, allusion, and language alike. Marlowe's bias is increasingly towards the full burlesque, and away from the impending tragic end of the story. (Morris 131)

Louis Cazamian describes the comic episodes in Marlowe's Doctor Faustus to be broad farce (Cazamian 140). Marlowe's Jew of Malta can also be analyzed from a comic point of view. Erich Segal has written an article entitled, "Marlowe's Schadenfreude: Barabas as Comic Hero," in which he defines Schadenfreude as a "delight at someone else's misfortune" (Segal 75). Segal contends that Marlowe, like Ben Jonson, wrote "savage comic humour," but further contends that critics seem to be much more aware of Jonson's brutality than they are that of Marlowe's (Segal 80). Barabas is Marlowe's "Jew of Malta." His humor can be compared to the poneria of Aristophanies, since he is "the self militant." In fact, Segal suggests that all of Marlowe's heroes are "monomaniac exponents of the first person" (Segal 81).

The most memorable confrontation in the Jew of Malta is that between the Jew Barabas and the Turk Ithamore. Barabas comes onto the scene brimming with "sweet hostility." He is not bitter or vengeful because he is as rich as he ever was and he can now devote himself entirely to mischief (Segal 85-86). In the tradition of the comic literature of Marlowe's day, Barabas and Ithamore each sings an aria of evil when they first meet each other (Segal 86). Barabas is Alazon par excellence as he brags his outrageous brag:

> As for my selfe, I walke abroad a nights
> And kill sicke people groaning under walls:
> Sometimes I goe about and poyson wells....
> And in the warres 'twixt France and Germanie,
> Under pretence of helping Charles the fifth,
> Slew friend and enemy with my strategems. (Segal 87)

Segal considers Barabas to be one of the grandest rogues of comedy (Segal 87).

The character of Barabas is grounded in medieval stereotypes of the Jew. Barabas's brag begins with the words "As for my selfe," and his preoccupation is much more with malice than it is with money. As a doctor he enjoyed enriching the priests (with burials). As a usurer he enjoyed causing pain (such as suicide and insanity). In "helping" Charles the fifth, he slew both friend and enemy. His cruelty was total, and non discriminating. "Marlowe's descriptions are intended to arouse the laugh of Schadenfreude through a comic hero who unabashedly relishes the inflicting of pain, "o qualunque rea cosa" (Segal 88).

At the beginning of the play, Barabas's exploits are merely imaginary; they are part of his brag. But by the end of the play, he has committed almost all of the atrocities he has boasted about. And Ithamore, who in the beginning of the play is one of Barabas's dupes, ends up by being one of his victims. Barabas flatters Ithamore as being "my second self," but he quickly lets the audience know that he is merely gulling Ithamore (Segal 88-89). Nevertheless, Ithamore prides himself in giving Barabas a helping hand in strangling a friar or whatever (Segal 89).

Barabas's single aim throughout the play is to outdo himself in evil. As he is poisoning the nuns, it is difficult for the audience to grieve for Abigail, the nun who is dying on stage, because they can hear the other nuns off stage who are all dying at the same time. Even after Barabas becomes governor, he must continue his malice, for that is his "humour" (Segal 89).

Barabas's last cruelty is his worst, since it has the most victims, and since he himself is one of these victims. Barabas and the other victims end up in a cauldron of boiling water. His last words, which were used to curse the "damn'd Christians, dogges, and Turkish Infidels" were intended to raise a "heartless laugh" (Segal 90). Segal concludes by saying that many psychologists define Schadenfreude as "childish pleasure," and by further saying that Marlowe often displayed "a rather adolescent delight in cruelty" (Segal 91).

Christopher Marlowe Bibliography

Cazamian, Louis. The Development of English Humor. Durham, NC: Duke University Press, 1952.

Crabtree, John H., Jr. "The Comedy in Marlowe's Dr. Faustus." Furman Studies NS9 (1961): 1-9.

Leech, Clifford. "Marlowe's Humor." Essays on Shakespeare and Elizabethan Drama in Honour of Hardin Craig. Ed. R. Hosley. Columbia, MO: University of Missouri Press, 1962.

Lynch, Stephen J. "Christopher Marlowe." Encyclopedia of British Humorists, Volume II. Ed. Steven H. Gale, New York, NY: Garland, 1996, 719-724.

Morgan, Gerald. "Harlequin Faustus: Marlowe's Comedy of Hell." The Humanities Association Review 18.1 (1967): 22-34.

Morris, Brian. "Comic Method in Hero and Leander." Christopher Marlowe. Ed. Brian Morris. New York: NY: Hill, 1968, 113-131.

Mulryne, J. R., and Stephen Fender. "Marlowe and the 'Comic Distance.' " Christopher Marlowe. Ed. Brian Morris. New York: NY: Hill, 1968, 47-64.

Segal, Erich. "Marlowe's Schadenfreude: Barabas as Comic Hero." Veins of Humor. Ed. Harry Levin. Cambridge, MA: Harvard University Press, 1972, 69-92.

William Shakespeare (1564-1616)

Northrop Frye says that Shakespearean comedy always "begins with some absurd, cruel, or irrational law: the law of killing Syracusans in the Comedy of Errors, the law of compulsory marriage in A Midsumer Night's Dream, the law that confirms Shylock's bond, the attempts of Angelo to legislate people into righteousness, and the like, which the action of comedy then evades or breaks" (Frye 166). Frye contrasts Shakespearean comedy with Shakespearean tragedy by saying that, "just as comedy often sets up an arbitrary law and then organizes the action to break or evade it, so tragedy presents the reverse theme of narrowing a comparatively free life into a process of causation. This happens to Macbeth when he accepts the logic of usurpation, to Hamlet when he accepts the logic of revenge, to Lear when he accepts the logic of abdication" (Frye 212). Frye continues that in comedy there tends to be a character which Frye calls the "tricky slave ("dolosus servus") that is an "eiron" figure who acts from pure love of mischief, and is able to set the comic action going. This "tricky slave," or "vice" can be as light-hearted as Puck in A Midsumer Night's Dream, or as malevolent as Don John in Much Ado about Nothing (Frye 173). Some of these "tricky slaves" or "vices" can be spiritual beings, such as Puck, or Ariel (Frye 174). Shakespeare's comedies also have a buffoon or "mad host," whom Frye describes as an "entertainer." He is jovial and loquacious and both Falstaff and Sir Toby Belch are examples (Frye 175).

Irene Makaryk compares the comedy of Shakespeare with that of Menander of Athens in that both of these authors celebrate the ongoing power of life and focus on how the individual matures in society. Makaryk goes on to discuss the structure of a Menander or a Shakespearean comedy.

> Although complications such as the separation of families or lovers, severe laws, negative or immature personality traits, threats of death, and so on begin the action of the comic play, meetings and reconciliations, marriages, and festivities involving dance, song, and feasting usually end it. Social order is re-established, individuals accept their proper roles, and the values of society are affirmed. (Makaryk viii)

Paul Grawe notes that by Shakespeare's time the comic traditions of Greece and Rome had become thoroughly intertwined with the earlier Judeo-Christian tradition of great spiritual force. Shakespeare tried to harmonize these divergent traditions from his earliest classical play, Comedy of Errors, to his latest romance, The Tempest. Twelfth Night, which Grawe considers to be the best of Shakespeare's stage comedies, is the most successful in blending the classical and the Christian ideals (Grawe 97). William Hazlitt contrasts Shakespeare's age with our own:

> Shakespeare's age was breaking into chaos, while today's age is trying to turn chaos into order. Yet his tragedy faced destiny with neither a bang nor a whimper and his comedy rose free of confusion and despair in humorous, unfettered laughter at the sheer absurdity of the passing spectacle. (53).

Larry Champion indicates that Shakespeare still employs many conventional elements of romantic comedy, but he moves to "comedies of identity" in which the humor arises not so much from the action itself as from the character's exposure arising from that action, what Champion calls "the comic gap between appearance and reality" (Champion 25).

According to J. B. Priestley, one of the archetypes of Shakespeare's comedies is the comic and highly poetic and unworldly atmospheres that keep recurring. In A Midsummer Night's Dream there is the magic wood. In As You Like It there is the amiable forest. In Twelfth Night there are the stately gardens, and this comedy-producing motif is reintroduced again and again. Whenever this fantasy world is produced,

> potential lovers advance, retreat, advance again, in a dance of glittering speeches. When humour arrives, as it does with the artisan-players in the Dream, with Touchstone and the rustics in As You Like It, with Sir Toby and Sir Andrew Aguecheek in Twelfth Night, it might be said to break in coming from some other world. (Priestley 18).

Helge Kökeritz notes that many modern researchers are squeamish about Shakespeare's puns. About half of Shakespeare's puns are still homonyms, and they carry the same connotations for the modern reader as for Shakespeare. "We have usually no difficulty in recognizing the pun, and only its possible indelicacy may prompt an editor to ignore it in his textual notes." Kökeritz is saying that Shakespearean texts are censored not so much by the omissions of text, but by the omissions of footnotes (Kökeritz 64).

Louis Cazamian indicates that Shakespeare was more brilliant than all of his rivals in word-play and wit, but that his real strength lie in his realistic comedy and humor and the implications that can be drawn about human nature from his comic depictions. Shakespeare would,

> either turn the absurdities of men and things to humorous purposes by painting them with liveliness which a wise reserve enhanced, or by uniting the gift of humor with the cognate one of psychological truth, create characters that were themselves humorists and radiated out the magic which they pretended that they did not feel. (Cazamian 206-207)

Shakespeare's earliest comedies (such as A Midsummer Night's Dream), like those of his contemporaries, were essentially situation comedies. "The humor arises from action rather than character. There is no significant development of main characters" (Champion 9). Even much of the characterization is visual and physical, established by such features as social rank (king), being a fairy, etc. But as Shakespeare matured as a writer, his characters developed increased complexity (as in As You Like It), so that the comedy is derived more from the characters' identities than from their appearances and actions. In this phase, the audience laughs not at the events, but at and with the characters who are involved in those events. Since it is no longer possible under these conditions to keep the audience detached emotionally, Shakespeare assures the audience throughout the plays that there will be a happy ending. "The perspective is such that we are forced to assume that normality will ultimately prevail and that [the characters] will never be allowed to engage in activities of permanent consequence" (Champion 10). Shakespeare's final works (such as The Tempest) are the most controversial. These plays are much more dramatic than are his previous comedies. The issues dealt with are far more serious, and this creates a problem for the comic artist--the problem of maintaining a comic perspective for the audience. In addition to increased dramatization, there is an increase of character complexity. However, in light of these differences, Shakespeare is probably at the peak of his comic ability. He is able to use character personality and change as a catalyst for humor and an assurance to the audience of a happy ending. These plays can therefore be appreciated in regard to their realistic depictions of humanity and social issues which provide an entertaining release. Note that only in this third and final stage, must there be a transformation, a development, a maturing of the character (Champion 10).

Alice Rayner points out that the interpretation of such Shakespearean characters as Malvolio, Shylock, and Katherine is constantly being revised, since it is a function of the external perception of equity, fairness, or sympathy of a particular time. Interpretations are subject to the currents of ethical taste and can shift greatly from one time to another (Rayner 26).

Kristian Smidt has written a book entitled Unconformities in Shakespeare's Early Comedies in which she discusses the unconformities in Comedy of Errors, The Two Gentlemen of Verona, The Taming of the Shrew, Love's Labour's Lost, A Midsummer Night's Dream, The Merry Wives of Windsor, and The Merchant of Venice. Smidt is using the term "unconformities" to refer basically to "breaks in narrative continuity, contradictions as to cause and effect, impossible or incredible sequences of events, or unexplained and surprising changes in the characters portrayed" (Smidt ix). Smidt continues,

> As this study of the early comedies should have amply demonstrated, he never adhered rigidly to a consistent preconceived design or to the details or even outlines of borrowed stories. He amplified and omitted, changed and revised, as the spirit moved him, his momentum impelled him, and his memory served him. And he often left signs and remains of abandoned or modified apparent intentions. (Smidt 177)

Zvi Jagendorf believes that change is such an important element in the resolution of Shakespeare's comedies that it is the rule rather than the exception. In Shakespeare's comedies, there are two types of changes. One of these is related to instability. It is the change that causes the tangle of errors produced by passions, disguises, interchangeable twins, accidents, and malice. The other type of change is the opposite. This second type of change puts an end to the error and the instability and provides the transformation into truth and stability (Jagendorf 111-112).

> In Shakespeare's comedies, the magic, the coincidences, and the devices that lead to resolution keep us aware of the part played by art in contriving the happy end. But this is an art that despite its transparency and its transience as performance redeems itself not only by gratifying our desire for pleasure but by giving us grounds for belief. (Jagendorf 161)

Many critics have suggested that Shakespeare inserted comic elements into his tragedies in order to relieve his audiences of the arousal from the distressing events that are occurring in the stories; however, Peter Derks suggests that the opposite is often the case. Rather than decreasing the level of arousal, the comic elements often increase the level of arousal (Derks 51). Derks noted that there are three types of humor in the tragedies: comic scenes, comic characters, and comic "spice." The two best known comic scenes in the tragedies are the "drunken porter" scene from Macbeth, and the "grave digger" scene from Hamlet. In terms of comic characters the evil comics of Shakespeare's tragedies are some of the most prized villains in all of literature. Richard III is funny as Glouster, but becomes serious as he becomes the king. Edmund is a comic villain in King Lear, as is Iago in Othello. Even the three witches in Macbeth can be viewed as comic villains if their incongruities and ironies can be perceived as humorous. The comic foils in Shakespeare's tragedies are also humorous. There is Polonius, and there are the "citizens" of Julius Caesar and Coriolanus whose quick-changing affections can be viewed as amusing. But the most important "foil" of Shakespeare's tragedies is Cleopatra, because she is constantly falling victim to her own desires and pomposity (Derks 52).

Charles Laurence Barber has written a book entitled Shakespeare's Festive Comedy in which he relates Shakespeare's comedies, at least those merry comedies written up to the time of Hamlet and the problem plays, as saturnalian. Barber points out that the saturnalia are presented in many different forms, but they all "involve inversion, statement and counterstatement, and a basic movement which can be summarized in the formula, through release to clarification (Barber 4). Barber also relates the saturnalian tradition to the tradition of theatrical clowning, saying that during Shakespeare's time the Clown, or Vice, "was a recognized anarchist who made aberration obvious by carrying release to absurd extremes" (Barber 5). Barber shows the relationship between "saturnalia," "festivity," and "the holiday spirit" by demonstrating Shakespeare's festive occasion not only in his holiday comedies like Love's Labour's Lost, A Midsummer Night's Dream, and Twelfth Night, but also in his non-holiday comedies like As You Like It and Henry IV. Shakespeare explains the relationship between holiday on the one hand and festivity and saturnalia on the other in the following way:

> "Merry England" was merry chiefly by virtue of its community observances of periodic sports and feast days. Mirth took form in morris-dances, sword-dances, wassailings, mock ceremonies of summer kings and queens and of lords of misrule, mummings, disguisings, masques--and a bewildering variety of sports, games, shows, and pageants improvised on traditional models. (Barber 5)

And in merry England these holidays tended to be formalized, and tended to be celebrated on an annual basis:

> Such pastimes were regular part of the celebration of a marriage, of the

village wassail or wake, of Candlemas, Shrove Tuesday, Hocktide, May
Day, Whitsuntide, Midsummer Eve, Harvest-home, Halloween, and the
twelve days of the Christmas season ending with Twelfth Night. (Barber 5)
Barber feels that there was also a tradition in England relating the holiday tradition with
the theatrical comedy in that both were ways of helping people cope with life; clearly
Shakespeare did a great deal to sustain and support this tradition.

Joan Hartwig believes that the plays toward the end of Shakespeare's career form
a cohesive group quite distinct from the rest of the canon. These plays include Pericles,
Cymbeline, The Winter's Tale, and The Tempest. These four plays were all written in the
five-year period from 1606 to 1611, and they all tell similar stories: a royal child is lost and
refound; sea journeys change men's lives; scenes occur in countries far from England; the
main characters struggle against adversity and in the end are rewarded; characters that were
thought dead are miraculously found to be alive; and the denouement at the end is achieved
through the agency of young people (Hartwig Tragicomic 3-4). In these four plays, the
main characters also aspire toward a perfect relationship, and that aspiration is shattered for
a while, but is later fulfilled in a manner which leaves the characters amazed (Hartwig
Tragicomic 5).

Joan Hartwig believes that in Shakespeare's last plays "the tragicomic vision evolves
through the separation of the central characters from the values they had held to be
significant" (Hartwig Tragicomic 32). She feels further that the important difference
between the characters at the beginning of the plays, and these same characters at the end
of the plays is that they have become aware of their own fallibility. They finally realize
that they are limited in their ability to sustain human relationships, and even in their ability
to endure. "The pattern of Shakespeare's tragicomic action, in the simplest terms, is to
dislocate settled perceptions through adversity and then to liberate perception through
unexpected prosperity" (Hartwig Tragicomic 32). The key to Shakespeare's tragicomedies
is a balancing of antithetical relationships. There is a balancing of the ideal with the actual,
of the artificial with the natural, and of sadness and joy. "These contradictory impulses
which the audience experiences simultaneously dislocate typical perspectives and force
judgment to wait for the plays concluding vision (Hartwig Tragicomic 176). But in
addition to the balancing of antithetical and ambivalent relationships, the tragicomic vision
of Shakespeare's latest plays also tends to affirm and revitalize the power of the
imagination, and thus "brings the playwright and his audience into a spiritual community
which remains active long after the playhouse darkens" (Hartwig Tragicomic 174).

1 Henry VI (1589), 2 Henry VI (1590), and 3 Henry VI (1591) are Shakespeare's
three earliest histories. Donald Watson has written an article entitled "The Dark Comedy
of the Henry VI Plays," in which he concentrates on those scenes which are essentially
comic, ironic, macabre, or grotesque as he investigates the theatricality of these plays.

As the comedy in the first tetralogy progressively darkens from the laughter
of derision in Part 1 to the macabre violence of Richard III, its place in each
play expands from pervasive but limited farce to mockery to grotesque
villainy and satanic horror. (Watson 11)

Richard III is a hunchbacked murderer who is more grotesque on the inside than on
the outside, and Sidney Homan says that Richard III is the "sole source of humor in
Shakespeare's early history play, The Tragedy of Richard III (1592)." In one scene of this
play, Lady Anne's servants are carrying the coffin containing her husband whom Richard
has murdered, and when she confronts Richard with the fact that he is a murderer, he
comically converts her insult into a benefit. Since her husband was a "saint," he had only
done him a favor in murdering him, thereby releasing his soul back to Heaven. As a saint,
he "was fitter for that place than earth." Richard then offers his sword to Lady Anne and
allows her to wound his "true breast." He gives her two alternatives. Either she can take

the sword and kill the murderer of her husband, or she can "take up" the murderer of her husband, this second possibility being laced with sexual innuendo. Lady Anne is disarmed both literally and figuratively by Richard's wit, and she incredulously takes him as a lover. When Anne exits, Richard turns to the audience and asks in a plaintive manner, "Was ever woman in this humor wooed?" and then says, "Was ever woman in this humor won?" Although Richard is morally repulsive, the audience is bonded to him because "he is a villain not only with a sense of humor but one whose humor is his chief weapon" (Homan 942).

The Comedy of Errors (1592) was Shakespeare's earliest comedy. Harry Levin calls this play a "knockabout farce," but J. A. Bryant adds that it is a knockabout farce with a difference, because to the characters in the play, the issues being presented are serious ones--love, fidelity, and personal honor (Bryant 25). Dorothea Kehler suggests that, "Many elements combine in The Comedy of Errors to create a genera mista: the tragicomedy of the Egeon frame, the romantic comedy of S. Antipholus's love for Luciana, the predominant farce of a mistaken-identity plot with its knockabout humor" (Kehler 229).

Kehler further points out that even though The Comedy of Errors exhibits renewal, this renewal is not in the form of a union of a man and his wife, for the perception of marriage in this play is rather pessimistic. Rather, the renewal results from the reunion of the twins with each other, and the reunion of the twins with their parents (Kehler 230). Kehler feels that The Comedy of Errors is successful. There are demons which frighten us, but they also evoke a most cathartic laughter. "The farce of mistaken identities and hallucinatory situations creates the verfremdungseffekt that allows us to laugh when the pain of human isolation brings us closer to tears" (Kehler 236).

Robert Ornstein feels that The Comedy of Errors owes its skillful design to Plautus's Menachmi. Partly because of its slapstick scenes, and partly because of its intricate and ingenious plot, it has to be seen on stage to be fully appreciated. The playwright is in total control of the lives of the comic characters, who must enter and exit on cue and meet or avoid each other as the comic plot requires (Ornstein 35). The plot revolves around twin brothers who have twin servants. This results in numerous confusions, arguments, threatenings, threshings, and a general rough-and-tumble comedy. Shakespeare multiplies the farcical complications of the plot by adding to the cast of characters a goldsmith who turns officers of the law against Antipholus E. The concluding scene of The Comedy of Errors is far more intricate and hilarious than was the final scene of Plautus's original (Ornstein 27). Ornstein considers the cheeky twin Dromio brothers to be more than merely grumbling servants born to be constantly yelled at and beaten by their masters. "The Dromios have the last words in Errors as they exit arm in arm rejoicing in a world that can produce two such remarkable creatures" (Ornstein 34).

Carol Neely suggests that in Shakespeare's comedies there are four women whose skills at logic, wit, and language play make them as strong as the strongest of Shakespeare's men. These women are Katharina in The Taming of the Shrew (1593), Portia in The Merchant of Venice (1596), Beatrice in Much Ado About Nothing (1598), and Rosalind in As You Like It (1599). Katharina ends up subjecting herself to marriage, but is able to keep her own independence in the end. Portia, the most intellectual of the women, takes on the disguise of a male lawyer in order to prove her superior intellect to the men of Venice. Beatrice uses her charming intellect to match wits with Benedick, thus proving her equality. And Rosalind disguises herself as a man, in which guise she befriends her own lover and takes control of all the events around her, making sure that everything comes to a happy conclusion. These plays all begin in a man's world, but the women come in and take over, and by their intelligence and wit, they "transform the men from foolish lovers into--we hope--sensible husbands" (Neely 215). Jeanne Roberts makes the interesting observation that crossdressing in Shakespeare's comedies works well for

women, but doesn't work at all well for men.   "Portia and Rosalind reach triumphant
heights as males, but Falstaff is beaten as Mother Prat" (Roberts Shakespeare's English
Comedy 119).

The Taming of the Shrew (1593) begins in Act I, Scene 1 with Katherine and
Petruchio first meeting each other.   This is when their argument begins.   Their rapid
punning has a number of functions.   In the first place, there is simply the humor and
entertainment of the exchange.   In the second place, the richness and rapidity of their
punning illustrates to the audience that they are well matched in intelligence and facility
of language.   In the third place, the bawdy nature of the punning reveals the sexual tension
which underlies the banter.   "Thus, in this first meeting, Shakespeare has economically
shown three levels of meaning by utilizing the rich language of puns" (Blackwell 1).   J. A.
Bryant points out that the turning point for Kate comes in Act 4, Scene 5, as Kate and
Petruchio are on the road back from Petruchio's country house.   In her weariness she
concedes to her husband that the sun might be the moon: "Be it moon, or sun, or what you
please;/ And if you please to call it a rush-candle,/ Henceforth I vow it shall be so for me."
From that point on, Katherine--Kate--is the true winner in this battle of the sexes (Bryant
113).

Richard Burt feels that while Petruchio claims to want to tame Katherine, he in truth
does not want a "traditional patriarchal relationship in which the husband rules the wife"
(Burt 297).   Rather, Petruchio wants an equal, with whom he can share intelligent
conversation and playful wit.   This is why he takes such pains to make her into a sensitized
human, one who can be an equal and respected for it.   This version of the shrew-taming
story changes the more typical male tyranny into a "nontyrannical hierarchy informed by
mutual affection" (Bean 70).

The bawdiness of Petruchio's and Katherine's punning is illustrated in the following
dialogue:

> PETRUCHIO: ...come sit on me.
> KATHERINE: Asses are made to bear, and so are you.
> PETRUCHIO: Women are made to bear, and so are you.
> KATHERINE: No such jade as you, if me you mean. (Colby 156)

Here can be seen the triple pun on the word "bear" (loads, children, and men).   Here also
can be seen the put-down of Petruchio's being compared to a "jade" (a horse that easily
tires).   But the punning becomes even stronger and more sexual:

> KATHERINE: If I be waspish, best beware of my sting.
> PETRUCHIO: My remedy is then to pluck it out.
> KATHERINE: Ay, if the fool could find it where it lies.
> PETRUCHIO: Who knows not where a wasp does wear his sting?   In his
>   tail.
> KATHERINE: In his tongue.
> PETRUCHIO: Whose tongue?
> KATHERINE: Yours, if you talk of tales, and so farewell.
> PETRUCHIO: What, with my tongue in your tail?   Nay come again, Good
>   Kate; I am a gentleman-- (Colby 156)

Interestingly, Kate is more amused and shocked by this gross conclusion to the punning
exchange (Colby 157).   Coppelia Kahn also discusses the sexual innuendoes of Shakespeare
in terms of how their feelings of sexuality make them like beasts in the fields.   She
indicates that the use of the "horn" vision, representing cuckoldry, runs deep within all of
Shakespeare's plays.   It is a "visual pun on the well-known emblem of marriage, the yolk;
what joins husband and wife together; [it] is also what degrades the man to the level of a
dumb beast--the destiny of being cuckold" (Kahn 125).

Shakespeare's witty dialogues in The Taming of the Shrew are not all between men and women. Petruchio also has a witty exchange with Grumio:

> Petruchio: Here, sirrah Grumio, knock, I say.
> Grumio: Knock sir? Whom should I knock? Is there any many has rebus'd your worship?
> Petruchio: Villain, I say, knock me here soundly.

> Grumio: Knock you here, sir? Why, sir, what am I sir that I should knock you here, sir? (Act I, Scene ii, Lines 5-10)

About this dialogue, Irene Dash writes, "Both men know that Petruchio wants him to knock on the gate of a friend's house. But the opportunity to play with words is too much to resist. They delight in puns and in extended misunderstanding of the most direct language" (Dash 38).

Robert Ornstein feels that only in The Taming of the Shrew does Shakespeare have a "Punch-and-Judy" farce in which a "bully-boy hero imposes his will on a wild-eyed but ultimately supine heroine" (Ornstein 63). The Taming of the Shrew is always a box-office favorite at modern Shakespeare festivals because the action can be vulgarized, and the characters can be reduced to cartoon figures, and it can then be "pitched to the lowest denominator of audience taste with mugging and leering, shouting, thumping, and chasing across the stage." Taming is described by Ornstein as an "Elizabethan romp." The slapstick and farcical comedy make the "taming" too preposterous to be offensive. Another way that critics have attempted to rescue the sexual stereotypes portrayed in Taming is to claim that in fact Kate is the subtle manager of her husband, whom she pretends to obey (Ornstein 63).

Both The Taming of the Shrew (1593) and Much Ado about Nothing (1598) describe a situation involving a pleasant and marriageable female contrasted with a shrewish unmarriageable female, and in both plays the plots involve disguises and mistaken identities. The earliest comedies also contained disguises and mistaken identities, but they were of a more contrived nature--twins who happened to look alike, women who put on men's clothes, dancers masked, and nighttime wanderers transformed by magic. J. A. Bryant feels that in The Taming of the Shrew, "Shakespeare seems to have gone out of his way to enliven his basic text with mistakes of the more superficial variety" (Bryant 99). Bryant suggests that one of the reasons for the critics' neglect of the subtleties in The Taming of the Shrew is its frame structure, with its crude but funny practical joke on the drunken Christopher Sly. This frame structure prepares the audience to interpret the play as a farce (Bryant 99). Bryant himself considers the play to be an amusing and uncomplicated farce with clean lines, with echoes of Christopher Marlowe appearing throughout the play (Bryant 100).

In Act II, Scene i of The Taming of the Shrew, Petruchio's ironic speech foreshadows Kate's ironic speech which appears at end of the play. Petruchio says,

> "Say that she rail, why then I'll tell her plain
> She sing as sweetly as a nightingale;
> Say that she frown, I'll say she looks as clear
> As morning roses newly wash'd with dew;
> Say she be mute, and will not speak a word,
> Then I'll commend her volubility." (qtd. in Evans 121)

Contrast Petruchio's speech above with Katherine's speech at the end of The Taming of the Shrew. Kate shows a last bit of defiance by saying that the sun is not the moon although Petruchio claims it to be. But she relents and through ironic exaggeration knows it is the moon (Bamber 35):

> KATHERINE: Forward, I pray, since we have come so far,
> And be it moon, or sun, or what you please;

An if you please to call it a rush candle,
Henceforth I vow it shall be so for me.
PETRUCHIO: I say it is the moon.
KATHERINE: I know it is the moon.

Thus Kate is tamed and Petruchio wins his wager; but Kate nevertheless retains her independence. By the end of the play, "Katharina is if anything more dominant than ever because she has learned how to phrase her attacks irresistibly, by humbly recognizing her own limitations and disarming resistance" (Richmond 91). Kate uses her wit and intelligence and her undefiled spirit to show her equality to men, and teach the other women the rules by which to govern their marriages if they are to be independent as well (Madden 7-8). In a book entitled What's in Shakespeare's Names, Murray Levith points out that Petruchio's name comes from the Greek word petros which means "stone or rock." This meaning is consistent with Petruchio's strong and willful nature." Levith also points out that Petruchio tames Katherine, and finally proves that he has done so by saying, "Why there's a wench! Come on, and kiss me, Kate" (Taming 5.ii)(Levith 70).

The Two Gentlemen of Verona (1594) has a number of important echoes to John Lyly's work, and it also has affinities with Italian "commedia dell'arte." It is a play which could have been written only after England had had some contact with continental urban sophistication (Bryant 27). Launce is the clown in this play, and he is an example of a clown who is not wholly conscious of himself as a source of amusement (Cazamian 323). Launce's descriptions of his family, his new sweetheart, and his mongrel dog Crab are an engaging blend of native intelligence with independence of spirit. These descriptions are oblique assaults on the pretentiousness of the society Launce has been destined from birth to serve (Bryant 28). Speed, the other clown of Two Gentlemen, also has lively moments, though perhaps not enough of them (Bryant 29). In this play, the audience must accept the expectations of romantic comedy that Valentine and Silvia will live happily ever after; however, for Proteus and Julia the romantic tradition offers no such guarantees, even though they do wish for constancy, for Proteus and Julia are brought down to earth by their passions, and for such people, the romantic happy endings do not apply. Nevertheless, as Bryant notes, "lovers who once naively thought themselves constant, as here, have confronted the realities of their circumstances and condition, discovered the inevitable imperfections in one another, and found in themselves the charity to forgive and accept" (39).

Robert Ornstein considers The Two Gentlemen of Verona interesting enough to hold the audience's attention in spite of the unaccountably silly final scene. Two Gentlemen is "low comedy" in which Launce and Speed steal every scene they are in and "make their supposed betters look like cardboard figures" (Ornstein 48).

Love's Labor's Lost (1594) is a play filled with lovers, but by the end of the play, none of them has found a mate. Not only is there no renewal in the play, but in addition, the offstage death of the "senex" (parent archetype, in this case the King of France) "removes from the stage the most determined and forthright advocate of mating that the plot has to offer" (Bryant 40). As Berowne says in Act 5, Scene 2, "Our wooing doth not end like an old play. Jack hath not Gill" (Bryant 40). It may be that Love's Labor's Lost is an experiment, or a brilliant apprentice work, as some critics have said. What it does is to put comedic action to the test of external reality, a test which Shakespeare always used, from his first play to his last, his comedies as well as his histories and tragedies (Bryant 56). Love's Labor's Lost, which was influenced by the comedies of John Lyly, is filled with puns and paradoxes. "The verbal brilliance and dullness of Love's Labor's are unique in the comedies. No later play so persistently aims at bravura displays of acrobatic wit and none devotes so much space to figures like Holofernes and Nathaniel, who preen themselves on their turgidities" (Ornstein 35). Ornstein concludes by saying that "critics can forgive what is tedious in <u>Love's Labor's</u> for the sake of its witty heroes and heroines" (Ornstein 48).

<u>Romeo and Juliet</u> (1595) has a humorous death scene to advance its plot. Mercutio has been portrayed in this play as a likeable and easy-going fellow, and in Act 3, Scene 1, Mercutio, who has been mortally wounded, reacts in his usual humorous fashion:

> ROMEO: Courage, man, the hurt cannot be so much.
>
> MERCUTIO: No, 'tis not so deep as a well, nor so wide as a church-door, but 'tis enough; 'twill serve. Ask for me to-morrow, and you shall find me a grave man. I am pepper'd, I warrant, for this world.
>
> (Evans 99)

Later, in Act 4, Scene 5, Paris refers to "amorous Death," and later the old father Capulet uses a number of melancholic puns to comprehend the tragic death of his daughter. He says to Paris, "O son, the night before thy wedding day hath death lain with thy wife. There she lies flower as she was, deflowered by him. Death is my son-in-law" (Roberts <u>Shakespeare's English Comedy</u> 8).

Juliet's nurse in <u>Romeo and Juliet</u> is a constant source of amusement both for Juliet and for Shakespeare's audiences; however, her humor seems to be quite unintentional, and she is often unconscious of the fact that she is indeed a humorous person (Cazamian 323).

<u>A Midsummer Night's Dream</u> (1594) stretches the audience's ability for suspension of disbelief because it contains fairies and creatures so tiny that they are dwarfed by cowslips, but they are all acted by people of average height and weight. "Yet the drastic illusion holds because believing is seeing, and because on stage one need not nibble a mushroom to shrink in stature Hermia dwindles to a mere bead once Helena and Lysander begin to slang her" (Ornstein 84). Lysander finds himself alone in the forest with Hermia, and they are tired and lost, and need rest. Hermia suggests that she will sleep "here," and Lysander can find a bed "over there," but Lysander suggests that they share the same sleeping area since they have "one heart," and "one troth," why should they not share "one pillow?" Hermia in punning in his sexual arguments when she says, "Lie further off yet, do not lie so near." Thus Lysander's humor is a tool for seduction, but it is an unsuccessful tool (Homan 943).

<u>A Midsummer Night's Dream</u> presents Nick Bottom, the Weaver, as part of a group of men who are planning a performance to celebrate the wedding of Duke Theseus to Queen Hippolyta. In Act I, Scene ii, Bottom (vain as always) tells the other characters that he would like to run the entire show. Bottom has already been given the role of Pyramus, but he also wants to play Thisby and the Lion as well. "Let me play the lion too. I will roar, that I will do any man's heart good to hear me. I will roar, that I will make the Duke say, 'let him roar again; let him roar again.' " (Evans 70-73). In the guise of Bottom's inept rustic troupe, <u>A Midsummer Night's Dream</u> Shakespeare mocks himself and the theatrical profession by parodying his company and the relationships among playwrights, directors, and actors (Homan 941).

As they are planning to enact the play to be entitled, "The Most Lamentable Comedy About the Most Cruel Death of Pyramus and Thisby," Bottom wants to enact all of the parts. Bottom wants to play not only the part of Pyramus, but says, "let me play Thisby too. I'll speak in a monstrous little voice.... Let me play the lion too. I will roar, that I will do any man's heart good to hear me...." (Evans 226). Bottom attempts to add drama and suspense to the play by prolonging the death scene of his character, but in the process, he mixes up his lines and ends with a comical adlib: "Thus die I, thus, thus, thus. Now am I dead. Now am I fled.... Tongue lose thy light, Moon take thy flight, Now die, die, die, die, die" (qtd. in Evans 245).

After the players are assigned their parts, Snug, who plays the part of the lion only has to roar, but even this simple line he can't remember. Similarly, Robin Starveling, who has the simple job of assuming the role of the Moonshine also has troubles with his lines. Francis Flute objects to the fact that he has to play the part of Thisby--a woman. Tom Snout is probably the most amusing character in this "play within a play," for he must assume the role of "a wall." He dons stones and mortar as a costume, and during the play, he spreads his fingers to symbolize a hole in the wall through which Pyramus and Thisby must kiss" (Woodford 3-4).

It is interesting to note how the suspension of disbelief functions in the play within the play. In the "Pyramus and Thisbe" play, it is necessary for Pyramus to draw a sword and kill himself, but Bottom suggests that ladies would not be able to abide such action. When Starveling suggests that they must therefore leave the killing out, Bottom responds:

> Not a whit. I have a device to make all well. Write me a prologue, and let the prologue seem to say, we will not do harm with our swords, and that Pyramus is not killed indeed; and for the more better assurance, tell them I, Pyramus, am not Pyramus, but Bottom the weaver; this will put them out of fear. (L'Estrange 256)

When it is suggested that the ladies of the audience might also be frightened by the lion, Snout suggests that another prologue might be in order, saying that the lion is not really a lion, but again Bottom protests:

> Nay, you must name his name, and half his face must be seen through the lion's neck; and he must himself speak through, saying thus, or to the same effect--"Ladies," or "Fair ladies, I would wish you." or "I would request you," or "I would entreat you not to fear, nor to tremble: my life for yours. If you think I come hither as a lion, it were pity of my life: no, I am no such thing. I am a man as other men are, and there then let him name his name and tell them plainly he is Snug the joiner." (L'Estrange 256)

In Act III, Scene i, Puck decides to have a bit of fun with Bottom. Puck replaces Bottom's head with the head of an ass, and because the "Love in Idleness" potion has already been placed in the eyes of Titania, the queen of the fairies, she immediately falls in love with Bottom, bearing an ass's head, as soon as she sees him. Titania tells Bottom that she loves him, and Bottom, who does not realize that he is wearing an ass's head, responds, "And yet, to say the truth, reason and love keep little company together now-a-days" (Evans 143-144).

Many of the names of the players in A Midsummer Night's Dream are sexual puns. "Bottom" is an example. Another example is "Snug the Joiner, since a joiner is a person who fits things together as people do in sex. "Flute" and "Snout" are English slang words for penis. "Quince" is a play on the word "quointes," which was the Middle English spelling for "cunt." Quince is a carpenter, and works with "wood," which rhymes with "wode" (madness), and which is also slang for a penis; an erection in England is often called a "woody." (Brewer 148).

Frank Kermode suggests that A Midsummer Night's Dream is Shakespeare's finest comedy. It contains everything that a comedy of Shakespeare's day should contain. It has rustic clowns in three of the first four acts, and these clowns dominate the last act. It contains the lyric voices of children reminiscent of John Lyly's earlier productions. It also contains diminutive fairies (also reminiscent of Lyly), and a mysterious wood and lovers that are both reminiscent of George Peele's best comedy. But most importantly, it contains "an action which expands the conflict of Roman comedy to include oppositions of generations, sexes, and social strata, to say nothing of the orders of creation, and contributes significantly to the continuing Renaissance inquiry into the nature of love" (Bryant 57-58). In A Midsummer Night's Dream there is a concatenation of disparate actions that include an enforced marriage, a marital quarrel, a tragedy, a romantic adventure of lovers in a wood, and all are presented as forms of comedy, not tragedy (Bryant 78).

The Merchant of Venice (1596) was the first of Shakespeare's comedies which shows a disturbing kind of somber, almost tragic, confusion. In The Merchant of Venice (1596), and also in the later Troilus and Cressida (1601), All's Well That Ends Well (1602), and Measure for Measure (1604) the tragic tones seem to be mingled indiscrimately with comic gaiety, and these "middle comedies" are therefore sometimes dubbed "dark comedies," "problem comedies," or "problem plays" (Bryant 81). In contrast to these middle comedies, Shakespeare's later comedies are filled with odd things like monsters, brothels, beheaded villains, and dead children, and such inclusions have prompted many critics to dub these later comedies "romances" or even "tragi-comedies" rather than "comedies" (Bryant 82). There is one comic scene in The Merchant of Venice where Launcelot Gobbo tricks his father into thinking that he is dead. He then leaps merrily around the stage causing his blind father to stumble and fall in a series of pratfalls that Sidney Homan considers to be reminiscent of modern theater of the absurd (Homan 940).

Paul Grawe points out that although some people become morally indignant at The Merchant of Venice, it has been repeatedly defended as a funny play, but it has been criticized as a hodgepodge of discordant elements, and it has also been criticized as a barbarous account of anti-Semitism. Many who don't like the play tend to see Shylock as a hero; those who do like the play tend to see him as a comedic villain. Some people argue that Shylock is a great individualist, fighting an unjust society; others laugh at him because he is the butt of the humor, and because he brings about his own well-deserved downfall (Grawe 186). In The Merchant of Venice, Shylock's daughter, Jessica, is forbidden by her father to marry a gentile, so she elopes with a Christian and steals her father's money. Shylock's reaction to this is comical--he doesn't know which he values more, his money or his daughter. "My daughter! O my Ducats!--O my Daughter! Fled with a Christian!--O my Christian ducats! (Merchant II.viii; Complete 19).

Shakespeare's early comedies tended to celebrate the power of love, to make an imperfect world better, and to restore a viable social order. Beginning with The Merchant of Venice, however, Shakespeare turned to the darker aspects of comedic survival. From this play on, Shakespeare asserted that love is not enough. There must also be mercy, and recognition of human imperfections if the human race is to survive (Grawe 201). The Merchant of Venice presents the audience with a "double bind" in Gregory Bateson's sense of the word. In the first place, there are a number of coherent patterns that present themselves in the play--love and likeness, release and bondage, and so on. Some of these coherent patterns are antithetical--law versus love, etc. But even though there are coherent patterns, there are also details that complicate, oppose, and frustrate the audience's efforts to understand the subtleties of meaning. Gregory Bateson has suggested that "play" is one of the "hot spots" for studying the double binds, the paradoxes, the categorical crosscuts and the confusions that characterize ordinary communication. In The Merchant of Venice, Shakespeare is "playing" with his audience, and Ron Klingspon feels that "by utilizing the concept of play we can...clarify aspects of the extraordinary process by which Shakespeare, through The Merchant of Venice, communicates with an audience" (Klingspon 36). For example, there is reciprocal play between Lorenzo and Jessica at the beginning of the last act. "In such a night" is a repeated formula that suggests a teasing competitiveness of the characters, and when the messenger arrives, there is a sudden change in both the content and the expression of the language that marks this interlude as "bilateral play." Portia also puts on a "play face" which is screened from the Venetians, but at the same time is not screened from the audience. "Much of our fun comes from catching the contextual clues [like the echoic parallelism, and the double entendres] the three males miss, that Portia is using to toy with them" (Klingspon 37). Ron Klingspon considers The Merchant of Venice to be a "comedy of play."

Yet it is play of such a perplexing kind that we will never have the instruments or the wit to construct an interpretive map exactly congruent with the orderly but turbulent, meaningful but puzzling, pleasurable but unsettling experience it provides. In the case of The Merchant of Venice, as of Shakespeare's other dramas, the only true map is the territory. (Klingspon 46).

Shylock in The Merchant of Venice is a character of contradictions. He is both unjustly sinner, and sinned against. Shylock appears in the midst of much pageantry, singing, dancing, and lovemaking, and he is seen as an intruder, "oftentimes vicious, usually devious, sometimes almost admirable, and occasionally pitiable" (Bryant 83). At the end of The Merchant of Venice there Shylock is exposed through a deception as a murderous, and merciless villain. Antonio loses his ships at sea and is therefore late in paying back the debt. The court is reluctantly forced to uphold Shylock's legal but immoral right to kill him. Though the court pleads with Shylock to have mercy, Shylock refuses, even though he is offered three times the price of the debt. "The pound of flesh which I demand of him / is dearly bought, is mine, and I will have it: / If you deny me, fie upon your law!" (Merchant IV.1; Complete 118). But then Portia traps Shylock by arriving in the courtroom disguised as a judge. She outwits Shylock by saying, "Tarry a little; there is something else.-- / This bond doth give thee here no jot of blood; / The words expressly are a pound of flesh; / Take then thy bond... / But, in the cutting, if thou dost shed / One drop of Christian blood, thy lands and goods / Are, by the laws of Venice, confiscate..." (Merchant IV.2; Complete 273). By this clever strategy, not only is Shylock outmaneuvered and prevented from killing Antonio, but he is fined the price of the loan and half of his wealth.

In the final scenes of The Merchant of Venice, the dialogue is charming; the heroes and heroines are appealing. All of the obstacles that had lain in the paths of the lovers have been removed, and news comes that Antonio's ships have come safely to port so that once again he can be a prosperous merchant of Venice. Robert Ornstein suggests that few endings in Shakespeare's comedies are as relaxed and playful as that of The Merchant (Ornstein 90).

The character Sir John Falstaff appeared in Henry IV Parts 1 and 2, in Henry V, and in The Merry Wives of Windsor. Falstaff is generally regarded as one of England's greatest comic characters. Marc Pulsifer considers Falstaff to exhibit both vice and charm:

> Shakespeare has maintained in Falstaff a perfect balance between complete villainy and redeeming charm through the end of Henry IV, Part I. Shakespeare accomplishes this mainly by openly showing Falstaff for what he is, and then brushing it over with some good and hearty humor. However, this is the most obvious of his tactics; the subtler ones include Falstaff's use of proverbs, his childlike characteristics, and the competent Hal's acceptance of him. (Pulsifer 1)

In an article entitled "No Abuse: The Prince and Falstaff in the Tavern Scene of Henry IV," J. McLaverty discusses the paradox that the Prince and Falstaff are closest to each other when they are exchanging abuse or when they are most in conflict (McLaverty 106).

There is one scene in 1 Henry IV where Falstaff plays Hal's father, and Falstaff plays Hal, so that their roles become reversed. "For Falstaff it is all good fun, besides being a chance to buff up his tarnished reputation as a coward. For Hal, it is no less fun." Falstaff tries to be a responsible, wise, old man. This scene is funny, but it is also revealing, for Hal now sees what he must do. He must banish Falstaff from his presence. According to Sidney Homan, "the divisions between comedy and tragedy have been erased" (Homan 948).

Willard Farnham suggests that the imagery that refers to Falstaff's enormous body tends to lean toward the unappealing, as he is referred to as a "woolsack," a "tun of man," a "swol'n parcel of dropsies," a "gross watery pumpion," and a "stuff'd cloakbag of guts" (Bloom 157).

> Falstaff owes his predominant position among comic figures to the fact that in him there meet the clown that delights the crowd, who love a person to laugh at; and the subtle character that engages the philosopher, who loves a person to laugh with (Priestley 94).

Falstaff's character changes greatly from play to play. "We begin with a bloated old buffoon, whose gluttony, cowardice, and lying are on such a colossal scale that we cannot help being amused by them; we end with the comic genius, busy dramatizing himself" (Priestley 92). Scholars have suggested that Falstaff's character developed beyond even Shakespeare's original intent. "Shakespeare's less conscious creative purpose...made his bragging coward grow into something much more rare, interesting, and original" (Cazamian 240).

In Henry IV (1596-1598), Falstaff reflects on the true worth of honor:

> Can honor set to a leg? No...Or take away the grief of a wound? No...Honor hath no skill in surgery then? No...What is honor? A word. What is in that word honor?...Air...Who hath it? He that died a' Wednesday. Doth he feel it? No. Doth he hear it? No...Therefore I'll none of it, honor is a mere scutcheon..." (Evans 876).

During a battle in Henry IV where Falstaff stayed in character by avoiding fighting, the Prince requests Falstaff's sword, and Falstaff instead offers him the gun in his case. But to the Prince's surprise it is not really a gun at all, but a bottle of sack. Falstaff very much enjoys his own joke and laughs, "Ay...'tis hot, 'tis hot. There's that will sack a city" (Evans 878). Later in the battle, Falstaff decides to avoid death by playing dead. But when he sees the Prince kill one of the enemy's best warriors, and then leave the scene, Falstaff decides to take advantage of the situation. He jumps up, and stabs the dead man in the thigh. Then he carries the dead body on his shoulders to claim the victory, much to the surprise and suspicion of the others, who had thought them both dead. This act was perfectly consistent with Falstaff's lifestyle. He explains that he has led a "virtuous" life, having "swore little, dic'd not above seven times--a week, went to a bawdy house not above once in a quarter--of an hour, [and] paid money that [he] borrow'd--three or four times" (Evans 869).

Marc Pulsifer notes that Falstaff is a self-serving, dishonest whoremonger and opportunist, but he points out that we nevertheless love his wit; we revel with him in his mirth; we feel deeply for him when he is banished by his long-time friend, the newly crowned Henry V. We sympathize with such a rogue because in the honesty of our souls, we can not deny that potentially we are every inch a Falstaff (Pulsifer 7). We also sympathize with Falstaff because of his humor, his ironic use of proverbs, and Hal's royal support of Falstaff's child-like characteristics. Shakespeare has meticulously balanced Falstaff's loathsome vice with his winning charm (Pulsifer 8). The Merry Wives of Windsor (1597) is Shakespeare's only comedy with an announced English setting. It is interesting to note that during his writing career, Shakespeare created two different Falstaffs. One Falstaff was the fat knight of 1 Henry VI and 2 Henry VI. The other Falstaff was a pallid reflection of this same knight who appeared in The Merry Wives of Windsor. This second Falstaff was seen by audiences of Shakespeare's time as little more than a discredited and banished rogue who had been sadly reduced from the irrepressible figure they had taken to their hearts in the earlier plays (Bryant 114-115). When Falstaff is being impulsive in his rollicking fun, he is farcical, and not humorous. But when he gains shrewd control over his language and actions he becomes humorous. His resulting cool judgment adds a bit of self-mockery to the absurdity of his pranks. Humor doesn't reside in what is said or done, but rather in the relationship between what is said or done and the environment. And part of this environment happens to be the other characters in the play (Cazamian 26). And of these other characters, Falstaff declares, "I am not only witty in myself, but the cause that wit is in other men" (Levin 12).

The language of Justice Shallow in Merry Wives is based on how he says things. Pistol's language, on the other hand, is based on what he says. Pistol's humor stems from, "a mouthful of silly phrases, and an idea or two, kept together only by his notation of his own importance" (Priestley 81). Pistol is the basic English braggart. He is the common tavern bully "who tries to make up for his want of courage and ability by boldness and address. A loud-voiced craven, whose scars are the mark of pots hurled in tavern brawls and of public beatings" (Priestley 73).

In Merry Wives young love triumphs over a series of obstacles imposed by the girl's ambitious parents. Master Page, her father, wants his daughter to marry the young Abraham Slender, the village ninny. Master Page's cousin, Justice Shallow, and the Welsh parson, Sir Hugh Evans both support Master Page's decision. On the other hand, Mistress Page, and Mistress Quickly as well, both want the daughter to marry a French physician by the name of Dr. Caius. Fenton, the young country gentleman of sound mind and limb, is the boy that the girl wants to marry, but of course he has no support at all. Fenton nevertheless eventually wins out after he is able to win the affections of the girl herself (Bryant 116).

It should be noted (pun intended) that the title of Much Ado about Nothing (1598) contains a pun. In Elizabethan English, "nothing" is pronounced very much like "noting." This play in fact dramatizes much ado which the characters make in their interpretation and understanding of the world, and each other (Tuverson 1). "The sophisticated gentlemen of Much Ado about Nothing tend to take noting in the sense of interpreting, resulting in a comedy of misunderstandings" (Tuverson 2).

Much Ado about Nothing has three plots, and it is basically humor that holds these three plots together in a single play. The main plot is about Claudio and Hero, and the two subplots feature the witty arguments of Beatrice and Benedick on the one hand, and the comic fumbling of Dogberry and his friends on the other hand. The wit that is shown by Beatrice and Benedick in arguing their cases ranges from puns to conceptual wit, in which the characters use "allusive understatement and sophistical logic" (McCollom 73). Graham Storey says that Dogberry's self-deception is the most humorous part of this particular character. "No one in the play is more mentally intoxicated than Dogberry." He thinks of himself as "king of all he surveys," but "words constantly trip him up" (Davis 23). When Dogberry gets excited his words get especially confused, "Marry, sir, they have committed false report; moreover they have spoken untruths; secondarily, they are slanders; sixth and lastly, they have belied a lady; thirdly, they have verified unjust things; and to conclude, they are lying knaves" (Evans 358). Dogberry gives the following orders to the watchmen, "Make no noise in the streets; for, for the watch to babble and to talk is most tolerable, and not to be endured." When the watchmen reply that they would rather sleep than talk, Dogberry responds with a different kind of logical fallacy: "I cannot see how sleeping should offend; only have a care that your bills [weapons] be not stol'n" (Evans 348). Herbert Weil suggests that Dogberry is not actually stupid, even though he is constantly tripped up with words. Weil says that "no one in the play is more mentally intoxicated than Dogberry. He is king of all he surveys" (Weil 42). J. A. Bryant suggests that Dogberry's outrageous malapropisms and utter stupidity, such as "They are "condemn'd into everlasting redemption" (Much Ado IV.ii. 56-57) in general provide occasion for some of the memorable merriment in this play (Bryant 142).

Dinesh Biswas considers Dogberry to play a major part in the action of Much Ado about Nothing, which is not normally the case for clowns. It is Dogberry who discovers and delays the exposure of the scene that provides the major tension of the play. It is his blunders that make the play's most suspenseful moments possible. By giving this critical role to a minor character, Shakespeare shows that "much ado" has been made about a matter that really was "nothing" (Biswas 189-190).

In <u>Much Ado about Nothing</u>, Benedick is ridiculously critical of Hero, and says, "methinks she is too low for a high praise, / too brown for a fair praise, and too little for a great praise... / she were unhandsome; and being no other but as she is, I do not like her" (<u>Much Ado</u> 1.1; <u>Complete</u> 180). Claudio continues Benedick's criticism. When he concludes that Hero has been unchaste, Claudio is overly judgmental, and cruel in denouncing her in public during the wedding ceremony without listening to any other point of view. "Behold, how like a maid she blushes here! / O, what authority and show of truth / Can cunning sin cover itself withall /...Would you not swear, all you that see her, / That she were a maid, by these exterior shows? / But she is none: She knows the heat of a luxurious bed" (<u>Much Ado</u> 4.1; <u>Complete</u> 46).

William McCollom suggests that the ways that many of the characters speak during many serious moments are actually parodies of language which Shakespeare's audience would have recognized as parodies, providing a precarious balance between seriousness and levity (McCollom 70). Sexual jealousy is the central theme of the main plot, and A. P. Rossiter points out that the play is created in such a way that if things didn't work out at the end of the play, the play would be a tragedy rather than a comedy. Shakespeare would only have had to change the ending so that Hero was indeed dead in order for the play be classified as a tragedy rather than a comedy. But instead, Hero is proved innocent and everyone lives happily ever after, and the play therefore becomes a comedy (Muir 55).

Shakespeare establishes the comic nature of the play for the audience so that when the possibly tragic events begin to happen the audience is sure that things will work out well in the end. He does this partly by means of the wit of such characters as Beatrice and Benedick whose "play of wit indicates in advance the way the action will go" (McCollom 71). Beatrice and Benedick are the wisest and the wittiest characters in the play and when Claudio rejects Hero at the alter, they are the first ones to "reject the rejection" and stick up for her (McCollom 71). McCollom says that this is one of the ways that the audience knows that everything will work out all right. Graham Storey agrees, saying that if Beatrice and Benedick had been as easily deceived as the other characters then the audience might have been worried (Davis 25).

Beatrice and Benedick aren't as hostile toward each other as it would appear on the surface, since there is an underlying affection in their words and actions. In the first scene, Beatrice makes insulting inquiries about Benedick, inquiries which show that at the very least she is very interested in him. Benedick, on the other hand, has a tendency to reject suggestions that have never been made. "I would not marry her, though she were endow'd with all that Adam had left him before he transgress'd" (<u>Much Ado</u> II.i 250-252). Beatrice and Benedick don't so much disdain each other as they enjoy the enactment of disdain. Benedick shows his affection for Beatrice in an ironic way at the ball, when Beatrice has insulted him and he then asks Don Pedro for any excuse to leave the party. The fact is that he could have left at any time on his own accord:

> "Will your Grace command me any service to the world's end? I will go on the slightest errand now to the Antipodes that you can devise to send me on; I will fetch you a toothpicker now from the furthest inch of Asia, bring you the length of Prester John's foot, fetch you a hair off the great Champs berare, do you an embassage to the Pygmies, rather than hold three words' conference with this harpy. You have no employment for me?" (<u>Much Ado</u> II.i.; <u>Complete</u> 263-271)

<u>Much Ado about Nothing</u> is warm and witty, with a compassionate view of human frailties and limitations. Among the characters, it is only Don John who is morose.

Shakespeare holds up Don John, the illegitimate brother of the King, to scorn. Don John is the prototypical misanthropic villain. He is so twisted with envy, hatred, and rage that he would ruin the reputation of Hero, a virtuous and innocent young woman, to get even with his brother. He is so obviously evil and pitiful that Shakespeare needs to spend very little time in mocking him, or in developing his character (Anderson 83).

Except for Don John, all of the other characters in Much Ado about Nothing are engaging and sympathetic (Ornstein 119). Alfred Gu L'Estrange considers Beatrice to be the liveliest character in all of Shakespeare, and he gives an example of her wit:

> BEATRICE: For hear me, Hero; wooing, wedding, and repenting, as a
>   Scotch jig, a measure and a cinque-pace; the first suit is hot and
>   hasty, like a Scotch jig, and full as fantastical; the wedding
>   mannerly-modest, as a measure full of state and anciently; and then
>   comes repentance, and with his bad legs, falls into the cinque-pace
>   faster and faster, till he sinks into his grave. (L'Estrange 251).

Beatrice is strong in her resolve to avoid being dominated either physically or in spirit. In Act 2, Scene 1, she can be seen as rebellious, and unwilling to be restored to her "natural state" as she states her demanding criteria for a husband: "He that hath a beard is more than a youth, and he that hath no beard is less than a man; and he that is more than a youth is not for me, and he that is less than a man, I am not for him."

Clara Park feels hat Benedick and Beatrice were made for each other: "The young woman and the young man are endowed with the same kind of wit and the same enjoyment of verbal competitiveness. The pleasure of watching them lies in the equality of the match" (Park 104).

Beatrice and Benedick, the protagonists of Much Ado about Nothing, are "the most attractive pair of lovers in the comedies--the only ones perhaps who are equally matched in intelligence, humor, and humanity" (Ornstein 119). Much Ado is possibly Shakespeare's most realistic comedy because it comes closest to representing the give and take of casual conversation and the daily routine of an actual sixteenth century household--that of Leonato (Ornstein 120). It is often regarded as Shakespeare's first "mature" or "joyous" comedy (Bryant 123). Like The Taming of the Shrew, this play is about the war between the sexes, and it has moments of high hilarity. Most audiences applaud the lively sparring between the lovers, and they also usually applaud Benedick's amusing but futile efforts to play the courtly lover, as he marches off to get the lady's picture in Act 2, Scene 3, or shaves off his beard, washes his face, and puts on perfume in Act 3, Scene 2. In Act 5, Scene 2, Benedick is finally forced to ask Margaret for help with his writing of courtly-love poetry:

> "Marry, I cannot show it in rhyme; I have tried. I can find out no rhyme
> to 'lady' but 'baby,' an innocent rhyme; for 'scorn,' 'horn,' a hard rhyme;
> for 'school,' 'fool,' a babbling rhyme: very ominous endings. No, I was not
> born under a rhyming planet." (Bryant 129)

In a book entitled Shakespearean Comedy, Chintamani Desai notes that whenever Shakespeare has a battle of wits between a man and a woman the woman is bound to win. Much of Shakespearean Comedy is the result of the clash between the male and female intelligences. They hinge on the conflict between their wits. "And in this conflict, man is the loser. For wit is woman's special quality as well as weapon" (Desai 45).

Henry V (1598) tells about how Henry V was mentored by Falstaff. In his speech before the battle of Agincourt, Hal knows what he has given up to become king--his playful, private, irresponsible, joyous self. He has given up that half of him that was tutored by Falstaff, and he realizes that this loss is the price he must pay to become king (Homan 948).

Carrie Morene says that much of the humor, satire and irony of As You Like It (1599) resides in the words and actions of Rosalind, Jaques, and Touchstone. As You Like

It is a cheerful play, despite the fact that it begins in a world turned upside down, a world where the reigning duke is a usurper who has forced his older brother into exile, and a world in which Oliver tyrannizes over his younger brother, Orlando, by depriving him of his inheritance, treating him as a common herdsman, and a person whom he would like to murder (Ornstein 141). Despite this plot, Ornstein considers As You Like It not only a "cheerful," but even a "sunny" play. The third, fourth, and fifth acts are set in Arden, a never-never land that is full of laughter, and song, and warmhearted sentiment, and a land free from anxieties. The interplay between the serious--often tragic-- and the light--often comic--elements have caused some critics to call this play a satire, and there are indeed satiric elements, but none cut very deep. "Rosalind and Touchstone are whimsical yea-saying skeptics who affirm the values they seem to mock" (Ornstein 141).

In As You Like It Rosalind exhibits both intelligence and independence of mind. She uses her talent for wit to make the exploration of Orlando's love "both funny and satiric, both delightful and instructive, as well as romantically satisfying." Rosalind adopts the role of a saucy lackey, and in this guise she assures Orlando that he can't be Rosalind's true lover because he lacks the marks of a lover: "a lean cheek...a blue eye and sunken.... an unquestionable spirit...a beard neglected...hose...ungartered...bonnet unbanded...sleeve unbuttoned...shoe untied...and everything about [him] demonstrating a careless desolation." At the end of this speech Rosalind (as Ganymede) says that Orlando's being well-groomed is suggestive of his "loving himself [more] than seeming the lover of any other" (Bloom 59). Orlando tries to suggest that he is a "courtly lover," and he suggests that if Rosalind rejects him he will die, but Ganymede (Rosalind) responds, "Men have died from time to time, and worms have eaten them, but not for love" (Bloom 60).

Keir Elam notes that in Shakespeare's comedies lovers or husbands are totally unable to recognize their women while in men's costumes. They fail to make the proper connections because they are distracted by other important matters. Thus Orlando is so distracted by his thoughts of Rosalind that he doesn't recognize her even as she stands in front of him as Ganymede and speaks. Even in the conversation which follows, words like "pretty" and "petticoat" do not give Orlando a hint. As Ganymede, Rosalind finally proclaims, "I thank God I am not a woman," and when Orlando continues to address her as a youth, she insists, "you must call me Rosalind" (Elam 17).

Touchstone in As You Like It has the role of a Court Jester, but he also contributes to the action of the play, and is even more amusing as a commentator. One of Touchstone's monologues is very similar to Cyrano de Bergerac's monologue about his nose, as he attempts to "quarrel by the book." He describes the different degrees of argument as the "Retort Courteous," the "Quip Modest," the "Reply Churlish," the "Reproof Valiant," and so on. (Evans 399). Touchstone's most used comic techniques are exaggeration and parody (Parrott 170). E. A. M. Colman describes Touchstone as "the cynic that attacks lovers with dry wit of would-be realism, but the lovers too are realistic, and more capriciously so than the cynic. Consequently, while his cynicism saves the play from cloudy idealism, it falls far short of debunking the lovers who stand at the play's emotional centre" (Colman 109). When Touchstone hears the romantic love poems which Orlando has written for Rosalind, Touchstone taunts Rosalind by creating some parody verse of his own: "Sweetest nut hath sourest rind, / Such a nut is Rosalind" (Evans Riverside 109-110). Clearly, Touchstone is not enamoured with the notion of being in love. It is ironic, therefore, that he falls in love with Audry and takes Orlando's place as the fool (Woodford 2).

In As You Like It, Jaques expresses the speech that probably gives the best glimpse into Shakespeare's conception of drama. The speech occurs in Act 2: "All the world's a stage, and all the men and women merely players: They have their exits and their entrances; and one man in his time plays many parts" (Bigaldi and Achtert 52). Jaques is a "humors" character, and his "humor" displays the features of cynicism and melancholy. In a single word, he is a "malcontent" (Parrott 169). Jaques is always argumentative, and he always indiscrimately takes the opposing view of any discussion. He is never pleased with anything or with anybody. His humor is, however, ironic, as when he comments that Duke Senior is too argumentative. It is Jaques himself who is too argumentative (Smith 26). The only time in the play when Jaques is content is when he meets Touchstone. Jaques is impressed by Touchstone's pessimism, and even attempts to quote him, not realizing that Touchstone is only pretending to have the same pessimistic and obscure view of the world that Jaques has (Smith 29).

One comic segment of <u>As You Like It</u> is Jaques's "Ages of Man" speech, in which he divides human beings into seven stages. He then talks about the infant "puking in his nurse's arms," and the tardy schoolboy, and the creator of such ballads as "His Mistress's eyebrow," and the soldier who wants more of a reputation than just a "bubble," and the fat country justice who has profited unduly from his office, and the old man who looks and acts ridiculous, and finally, the senile old man who goes through life very much like a child, "sans teeth, sans eyes, sans taste, sans every thing" (Homan 940-941).

<u>As You Like It</u> is based on a novel entitled <u>Rosalynde</u>, and written by Thomas Lodge (Bryant 146); however, as J. A. Bryant notes, "It is Jaques, in short, who directs us to see the potential for true comedy in Lodge's <u>Rosalynde</u>, and without him the play would be as dated as its source" (Bryant 164). In <u>As You Like It</u>, It is ironic when Rosalind dresses up as a man, Ganymede, and them meets up with Orlando (Rosalind's lover) in the forest, and takes on the task of curing him of his love for Rosalind. She advises, "Love is merely a madness and, I tell you, deserves as well a dark house and a whip as madmen do; and the reason why they are not so punished and cured is that the lunacy is so ordinary that the whippers are in love too (Madden 3). Both Celia and Rosalind decide to gout forth alone in the world in disguise. This scene is very ironic and humorous because the character of Rosalind is played by a boy pretending to be a girl disguised as a boy. Rosalind chooses the name of Ganymede as her alias, and of course in Greek mythology, Ganymede was a beautiful Trojan prince with whom Jupiter fell in love. It is appropriate that Ganymede, who was the object of homosexual love, provides the name for the effeminate Rosalind, a young lady who is disguised as a young man. The name which Celia chooses for herself is Aliena, which is again appropriate because Aliena is the feminine form of a Latin word that means "stranger" (Asimov 565). The irony becomes more intense when a pact is drawn between Rosalind (Ganymede) and Orlando, and when Rosalind finds herself in a position to hear her lover extol her virtues and declare his love for her without being aware that he is in fact talking to her. The dramatic irony here is a touch of brilliance" (Smith 33).

<u>Twelfth Night</u> (1599) is based on a sixteenth century ritual called "Twelfth Night." Christ was supposedly revealed to the Magi, who represented the Gentile world, on the twelfth night. The "Twelfth Night" was, therefore, the night of the Epiphany. It also became celebrated as a festive day of misrule. ·

> Servants took their masters' places for a day and the lower orders were allowed impertinence against their betters that would have been heavily fined any other time of year. The festivity generally celebrated the age of grace that Christ ushered in, the age in which it was revealed that human sins were already cleansed in the blood of God's Son. (Grawe 110-111)

Grawe continues by saying that while the Renaissance English were celebrating the "Twelfth Night" with their festive misrule, they were at the same time terribly conscious that the "misrule was itself the basis of social destruction. Misrule must have its day, but if society is to survive, misrule must have no more than its day" (Grawe 111).

In <u>Twelfth Night</u>, everyone is a fool except for the fool. Viola fools others by dressing up as a man. Sir Toby fools Malvolio. The lovers fool themselves by pursuing characters who are not interested in them. Feste, on the other hand, knows them all for the fools they are (Draper 211-212). Twelfth Night may not have a single central character. Various critics have presented Viola, Orsino, Olivia, Sir Toby Belch, Malvolio, and even Feste as the central character of the play, and this has created something of a cacophony of criticism. However Paul Grawe feels that there is a pattern to the cacophony. Grawe says that throughout Shakespeare, whether in The Comedy of Errors, or in Love's Labour's Lost, or in Merchant of Venice, or in The Tempest, the comedy "never symbolizes the survival of mankind in a single character or in a single romantic couple:

> Shakespeare's inability to form his comedies around single characters or couples is basic to the implicational import of the comedies. For Shakespeare, there is no survival if one is an island unto oneself. Survival must be shared with and partially created by society at large. For Shakespeare, the hero of every comedy is society itself, threatened as it is from within and from without. (Grawe 98)

Feste is perhaps the shrewdest character in Twelfth Night. He is an excellent manipulator and can quickly adapt his talents and wit to serve him in any situation. The tools of music, speech, and action are always in close reach of his clever mind. He entertains the Duke and Sir Toby Belch with songs, fends off Maria with impudence, confounds Sir Andrew with nonsense, and outwits his mistress with logical paradoxes. He wisely ascertains that he cannot entertain Malvolio at all and so he entertains himself at Malvolio's expense (Draper 204). Malvolio is a parody of the strait-laced, humorless Puritans of Elizabethan England (Homan 940). In Act 3, Scene 2, Viola recognizes the intelligence behind Feste's constant word play and comments, "This fellow is wise enough to play the fool, and to do that craves a kind of wit" (Draper 204). Feste is portrayed both as a reveler and an ironic commentator in Twelfth Night. Even though Feste lacks both specific motive and personal drive in the play, he is the internal ironic voice as he speaks more to the audience than to the other characters. Ironically, it is his distance from the other characters that allows their full acceptance of him in their midst. He functions both inside, and outside, of the play in his role as singer, performer, and poet. In sum, he is "the emblem of comic pleasure always aware of the limitations and cost of that pleasure" (Rayner 37). Unlike Shakespeare's earlier clowns, Feste is never given to exuberant fancies. For Feste, laughter does not come easily, and in fact Feste tells Cesario that foolery "does walk about the orb like the sun, it shines everywhere" but in Twelfth Night the high-spirited and good natured foolery is intertwined with sharp-edged and denigrating wit (Ornstein 172).

Leslie Hotson points out that Feste, the fool in Twelfth Night is a character highly reminiscent of the character of Vice in the Tudor morality plays. Vice was a crude character who taunted the Devil with a wooden dagger and rode off the stage on the Devil's back (Hotson 84). Feste leaves the stage in the same way:

> I am gone, sir, / And anon, sir, / I'll be with you again, / In a trice, / Like to the old vice, / Your need to sustain; / Who, with dagger of lath, / In his rage and his wrath, / Cries, ah, ha! to the devil: / Like a mad lad, / Pare thy nails, dad; / Adieu, goodman devil (Evans 132).

Robert Goldsmith notes that the professional fool of Shakespeare's time probably descended from the medieval minstrels who roamed around Europe after the breakup of the Roman Empire. These wandering minstrels gradually took on the role of the "natural fool." The practice of keeping natural fools, idiots, or dwarfs, can be traced back to Roman times, when people kept them as pets. This practice grew during the Middle Ages, and many nobles became guardians for fools (Goldsmith 5-6). Although they were treated as pets, the fools were viewed as a cross between a victim and a lucky charm, and they were therefore dearly loved by their masters (Belkin 40). Erasmus described these "innocents" as follows: "These my selie paches. Who not onelye them selues are euer mery, playing, singing, and laughynge: but also whateuer they doo, are prouoker of others lykewyse to pleasure, sporte, and laughter" (Goldsmith).

In Twelfth Night, the appetites for music, food, drink, love, and the sea are equated (Rayner 27). For example, Sir Toby Belch makes the oceanic theme physical when he says that he has an unquenchable thirst for ale and will drink toasts to Olivia "as long as there's passage in my throat and drink in Illyria" (Rayner 28). But Paul Grawe suggests that even Sir Toby Belch's humor is not individual, but is rather communal, as Toby is matched off against the other characters of the play. He is seen in the company of Sir Andrew Aguecheek, who is "as lacking in will as Sir Toby is ruled by it," or he is matched against Malvolio ("bad wishing"), who is opposite to Toby in superficial behavior, but just as self-willed, and in the end, just as incapable of self-control (Grawe 107). Sir Toby's actions and language are also seen in relation to those of his wife. Sir Toby has married below his station. He has married a women with little sympathy for his carousing drunkenness, and this sets up a fine background for Toby's words and actions (Grawe 110).

Some of the bawdiest language in Shakespeare appears in Act 2, Scene 5, of Twelfth Night. It is here that Malvolio is trying to figure out if a particular letter has been written by a particular lady or not. To understand the pun, the audience must know that in the sixteenth century the expression "cut" was a slang word for "vulva," and that the plural of "P" was a long-established euphemism for "piss." Taking up the letter, Malvolio says, "By my life, this is my lady's hand: these be her very C's, her U's, and her T's, and thus makes she her great P's" (Turell 253).

J. Dover Wilson considers Twelfth Night to be Shakespeare's finest play. Wilson uses such descriptions as "that gem of his comic art," "that condensation of life and (for those who know how to taste it rightly) elixir of life." Wilson goes on to say, "He could never better this--and he never attempted to. He broke the mold--and passed on" (Bryant 165). J. A. Bryant suggests that the high praise of Twelfth Night is because it is an excellent representation of romantic comedy, or more specifically, the romantic version of Italianate comedy, in which the audience is reassured about civilized society's ability to renew itself (Bryant 166). But although Twelfth Night superficially resembles Italianate comedy, it is actually "the apotheosis of a development that Shakespeare had been anticipating ever since he portrayed the French ladies at the court of Navarre" (Bryant 178).

There is much irony in Hamlet (1600). John Peter points out, for example, that Hamlet is not being ridiculous when he speaks of women painting their faces an inch thick, and rotting in spite of it. Tragedy transcends and appears almost indifferent to preoccupations of individual characters with their personal perceptions (Peter 208). The most famous pun in Hamlet occurs after Hamlet decides to obey the ghost. Horatio's question, "To what issue will this come?" is a play on that which issues from an arse, i.e. a fart, and Marcellus answers that "Something is rotten in the state of Denmark." Claudius, of course, is the state, and it is Claudius which is rotten (Rubinstein 186). When Horatio mentions that the funeral of Hamlet's father and the marriage of Hamlet's mother come very close together, Hamlet ironically replies, " 'Thrift, thrift, Horatio! the funeral bak'd meats / Did coldly furnish forth the marriage tables' " (qtd. in Booth 177). Hamlet gives this ridiculous explanation of his mother's hasty wedding ironically, in order to intensify his revulsion at the lust which he and Horatio both recognize as the real explanation (Booth 177).

Hamlet's feigned madness ia a bizarre reversal--"a sane man convincing others that he is mad by speaking the truth disguised as madness. He engages in punning battles with everyone, especially with the king's chief advisor, who loses every time. The battles are designed to show his madness, but are so clever in double entendres that Polonius exclaims, "though this be madness, yet there is method in't" (Hamlet Act 2, Scene 2).

Hamlet contains an ironic joke that is pivotal to the performance of the play. If the King's attendants laugh at Hamlet's joking, they shift their allegiance from Claudius to Hamlet by doing so, and the tension in the scene is thereby intensified, because the audience cannot then be sure whether the attendants will obey the King's command. On the other hand, if they remain silent, Hamlet's jokes fail, and his vulnerability becomes all the greater (Pfordresher 204).

Much of the wit in Shakespeare's plays comes not from the words, which are actually rather dull in most cases, but the wit comes from the particular words being associated with particular ludicrous characters. The words become highly amusing when coming from men of certain peculiar views. For example, much of the humor in the conversation between the two gravediggers in Hamlet comes not from the words themselves, but rather comes from the contrast between the language of the men and their occupation (L'Estrange 255).

> HAMLET: Whose grave's this, sirrah?
> CLOWN/GRAVEDIGGER: Mine, sir....
> HAMLET: What man dost thou dig it for?
> CLOWN: For no man, sir.
> HAMLET: What woman then?
> CLOWN: For none neither.
> HAMLET: Who is to be burried in't?
> CLOWN: One that was a woman, sir; but, rest her soul, she's dead.
> HAMLET: How absolute the knave is! We must speak by the card, or equivocation will undo us. (Act 5, Scene i).

Hamlet's soliloquy as he talks to poor Yorick's skull in this same scene seems less concerned that the life is gone than that the laughter is gone.

> He hath borne me on his back a thousand times. And now how abhorred in my imagination it is! My gorge rises at it. Here hung those lips that I have kiss'd I know not how oft. Where be your gibes now? your gambols? your songs? your flashes of merriment that were wont to set the tables on a roar? Not one now, to mock your own grinning? Quite chapfall'n? Now get you to my lady's chamber, and tell her, let her paint an inch thick, to this favour she must come. Make her laugh at that. (Hamlet V, i).

Hamlet considered Yorick to be "...a fellow if infinite jest, of most excellent fancy. Hamlet mused over Yorick's skull about life and death, showing that in this case, "even long after death, one of Shakespeare's clowns was causing someone to look at things in a different way, to see the hidden truth" (Sease 1). Hamlet asks Ophelia, "What should a man do but be merry." Sidney Homan says that "the paradox is that the grieving young man who refuses to change out of his funeral clothes, much to the anguish of his mother and step-father, with his puns and jokes is also Shakespeare's most profound and intense comedian. Hamlet models himself after Yorick, whose skull he addresses as 'a fellow of infinite jest, of most excellent fancy'" (Homan 948).

Troilus and Cressida (1601) is a satire in the sense that it is a serious criticism of life. Nevertheless, it puts emphasis on those features which Elizabethans expected to find in their comedies, and it is usually classified, therefore, as a comedy. Kenneth Steele White uses the following adjectives to describe Troilus and Cressida: "scathing," "darkly comic," "iconoclastic," and "far-sighted." He says that the comedy in this play "insinuates affinities of lust and war-making" (White 2). J. A. Bryant considers Troilus and Cressida to be at a crucial juncture in the development of Shakespeare's exploration of the comic genre. Here Shakespeare presented themes and subject matter as a way of reassuring audiences and ameliorating their peace of mind (179). The play contains a great deal of conventional satire in its barbed criticism of manners and morés, its recognizable specific personages, and its relationship to rival theatres. Shakespeare's critical knife cuts at some of the fundamental assumptions of Elizabethan life (Bryant 180). J. A. Bryant evaluates the play as follows:

> There are no perfections in Troilus and Cressida, and there will be none in any of Shakespeare's comedies to follow, whether we call them problem plays or romances. Comedy henceforth in Shakespeare's practice of it will find its love and devotion in a world where unadulterated truth and beauty are illusions and where the viewer or reader is constrained to accept a human approximation of these ideals in something like charity and forgiveness. (Bryant 202)

All's Well that Ends Well (1602) is Shakespeare's only play that is based on a single love (or in this case a single love-hate) relationship (Ornstein 173). Except for Bertram's mistaken assumption that he has made love to Diana, there are no scenes in this play that turn on mistaken identities. In the final scene, most of the comedy derives from Helena's artful interpretations of Diana's accusations against Bertram and her provocative riddling about her (Helena's) ring. Shakespeare makes Helena's case stronger by allowing Diana to enter just as the bewildered Bertram, who is suspected of wicked deeds, is being led away under guard (Ornstein 190).

All's Well that Ends Well is like Troilus and Cressida (1601) and Measure for Measure (1604) in being an anomalous play. These three plays, which were written in a four-year period from 1601 to 1604 have been called not only "anomalous plays;" they have also received such designations as "dark comedies," "problem comedies," "problem plays," and even "tragicomedies." But whatever a person calls these "middle plays," they address themselves to the basic function of comedy, which is to reassure the audience that society is able to provide the processes which are necessary for self renewal, in all but the most extraordinary circumstances (Bryant 203). These three "middle comedies" are distinguished from the ten comedies that preceded them in that neither the validity of established social institutions, nor the psychology of human beings, or even the physical and moral order of the universe is taken for granted (Bryant 204). "These middle comedies present what appears to be an indiscrimate mixture, and with them the hope of a conclusive sorting out--light from dark, good from evil, justice from injustice--vanishes, never to return" (Bryant 204). Mary Bly says that around 1600 several comedies experimented with the female expression of desire, where these females did not answer either by death or by repentance. Shakespeare's Helena in All's Well that Ends Well is one such female. Helena "is a master of Petrarchan idiom, yet her initial sonnet-like revelation of love for a 'bright particular star' is immediately followed by a jest regarding her virginity: 'How might one do, sir, to lose it to her own liking?' " (Hunter 147) a question far from lyrical chastity (Bly 36).

In Measure for Measure (1604), Isabella's brother Claudio has been imprisoned for the crime of having premarital sex with Juliet, and Isabella, who is about to enter a convent is propositioned by Angelo, a wicked officer (Homan 943). Claudio is so eager to prove to Isabella that he is a loving brother that he vows to die for his sister's honor. Isabella cheerfully responds, "Be ready for death tomorrow." Suddenly, Claudio realizes what she is saying and says to her, "Death is a fearful thing." When Isabella sees that Claudio is going back on his vow, he calls him a "beast" and a "faithless coward" because he seeks to preserve his own life at the cost of his sister's shame. Then Isabella offers the coup de grace with her exit line, as she prays a thousand prayers for her brother's death. In Elizabethan England, the expression "to die" had two meanings. It meant "to cease to be alive," and it also meant "to have sexual intercourse." "The act that ends life was thus, paradoxically, lined with the physical act that begins life" (Homan 944).

Northrop Frye says that in <u>King Lear</u> (1605), Shakespeare is ironicically parodying a tragic situation, and Frye further says that Shakespeare's plot is very elaborately developed, so elaborately developed, in fact, that Frye considers <u>King Lear</u> to be a "comedy of the grotesque" (Frye 237). <u>King Lear</u> has probably aroused more contradictory or paradoxical commentary than has any other Shakespearean tragedy. It is acclaimed by many scholars to be Shakespeare's finest tragedy, but it has also been derided as structurally weak, as unrealistic and artificial in dramatic development, and as filled with anachronisms, incongruities, inconsistencies, and superfluous characters (Martin 1). There is even controversy as to whether to classify <u>King Lear</u> as a tragedy or a comedy. Aristotle tells us that comedy "aims at representing man as worse, tragedy as better than in actual life," and by this definition, <u>King Lear</u> is a comedy, since the play is filled with examples of human behavior which is below the norm. There are certainly crass stupidities, and absurd misapprehensions of reality (Martin 7). Or it would be possible to consider <u>King Lear</u> a tragicomedy in which the tragic and the comic elements are indistinguishably melted together, but this is an over-simplification which misses the rich complexity of the drama.

> Shakespeare...has not merely reconciled tragedy and comedy, but he has amalgamated all the notable dramatic genres familiar to Elizabethan playwrights.... <u>King Lear</u>, in fact, comprises the tragic, comic, chronicle, morality, and miracle dramatic traditions. Shakespeare, perhaps disenchanted by, or at least dissatisfied with, the limited views of life presented by each of the conventional dramatic types, has indissolubly knit all these traditions and formed a composite drama which deals with the manifold complexities of life. (Martin 16)

Martin continues that each of the conventional dramatic forms concentrates on a single aspect of man's nature.

> tragedy emphasizes the nobility and pathos of man's predicament; comedy concentrates upon man's absurdity; the chronicle deals with the deeds and historical accomplishments of man; the morality plays and the miracle plays accentuate man's moral nature and its religious proclivities (Martin 16).

In Martin's opinion, tragedy appeals mainly to the emotions while comedy appeals mainly to the intellect. The morality and miracle plays appeal to the spirit; and the chronicles appeal to man's sense of accomplishment. But Martin further suggests that no person's life can be totally explained by knowing its pathos, its comedy, its spirituality, or its works. A legitimate view of human life must include all facets of a person's life, and <u>King Lear</u> attempts this comprehensive view of the human predicament (Martin 16). The resultant patchwork shows man as he is, for he is inept, pathetic, absurd, spiritual, and great; and he is all of these things at the same time. Because a person's predicament is filled with aberrancies, contradictions, and inconsistencies, it is basically ironic, and <u>King Lear</u> investigates the ironic nature of man in a different way. "Whereas other dramas had utilized irony to point up tragedy or comedy, <u>King Lear</u> employs comedy and tragedy to point up irony" (Martin 17).

Many of Shakespeare's plays contain a fool, a clown, a jester, or a madman, but the "fool" in <u>King Lear</u> is not so much of a "fool" as the King is. In fact, at one point in the play, the fool in <u>King Lear</u> ends up by saying, "Nuncle! Would I had two coxcombs and two daughters!" Lear asks, "Why, my boy?" and the fool responds, "If I gave them all my living, I'll keep my coxcombs myself. There's mine; beg another of thy daughters" (Muir 39). The fool is here saying that he would give something to his daughters if he had daughters, but he would still keep the cap so that he could make a living. He is further telling Lear that he has given everything to his daughters, and this means that he must now beg his daughters for a living (Lin 8). When the King says, "Dost thou call me a fool, boy?" the fool replies, "All thy other titles thou hast given away; that thou was't born with." (Evans Riverside 441).

Cleopatra's death scene in The Tragedy of Antony and Cleopatra (1606) is grim comedy, as the clown brings Cleopatra a basket containing two small very poisonous snakes called asps. These asps live in the mud on the banks of the Nile, and the Clown, who knows about Cleopatara's sexual reputation, makes crude puns on "dying" and "death," suggesting that the snakes will "function as some sort of sexual surrogate for Cleopatra." When the Clown exits, Cleopatra takes the first asp to her breast, and when it bites her, she compares the bite to a "lover's pinch," in that it "hurts, and is desired." After the second asp has also bitten her, she takes both of the asps to her breast and calls the first one "Antony." In the scene of Cleopatra and the two asps at her breasts, we have "an idyllic picture, the nuclear family--mother, father, and child sleeping at its mother's breast, full of mother's milk." Homan concludes therefore that "Cleopatra's death is, in a way, pleasurable, as comedy itself is" (Homan 946).

In Macbeth (1606), there is very dark humor in the irony of Lady Macbeth's taunting her husband by equating his desire to kill the king with his sexual promises. "She then links his twin deeds of assassination and lovemaking" (Homan 940). Macbeth also contains the famous "drunken porter scene" of Act 2, Scene 3. This scene comes between the murder of King Duncan and the discovery of his body, and is therefore the most tense moment of the play. The audience is in an extreme state of arousal, as the drunken porter, before answering the loud knocking at the castle gate, decides to play the role of the gate keeper in Hell. In his fantasy, he opens the gates of hell to admit a failed farmer, an equivocator, and an English tailor, before he, in realty, actually opens the castle gate and admits the messenger. It is difficult to determine whether the "drunken porter scene" increases, or decreases the arousal, or whether it does both, but in any case, the scene at this point is in need of a delay tactic to force the audience to keep the tension of the King's undiscovered murder longer in their minds before the discovery lessens the tension of the moment (Derks 52).

Pericles (1607) is sometimes classed with Cymbeline (1609), The Winter's Tale (1610), and The Tempest (1611) as being Shakespeare's "late comedies;" however, recently, these four plays are usually classed as "romances" or "comic romances" rather than "comedies" (Bryant 221). Pericles is different from all of Shakespeare's other plays in the appearance of John Gower, the poet, as one of the characters. Gower, who had died in 1408, is resurrected in order to present the play (Hartwig Tragicomic 34). But Pericles contains a number of special rhetorical devices in addition to the appearance of Gower. There is the dumb show, the tournament, the ritual use of music, and the dance. These devices control the audience in two significant ways. In the first place, the show of artificiality requires the audience to see the play as remote from actual life. In the second place, the lack of dramatic development has a static, disconnected effect. Therefore, both of these devices serve to place a distance between the staged illusion and the audience. A reason for establishing the distance is to force the play to be interpreted on a more universal (rather than local) level. Another reason is to shape the perception of the play itself. Instead of seeing the episodes as part of a developing dramatic continuum, we see them instead as individual pictures, like pictures in an exhibition. Each scene, then, should be viewed as a work of art in itself, and Gower acts as the guide who supplies the necessary links between the various pictures (Hartwig Tragicomic 43).

Cymbeline (1609) is adapted from the Ninth Story of the Second Day of Giovanni Boccaccio's Decameron, but the play also borrows touches from The Rare Triumphs of Love and Fortune, published anonymously in 1589, and from Holinshed's Chronicles to localize and extend the context. This is a romantic comedy in which the comic action is spread through the entire play (Bryant 223). Cymbeline has three basic plot lines, but each of these contains a number of subsidiary plots, and their interweaving is intricate indeed.

> First, there is the suit for the hand of Imogen, which includes Iachimo's "wager" and Cloten's "revenge" as well as Posthumus's banishment and return. A second plot concerns the lost sons of Cymbeline and their abductor-guardian Belarius; and the third is the separation and reunion of Britain and Rome. (Hartwig Tragicomic 61)

Even though Cymbeline ends happily, it is not a comedy in the ordinary sense, because it contains only one unmistakably comic scene--that between Posthumus and a jailer who has learned his trade from Pompey and his philosophy of life from the Clown who brings Cleopatra a basket of figs. But even though the rest of the play is serious, there are moments of laughter, either because the events are too preposterous to be taken seriously, or because, as in the final scene, there is a deadpan parody of John Fletcher's sensational and contriving style. Furthermore, Cymbeline has a farcical, even a silly, ending (Ornstein 195). "The silliness of the denouement of Cymbeline is far more ingenious and entertaining than the silliness of the denouement of Two Gentlemen, but it is not more artistically defensible, for in parodying Fletcherian tragicomedy, Shakespeare makes a joke of his own play" (Ornstein 212).

Cymbeline, The Winter's Tale, and The Tempest all seriously and specifically call the audience's attention to an analogous and much wider context that exhibits its own conflict and resolution as the plays proceed. They are not presented as "divine comedy," but they do present comedy that is filled with clear implications for Shakespeare's audiences and to a large extent for audiences today as well. These three plays represent a kind of comedy that might be called international, or intercultural, if not divine (Bryant 226).

The Winter's Tale (1610) contrasts sharply with Cymbeline in that it has a comic action that seems subsidiary to its main action, which is a near-domestic tragedy that frames the comedy like a matrix (Bryant 225). Laughter is created in Act 3, Scene 3 when a bear suddenly appears and chases Antigonas off the stage. At first the audience thinks it is laughing at a bear, but then the audience realizes that it is laughing at more, for the bear is an enactment of death, and when this is realized, the audience experiences a startling dislocation (Hartwig Tragicomic 5).

Kathleen Latimer points out that the first half of The Winter's Tale is distinctly tragic, while the second half is exceptionally joyous. This may be a problem for some critics; and in fact this play has been studied not only as a comedy, a tragi-comedy, and a romance, but E. M. W. Tillyard, in his important study of Shakespeare's last plays considers it to be a tragedy. Against our decision to classify the play as a comedy, we must consider "its lack of social criticism, its troubled hero, its generally somber tone, and its actual, not merely threatened deaths" (Latimer 125); however, Latimer categorizes the play as a comedy nevertheless, based on F. M. Conford's study of the origins of comedy as opposed to the origins of tragedy. Conford traces comedy and tragedy to different parts of the same ritual:

> The first half of the ritual, the death of the scapegoat figure, suggests the tragic pattern; the second half, which includes the figure's rebirth or replacement, reveals the comic pattern.... The Winter's Tale...enacts the entire pattern of the ancient ritual from which tragedy and comedy derive. Through it we can see not only the ultimately comic shape of the total action, but also the means by which the comic pattern is obtained. (Latimer 126)

Latimer notes further that The Winter's Tale presents a harmonious society, one with feelings of community. According to Latimer, "comedy serves as a ritual through which the image of the communal action is conveyed to the society of its audience" (Latimer 140), and by this criterion as well, The Winter's Tale should be classed as a comedy.

Hermione dies in The Winter's Tale, but her memory pervades every scene in Act 5, and the audience will therefore accept Hermione's statue being unveiled and Hermione's descending from the pedestal, alive. One reason that the audience accepts this is the earlier tradition of inanimate or dead objects coming to life that are archetypes in pagan fables, and in Christian legend, and in literary analogues. The most obvious analogue for Shakespeare's audiences would be Ovid's tale of Pygmalion's statue coming to life, but it also echoes many medieval stories of religious statues that miraculously wept or bled or came momentarily to life (Ornstein 233).

According to Joan Hartwig, The Winter's Tale is Shakespeare's only tragicomedy which does not reveal to the audience the resolution of the play. This concealment intensifies the audience's sense of dislocation, and it encourages the audience to alter their perspective in an important way, for the audience realizes, just as the play's characters realize, that people's actions do not produce irrecoverable effects. It is clear from the play that there is a benevolent power which is controlling events in a way that surpasses even the hopes and dreams of the characters. "The tragicomic perspective that Shakespeare creates in The Winter's Tale forces us to suspend rational judgement so that for a special moment we may glimpse the wonder of the world of human action" (Hartwig Tragicomic 136).

The Tempest (1611) can be described as a "romantic comedy" from beginning to end (Bryant 225). J. A. Bryant feels that to call this play a "tragicomedy" is an evasion, and to call it "divine comedy" is more than the play deserves and more than Shakespeare intended. But what is clear about The Tempest is that it ends with people accepting each other--their enemies as well as their loved ones and not excluding any person who by choice or chance has become one of our neighbors (Bryant 251).

In each of the three plays which preceded The Tempest there is a "divine controller" which manifests itself directly. Diana comes to Pericles; Jupiter descends on his eagle in Posthumus's dream-vision; and Apollo is very much present in his oracle at Hermione's trial. However, there is no such direct manifestation of divinity in The Tempest. Rather, Prospero, who is both a man and a magician, incorporates his power with that of the divinity (Hartwig Tragicomic 137). The action of The Tempest involves the education of the characters as to how the concept of tragicomedy relates to them. "The magic island is their 'schoolroom,' and Prospero is their 'schoolmaster' " (Hartwig Tragicomic 138). The Epilogue of The Tempest functions on a number of different levels simultaneously. The magic island becomes the actual world in which the characters live. The magic is no longer an illusion; it has become instead an actual power which the audience itself controls through the power of the imagination. And the audience, realizing that it has been in control the whole time is aware of the extreme power of the imagination, a power it is now not willing to so easily relinquish, because, "a beautiful vision, no matter how illusory, is not easy to give up" (Hartwig Tragicomic 171).

The Tempest has a special place in the Shakespeare repertoire. It is the last play of Shakespeare's sole authorship, and it has a special significance and poignancy not only for Shakespeare scholars, but for Shakespeare as well. "It succeeds as a fairy tale where Cymbeline fails because it creates a wholly consistent imaginative world; it does not intermingle realism and fantasy, moral drama and Fletcherian theatricality" (Ornstein 235).

Shakespeare's significant contribution was based on his ability as a dramatist, as a poet, and as a realist. Some of his plays which we now call comedies were originally classed as histories (L'Estrange 250). Shakespeare's genius for the comic was equal to his genius for the tragic, and "everybody would think so, were it possible for comedy to impress the mind as tragedy does" (Hunt 111). Samuel Johnson suggested that Shakespeare's tragedy is based on skill; his comedy is based on instinct (Hunt 111). Shakespeare's plays, especially his later ones, suggest that "although men do not always realize it, absolute independence is not their goal. Men wish to be led, not driven, so that their own choice is a determinant in the plan that ultimately exceeds their own comprehension" (Hartwig Tragicomic 179).

Susan Snyder finds that Shakespeare uses a number of traditional comic structures in his tragedies. These comic structures set up expectations which often prove false, or they reinforce the movement into tragic inevitability, or they underline a tragic awareness by a pointed irrelevance and establish a point of departure when comedy's assumptions reveal a darker and more evil side, or they become part of the tragedy itself, as when comic elements threaten the hero with absurdity (Snyder 1).

During Shakespeare's time, fools were felt to be especially protected by God, and they were often granted special insights not available to the sane (Hotson 101). The Fool was supposed to be able to bring the king to his senses by jesting him out of his dark mood. But the fools in Shakespeare's tragedies failed to make the kings happy, making their jesting all the darker. Hamlet took refuge from his problems by becoming a fool. By acting the fool, he was free to speak his mind without being in too much danger (Hotson 92).

Shakespeare's clowns, fools, and jesters are the wisest of men: "They talk of Aesop and Solomon in every jest. Yet they amuse as much as they instruct us. The braggart Parolles, whose name signifies 'words,' as though he spoke nothing else, scarcely utters a sentence that is not rich with ideas" (Hunt 113). Leslie Hotson points out that during Shakespeare's time, the word "motley" was not an adjective describing many colors. Instead, it described a coarse fabric woven from various colored threads, the overall color of which was often a dull green (Hotson 7-10). Will Summers, the court fool of Henry VIII wore such an outfit, as did Robert Armin, a lead actor in Shakespeare's company. Armin, who played all of Shakespeare's wise fools--Touchstone in As You Like It, Feste in Twelfth Night, Lavache in All's Well that Ends Well, and the Fool in King Lear--may have significantly changed the character of the on-stage fool. The roles of Touchstone, and Feste, and Lavache, and the Fool in King Lear were in fact written specifically for Armin. When Armin joined Shakespeare's company around 1599, there was a change n Shakespeare's comic characters from the low-brow comedy (made famous by Kempe) to the more high-comedy of the wise fool, and the wearing of the traditional fool's coat may have been a way to distinguish this character from the earlier stage clowns (Hotson 84).

Sidney Homan says that "as the sense of comedy in Shakespeare's comedies deepens to include important human issues (tha nature of justice, the treatment of women, the ability of a community to be inclusive rather than exclusive), so too does comedy invade the writer's histories and tragedies" (Homan 948). Homan feels that a general pattern emerges in Shakespeare's canon: "Humor based on plot, language, and character in the early works; humor that is inseparable from the entertainment of serious issues in the middle works; and, in his final dramas, a comic view of life where humor aided by time is the key to a happy resolution" (Homan 949).

In A Kind of Wild Justice--Revenge in Shakespeare's Comedies, Linda Anderson discusses the ends of Shakespeare's plays. By the end of the play, it is obvious to the audience which of the characters the playwright feels have or have not learned their lessons. If they have not, they end up with a smaller fortune, a weak husband, or a bad reputation. Those who have learned their lessons, however, or who were good from the start, get rewarded with good fortune and the blessings of their friends, family, and society in general. Irene Makaryk calls this "Comic Justice" (Makaryk i), and Linda Anderson calls it "Comedic Revenge." "Overall, the theme of comedic revenge as a social instrument for educating and transforming the behavior of foolish or evil characters...[is] a theme prominent in many of the later comedies" (Anderson 23). "Those characters with true wit and humor can change because they can become aware of their own deficiencies. But those without a sense of humor--Don John, Shylock, Malvolio--have little or no hope of recovering from their egocentricity" (Makaryk 79).

Shakespeare used humor not only in his plays, but in his sonnets as well. Sonnet 130 for example is not a love poem; rather, it is a parody of a love poem. It reads as follows:

> My mistress' eyes are nothing like the sun.
> Coral is far more red than her lips' red.
> If snow be white, why then her breasts are dun.
> If hair be wires, black wires grow on her head.
> I have seen roses damasked, red and white
> But no such roses see I on her cheeks.
> And in some perfume there is more delight
> Than in the breath that from my mistress reeks. (Lederer 187)

Part of the power of this parody lies in the fact that the word reek was just beginning to undergo a semantic shift at this time to a more negative connotation. Shakespeare was aware of this on-going shift of meaning, and was using the fact for comic effect (Lederer 187).

Shakespeare had an extraordinary sense of irony, humor, and wit. Shakespeare invented the phrase, "setting the table on a roar," and he almost invented the concept as well. Shakespeare also invented the memory of Yorick, and the stomach of Falstaff, "stuffed as full of wit as of sack" (Hunt 112). It was Shakespeare's clowns, simpletons, and profligates who engaged in wit. His grander characters tended to be much less witty (L'Estrange 254). It is said that Shakespeare died while he was getting out of his sick-bed to entertain his friends, Michael Drayton and Ben Jonson, who had come to visit him from London (Hunt 112).

William Shakespeare Bibliography

Alden, Raymond Macdonald. "The Use of Comic Material in the Tragedy of Shakespeare and His Contemporaries." Journal of English and Germanic Philology 13 (1914): 281-298.

Anderson, Linda. A Kind of Wild Justice--Revenge in Shakespeare's Comedies. Newark, DE: University of Delaware Press, 1987.

Asimov, Isaac. Asimov's Guide to Shakespeare. New York, NY: Avenel Books, 1978.

Bamber, Linda. Comic Women, Tragic Men: A Study of Gender and Genre in Shakespeare. Stanford, CA: Stanford University Press, 1982.

Barber, Charles Laurence. "From Ritual to Comedy: An Examination of Henry IV." English Stage Comedy: English Institute Essays 1954. Ed. W. K. Wimsatt, Jr. New York, NY: Columbia Univ Press, 1955, 22-51.

Barber, Charles Laurence. "The Saturnalian Pattern in Shakespeare's Comedy." Comedy: Meaning and Form. Second Edition. Ed. Robert W. Corrigan. New York, NY: Harper and Row, 1981, 363-377.

Barber, Charles Laurence. "Shakespearean Comedy in The Comedy of Errors. College English 25 (1964): 493-497.

Barber, Charles Laurence. Shakespeare's Festive Comedy: A Study of Dramatic Form and Its Relation to Social Custom. Princeton, NJ: Princeton Univ Press, 1959.

Barber, Lester E. "The Tempest and New Comedy." Southern Quarterly 21 (1970): 207-211.

Baxter, John S. "Present Mirth: Shakespeare's Romantic Comedies." Queen's Quarterly 72 (1965): 52-77.

Bean, John C. "Comic Structure and the Humanizing of Kate in The Taming of the

Shrew." The Woman's Part: Feminist Criticism of Shakespeare. Eds. Carolyn Ruth Swift Lenz, Gayle Greene, and Carol Thomas Neely. Urbana, IL: Univ of Illinois Press, 1980, 65-78.

Bennett, Josephine Waters. "New Techniques of Comedy in All's Well That Ends Well." Southern Quarterly 18 (1967): 337-362.

Bergeron, David M. "Come Hell or High Water: Shakespearean Romantic Comedy." Shakespearean Comedy. Ed. Maurice Charney. New York, NY: Literary Forum, 1980, 111-120.

Berman, Ronald. "Shakespearean Comedy and the Uses of Reason." South Atlantic Quarterly 63 (1964): 1-9.

Berry, Edward. Shakespeare's Comic Rites. Cambridge, England: Cambridge Univ Press, 1984.

Berry, Ralph. "Discomfort in The Merchant of Venice." Thalia: Studies in Literary Humor 1.3 (1979): 9-16.

Berry, Ralph. "The Season of Twelfth Night. Comedy: New Perspectives. Ed. Maurice Charney. New York, NY: New York Literary Forum, 1978. 139-150.

Berry, Ralph. Shakespeare's Comedies: Explorations in Form. Princeton, NJ: Princeton Univ Press, 1972.

Bethell, S. L. "The Comic Element in Shakespeare's Histories." Anglia 71 (1952): 82-101.

Bigaldi, Joseph, and Walter S. Achtert, eds. MLA Handbook for Writers of Research Papers. 2nd edition. New York, NY: MLA, 1984.

Biswas, Dinesh. Shakespeare's Treatment of His Sources in the Comedies. Calcutta, India: Jadavpur, 1971.

Blackwell, Julie. "The Pun in 1 Henry IV: Saying Much by Saying Little." Unpublished Paper. Tempe, AZ: Arizona State University, 1991.

Blake, Ann. "The Comedy of Othello." Chesterton Review 15 (1972): 46-51.

Blanshard, Rufus A. "Shakespeare's Funny Comedy." College English 21 (1959): 4-8.

Bloom, Donald A. "Dwindling into Wifehood: The Romantic Power of the Witty Heroine in Shakespeare, Dryden, Congreve, and Austen." Look Who's Laughing: Gender and Comedy. Ed. Gail Finney. New York, NY: Gordon and Breach, 1994. 53-80.

Bloom, Harold, ed. Falstaff. Ed. Harold Bloom. New York, NY: Chelsea House, 1992.

Bly, Mary. "Imagining Consummation: Women's Erotic Language in Comedies of Dekker and Shakespeare." Look Who's Laughing: Gender and Comedy. Ed. Gail Finney. New York, NY: Gordon and Breach, 1994. 35-52.

Bonazza, Blaze. Shakespeare's Early Comedies: A Structural Analysis. The Hague, Netherlands: Mouton, 1966.

Boose, Lynda E. "Scolding Brides and Bridling Scolds: Taming the Woman's Unruly Member." Shakespeare Quarterly. Summer, 1991: 179-213.

Booth, Wayne C. The Rhetoric of Irony. Chicago, IL: University of Chicago Press, 1974.

Borthwick, E. Kerr. " 'So Capital a Calf': The Pun in Hamlet, III.ii.105." Shakespeare Quarterly 35 (Summer, 1984): 203-204.

Bradbury, Malcolm, and David Palmer, eds. Shakespearian Comedy. Stratford-upon-Avon Studies 14. New York, NY: Crane, 1972.

Braunmuller, A. R., and J. C. Bulman, eds. Comedy from Shakespeare to Sheridan. Newark, DE: University of Delaware Press, 1986.

Brewer, Ebenezer Cobham. Brewer's Dictionary of Phrase and Fable. 100th edition. New York, NY: Harper and Row, 1981.

Brown, John Russell. "Laughter in the Last Plays." Later Shakespeare. Eds. John Russell Brown, and Bernard Harris. Stratford-upon-Avon Studies 8. New York, NY: St. Martin's, 1966, 103-125.

Brown, John Russell. "The Presentation of Comedy: The First Ten Plays." Shakespearian

Comedy. Ed. Malcolm Bradbury and David Palmer. New York, NY: Crane, 1972, 9-30.

Brown, John Russell. Shakespeare and His Comedies. London, England: Methuen, 1957.

Brucher, Richard T. " 'Tragedy, Laugh On': Comic Violence in Titus Andronicus." Renaissance Drama NS10 (1979): 71-91.

Bruster, Douglas. "Comedy and Control: Shakespeare and the Plautine Poeta." Comparative Drama (Fall, 1990): 217.

Bryant, J. A., Jr. Shakespeare and the Uses of Comedy. Lexington, KY: University Press of Kentucky, 1986.

Burt, Richard A. "Charisma, Coercion, and Comic Form in The Taming of the Shrew. Criticism 26 (1984): 295-311.

Campbell, Oscar J. "The Two Gentlemen of Verona and Italian Comedy." Studies in Shakespeare, Milton, and Donne. New York, NY: Phaeton, 1970, 49-63.

Carroll, C. William. The Metamorphosis of Shakespearean Comedy. Princeton, NJ: Princeton University Press, 1985.

Cazamian, Louis. "Shakespeare's Humor." The Development of English Humor. Durham, NC: Duke University Press, 1952, 180-307.

Champion, Larry S. The Evolution of Shakespeare's Comedy: A Study in Dramatic Perspective. Cambridge, MA: Harvard Univ Press, 1970.

Charlton, H. B. Shakespearian Comedy. London, England: Methuen, 1938.

Charney, Maurice. "Comic Premises of Twelfth Night." Comedy: New Perspectives. Ed. Maurice Charney. New York, NY: New York Literary Forum, 1978. 151-167.

Charney, Maurice. "Comic Villainy in Shakespeare and Middleton." Shakespearean Comedy. Ed. Maurice Charney. New York, NY: Literary Forum, 1980, 165-173.

Charney, Maurice. "Twelfth Night and the 'Natural Perspective' of Comedy." De Shakespeare à T. S. Eliot: Mélanges Offerts à Henri Fluchère. Paris, France: Didier, 1976, 43-51.

Clubb, Louise George. "Italian Comedy and The Comedy of Errors." Comparative Literature 19 (1967): 240-251.

Clubb, Louise George. "Shakespeare's Comedy and Late Cinquecento Mixed Genres." Shakespearean Comedy. Ed. Maurice Charney. New York, NY: Literary Forum, 1980, 129-139.

Clubb, Louise George. "Woman as Wonder: A Generic Figure in Italian and Shakespearean Comedy." Studies in the Continental Background of Renaissance English Literature: Essays Presented to John L. Lievsay. Eds. Dale B. J. Randall and George Walter Williams. Durham, NC: Duke Univ Press, 1977, 109-132.

Coghill, Nevill. "The Basis of Shakespearean Comedy." Essays and Studies NS3 (1950): 1-28.

Coghill, Nevill. "Comic Form in Measure for Measure." Shakespeare Studies 8 (1955): 14-27.

Colby, Arthur L. "Shakespeare's Bawdy Ladies: Sexual Humor in the Conversations of Shakespeare's Aristocratic Female Characters." WHIMSY 1 (1983): 156-157.

Cole, Howard C. "Shakespeare's Comedies and their Sources: Some Biographical and Artistic Inferences." Shakespeare Quarterly 34 (1983): 405-419.

Colman, E. A. M. The Dramatic Use of Bawdy in Shakespeare. London, England: Longman, 1974.

Coursen, H. R. "Shakespearean Comedy and the Moral Limits of Art." Christianity and Literature 26.4 (1977): 4-12.

Cowling, George. "Shakespearean Comedy." Shelley and Other Essays. Freeport, NY: Books for Libraries Press, 1936.

Cox, Roger L. Shakespeare's Comic Changes. Boston, MA: Houghton Mifflin, 1974.

Crane, Milton. "Twelfth Night and Shakespearean Comedy." Shakespeare Quarterly 6 (1955): 1-8.

Crewe, Jonathan V. "God or the Good Physician: The Rational Playwright in The Comedy of Errors." Genre 15 (1982): 203-223.

Cubeta, Paul M. "Lear's Comic Vision: 'Come, Let's Away to Prison.' " Teaching Shakespeare. Eds. Walter Edens, et. al. Princeton, NJ: Princeton Univ Press, 1977, 138-152.

Cunningham, Dolora G. "Wonder and Love in the Romantic Comedies." Shakespeare Quarterly 35 (1984): 262-267.

Curtis, Harry, Jr. "Four Woodcocks in a Dish: Shakespeare's Humanization of the Comic Perspective in Love's Labour's Lost." Southern Humanities Review 13 (1979): 115-124.

Dash, Irene G. Wooing, Wedding and Power. New York, NY: Columbia University Press, 1981.

Davis, Lisa Ivy. "A Discussion of Humor in Four Shakespearean Plays." Unpublished Paper. Tempe, AZ: Arizona State University, 1992.

Davis, Walter C. ed. Twentieth Century Interpretations of "Much Ado About Nothing". Englewood Cliffs, NJ: Prentice-Hall, 1969.

Dean, Leonard F. "Three Notes on Comic Morality: Celia, Bobadill, and Falstaff." Studies in English Literature 1500-1900 16 (1976): 263-271.

Derks, Peter L. "Clockwork Shakespeare: The Bard Meets the Regressive Imagery Dictionary." Empirical Studies of the Arts 12.2 (1994): 131-139.

Derks, Peter L. "Pun Frequency and Popularity of Shakespeare's Plays." Empirical Studies of the Arts 7.1 (1989): 23-31.

Derks, Peter L. "Shakespeare's Use of Humor in Tragedy: Comic Relief or Tragic Reversal?" WHIMSY 6 (1988): 51-53.

Desai, Chintamani N. Shakespearean Comedy. New York, NY: AMS, 1975.

Draper, J. W. "Falstaff, a 'Knave-Fool.' " Stratford to Dogberry: Studies in Shakespeare's Earlier Plays. Pittsburgh, PA: Univ of Pittsburgh Press, 1961, 189-199.

Draper, John W. "The Humor of Corporal Nym." Stratford to Dogberry: Studies in Shakespeare's Earlier Plays. Pittsburgh, PA: Univ of Pittsburgh Press, 1961, 233-239.

Draper, John W. "Mistaken Identity in Shakespeare's Comedies." Stratford to Dogberry: Studies in Shakespeare's Earlier Plays. Pittsburgh, PA: Univ of Pittsburgh Press, 1961, 40-47.

Draper, John W. The Twelfth Night of Shakespeare's Audience. Stanford, CA: Stanford University Press, 1975.

Draper, R. P. "Shakespeare's Pastoral Comedy." Etudes Anglaises 11 (1958): 1-17.

Durant, Geoffrey. "Measure for Measure: A Comedy." Stratford Papers 1968-69. Ed. B. A. W. Jackson. Hamilton, Canada: McMaster Univ Library, 1972, 21-39.

Elam, Keir. Shakespeare's Universe of Discourse, Language-Games in the Comedies. Cambridge, England: Cambridge University Press, 1984.

Epstein, Harry. "The Divine Comedy of The Tempest." Shakespeare Studies 8 (1976): 279-296.

Evans, Bertrand. Shakespeare's Comedies. Oxford, England: Clarendon, 1960.

Evans, G. Blakemore, ed. The Riverside Shakespeare. Boston, MA: Houghton Mifflin, 1974.

Evans, Garth Lloyd. "Shakespeare's Fools: The Shadow and the Substance of Drama." Shakespearian Comedy. Ed. Malcolm Bradbury and David Palmer. New York, NY: Crane, 1972, 142-159.

Evans, James E. "Shakespeare." Comedy: An Annotated Bibliography of Theory and

   Criticism. Metuchen, NJ: Scarecrow Press, 1987, 128-148.
Farley-Hills, David. The Comic in Renaissance Comedy. Totowa, NJ: Barnes, 1981.
Felheim, Marvin. "Comic Realism in Much Ado about Nothing." Philological Pragensia 7
   (1964): 213-225.
Fisher, Claudine G. "Réfractions Shakespeariennes et Humour Noir Chez Hélène Cixous."
   Thalia: Studies in Literary Humor 10.1 (1989): 30-34.
Fleissner, Robert F. "Sherlock Holmes and Shakespeare's Second Most Famous Soliloquy:
   The Adventure of Hamlet's Polluted Flesh." Thalia: Studies in Literary Humor 10.1
   (1989): 43-47.
Foakes, R. A. "The Owl and the Cuckoo: Voices of Maturity in Shakespeare's Comedies."
   Shakespearian Comedy. Ed. Malcolm Bradbury and David Palmer. New York, NY:
   Crane, 1972, 121-141.
Foakes, R. A. Shakespeare: The Dark Comedies to the Last Plays: From Satire to
   Celebration. Charlottesville, VA: Univ Press of Virginia, 1971.
Freedman, Barbara. "Errors in Comedy: A Psychoanalytic Theory of Farce."
   Shakespearean Comedy. Ed. Maurice Charney. New York, NY: Literary Forum,
   1980, 233-243.
Frey, Charles. "The Sweetest Rose: As You Like It as Comedy of Reconciliation."
   Comedy: New Perspectives. Ed. Maurice Charney. New York, NY: New York
   Literary Forum, 1978. 167-186.
Frye, Northrop. "Characterization in Shakespearean Comedy." Shakespeare Quarterly 4
   (1953): 271-277.
Frye, Northrop. Anatomy of Criticism. Princeton, NJ: Princeton University Press, 1957.
Frye, Northrop. The Myth of Deliverance: Reflections on Shakespeare's Problem
   Comedies. Toronto, Canada: Univ of Toronto Press, 1983.
Frye, Northrop. A Natural Perspective: The Development of Shakespearean Comedy and
   Romance. New York, NY: Columbia Univ Press, 1965.
Frye, Northrop. "Shakespeare's Experimental Comedy." Stratford Papers on Shakespeare,
   1961. Ed. B. W. Jackson. Toronto, Canada: Gage, 1962, 1-14.
Galway, Margaret. "Flyting in Shakespeare's Comedies." Shakespeare Association Bulletin
   10 (1935): 183-191.
Garber, Marjorie. " 'Wild Laughter in the Throat of Death': Darker Purposes in
   Shakespearean Comedy." Shakespearean Comedy. Ed. Maurice Charney. New
   York, NY: Literary Forum, 1980, 121-126.
Garner, Shirley Nelson. "A Midsummer Night's Dream: Jack shall have Jill/Nought shall
   go ill." Women's Studies 9 (1981): 47-63.
Gay, Penny. As She Likes It: Shakespare's Unruly Women. New York, NY: Routledge,
   1994.
Gelb, Hal. "Duke Vincentio and the Illusion of Comedy or All's Not Well That Ends
   Well." Shakespeare Quarterly 22 (1971): 25-34.
Gianakaris, C. J. "Folk Ritual as Comic Catharsis and The Merry Wives of Windsor."
   Mississippi Folklore Register 10 (1976): 138-153.
Goldsmith, Robert H. Wise Fools in Shakespeare. East Lansing, MI: Michigan State
   University Press, 1955.
Goldstein, Melvin. "Identity Crises in a Midsummer Nightmare: Comedy as Terror in
   Disguise." Psychological Review 60 (1973): 169-204.
Gordon, George. Shakespearian Comedy and Other Studies. Oxford, England: Oxford Univ
   Press, 1944.
Gowda, H. H. Anniah. Shakespeare's Comedies and Poems: A Critical Introduction. New
   York, NY: Envoy Press, 1986.
Grawe, Paul H. "The Merchant of Venice." Comedy in Space, Time and the Imagination.

Chicago, IL: Nelson-Hall, 1983, 183-203.

Grawe, Paul H. "Twelfth Night." Comedy in Space, Time and the Imagination. Chicago, IL: Nelson-Hall, 1983, 97-112.

Gruber, William E. "Heroic Comedy and The Tempest." Classical and Modern Literature 1 (1981): 189-204.

Habicht, Werner. "The Wit-interludes and the Form of Pre-Shakespearean 'Romantic Comedy.' " Renaissance Drama 8 (1965): 73-88.

Hale, John K. " 'We'll Strive to Please You Every Day': Pleasure and Meaning in Shakespeare's Mature Comedies." Studies in English Literature 21 (1981): 241-255.

Hardison, O. B., Jr. "Logic Versus the Slovenly World in Shakespearean Comedy." Shakespeare Quarterly 31 (1980): 311-322.

Harrison, G. B. "Shakespearean Comedy." Stratford Papers on Shakespeare, 1962. Ed. B. W. Jackson. Toronto, Canada: Gage, 1963, 36-63.

Hart, John A. Dramatic Structure in Shakespeare's Romantic Comedies. Pittsburgh, PA: Carnegie-Mellon University, 1980.

Hartwig, Joan H. Parody as Structural Syntax: Shakespeare's Analogical Scene. Lincoln, NE: University of Nebraska Press, 1983.

Hartwig, Joan H. Shakespeare's Tragicomic Vision. New Orleans, LA: Louisiana State University Press, 1972.

Hassel, R. Chris, Jr. Faith and Folly in Shakespeare's Romantic Comedies. Athens, GA: Univ of Georgia Press, 1980.

Hawkes, Terence. "Comedy, Orality, and Duplicity: A Midsummer Night's Dream and Twelfth Night."." Shakespearean Comedy. Ed. Maurice Charney. New York, NY: Literary Forum, 1980, 155-163.

Hawkins, Sherman. "The Two Worlds of Shakespearean Comedy." Shakespeare Studies 3 (1967): 62-80.

Hayles, Nancy K. "Sexual Disguise in As You Like It and Twelfth Night." Shakespeare Studies 32 (1979): 63-72.

Hazlitt, William. Lectures on the English Comic Writers. London, England: J. M. Dent and Sons, 1910.

Hazlitt, William, Ed. Wit and Mirth--Volume 3: Shakespeare Jest Books. London, England: Willis and Sotheran, 1864.

Herbert, T. Walter. "The Villain and the Happy End of Shakespeare Comedy." Renaissance Papers 1966 (1967): 69-74.

Hill, R. F. "The Merchant of Venice and the Pattern of Romantic Comedy." Shakespeare Studies 28 (1975): 75-87.

Hinely, Jan Lawson. "Comic Scapegoats and the Falstaff of The Merry Wives of Windsor." Shakespeare Studies 15 (1982): 37-45.

Hogan, Robert. Comedy from Shakespeare to Sheridan. New York, NY: Associated University Press, 1986.

Homan, Sidney. "William Shakespeare." Encyclopedia of British Humorists, Volume II. Ed. Steven H. Gale, New York, NY: Garland, 1996, 938-950.

Hosley, Richard, ed. Essays on Shakespeare and Elizabethan Drama in Honor of Hardin Craig. Columbia, MO: Univ of Missouri Press, 1962.

Hotson, Leslie. Shakespeare's Motley. New York, NY: Oxford University Press, 1952.

Hoy, Cyrus. "Love's Labour's Lost and the Nature of Comedy." Shakespeare Quarterly 13 (1962): 31-40.

Huber, Edward. "The Range of Shakespeare's Comedy." Shakespeare Quarterly 15.2 (1964): 55-66.

Hunt, Leigh. "Shakespeare." Wit and Humour from the English Poets. New York, NY: Folcroft, 1972, 111-138.

Hunter, G. K., ed. All's Well that Ends Well. London, England: Methuen, 1959.

Hunter, G. K. William Shakespeare: The Late Comedies. New York, NY: Longmans Green, 1962.

Hunter, Robert Grams. Shakespeare and the Comedy of Forgiveness. New York, NY: Columbia Univ Press, 1965.

Hunter, Robert Grams. "Shakespeare's Comic Sense As It Strikes Us Today: Falstaff and the Protestant Ethic." Shakespeare, Pattern of Excelling Nature: Shakespeare Criticism in Honor of America's Bicentennial. Eds. David Bevington, and Jay L. Halio. Newark, DE: Univ of Delaware Press, 1978, 125-132.

Huston, J. Dennis. Sheakespeare's Comedies of Play. New York, NY: Columbia Univ Press, 1980.

Hyland, Peter. "Shakespeare's Heroines: Disguises in the Romantic Comedies." Ariel 9.2 (1978): 23-39.

Jackson, Margaret Y. " 'High Comedy' in Shakespeare." College Language Association Journal 10 (1966): 11-22.

Jacobs, Henry E. and Claudia D. Johnson. An Annotated Bibliography of Shakespearean Burlesques, Parodies, and Travesties. New York, NY: Garland, 1976.

Jagendorf, Zvi. "Patterns of Resolution in Shakespeare's Comedies." The Happy End of Comedy: Jonson, Molière, and Shakespeare. Newark, DE: University of Delaware Press, 1984, 111-161.

Jensen, Ejner J. Shakespeare and the Ends of Comedy. Indianapolis, IN: Indiana University Press, 1991.

Jessup, Katherine E. "Shakespeare's Comic Lovers." Shakespeare Association Bulletin 4 (1929): 104-116.

Kahn, Coppelia. Man's Estate: Masculine Identity in Shakespeare. Berkeley, CA: University of California Press, 1981.

Kaul, A. N. The Action of English Comedy: Studies in the Encounter of Abstraction and Experience from Shakespeare to Shaw. New Haven, CT: Yale Univ Press, 1970.

Kehler, Dorothea. "The Comedy of Errors as Problem Comedy." Rocky Mountain Review of Language and Literature 41.4 (1987): 229-241.

Kermode, Frank. "The Mature Comedies." The Early Shakespeare. Eds. John Russell Brown, and Bernard Harris. New York, NY: St. Martin's, 1961, 211-227.

Klingspon, Ron. "Play and Interplay in the Trial Scene of The Merchant of Venice." Thalia: Studies in Literary Humor 9.1 (1986): 36-47.

Knox, Bernard. "The Tempest and the Ancient Comic Tradition." English Stage Comedy: English Institute Essays 1954. Ed. W. K. Wimsatt, Jr. New York, NY: Columbia Univ Press, 1955, 52-73.

Kökeritz, Helge. Shakespeare's Pronunciation. New Haven, CT: Yale University Press, 1953.

Kott, Jan. "The Bottom Translation." Shakespeare: The Comedies: A collection of Critical Essays. Englewood, NJ: Prentice Hall, 1965, 73-85.

Krieger, Elliot. A Marxist Study of Shakespeare's Comedies. Totowa, NJ: Barnes, 1979.

Kreiger, Murray. "Measure for Measure and Elizabethan Comedy." Publications of the Modern Language Association 66 (1951): 775-784.

L'Estrange, Alfred Gu. "Shakespeare--Ben Jonson--Beaumont and Fletcher--The Wise Men of Gotham." History of English Humour. New York, NY: Burt Franklin, 1878, 250-270.

Labriola, Albert C. "Twelfth Night and the Comedy of Festive Abuse." Modern Language Studies 5.2 (1975): 5-20.

Langman, F. H. "Comedy and Saturnalia: The Case of Twelfth Night." Southern Review: Australia 7 (1974): 102-122.

Lascelles, Mary. "Shakespeare's Comic Insight." Proceedings of the British Academy 48 (1962): 171-186.

Lascelles, Mary. "Shakespeare's Pastoral Comedy." More Talking of Shakespeare. Ed. John Garrett. New York, NY: Theatre Arts. 1959, 70-86.

Latimer, Kathleen. "The Communal Action of The Winter's Tale." The Terrain of Comedy. Ed. Louise Cowan. Dallas, TX: Dallas Institute of Humanities, 1984, 125-142.

Lawrence, William Witherle. Shakespeare's Problem Comedies. London, England: Macmillan, 1931; Penguin, 1969.

Lederer, Richard. Crazy English. New York, NY: Pocket Books, 1989.

Leech, Clifford. "Shakespeare's Comic Dukes." Review of English Literature 5.2 (1964): 101-114.

Leech, Clifford. Twelfth Night and Shakespearean Comedy. Toronto, Canada: Univ of Toronto Press, 1965.

Leggatt, Alexander. Citizen Comedy in the Age of Shakespeare. Toronto, Canada: Univ of Toronto Press, 1973.

Leggatt, Alexander. Shakespeare's Comedy of Love. London, England: Methuen, 1973.

Leonard, Nancy S. "The Persons of the Comic in Shakespeare and Jonson." Research Opportunities in Renaissance Drama 22 (1979): 11-15.

Leonard, Nancy S. "Shakespeare and Jonson Again: The Comic Forms." Renaissance Drama NS10 (1979): 45-69.

Leonard, Nancy S. "Substitution in Shakespeare's Problem Comedies." English Literary Renaissance 9 (1979): 281-301.

Lever, J. W., ed. Shakespeare's "A Midsummer Night's Dream. Essex, England: Longman Group, 1992.

Levin, Harry. Playboys and Killjoys: An Essay on the Theory and Practice of Comedy. New York, NY: Oxford Univ Press, 1987.

Levith, Murray J. What's in Shakespeare's Names? New York, NY: The Shoe String Press, 1978.

Lewis, Allan. "Shakespeare's Open-Ended Comedy: A Challenge to Performance." Queen's Quarterly 78 (1971): 219-226.

Lin, Luna Y. H. "The Fool in King Lear Is a Fool." Unpublished Paper. Tempe, AZ: Arizona State University, 1991.

Logan, Thad Jenkins. "Twelfth Night: The Limits of Festivity." Studies in English Literature 22 (1982): 223-238.

Love, John M. " 'Though many of the rich are damn'd': Dark Comedy and Social Class in All's Well That Ends Well." Tulane Studies in Romance Languages and Literature 18 (1977): 517-527.

MacCary, W. Thomas. "The Comedy of Errors: A Different Kind of Comedy." New Literary History 9 (1978): 525-536.

MacCary, W. Thomas. Friends and Lovers: The Phenomenology of Desire in Shakespearean Comedy. New York, NY: Columbia University Press, 1985.

McCollom, William G. "The Role of Wit in Much Ado About Nothing." Twentieth Century Interpretations of Much Ado About Nothing. Ed. Walter C. Davis. Englewood Cliffs, NJ: Prentice-Hall, 1969.

MacDonald, Ronald R. William Shakespeare: The Comedies. New York, NY: MacMillan, 1992.

McDonald, Russ. "Skeptical Visions: Shakespeare's Tragedies and Jonson's Comedies." Shakespeare Studies 34 (1981): 131-147.

McFarland, Thomas. Shakespeare's Pastoral Comedy. Chapel Hill, NC: Univ of North Carolina Press, 1972.

McLaverty, J. "No Abuse: The Prince and Falstaff in the Tavern Scene of Henry IV."

Shakespeare Survey 34 (1981): 105-110.

McNamara, Peter L. "King Lear and Comic Acceptance." Erasmus Review 1 (1971): 95-105.

Madden, Amie. "Women in Shakespeare's Comedies: Using Wit and Wordplay as a Tool against Patriarchal Domination." Unpublished Paper. Tempe, AZ: Arizona State University, 1994.

Mahood, Molly. Shakespeare's Wordplay. London, England: Methuen, 1979.

Makaryk, Irene Rima. Comic Justice in Shakespeare's Comedies. Salzburg, Austria: Institut fur Anglisk und Amerikanistik, Universitat Salzburg, 1980.

Mares, F. H. "Viola and Other Transvestist Heroines in Shakespeare's Comedies." Stratford Papers 1965-67. Ed. B. A. W. Jackson. Hamilton, Canada: McMaster University, 1969, 96-109.

Markels, Julian. "Shakespeare's Confluence of Tragedy and Comedy: Twelfth Night and King Lear." Shakespeare Quarterly 15.2 (1965): 75-88.

Marshall, Cynthia. "Wrestling as Play and Game in As You Like It." Studies in English Literature (1993): 265.

Martin, William F. The Indissoluble Knot: "King Lear" as Ironic Drama. New York, NY: University Press of America, 1987.

Martz, William J. The Place of Measure for Measure in Shakespeare's Universe of Comedy. Lawrence, KS: Coronado, 1982.

Martz, William J. The Place of The Merchant of Venice in Shakespeare's Universe of Comedy. New York, NY: Revisionist, 1976.

Martz, William J. The Place of The Tempest in Shakespeare's Universe of Comedy. Lawrence, KS: Coronado, 1978.

Martz, William J. Shakespeare's Universe of Comedy. New York, NY: David Lewis, 1971.

Mehl, Dieter. "Chaucerian Comedy and Shakespearean Tragedy." Shakespeare-Jahrbuch 81 (1984): 111-127.

Mellamphy, Ninian. "Pantaloons and Zanies: Shakespeare's 'Apprenticeship' to Italian Professional Comedy Troupes." Shakespearean Comedy. Ed. Maurice Charney. New York, NY: Literary Forum, 1980, 141-151.

Miller, Ronald F. "King Lear and the Comic Form." Genre 8 (1975): 1-25.

Mindess, Harvey. "If Hamlet Had Had a Sense of Humour." It's a Funny Thing, Humour. Eds. Antony J. Chapman and Hugh C. Foot. New York: Pergamon Press, 1977, 3.

Montrose, Louis Adrian. " 'Folly, in wisdom hatch'd: The Exemplary Comedy of Love's Labour's Lost." Comparative Drama 11 (1977): 147-170.

Montrose, Louis Adrian. " 'The Place of a Brother' in As You Like It: Social Process and Comic Form." Shakespeare Quarterly 32 (1981): 28-54.

Moran, Jeffrey B. "Shakespeare's Starling." Journal of Irreproducible Results. 1988, 3-5.

Morene, Carrie. "Shakespeare's As You Like It: Love and Laughs Among the Trees." Unpublished Paper. Tempe, AZ: Arizona State University, Tempe, AZ, 1994.

Mueschke, Paul and Jeannette Fleisher. "Jonsonian Elements in the Comic Underplot of Twelfth Night." Publications of the Modern Language Association 48 (1933): 722-740.

Muir, Kenneth, ed. King Lear. London, England: Methuen, 1972.

Muir, Kenneth, ed. Shakespeare: The Comedies: A Collection of Critical Essays. Englewood Cliffs, NJ: Prentice-Hall, 1965.

Muir, Kenneth. Shakespeare's Comic Sequence. Totowa, NJ: Barnes and Noble, 1979.

Nahm, Milton C. "Falstaff, Incongruity and the Comic: An Essay in Aesthetic Criticism." Person 49 (1968): 289-321.

Neely, Carol Thomas. "Women and Men in Othello: What should such a fool / Do with so good a woman?' " The Woman's part: Feminist Criticism of Shakespeare. Ed.

Carolyn Ruth Swift Lenz, Gayle Greene and Carol Thomas Neely. Chicago, IL: University of Illinois Press, 1983, 211-239.

Nelson, Thomas Allen. Shakespeare's Comic Theory: A Study of Art and Artifice in the Last Plays. The Hague, Netherlands: Mouton, 1972.

Nelson, Timothy G. A. "The Fool as Clergyman (and Vice-Versa): An Essay on Shakespearian Comedy." Jonson and Shakespeare. Ed. Ian Donaldson. London, England: Macmillan, 1983, 1-17.

Nelson, Timothy G. A. "The Rotten Orange: Fears of Marriage in Comedy from Shakespeare to Congreve." Southern Review--Australia 8 (1975): 205-226.

Nevo, Ruth. Comic Transformations in Shakespeare. London, England: Methuen, 1980.

Nevo, Ruth. "Shakespeare's Comic Remedies." Shakespearean Comedy. Ed. Maurice Charney. New York, NY: Literary Forum, 1980, 3-15.

Nichols, Mary Pollingue. "The Winter's Tale: The Triumph of Comedy over Tragedy." Interpretation: A Journal of Political Philosophy 9 (1981): 169-190.

Novy, Marianne L. " 'And You Smile Not, He's Gagged': Mutuality in Shakespearean Comedy." Philological Quarterly 55 (1976): 178-194.

Novy, Marianne L. "Patriarchy and Play in The Taming of the Shrew." Modern Critical Interpretations: The Taming of the Shrew. Ed. Harold Bloom. New York, NY: Chelsea House, 1988, 13-27.

Nugent, S. Georgia. "Ancient Theories of Comedy: The Treatises of Evanthius and Donatus." Shakespearean Comedy. Ed. Maurice Charney. New York, NY: Literary Forum, 1980, 259-280.

Ornstein, Robert. Discussions of Shakespeare's Problem Comedies. New York, NY: D. C. Heath, 1961.

Ornstein, Robert. "The Human Comedy: Measure for Measure." University of Kansas City Review 24 (1957): 15-22.

Ornstein, Robert. Shakespeare's Comedies: From Roman Farce to Romantic Mystery. Newark, DE: University of Delaware Press, 1986.

Ornstein, Robert. "Shakespearian and Jonsonian Comedy." Shakespeare Survey 22 (1969): 43-46.

Owen, Charles A., Jr. "Comic Awareness, Style, and Dramatic Technique in Much Ado about Nothing." Boston University Studies in English 5 (1961): 193-207.

Oz, Avraham. "The Doubling of Parts in Shakespearean Comedy: Some Questions of Theory and Practice." Shakespearean Comedy. Ed. Maurice Charney. New York, NY: Literary Forum, 1980, 175-182.

Palmer, John. Comic Characters of Shakespeare. London, England: Macmillan, 1946.

Park, Clara Claiborne. "As We Like It: How a Girl Can Be Smart and Still Popular." The Woman's Part: Feminist Criticism of Shakespeare. Eds. Carolyn Ruth Swift Lenz, Gayle Greene, and Carol Thomas Neely. Chicago, IL: University of Illinois Press, 1983, 100-116.

Parrott, Thomas M. Shakespearean Comedy. New York, NY: Russell and Russell, 1946.

Partee, Morris Henry. "The Comic Unity of Measure for Measure." Genre 6 (1973): 274-297.

Partee, Morris Henry. "The Divine Comedy of King Lear." Genre 4 (1971): 60-75.

Partridge, Eric. Shakespeare's Bawdy. London, England: Routledge, and Kegan Paul, 1968.

Peck, Russell A. "Edgar's Pilgrimage: High Comedy in King Lear." Studies in English Literature 7 (1967): 219-237.

Peter, John. Complaint and Satire in Early English Literature. Oxford, England: The Clarendon Press, 1956.

Peterson, Douglas L. "The Tempest and Ideal Comedy." Shakespearean Comedy. Ed. Maurice Charney. New York, NY: Literary Forum, 1980, 99-110.

Pfordresher, John. "On Teaching Jokes in the High School Classroom." WHIMSY 1 (1983): 202-204.

Philias, Peter G. "Comic Truth in Shakespeare and Jonson." South Atlantic Quarterly 62 (1963): 78-91.

Philias, Peter G. Shakespeare's Romantic Comedies: The Development of Their Form and Meaning. Chapel Hill, NC: Univ of North Carolina Press, 1966.

Price, Joseph G. The Unfortunate Comedy: A Study of All's Well That Ends Well and Its Critics. Toronto, Canada: Univ of Toronto Press, 1968.

Priestley, J. B. The English Comic Character. New York, NY: Dodd, Mead, and Co., 1925.

Priestley, J. B. English Humour. New York, NY: Stein and Day, 1976.

Prior, Moody E. "Comic Theory and the Rejection of Falstaff." Shakespeare Studies 9 (1976): 159-171.

Pulsifer, Marc. "Falstaff: Shakespeare's Balance between Vice and Charm." Unpublished Paper. Tempe, AZ: Arizona State University, 1995.

Putney, Rufus. "Sir John Falstaff: Comic Hero." Theatre Annual 15 (1957-58): 28-34.

Rayner, Alice. "Shakespeare's Poesis: Use and Delight in Utopia." Comic Persuasion: Moral Structures in British Comedy from Shakespeare to Stoppard. Berkely, CA: University of California Press, 1987, 24-40.

Richmond, Hugh M. Shakespeare's Sexual Comedy: A Mirror for Lovers. New York, NY: The Bobbs-Merrill Co., 1971.

Riemer, A. P. Antic Fables: Patterns of Evasion in Shakespeare's Comedies. New York, NY: St. Martin's, 1980.

Roberts, Jeanne Addison. "Animals as Agents of Revelation: The Horizontalizing of the Chain of Being in Shakespeare's Comedies." Shakespearean Comedy. Ed. Maurice Charney. New York, NY: Literary Forum, 1980, 79-96.

Roberts, Jeanne Addison. Shakespeare's English Comedy: The Merry Wives of Windsor in Context. Lincoln, NE: Univ of Nebraska Press, 1979.

Roberts, Susan. "Puns in Romeo and Juliet." Unpublished Paper. Tempe, AZ: Arizona State University, 1988.

Rosador, K. Tetzei von. "Plotting the Early Comedies: The Comedy of Errors, Love's Labour's Lost, The Two Gentlemen of Verona." Shakespeare Studies 37 (1984): 13-23.

Rossiter, A. P. Modern Critical Views: William Shakespeare's Comedies and Romances. New York, NY: Chelsea House, 1986.

Rubenstein, Frankie. Sexual Puns in Shakespeare. London, England: MacMillan, 1984.

Rukkila, Elyse. "Puns in Shakespeare." Unpublished Paper. Tempe, AZ: Arizona State University, 1993.

Sale, Roger. "The Comic Mode of Measure for Measure." Shakespeare Quarterly 19 (1968): 55-61.

Salinger, Leo. Shakespeare and the Tradition of Comedy. Cambridge, England: Cambridge Univ Press, 1974.

Sanders, Norman. "The Comedy of Greene and Shakespeare." The Early Shakespeare. Eds. John Russell Brown and Bernard Harris. New York, NY: St. Martin's, 1961, 35-53.

Schmerl, Rudolf B. "Comedy and the Manipulation of Moral Distance: Falstaff and Shylock." Bucknell Review 10 (1961): 128-137.

Schoenbaum, Marilyn. A Shakespeare Merriment. New York, NY: Garland, 1988.

Schwartz, Elias. "Twelfth Night and the Meaning of Shakespearean Comedy." College English 28 (1967): 508-514.

Schwartz, Helen J. "The Comic Scenes in Henry V." Hebrew University Studies in Literature 4 (1976): 18-26.

Scott, William O. The God of Arts: Ruling Ideas in Shakespeare's Comedies. Lawrence,

KS: Univ of Kansas, 1977.

Scoufos, Alice Lyle. Shakespeare's Typological Satire. Athens, OH: Ohio University Press, 1979.

Sease, Windee. "Shakespeare's Fools: Custom-Tailored Morality." Unpublished Paper. Tempe, AZ: Arizona State University, 1992.

Sen Gupta, S. C. Shakespearean Comedy. London, England: Oxford Univ Press, 1950.

Shaaber, M. A. "The Comic View of Life in Shakespeare's Comedies." The Drama of the Renaissance: Essays for Leicester Bradner. Ed. Elmer M. Blistein. Providence, RI: Brown Univ Press, 1970, 165-178.

Shakespeare, William The Complete Works of William Shakespeare. New York, NY: Avenel Books, 1975.

Shakespeare, William Much Ado about Nothing. Oxford, England: Clarendon Press, 1993.

Shaw, Catherine M. "The Conscious Art of The Comedy of Errors." Shakespearean Comedy. Ed. Maurice Charney. New York, NY: Literary Forum, 1980, 17-28.

Sheriff, William E. "The Grotesque Comedy of Richard III." Studies in the Literary Imagination 5.1 (1972): 51-64.

Shickman, Allen R. "The Fool's Mirror in King Lear." English Literary Renaissance 21.1 (1991): 75-86.

Sider, John Wm. "The Serious Elements of Shakespeare's Comedies." Shakespeare Quarterly 24 (1973): 1-11.

Siegel, Paul N. "Malvolio: Comic Puritan Automaton." Shakespearean Comedy. Ed. Maurice Charney. New York, NY: Literary Forum, 1980, 217-230.

Siemon, James Edward. "The Canker Within: Some Observations on the Role of the Villain in Three Shakespearean Comedies." Shakespeare Quarterly 23 (1972): 435-443.

Silverman, J. M. "Two Types of Comedy in All's Well That Ends Well." Shakespeare Quarterly 24 (1973): 25-34.

Simonds, Peggy Munoz. "Overlooked Sources of the Bed Trick." Shakespeare Quarterly 34 (1983): 433-434.

Smidt, Kristian. Unconformities in Shakespeare's Early Comedies. New York, NY: St. Martin's, 1986.

Smidt, Kristian. Unconformities in Shakespeare's Later Comedies. London, England: MacMillan, 1993.

Smith, J. Percy. "Imaginary Forces and the Ways of Comedy." Stratford Papers 1968-69. Ed. B. A. W. Jackson. Hamilton, Canada: McMaster University, 1972, 1-20.

Smith, Tom. As You Like It. Omaha, NE: Cliff Notes, 1981.

Snyder, Susan. The Comic Matrix of Shakespeare's Comedies. Princeton, NJ: Princeton University Press, 1979.

Snyder, Susan. The Comic Matrix of Shakespeare's Tragedies: Romeo and Juliet, Hamlet, Othello, and King Lear. Princeton, NJ: Princeton Univ Press, 1979.

Somerset, J. A. B. "Shakespeare's Great State of Fools, 1599-1607." Mirror up to Shakespeare. Ed. J. C. Gray. Toronto, Canada: University of Toronto Press, 1984, 68-81.

Spevack, Marvin. "Shakespeare's Early Use of Wordplay: Love's Labor's Lost." Festschrift für Edgar Mertner. Eds. Bernard Fabian and Ulrich Suerbaum. Munich, Germany: Wilhelm Fink, 1969, 157-168.

Spivack, Charlotte. The Comedy of Evil on Shakespeare's Stage. Rutherford, NJ: Fairleigh Dickinson Univ Press, 1978.

Stockholder, Katherine. "The Multiple Genres of King Lear: Breaking the Archetypes." Bucknell Review 16.1 (1968): 40-63.

Stoll, Elmer Edgar. "The Comic Method." Shakespeare Studies, Historical and Comparative in Method. New York, NY: Macmillan, 1927, 147-186.

Swinden, Patrick. An Introduction to Shakespeare's Comedies. New York, NY: Barnes,
    1973.
Thaler, Alwin. "Shakespeare and the Unhappy Happy Ending." Publications of the Modern
    Language Association 42 (1927): 736-761.
Thompson, Karl F. "Shakespeare's Romantic Comedies." Publications of the Modern
    Language Association 67 (1952): 1079-1093.
Thorndike, Ashley H. "Shakespeare: The Earlier Comedies." English Comedy. New York,
    NY: Macmillan, 1929. 95-119.
Thorndike, Ashley H. "Shakespeare: The Later Comedies." English Comedy. New York,
    NY: Macmillan, 1929. 120-139.
Tillyard, E. M. W. The Nature of Comedy and Shakespeare. London, England: Oxford
    Univ Press, 1958.
Tillyard, E. M. W. Shakespeare's Early Comedies. New York, NY: Barnes and Noble,
    1965.
Traugott, John. "Creating a Rational Rinaldo: A Study in the Mixture of the Genres of
    Comedy and Romance in Much Ado about Nothing." Genre 15 (1982): 157-181.
Traversi, Derek. Shakespeare: The Early Comedies. London, England: Longmans, Green,
    and Co., 1960.
Tromly, F. B. "Twelfth Night: Folly's Talents and the Ethics of Shakespearean Comedy."
    Mosaic 7.3 (1974): 53-68.
Trousdale, Marion. "Semiotics and Shakespeare's Comedies." Shakespearean Comedy. Ed.
    Maurice Charney. New York, NY: Literary Forum, 1980, 245-255.
Tucker, Kenneth. "The Politics of Tragicomedy: Shakespeare and After." The Shakespeare
    Newsletter 44.2 (Summer, 1994): 27, 37.
Turell, Maite. "Some Humorous Speech-Acts in Twelfth Night." Literary and Linguistic
    Aspects of Humour. Barcelona, Spain: University of Barcelona, 1984, 251-256.
Tuverson, Andrea. "Humor in Shakespeare's Much Ado about Nothing." Unpublished
    Paper. Tempe, AZ: Arizona State University, 1995.
Uphaus, Robert W. "The 'Comic' Mode of The Winter's Tale." Genre 3 (1970): 40-54.
Vaughn, Jack A. Shakespeare's Comedies New York, NY: Frederick Ungar, 1980.
Walker, Marshall. "Shakespeare's Comedy (or Much Ado about Bergson)." Interpretations
    3 (1971): 1-12.
Watson, Donald G. "The Dark Comedy of Shakespeare's Henry VI Plays." Thalia: Studies
    in Literary Humor 1.2, 11-21.
Watts, Robert A. "The Comic Scenes in Othello." Shakespeare Quarterly 19 (1968): 349-
    354.
Weil, Herbert. Discussions of Shakespare's Romantic Comedy. New York, NY: D. C.
    Heath, 1966.
Weiss, John. Wit, Humor, and Shakespeare. Boston, MA: Roberts Brothers, 1889.
Wells, Stanley. "Happy Endings in Shakespeare." Shakespeare-Jahrbuch 102 (1966): 103-
    123.
West, Gilian. "Falstaff's Punning." English Studies 69 (1988): 541-558.
Westlund, Joseph. Shakespeare's Reparative Comedies: A Psychoanalytic View of the
    Middle Plays. Chicago, IL: Univ of Chicago Press, 1984.
Wheeler, Richard P. Shakespeare's Development and the Problem Comedies: Turn and
    Counter-Turn. Berkeley, CA: Univ of California Press, 1981.
Whilcher, Robert. "The Art of the Comic Dialogue in Three Plays by Shakespeare."
    Shakespeare Survey 35 (1982): 87-100.
Whitaker, Virgil K. "Philosophy and Romance in Shakespeare's 'Problem' Comedies." The
    Seventeenth Century. Stanford, CA: Stanford Univ Press, 1951, 339-354.
Whitcher, Robert. "The Art of the Comic Dialogue in Three Plays by Shakespeare."

Shakespeare Studies 35 (1982): 87-100.

White, Kenneth Steele. "Savage Comedy Since King Ubu: A Tangent to 'The Absurd.' "
New York, NY: University Press of America, 1977.

Williams, Gwyn. "The Comedy of Errors Rescued from Tragedy." Review of English
Literature 5.4 (1964): 63-71.

Wilson, Elkin C. Shakespeare, Santayana, and the Comic. Birmingham, AL: University of
Alabama Press, 1973.

Wilson, John Dover. The Fortunes of Falstaff. Cambridge, England: Cambridge University
Press, 1964.

Wilson, John Dover. Shakespeare's Happy Comedies. Evanston, IL: Northwestern
University Press, 1962.

Woodford, Trevor. "Shakespeare's Comic Characters." Unpublished Paper. Tempe, AZ:
Arizona State University, 1994.

John Davies of Hereford (c1565-1618)

In October of 1610 John Davies of Hereford published his The Scourge of Folly,
Consisting of Satyricall Epigramms, and Others in Honor of Many Noble and Worthy
Persons of our Land. Together with a Pleasant (though Discordant) Descant upon most
English Proverbs: and Others (Alden 174). This is a satire in the loose sense of the word.
In fact, John Davies of Hereford is more of an epigramist than a satirist, since his attitude
toward life is lighter and less pessimistic than that of most satirists. Nevertheless, this work
is a series of satirical verses in epigramatic form. Davies wrote in decasyllabic couplets
such as the following:

> Papers Complaint, compiled in ruthfull Rimes
> Against the Paper-spoylers of these Times.... (Alden 175)

In total there are 292 epigrams in The Scourge of Folly targeting such subjects as tobacco,
lust, superstition, usury, bad poetry, and the granting of favors. As an example of his
approach, consider a verse comparing alchemists with satirists. He says that the alchemist
is trying to make lead into silver or gold, while the satirist is trying to make a beast into
a man. In both cases, "By heat of strange Fires, / They seeke their desires" (Alden 175).

John Davies of Hereford Bibliography

Alden, Raymond MacDonald. "John Davies of Hereford." The Rise of Formal Satire in
England under Classical Influence. New York, NY: Archon, 1961, 174-175.

William Kempe (c1565-c1603)

William Kempe was Shakespeare's first clown, and it was Kempe who first
developed the roles of Costard in Love's Labour's Lost, of Launce in The Two Gentlemen
of Verona, of Peter in Romeo and Juliet, of Launcelot Gobbo in The Merchant of Venice,
of Dogberry in Much Ado about Nothing, of Bottom in A Midsummer Night's Dream, and
Kempe may have developed the role of Falstaff as well. In his time, he was famous as a
dancer and a comic writer. His specialties were "jigs" and "merriments," two different
types of short musical comic entertainments that were very popular in Elizabethan England
(Timpane 621). People hummed Kempe's tunes throughout London, and in 1598 Edward
Guilpin wrote that anywhere in London a person went, there would be "whores, belles,
bawdes, and sergeants" filthily chanting his jigs (Timpane 622).

"Kemps Applauded Merriments of the Men of Goteham, in Receiving the King into Goteham" (1992) is the only piece of extant comic writing that is almost certainly written by William Kempe. Nevertheless, there are very many anonymous jigs from the period which were probably written by Kempe as well (Timpane 624). Kempe may also have helped to write A Knack to Know a Knave (1592).

In February of 1600, Kempe accepted a three-for-one wager that he would not be able to dance a morris dance all the way from London to Norwich. With his drummer, and two servants, and the fans and camp followers who went with him, Kempe claimed to have completed the dance in nine days, but in fact the dance took twenty-three days, because Kempe didn't count the days off for bad weather, muddy roads, and fatigue. It is true that Kempe spent only nine days on the road, all of the time dancing and leaping, and his adventures are recorded both in his own writings and in those of other local authors (Timpane 622). The most straight-forward account of the event is entitled Kemp's Nine Daies Wonder, and it describes Kempe as being mobbed all along the way. At one point the crowds became so intense that he had to lock himself in his inn and wave out of his window rather than perform his dance. During the dance, there were many people who couldn't resist dancing along, and on a number of occasions, Kempe took them on in good-natured competitions. Of course Kempe always won (Timpane 623).

William Kempe Bibliography

Timpane, John. William Kempe, Kemp, or Kempt." Encyclopedia of British Humorists,
      Volume I. Ed. Steven H. Gale, New York, NY: Garland, 1996, 621-624.

Thomas Nashe (1567-1601)

Mary Free says that Thomas Nashe's prose style was influenced by Robert Greene and other "University Wits. She also says that his writing style has become a hallmark for invective and satire (Free 782).

Nashe had difficulty writing satire because his feelings were more than just critical--they were filled with invective and personal abuse. His animosity for Gabriel Harvey was so great that in 1599 the Archbishop of Canterbury and Bishop of London issued an order that his books be "taken wheresoever they be found, and that none of the said books be ever printed hereafter" (L'Estrange 240-241). Nevertheless, Nashe had a humorous side as well. He enjoyed coining long and almost unintelligible words, and when someone translated his "Piers Penniless" into more readable prose, he attacked the translator wrathfully, saying that his writing had become "macaronical language" (L'Estrange 241). Invective was a common device for Nashe, and in his "Lenten Stuffe or Praise of the Red Herring," he called those who hated Homer during his life-time "dull-pated pennifathers," continuing that "those grey-beard huddle-duddles and crusty cum-twangs were strooke with stinging remorse of their miserable euchonisme and sundgery" (L'Estrange 241).

Louis Cazamian points out that Nashe was fond of the writings of François Rabelais, and much of Nashe's work echoes that of Rabelais, for Rabelais and Nashe had what Cazamian called an "affinity of temper" (167). Nashe was a master of biting, picturesque invective, but Cazamian feels that he lacked certain qualities for being a good humorist--the mental discipline that allows balance, and the cool judgement required to distance the author from the subject. Nevertheless, Nashe possessed the other requisites for humor, for he was able to present rich, concrete vivid pictures of things as they were. He also had an ability at comic invention, a verve, a mother wit, and an impressive command of some of the raciest words and phrases in the English language (Cazamian 168).

In the "Preface" to Menaphon Camillas Alarum to Slumbering Euphues (1589), Nashe blends satire, invective and irony with praise. Mary Free considers this "Preface" to be "a model of the vituperation that characterizes the pamphlet wars of the era. Nashe's invectives especially target university-educated "poetasters" for their use of "inkhorn" and "tapsterly" expressions. He uses parody to satirize hexameral verse, and he asks the reader to judge a piece of writing that describes a tempest by saying that the "heavens vault to rebounde, with rounce robble hobble / Of ruffe raffe roaring, with thwick thwack thurlery bouncing" (Free 782).

Thomas Nashe dedicated An Almond for a Parrat, or Cuthberg Curryknaues almes. Fit for the Knaue Martin (1589) to William Kempe, whom he describes as "Jest-monger and Vice-gerent generall to the Ghost of Dicke Tarleton" (Timpane 622).

All of Nashe's books are medleys. In The Unfortunate Traveller. Or, the Life of Jacke Wilton (1594), the only picaresque element is the freedom with which the story passes from one country, and from one theme, to another (Cazamian 168). The comedy in The Unfortunate Traveller is violent comedy. In an article entitled "The Comedy of Violence in Nashe's The Unfortunate Traveller," Charles Larson outlines the basic plot. A particular house in sixteenth-century Rome is robbed; the master of the house is stabbed; and his wife is brutally raped. These crimes are punished in curious ways. Esdras of Granada, the principal villain, is shot through the mouth by Cutwolfe, another small-time criminal. Cutwolfe in turn is publicly executed by a tribunal in Bologna. There are some who fail to see the humor potential in this plot; however Nashe's admirers see many instances of wit and comic invention in The Unfortunate Traveller, and Charles Larson states in his article that the book is "one of the most interesting pieces of comic prose fiction of the Elizabethan age" (Larson 15). Nashe uses violence in the story to "flout taboo and to demand of his readers the most wide-ranging explorations of their own perceptions of the comic." But violent comedy is not the only type of humor in this book. Larson concludes that the comedy of violence is not Nashe's only, or even his main, comic interest (Larson 27). Mary Free considers The Unfortunate Traveller to be Nashe's best known work. She also says that the humor in this work derives from Wilton's cavalier attitude and from his wit. Here Nashe is satirizing war by calling it a "wonderful spectacle" filled with people "wallowing in their gore," and which results in "a peace concluded" (Free 784). In The Unfortunate Traveller, Jack's countrymen question why Jack is a traveller, since travel brings nothing but evil. It is by travelling that the traveller learns that "the Italians are bloody minded, the French false, the Spanish braggarts, the Dutch and Danes drunkards" (Free 784).

In addition to The Unfortunate Traveller, Nashe also wrote The Anatomy of Absurdity: Contayning a Breefe Confutation of the Slender Imputed Prayses to Feminine Perfection (1589), the humor of which is mainly in the sauciness or in the coarseness of the gibes. The Anatomie of Absurditie shows the beginnings of Nashe's satiric style. The first part of this work is a satire on the failings of womankind (Free 782). Nashe's Pierce Pennilesse his Supplication to the Divell (1592) contains the humor of paradox, in that Elizabethan society often rewards outward appearances rather than inward worth. Nashe wrote this book with a twinkle in his eye that demonstrated that he was aware of the paradox he was developing (Cazamian 169). Pierce Penilesse employs satire, invective, alliteration, wit, and self-mockery as it transcends topical issues. Nashe laments the writers fate as having to spend "many years in studying how to live...without money." Nashe satirizes the Spaniards, the Italians, the French, and the Danes for their pride. This is the work in which Nashe fired his first salvo in the Harvey-Nashe debate. He calls Richard Harvey a "great baboon," and a "Pygmy braggart," and concludes that he is a "pamphleteer of nothing." When Pierce Penilesse first appeared, Gabriel Harvey was busy writing his Four Letters, an attack on Greene, but Nashe's work was so strong that is incensed Harvey into devoting the third letter to Nashe. Nashe in turn retaliated with <u>Strange Newes, of the</u> <u>Intercepting Certaine Letters</u> (1592), in which he begins his attack of Harvey as early as the "Epistle Dedicatory," where he talks about "a Doctor and his fart that have kept a foul stinking stir in Paul's churchyard." Because Harvey had condemned Greene, Nashe calls Harvey "a wisp, a wisp, a wisp, rip, rip, you kitchenstuff wrangler" (Free 783).

According to Mary Free, <u>A Pleasant Comedie, called Summers Last Will and</u> <u>Testament</u> (1600) is a dramatic comedy in which Bacchus knights Will as "Sir Robert Tosspot." In this piece, Nashe satirizes the Dutch by having Will say that his clothes are so drenched with beer than any "Dutchman within twenty miles...[could] claim kindred of him (Free 783).

Nashe's linguistic battle with Harvey continues in <u>Haue with You to Saffron-</u> <u>Walden. Or, Gabriel Harveys Hunt is Up</u> (1596). This is a work which uses invective to achieve its comic effect. The Harveys are described as "two blockheads, two blunderkins, having their brains stuffed with nought but balderdash" (Free 784). Nashe's <u>Nashes Lenten</u> <u>Stuffe, Containing, the Description of Great Yarmouth with a New Play of the Praises of</u> <u>the Red Herring</u> (1599) is described by Mary Free as a "mock encomium in praise of the red herring." It is also a parodic history of "The Isle of Dogs" (Free 784). Nashe was a staunch loyalist to English language, styles, and customs. He criticized <u>Grobianus</u> because it displayed the wit of German students. He railed against Italian vices, and criticized Euphuistic writing because it borrowed from the classics. His mindset was solidly rooted in English values (Cazamian 170).

In "Thomas Nashe and the Functional Grotesque in Elizabethan Prose Fiction" Barbara Mallard shows the grotesque to be one of the modes of Elizabethan expression, as she examines the relationship between the grotesque and the picaresque, and shows how the grotesque becomes the "center of the picaresque" (Timpane 786). In "Thomas Nashe and the Satirical Stance" Stanley Wells argues that the feud, which was responsible for some of Nashe's best writing, was the result of his personal feelings. Wells also argues that Nashe had the ability to produce superior satire because of his balance between the particular and the general (Timpane 786).

Thomas Nashe Bibliography

Cazamian, Louis. "Nashe." <u>The Development of English Humor</u>. Durham, NC: Duke
    University Press, 1952, 167-171.
Free, Mary. "Thomas Nashe." <u>Encyclopedia of British Humorists, Volume II</u>. Ed. Steven
    H. Gale, New York, NY: Garland, 1996, 781-786.
L'Estrange, Alfred Gu. "Robert Greene--Friar Bacon's Demons--The 'Looking Glasse'--
    Nashe and Harvey." <u>History of English Humour</u>. New York, NY: Burt Franklin,
    1878, 231-242.
Larson, Charles. "The Comedy of Violence in Nashe's <u>The Unfortunate Traveller</u>." <u>Cahiers</u>
    <u>Elisabéthains</u> 8 (1976): 15-29.
Mallard, Barbara. "Thomas Nashe and the Functional Grotesque in Elizabethan Prose
    Fiction." <u>Studies in Short Fiction</u> 15.1 (1978): 39-48.
Timpane, John. William Kempe, Kemp, or Kempt." <u>Encyclopedia of British Humorists,</u>
    <u>Volume I</u>. Ed. Steven H. Gale, New York, NY: Garland, 1996, 621-624.
Wells, Stanley. "Thomas Nashe and the Satirical Stance." <u>Cahiers Elizabethans</u> 9 (1976):
    1-7.

Robert Armin (c1569-c1616)

Robert Armin played many of Shakespeare's clowns, but he probably played many other clowns as well. He may very well have played the role of Sommers, Henry VIII's clown in Samuel Rowley's <u>When You See Me, You Know Me</u> (1604). In this play, Sommers is an aggressive, bawdy fool who makes insightful observations about the serious action, but the part also requires someone talented in physical humor and extemporizing (Timpane 40).

Robert Armin wrote <u>Foole upon Foole, or, Sixe Sorts of Sottes</u> (1600) and H. F. Lippincott says that this book shows Armin to have been more of a "natural" fool, numbskull, or village idiot than the "artificial" fool who tells wise and witty things in the guise of a clown (Timpane 39). Robert Armin was probably also the compiler of <u>Tarlton's Jests</u> (1616), which contains the famous story in which Dick Tarlton, the greatest clown in England "made Armin his adopted sonne, to succeed him" (Timpane 38). Here it says that Tarlton prophesies that Armin would "enjoy my clownes sute after me." It must be noted, however, that such statements can only be found in <u>Tarlton's Jests</u>, and that Armin is the probably compiler of this book. So Armin may well have written it as a self advertisement. In support of this argument is the statement in the book that "men may see [Armin] at the Globe." What is incongruous about this statement is that it appears in a book twelve years after Tarlton had died, and would not have been true while Tarlton was alive (Timpane 39).

Robert Armin Bibliography

Lippincott, H. F. ed. <u>A Shakespeare Jestbook. Robert Armin's "Foole upon Foole."</u> Salzburg, Austria: Salzburg Press, 1973.
Timpane, John. "Robert Armin." <u>Encyclopedia of British Humorists, Volume I</u>. Ed. Steven H. Gale, New York, NY: Garland, 1996, 38-41.

5

Humor in Seventeenth-Century British Literature

SEVENTEENTH CENTURY MONARCHS OF GREAT BRITAIN:

James I (VI of Scotland)	Stuart	1603-1625
Charles I	Stuart	1625-1649
Commonwealth	None	1649-1653
Oliver Cromwell	None	1653-1659
Charles II (the Merry Monarch)	Stuart	1660-1685
James II	Stuart	1685-1688
William III and Mary	Stuart	1689-1702

The seventeenth century was the time of Bacon, Bernini, Calderón, Cervantes, Corneille, Cromwell, Descartes, Donne, Dryden, Galileo, Herbert, Hobbes, Jonson, Kepler, Locke, Lope de Vega, Marvell, Milton, Molière, Newton, Purcell, Racine, Rembrandt, Richelieu, Rubens, Shakespeare, Van Dyck, Vermeer, and Wren. Alfred North Whitehead called the seventeenth century the "century of genius." "In these hundred years, England had her greatest periods of prose, comedy, and perhaps of lyric verse" (Holland 45). The comedies of the seventeenth century were especially notable. These comedies used disguise to probe some of the most basic assumptions of the seventeenth century, and in fact of all ages. In the seventeenth century, disguise developed cosmic significance, and became a fundamental element in ethical and metaphysical thought, and this was mainly because of the development of a new sense of science. The writers of comedies were connected in various ways to the newly formed Royal Scientific Society, and they were therefore exposed to this new way of looking at the world (Holland 45). Etherege, Wycherley, and Congreve used disguise, affectation, dissimulation, pretence, and hypocrisy on the stage, and all of this, like seventeenth-century physics, was a kind of cosmic disguise. "Their seventeenth-century metaphysic gave them a stage beyond their stage. And if Restoration comedy is merely a 'passionate dance-figure, or an arabesque of words and repartées,' as some critics say, the pattern of the dance is the metaphysic of modern science" (Holland 63).

Much of the satire of the early seventeenth century lacked subtlety and restraint:
> In the seventeenth century it [literary satire] was very unfavourable; for the journalists and pamphleteers had not yet learnt the lesson that a certain command of temper is necessary in order to be effective. Even so great a

man as Milton suffers himself to be abusive where a higher literary art
would have made him satirical. (Walker 180)

So strongly did the targets feel the sting of the invectives that were directed against them
that towards the end of the reign of King James I, satire was censored to the extent that it
virtually ceased to be written during that time. This was especially true of prose satire, but
it was somewhat true of verse satire as well. The satires that were written during this
period were not of good quality:

> In spite of the censorship, a great mass of material was produced in the
> shape of pamphlets and journals--Corantos, Mercuries, Newsletters and what
> not--only a small portion of it deserves to rank as literature at all, and a still
> smaller fraction as satire. (Walker 180)

Later in the seventeenth century the satire became much more sophisticated. Much
of the political satire of that period resulted from the hot debates and intrusive styles of
politicians of the day. What developed most during this period is "character satire." In his
Every Man Out of His Humour, Ben Jonson wrote some very effective satirical character
sketches. This was followed by the satirical character sketches in Joseph Hall's Characters
of Virtues and Vices, Sir Thomas Overbury's Characters, John Earle's Micro-cosmographie;
or, a Peece of the World Discovered; in Essays and Characters, and Samuel Butler's
Hudibras, which is considered by Raymond Alden to be the best example of the genre
(Alden 244-245). In addition to the excellent character satires, the seventeenth century also
had many witty treatments of contemporary events, and in fact, Alden sees such treatments
to be a revival of certain elements of medieval satire. The late seventeenth century was the
Age of Dryden, an age in which "the greatest poet in England could show his strength in
satire" (Alden 245).

King James I not only kept two clowns in his court for his own amusement, but he
also very much appreciated the humor of Ben Jonson, whom he made director of the Court
Masques. Sometimes the humor of King James I was filled with indignation and
didacticism. In his "Counterblaste to Tobacco" he observes that the custom of smoking
came from the American Indians, and then continues, "And now, good countreymen let us
(I pray you) consider what honour or policy can move us to imitate the barbarous and
beastly maneres of the wilde, Godlesse and slavish Indians.... Why doe wee not as well
imitate them in walking naked as they doe? in preferring glasses, feathers, and such toyes
to gold and precious stones, as they doe?" (L'Estrange 282-283).

In talking about the love which James I had of jesting, Joseph Addison observed
that

> The age in which the pun chiefly flourished was in the reign of King James
> the First. That learned monarch was himself a tolerable punster, and made
> very few bishops or privy-councillors that had not some time or other
> signalized themselves by a clinch or a conundrum. It was therefore in this
> age that the pun appeared with pomp and dignity. (L'Estrange 284)

Before James I the pun had been admitted into merry speeches and ludicrous compositions,
but during his reign it was "delivered with great gravity from the pulpit, or pronounced in
the most solemn manner at the council-table" (L'Estrange 284).

Verbal humor continued to be admired during the reign of Charles I, and there was
a jester named Archee in Charles's court. Archee dressed in motley clothes, and told
homely truths to his master. On one occasion he was ordered by the King to say grace,
since the chaplain was away, and Archee spoke as follows: "All glory be to God on high,
and little Laud to the devil." On hearing this, the courtiers all smiled, because it was a
reflection on the Archbishop of Canterbury, who was a little man. The King told Archee
that he was going to tell Laud, and asked Archee what he would do then. Archee
responded, "Oh! I will hide me where he will never find me." When the King asked where

that would be, Archee responded, "In his pulpit..., for I am sure he never goes there" (L'Estrange 286).

In Elizabethan and Jacobean comedy, sexual pleasure is incidental; During this time, sexual pleasure was a relatively limited concept which was both bounded and understood primarily "through the chaste sheets of marriage, or the monstrous expressions of demonic sexuality." However, after the Restoration, "pleasure becomes a more complex phenomenon, assuming diverse shapes and meanings" (Weber 51). Thus the Restoration changes marriage from a holy or sanctified union to more of a social institution, and although sexuality still appears in monstrous forms after the Restoration, these forms usually escape the condemnation and demonic explanations that were prevalent earlier (Weber 51).

The Civil War in England caused so many fears and jealousies that "politics and polemics had almost driven mirth and good humour out of the nation," and according to Alfred Gu L'Estrange humor did not make much progress under the Restoration (L'Estrange 312). L'Estrange further indicates that the humor in the court of Charles II was more in the line of jollity than of wit. Charles II was not reluctant to laugh heartily, even in church during a sermon. "He encouraged and led the way in an indelicate kind of jesting, which he seems to have learned during his travels in France" (L'Estrange 289). It should be noted that the poems of Sir Charles Sedley and John Wilmot, Earl of Rochester, are "as abundant in indelicacy as they are deficient in humour" (L'Estrange 292). During the sixteenth and seventeenth centuries, the character of the monarch gave the tone to society, and this was reflected in the dramatists.

> Thus we find the earnestness of Elizabeth in Shakespeare, the whimsicality of James in Jonson, the licentiousness of Charles II in the poets of the Restoration. The deterioration of men and of humour in the last reign is marked by the fact that ridicule was mostly directed not against vice as in Roman satire, but against undeserved misfortunes. (L'Estrange 291)

One of the traditions of the earliest part of the seventeenth century was that of extending a work's title to take up most of the title page. An illustration of the development of this practice can be seen by comparing an earlier William Goddard title with a later one. In 1599, William Goddard published A Satyrical Dialogue, or a Sharplye Invective Conference, betweene Alexander the Great and the Trulye Woman-Hater Diogynes. In 1600 Goddard published his A Mastif-Whelp, with Other Ruff-Island-Lik-Curs Fecht from amongst the Antipedes, Which Bite and Barke at the Fantastical Humorists and Abusers of the Time...Imprinted amongst the Antipedes, and are to be Sould Where They are to be Bought (Alden 191).

In The Rise of Formal Satire in England under Classical Influences, Raymond Alden mentions a series of satirical poems by Nicholas Breton published in 1600. They are entitled Pasquil's Madcap, Pasquil's Foolscap, Pasquil's Mistress, and Pasquil's Passe, and Passeth Not. These poems are satirical, but they are not formal satires. One year later, in 1601, John Weever published his The Whipping of Satyr. This book is addressed to the satirist, the epigrammatist, and the humorist (Alden 163).

Probably the most important contrast in genre development that happened during the seventeenth century was that between the satire and the epigram. John Peter considers the Epigram to be a "form" rather than a "mode." Its most salient features are its brevity and its conciseness rather than any particular temper or attitude. "English poets recognized the epigram as a distinct species like the sonnet; they knew that it could be either satirical or encomiastic, as can be seen from the practice of epigrammatists like Thomas Bastard, John Weever, and John Heath" (Peter 160). The epigram has its roots in classical literature. In the same way that Horace, Persius, and Juvenal developed three distinct types of satire whose antecedents can be clearly seen in seventeenth-century England, Martial developed the structure of the epigram, whose antecedents can again be clearly seen in seventeenth-century England (Peter 161).

Alden considers Samuel Rowlands to have been one of the most prolific of popular writers in London during the first decade of the seventeenth century. His most important satire was entitled The Letting of Humours Blood in the Head-Vaine (1600). Many of the epigrams in this book are offensive personal attacks, and in fact there is a note in the Stationers' Register that twenty-nine stationers had been fined for buying the book that had been newly printed after it had been forbidden and burned. Raymond Alden considers Rowlands's satires to be smooth and vigorous with an unusual number of feminine endings compared to other couplets of the period. Rowlands's vernacular style is so concrete as to suggest that the author always had his eye on the subject. The satires tend to give vivid pictures of real life. The Letting of Humours Blood begins with thirty-seven epigrams, some of which might pass for legitimate satires. The satires which follow the epigrams are seven in number, and they discuss dressing in fancy clothes, hypocrisy, servants, high-sounding words, contempt, "jolly William" and his praises of drink, and the triumph of Vice over Virtue. The book goes on to discuss the seven grand devils which rule the world: Pride, Covetousness, Lechery, Envy, Wrath, Gluttony, and Sloth, and ends as follows:

> The world is naught, and now upon the ending,
> Growes worse and worse, and farthest off from mending.

In 1604 Rowlands published Looke to It: for Ile Stabbe Ye which is a series of stabs promised by the allegorical figure of Death directed against tyrant kings, wicked magistrates, curious divines, covetous lawyers, up-start courtiers, wealthy citizens, greedy usurers, cursed swearers, quacksalver physicians, base gentlemen, counterfeit captains, dissembling soldiers, and so forth. In 1608 Rowlands published Humors Looking Glasse which contains twenty pieces, mostly in the form of epigrams and anecdotes that deal with the foibles and follies of the day. But the best known of Rowlands's work is the "Knave" series: Knave of Clubbes (1609), Knave of Harts (1612), Knaves of Spades and Diamonds (1613). The first of these books is a series of rough but vigorous accounts of London life. The second is a characterization of various types of knaves--the proud knave, the lying knave, the whoring knave, etc. The third book is more of a dignified satire. It reflects on a number of wise sayings, and deals with such topics as tobacco, Machiavellianism, usury, gluttony, the seven deadly sins, etc. Rowlands's last book appeared in 1615 and was called The Melancholie Knight. It is a burlesque depiction of a young gentleman of the period who had been inspired by the romances of Sir Launcelot, Sir Guy, and King Arthur. He laments the fact that he is not appreciated because of his constant demands for money. Raymond Alden considers the sketch to be very clever. It ends with samples of the Knight's romantic poetry, and presents further evidence that the qualities of romanticism that were prevalent during this time were often subject to rather strong ridicule (Alden 170).

Henry Parrot was considered the most prolific epigrammist of his time. In 1606, Parrot published his A Book of Epigrams called The Mouse-Trap; in 1608 he published Epigrams or Humors Lottery; and in 1612 he published Laquei Ridiculosi, or Springes to Catch Woodworks. The epigrams are generally both smart and coarse, and they are accompanied by clever Latin mottoes. Following the epigrams in Laquei Ridiculosi there are three satires and a paradox on war (Alden 190).

Between 1604 and 1611, Thomas Middleton, Ben Jonson, John Marston, and other playwrights developed a new genre called "city comedy." This genre had its roots in the genre of the medieval morality play that featured such stock characters as Vice and Avarice. It also had its roots in the Roman intrigue plays of Terence and Plautus, and in the genre of Commedia dell'arte that was coming from Italy. Like Commedia dell'arte,

City Comedy featured episodes of trickery, and also featured standard characters and plots. In City Comedy there was also a conflict between young lovers and their strict parents, and the plots were developed around ways of overcoming the parental restrictions. City Comedy was also filled with humours characters with such names as Allwit, Penitent Brothel, Epicure Mammon, and Sir Walter Whorehound. The names of these characters are indications of the vices which they embodied (Brunning 758).

In 1608 Richard Middleton published his Epigrams and Satyres, which contains decasyllabic couplets. Raymond Alden considers the style to be generally commonplace and lacking in both force and purpose. There are fifty epigrams, many of which are very coarse. His "satires" are included in a separate section of the book with a separate title-page and separate title--Metamorphosis. The "satires" do not have individual titles, and Alden feels that they should be called "epigrams" rather than "satires." In general they are brief character sketches in apostrophic form (Alden 172). The significance of these "quasi-satires" results not from their quality, but rather from the fact that they come after a considerable silence in formal satire dating from 1600 to 1608. But there is very little freshness in the satires, and they are not of the same quality as the satires that would later appear between 1613 and 1621. They indicate only a general familiarity with previous English satire, and only feebly suggest the later epigrams of Jonson. The local color of the satires relates to York in England. The targets of the satire include Morals (lust, pride, usury, hypocrisy), Fashions (gallants, clothes, hair, false gentility), and Literature (bad poets).

In 1617 Henry Fitzgeffrey published an anthology entitled Certain Elegies, Done by Sundrie Excellent Wits; with Satyrs and Epigrams. The elegies were written by Francis Beaumont, Michael Drayton, and Nathaniel Hookes. The epigrams and satires were written by Henry Fitzgeffrey. The satires took the form of couplets. The vernacular epigrams were vigorous, witty, and sometimes crude (Alden 207). Fitzgeffrey was familiar with earlier English satire, because he was a man who exhibited a classical education (Alden 209). Hugh Walker feels that Fitzgeffrey wrote with vigor and originality. His satires

> follow the example set by Hall, and satirize literature, condemning the fulsome adulation of patrons by the poets, their unscrupulousness in plagiarism, and their licentiousness. Above all, the satirist calls satire to account, condemning its excess and the spirit of prying into minute points of life and conduct. But by far the best and most interesting part of Fitzgeffrey's work is the third book, Notes from Blackfriars.... The conception of the spectator watching the throng at the Blackfriars theatre and noting down his observations, supplies a certain unity and affords a natural introduction to an endless variety of types. The sketches are pungent and amusing. (Walker 89)

Walker goes on to say that Fitzgeffrey is "the last satirist worthy of note before the temporary eclipse of satire in the reign of Charles I" (Walker 89).

Only one of Henry Hutton's works has survived to the present day, and it is a satire entitled, Follie's Anatomie: or Satyres and Satyricall Epigrams (1619). The satires in this book are vernacular couplets, generally end-stopped, and monotonous in effect. The style is dull, unilluminating, and an imitation of English-type satires (Alden 213). In addition to being not a very good writer, Hutton was also famous for his plagiarism. One critic uses understatement to claim that Follie's Anatomie is "not quite so great a plagiary as Parrot" (Alden 213). Hutton's humor is crude and rare. In his epigrams, Hutton's wit centers around his atrocious puns. His targets of satire are typical for the seventeenth century--Morals (hypocrisy, slander, gluttony, lust), Fashions (fashionable gallants, tobacco, women's artificial beauty), Classes (travelers), Personal Humors (love-sick gallants), and Literature (sonnets, madrigals, bad poets), etc.

In 1642 Puritan attacks on English dramas resulted in their being closed down. They were not reopened until Charles II was restored to the throne in 1660. Stephen Gossen explains what was so offensive about drama to the Puritan mind:

> The profe is evident, the consequent is necessarie, that in Stage Playes for a boy to put one the attyre, the gesture, the passions of a woman; for a meane person to take vpon him the title of a Prince with counterfeit porte, and traine, is by outwarde signes to shewe them selues otherwise then they are, and so with the compass of a lye. (MacCabe 14)

It is ironic, then, that women's absence from the Elizabethan stage was one of the Puritan motivations for having the theatre closed down in 1642. And it is even more ironic that when Charles II reopened the English theatres in 1660 he used Puritan logic to allow women to play women's roles on stage.

Anyone who studies seventeenth-century British humor must come into contact with The Merry Tales of the Wise Men of Gotham. One theory has it that these tales were written by Andrew Gotham, a physician of Henry VIII, and thereby derived their name. Another, and more credible, theory is that the term "Gotham" comes from the name of a village in Northamptonshire. The story goes that on one occasion King John was planning to pass through the city of Gotham, but the inhabitants placed some barriers in his way. Since the King was determined not to be deterred from his action, he sent his officers to the front to determine the nature of the opposition being offered. The Gotham townspeople were seized with panic, and pretended to have lost their senses. This, then, became the official explanation of how these tales were started (L'Estrange 268). There are many stories about the "Wise Men of Gotham." All of the stories involve a weird kind of non-linear logic. The most famous story about the Wise Men is about when they decide to go fishing, and some stand on dry land while others wade out into the water. One of the waders feels that they have ventured greatly in their wading, and he hopes that no-one has drowned. So they all begin to count how many Wise Men are there. Of course each of the Wise Men forgets to count himself, so they are all in agreement that there are eleven Wise Men and there should be twelve, and they make great lamentations. Then along comes a courtier who is able to convince them of their mistake by striking each of them with his whip. On being whipped, they cry out in turn, "Here's one," "Here's two," until finally all twelve are counted (L'Estrange 269-270).

George Kitchin suggests that burlesque, as a literary art form, did not flourish until the nineteenth century in England (Cazamian 153). During the second half of the seventeenth century, however, there developed a school of crude burlesque which consisted mainly of wild exaggeration. Kitchin considers this to be more travesty than the kind of artful burlesque that can be found in Austen's Northanger Abbey in the nineteenth century (252).

During the seventeenth century, little humor can be found in the writings of Milton, or in the writings of the religious poets in the semimystic category, or in the writings of the two Herberts, Vaughan, Crashaw, or Traherne. Samuel Pepys could not discover any fun in Samuel Butler's Hudibras. These writers were single-minded in their perspectives, and this single-mindedness did not allow for the double-meanings that are necessary for humor (Cazamian 388). On the other hand, there was much humor to be found in the writings of those authors who wrote for pleasure or for gain, and there was an increasing number of such authors during the seventeenth century. Most of John Cleveland's conceits were parodies. Andrew Marvell's writings were filled with quaint and fanciful images that were endowed with the virility of robust English humor; Marvell's writings are close to the writings of Jonathan Swift in their cleverness, intellect and irony. In Samuel Butler's Hudibras, there was both wit and humor. Samuel Butler's humor was dry, sardonic and kind, and in ways it foreshadows Swift. John Dryden is the greatest of the Restoration writers, and his satires are filled with a genuine and kind sort of humor. Sir George Etherege's plays and his letters contain much pointed humor. William Wycherly's writings contain both bitter humor and savage wit. Thomas Shadwell's writings display the "humors" in the older sense of the word. William Congreve's writings were brilliant and refined in their cynicism. In Sir John Vanbrugh's writings there is a Flemish influence in the robustness of the humor. George Farquhar's plays contain humor of a gentler variety. The humor in seventeenth-century England is therefore extensive and varied (Cazamian 388-389). Talking about Restoration repartee, John Sitter says, "The Rape of the Lock, Fielding's asides and prefaces, most of the poetry of Swift and Prior, and The Beggar's Opera are all witty (Sitter 49).

In 1660 English drama was influenced from two European movements. Out of the tradition of Italy's Commedia dell'Arte there developed the tradition of farce. And out of the tradition of France's Comédie Française (especially Molière) there developed the tradition of comedy of manners. According to Leo Hughes, the term "farce" was first used with vigor in 1660 during the Restoration. But in terms of farce, the restoration was not confined to the forty-year period of 1660 to 1700; rather it had to be extended for another decade to 1710, since this was the most important decade of all in the development of farce. And after Hughes had extended his period of inquiry to 1710, he discovered that he had to extend it even more--"on to the middle of the eighteenth century, by which point farce as a distinct dramatic genre seemed well set upon its course" (Hughes v). According to Hughes, farce is a great deal more than a bunch of words on a page.

> Farce is involved far more directly and intimately in the business of the theatre itself than any other dramatic form; it [therefore] cannot profitably be thought of apart from the theatre in which it was produced. For this reason I have found it necessary to devote much space...to the fortunes of the London theatres, to actors and companies, to bills and box-office receipts. (Hughes vi)

Jagdish Chander points out that in 1660, King Charles II gave letters to Thomas Killigrew and Sir William Davenant authorizing the incorporation of two companies of players. But the Restoration theatre that developed as a result of these two letters was very different from the Elizabethan theatre that had been in place before.

> The Elizabethan theatre was plain and simple with a half-lighted stage without any scenery or decorations. It was a narrow enclosure where the spectators jostled with the actors. There were no female actresses and the female parts were played by boys. But the new theatres saw great improvements. Lighting was introduced as a theatrical element. Instead of the old tapestry as the only decoration, the plays were now presented with an elaborate moving scenery. (Chander 1)

Women were first allowed to come on stage as actresses in 1661. Great actresses, such as Melantha and Nell Gwyn became prominent, and a new kind of verbal comedy--a comedy of wit--developed.

> From these theatres the great mass of people belonging to middle and lower classes remained away. The theatres became the exclusive haunts of aristocratic society, the courtiers and the attendants. The attendance at these theatres was invariably thin.... The audience...usually consisted of three types, the critics who came to judge the play, the gallants and their mistresses and the fops and coxcombs who wanted to be in the swim. Though small in number, the spectators were unruly and noisy. To them, theaters were like clubs where appointments were made, duels were arranged and mistresses were picked up. (Chander 2)

The genre which most developed in English theater at this time was comedy of manners. It was also theatre designed to be seen through the eyes of the young. In a book entitled Crabbed Age and Youth: The Old Men and Women in the Restoration Comedy of Manners, Elisabeth Mignon discusses the old men and women in the plays of Etherege, Wycherley, Dryden, Shadwell, Behn, Congreve, Vanbrugh, and Farquhar and indicates that

> Superannuated belles and timeworn rakes crowded the English stage between 1660 and 1700. The old women with their decayed charms are always pursuers, never pursued. The old men are predestined to wear the horns on their ugly foreheads. The aged of both sexes are loathsome to the gay young blades and precocious heroines who bewilder and victimize them. For it is the young who rule with arrogant ease the beau monde of these plays. It is the old who are intruders. To their highly sophisticated juniors they are merely old harridans and fossils. (Mignon 3)

Much of the plot of these Restoration comedies of manners was furnished by the conflict between the young and the old. This may be a legitimate battle for the first four acts, but the younger generation always triumph in the fifth act. The old people were termed by Mignon to be "miserable pretenders," and they are always completely frustrated by the end of the play. Although battles between the young and the old can be seen in many non-Restoration plays, and although the young and gay usually triumph in non-Restoration plays, there is something distinct in the Restoration comedies, for the battles are more intense, they occur more frequently, and the repercussions in language and character are wider in these plays (Mignon 3).

Harold Weber points out that the most significant quality of the Restoration comedy of manners is sexuality, and that the most significant character is the rake. But this rake is not just a sex machine. He is a complex and enigmatic figure. He loves disguises; he needs freedom; he has a fondness for play. It is true that the lives of characters like Wycherley's Horner and Etherege's Dorimant can be defined in terms of their lists of previous mistresses, but each sexual encounter is different. As Horner states,

> I love the frolick, the precise,
> The reverend Lady, that is wise;
> The Wife, the Maid, the Widow too,
> All that is Woman, and will Do. (Weber 3)

Weber points out that it was the women as well as the men of Restoration comedy who were rakes.

> Women were intimately involved in the transformation of sexual identity that separated the second half of the seventeenth century from the first. The female rake must differ from her male counterpart, for the male takes his definition precisely from those social conventions that assume male aggression and enforces female passivity. Yet Restoration comedy presents a select number of women determined to enjoy the sexual freedoms available to men. (Weber 11)

There were also some couples in Restoration comedy, and John Smith discusses them in The Gay Couple in Restoration Comedy. In the period of 1660 to 1675 he refers to "gay comedy" where love is treated as a game. In the period of 1675 to 1687 he refers to "cynical comedy" in which the character of the Gallant is in the process of ascending. From 1687 until 1690 he talks about forces in opposition--the reforming dramatists, and the "ladies." From 1690 until 1700 there is the gay couple on the defensive. And finally, after 1700, there is the decline of the gay couple and the triumph of the man and woman of sense (Smith xi).

All critics recognize that Molière's comedies in France had an influence in the development of English Restoration comedy; however, John Wilcox points out that there are four different positions that critics have taken in respect to the nature and extent of this influence. There are some critics who assert that English Restoration comedy was basically a child of France. There are other critics, like John Dryden, who assert that whatever Restoration received from France was essentially lost by the time that it reached the English stage. There were still other critics who asserted that Restoration comedy must have come from France, for otherwise, how could it be so immoral. And finally, there were those critics who asserted that the immorality of Restoration comedy is totally consistent with English thought and action, and therefore the indecency of the plays proves that they are thoroughly English (Wilcox vii).

Alice Rayner points out that in Restoration comedy there was a wide range of critical opinion, explained, perhaps, by the fact that Restoration comedy tended to intrude into the morally dangerous territory of sexuality without a consistent moral attitude toward that territory. "The broad range of appetites that appear in Shakespeare and Jonson is nowhere to be found in the Restoration, where the only appetite seems to be sexual" (Rayner 65). C. L. Knights dismissed Restoration comedy as "trivial, gross, and dull," (Knights 140) rather than calling it specifically immoral. William Makepeace Thackeray called Restoration comedy "miserable, rouged, tawdry, sparkling, [and] hollow-hearted" (Holland 3). Virginia Birdsall said,

> The "heroes" of the [Restoration] comedies seemed scarcely heroes at all. They were rakes, libertines, wits, gallants, painted with realistic strokes from living models; and court society, so one critical argument goes, merely thronged to the theater to see and admire themselves upon a stage. (Birdsall 3)

In an article entitled "Etherege and Comic Shallowness," Harold Brown attempts to define the heroes of Restoration comedy in terms of their shallowness in philosophy and in cultural schizophrenia, and Brown pays particular attention to the comedy of manners of Etherege. However for almost all writers of Restoration comedy, there is a disrespect for marriage and romantic love. There was also a certain "libertinism" which Brown defines as:

> the spirit of excess among the cavaliers and King Charles, and the heightened value of wit instead of human emotion or moral character in judgment of proper social conduct. To speak of libertinism in the late seventeenth century denotes worldliness, skepticism towards dogma, and a revulsion against all fanaticism, a freethinking spirit, easily spreading from irreligion towards antisacramental sexual indulgence.... The term "libertine" was current in England contemporary parlance with the comedy of manners, appearing in such titles as Shadwell's Libertine, a play, and Etherege's "The Libertine," a lyric. Wycherley and later Congreve sometimes call their rakish characters libertines. (Brown 675)

William Archer condemned Restoration comedy as "stupid, nauseous and abominable beyond anything else that can be found in the world's dramatic literature" (Archer 173). Ursula Jantz notes that although twentieth-century criticism of Restoration comedy has in general moved away from the devastatingly negative approach, such criticism did remain at least until 1956, when John Wain designated Restoration comedy as " 'immoral' because this comedy is one of the symptoms of a sick society." Wain discusses the "never-ending stream of filth that splashes across the stage" (Jantz 1; Wain 376). In The Memoirs of Count Grammont, Anthony Hamilton said that the Restoration was "the most licentious, wicked, and bawdy era in English history, and the comedies are an accurate reflection of the decadence of the audience" (Harwood xi). John Harwood discusses those critics who say that Restoration comedy "exposes the reader to the infectious disease of moral turpitude with which the dramatis personae are terminally ill," and those critics who feel that Restoration comedy "is entertaining (or boring) but nothing more" (Harwood ix).

But Harwood also discusses those critics who feel that Restoration comedy "is a bracing tonic, a healthful and stimulating criticism of sterile and repressive social conventions," and those who feel that Restoration comedy "allows the reader to enter a rarefied world of gallantry and rococo manners," seeing such an escape from the mundane world as salutary (Harwood ix).

In reaction to C. L. Knights's depiction above, F. W. Bateson finds in Restoration comedy a "serious social purpose," which is that of rationalizing the sex instinct and thereby buffering the battle between the Puritans and Royalists (Rayner 64). Norman Holland suggests that those critics who criticize Restoration comedy as being immoral are confusing immorality with indecency.

> The first kind of understanding involves such things as contrast, parallelism, images, or symbols; the second deals with lifelikeness, "character," probability, motivation, and the like.... If a play is true to its purpose, the pleasure of understanding, then I think it cannot be called immoral. The "morals" critics have made much of the fact that the dissolute rake-heroes of Restoration comedies marry the delectable heroines. The plays, they say, are immoral because vicious persons are rewarded.... A play cannot be called immoral because it shows a rake rewarded, for it is not immoral to represent the truth. (Holland 3-4)

In a book entitled Wild Civility, Virginia Birdsall says that we must evaluate Restoration comedy in the context of Restoration values. We need to know, not only the role of the rake in late seventeenth-century England in particular, but we must also acknowledge the essentially devilish, bad-boy nature of the English comic spirit in general. Restoration comedy represented a "rebellion of instinct and natural mirth against the repression of a faith too strictly bound up with the fear of hell." It represented a "free voice," and a "Rabelaisian note of frank, almost pagan naturalism." It was a "humor of release," as we "laugh in delighted responsiveness with the mischievous, high-spirited troublemakers" (Birdsall 7).

John Wain hailed Restoration comedy as a meaningful approach to life in expressing "not licentiousness, but a deep curiosity, and a desire to try new ways of living" (Wain 368). R. D. Hume suggests that the "value of the plays, beyond entertainment, lies in their vivid communication of complex and not wholly happy attitudes toward life. And they are designed to provide an experience, not a proposition for analytic dissection" (Hume Development 147). Thomas Fujimura says that Restoration comedy "gave a brilliant picture of its time rather than a new insight into man" (Fujimura 5):

> The comedy of manners, then, is the laughable born of the inability of men to conform to an artificial social standard (as in the country bumpkins), or of excessive attempts at conformity (as in the fops), or of conformity so successful that the individual loses his human elasticity (in a Bergsonian sense). Manners, in this sense, is extensive and ubiquitous; it is the faint gossamer thread of fashionable and artificial convention on which the characters cross the Niagara of this life. (Fujimura 6)

But while some critics see Restoration comedy as totally bad; and other critics see Restoration comedy as totally good, John Harwood and many other critics feel that Restoration comedy is both. They feel that it is a "treasure chest for the historian who wants an accurate picture of late seventeenth-century social conditions, values, and mores in England." Harwood continues, "Restoration comedy has been a bête noire for literary critics and historians for several centuries. No other literature seems as likely to propel its critics either into paroxisms of moral indignation or rhapsodies of lyrical praise" (Harwood ix).

An additional compounding factor is that the term "Restoration comedy" has no clear and unambiguous referent. Thomas Shadwell's The Virtuoso, Thomas Ravenscroft's The London Cuckolds, and William Congreve's The Way of the World have all been designated as "Restoration comedies." But this designation indicates "nothing but a rough time reference," and it ignores "substantial differences among the plays" (Harwood xi). Nor are the subjects and targets of Restoration comedy always the same.

> The London Cuckolds and The Country Wife are particularly concerned with questions of sexual politics, to use Kate Millett's phrase, and I am interested in the techniques by which Ravenscroft and Wycherley shape the response of the audience to their characters' sexual adventures. The Souldiers Fortune (and its sequel, The Atheist) offers a grimly pessimistic view of justice and human relationships. In such a world, Otway affirms only male friendship and drinking. The Squire of Alsatia is an "education" play, testing the values by which a young gentleman ought to live and illustrating the perils of raising a young man to maturity. I deal with Otway and Shadwell because they raise ethical questions not necessarily related to sexual conduct. (Harwood xiii)

Normand Holland notes that Restoration comedy "has almost always been the darling of audiences, but a strumpet to critics.... In the eighteenth century and early nineteenth, and increasingly in the twentieth, revivals of Restoration comedy have succeeded beyond any expectation reasonable for a drama so consistently maligned" (Holland 3). Holland continues that

> There is scarcely an important actor or actress of our day who has not starred in some Restoration comedy. Yet, ever since the seventeenth century, critics almost without exception have damned or belittled Restoration comedies: damned them for bad morals or belittled them by saying they deal only with "manners." (Holland 3)

At this point a special note needs to be made about the comedy of manners that developed in France mostly under the pen of Jean Baptiste Poquelin Molière (1622-1673), but which greatly influenced William Congreve in the late seventeenth century, Francis Sheridan in the late eighteenth century, Oscar Wilde in the late nineteenth century, and Sir Noel Coward in the late twentieth century. Congreve broke away from the Elizabethan traditions by adopting the continental play-writing techniques imported by Charles II and his court out of France. Congreve looms large as an innovator of this dramatic type in England.

> Congreve's five-act plays are much heavier in texture than any of the later plays considered. In them he satirizes pleasure-loving Restoration society for the most part through his characterizations. Sheridan, on the other hand, is more generous, frequently using an entire play to satirize one particular weakness of his age, as in The School for Scandal and The Rivals, where he shows up, respectively, slander and sentimentality. Oscar Wilde's satire finds expression in the verbal achievements of his characters. Noel Coward resembles Sheridan in that he devotes an entire play, such as Easy Virtue or Design for Living, to the ridicule of Victorian prudishness or the insignificance of present-day moral conventions. Also, he is close to Wilde in that he is invariably clever and flippant. (Snider 124)

But the comedies of manners of all of these varied authors has one thing in common. They all target the superficialities of the sophisticated upper-class society. English comedy of manners was like the French comedy of manners in targeting the aristocratic leisure class. Comedy of Manners is social criticism that concentrates on a very narrow coterie, high in the social scale with much leisure time on their hands, a condition conducive to cultivation of the intellect.

In both France and England, the comedy of manners has limited characterization, limited setting, and a sense of artificiality, but Stanley Ashby responds to the charge that it was artificial: "It was artificial, of course, but so was the society that it professed to exhibit.   At any rate, it had one characteristic element that made it significantly representative, namely, satire" (Snider iii). According to Rose Snider,

> There is in the comedy of manners a frankness which embraces satire as its greatest ally. The particular brand of satire involved is not the biting, often uncouth, variety of Swift, nor the purely ironical type of Defoe. It is a satire in which the criticism is crisp and sprightly, and alleviated by genuine humor. (Snider viii)

Snider continues by quoting George Jean Nathan who maintains that polite comedy "is polite only as a servant is polite, that is, for business reasons" (Snider viii).

John Clark points out that Sir George Etherege, and William Wycherley were two of the most important comic dramatists in the early Restoration (1660-1680). When the theaters were reopened in 1660, the so-called Restoration Comedy that came onto stage was flauntingly profligate and lubricious. This courtly or Cavalier comedy was the beginning of comedy of manners.

> There was a suitable mean of poised mannerly behavior, and upon either side of that mean were the attendant flaws of defect and excess. On the defective side was any coarseness or ignorance; the typical emblems of such folly were country bumpkins and middle-class London merchants and dissenters (the citizens or "cits," as they were derogatorily termed), who were presented as being devoid of manners, polish, class, and style. The figures of excess at the opposite extreme were the would-be-wits, awkwardly aspiring town gallants, and fops--those who tried too hard to be humorous, gentlemanly, and a la mode. (Clark 1228)

The line between the true wits and the foppish attempter at wit was very thin. Both of them idolized the glib tongue, the social disguise, the amorous tryst, and the sexual conquest (Clark 1229). The would-wits usually failed, however, in whatever they attemped; whereas the refined wits succeeded, and the play usually ended in a "perfect marriage." During the play, there was a great deal of drawing-room gossip, and intrigue, and lovers' deceits and assignations. there were fools who could not understand the machinations or the jests, and there were also the scandalous lovers who devoted their lives to rendezvous, repartee, and seduction. This Restoration Theater was a way of "getting even" for the recent civil wars that had exiled the courtiers from England (Clark 1228).

At the end of the seventeenth century there was a sudden decline in English comedy. During the 1690s about six great plays were written, but with the exception of The Beggar's Opera, there were no great plays written for the seventy years which followed (Myers 75).

Seventeenth-Century Bibliography

Alden, Raymond MacDonald. The Rise of Formal Satire in England under Classical Influence. New York, NY: Archon Books, 1961.

Aldridge, Alfred Owen. "Shaftesbury and the Test of Truth." PMLA 60 (1945): 129-156.

Alleman, Gellert Spencer. Matrimonial Law and the Materials of Restoration Comedy. Wallingford, PA: n.p., 1942.

Archer, William. The Old Drama and the New. London, England, 1923.

Bateson, F. W. "Second Thoughts: II. L. C. Knights and Restoration Comedy." Essays in Criticism 7 (1957): 56-67.

Bear, Andrew. "Restoration Comedy and the Provok'd Critic." Restoration Literature: Critical Approaches. Ed. Harold Love. London, England: Methuen, 1972, 1-26.

Berkeley, David S. "The Penitent Rake in Restoration Comedy." Modern Philology 49 (1952): 223-233.

Berkeley, David S. "The Précieuse, or Distressed Heroine, of Restoration Comedy. Stillwater, OK: Oklahoma State Univ Press, 1959.

Berkeley, David S. "Préciosité and the Restoration Comedy of Manners." Huntington Library Quarterly 18 (1955): 109–128.

Berman, Ronald. "The Comic Passions of The Man of Mode." Studies in English Literature, 1500-1900 10 (1970): 459-468.

Bevis, Richard. The Laughing Tradition: Stage Comedy in Garrick's Day Athens, GA: University of Georgia Press, 1980.

Birdsall, Virginia Ogden. Wild Civility: The English Comic Spirit on the Restoration Stage. Bloomington, IN: Indiana Univ Press, 1970.

Borkat, Roberta F. S. "Vows, Prayers, and Dice: Comic Values in The Man of Mode." University of Daton Review 12.3 (1976): 121-131.

Bradbrook, M. C. The Growth and Structure of Elizabethan Comedy. London, England: Chatto and Windus, 1955.

Brooke, Nicholas. Horrid Laughter in Jacobean Tragedy. New York, NY: Barnes and Noble, 1979.

Brown, Harold Clifford, Jr. "Etherege and Comic Shallowness." Texas Studies in Literature and Language 41.4 (Winter, 1975): 675-689.

Bruce, Donald. Topics of Restoration Comedy. New York, NY: St. Martin's, 1974.

Brunning, Alizon. "Thomas Middleton." Encyclopedia of British Humorists, Volume II. Ed. Steven H. Gale, New York, NY: Garland, 1996, 757-763.

Burns, Edward. Restoration Comedy: Crises of Desire and Identity. New York, NY: St. Martin's, 1987.

Canfield, J. Douglas. "Religious Language and Religious Meaning in Restoration Comedy." Studies in English Literature, 1500-1900. 20 (1980): 385-406.

Cazamian, Louis. The Development of English Humor. Durham, NC: Duke University Press, 1952.

Cecil, C. D. "Delicate and Indelicate Puns in Restoration Comedy." Modern Language Review 61 (1966): 572-587.

Cecil, C. D. " 'Une Espèce d'éloquence abrégée': The Idealized Speech of Restoration Comedy." Etudes Anglaises 19 (1966): 15-25.

Cecil, C. D. "Libertine and Précieux Elements in Restoration Comedy." Essays in Criticism 9 (1959): 239-253.

Cecil, C. D. "Raillery in Restoration Comedy." Huntington Library Quarterly 29 (1966): 147-159.

Chander, Jagdish. The Licentious Comedy of the Restoration Age. New York, NY: Folcroft Library, 1973.

Clark, John R. "William Wycherley." Encyclopedia of British Humorists, Volume II. Ed. Steven H. Gale, New York, NY: Garland, 1996, 1227-1231.

Crawford, Bartholow V. "High Comedy in Terms of Restoration Practice." Philological Quarterly 8 (1929): 339-347.

Croissant, DeWitt C. "Early Sentimental Comedy." Essays in Dramatic Literature: The Parrott Presentation Volume Ed. Hardin Craig. New York: Russell, 1967, 47-71.

Dobrée, Bonamy. Restoration Comedy, 1660-1720. Oxford, England: Clarendon, 1924.

Elkin, P. K. The Augustan Defence of Satire. Oxford, England: Oxford University Press, 1973.

Farley-Hills, David. The Benevolence of Laughter: Comic Poetry of the Commonwealth and Restoration. London, England: Macmillan, 1974.

Fujimura, Thomas H. The Restoration Comedy of Wit. Princeton, NJ: Princeton University Press, 1952.

Gewirtz, Arthur. Restoration Adaptations of Early Seventeenth-Century Comedies. Washington, DC: Univ Press of America, 1982.

Gibbons, Brian. Jacobean City Comedy: A Study of Satiric Plays by Jonson, Marston and Middleton. 2nd ed. London, England: Methuen, 1980.

Harwood, John T. Critics, Values, and Restoration Comedy. Carbondale, IL: Southern Illinois University Press, 1982.

Heilman, Robert B. "Some Fops and Some Versions of Foppery." Journal of English Literary History 49 (1982): 363-395.

Holden, William P. Anti-Puritan Satire 1572-1642. New Haven, CT: Yale University Press, 1954.

Holland, Norman N. The First Modern Comedies: The Significance of Etherege, Wycherley, and Congreve. Cambridge, MA: Harvard University Press, 1959.

Holland, Peter. The Ornament of Action: Text and Performance in Restoration Comedy. Cambridge, England: Cambridge Univ Press, 1979.

Horwich, Richard. "Wives, Courtesans, and the Economics of Love in Jacobean City Comedy." Comparative Drama 7 (1973-74): 291-309.

Hughes, Leo. A Century of English Farce. Princeton, NJ: Princeton University Press, 1956.

Hume, Robert D. "Concepts of the Hero in Comic Drama, 1660-1710." The English Hero, 1660-1800. Ed. Robert Folkenflik. Newark, DE: Univ of Delaware Press. London, England: Associated University Press, 1982, 61-78.

Hume, Robert D. The Development of English Drama in the Late Seventeenth Century. Oxford, England: Clarendon, 1976.

Hume, Robert D. The Rakish Stage: Studies in English Drama, 1660-1800. Carbondale, IL: Southern Illinois University Press, 1983.

Jantz, Ursula. "Targets of Satire in the Comedies of Etherege, Wycherley, and Congreve." Salzburg, Austria: Institut für Englische Sprache und Literatur/Universität Salzburg, 1978.

Jordan, Robert. "The Extravagant Rake in Restoration Comedy." Restoration Literature: Critical Approaches. Ed. Harold Love. London: Methuen, 1972, 69-90.

Kaufman, Helen. "The Influence of Italian Drama on Pre-Restoration English Comedy." Italica 31 (1954): 8-23.

Keller, Katherine Zapantis. "Re-Reading and Re-playing: An Approach to Restoration Comedy." Restoration 6 (1982): 64-71.

Kernan, Alvin. The Cankered Muse: Satire of the English Renaissance. New Haven, CT: Yale University Press, 1959.

Kirk, Eugene [Bud Korkowski]. Menippean Satire: An Annotated Catalogue of Texts and Criticism. New York, NY: Garland, 1980.

Kitchin, George. Survey of Burlesque and Parody in English. London, England: Oliver and Boyd, 1931.

Knights, L. C. "Restoration Comedy: The Reality and the Myth." Scrutiny 6 (1937): 122-143.

Kupersmith, William. Roman Satirists in Seventeenth-Century England. Lincoln, NE: Univ of Nebraska Press, 1985.

L'Estrange, Alfred Gu. History of English Humour. New York, NY: Burt Franklin, 1878.

LeCocq, Louis. La Satire en Angleterre de 1588 à 1603. Paris, France: Didier, 1969.

Leinwand, Theodore B. " 'This gulph of marriage': Jacobean City Wives and Jacobean City Comedy." Women's Studies 10 (1984): 245-260.

Lynch, Kathleen M. The Social Mode of Restoration Comedy. New York, NY: Octagon,

1965.
MacCabe, Colin. "Abusing Self and Others: Puritan Accounts of Shakespearian Stage." Critical Quarterly 30.3 (1988): 3-17.
McDonald, Charles O. "Restoration Comedy as Drama of Satire: An Investigation into Seventeenth Century Aesthetics." Studies in Philology 61 (1964): 522-544.
McDonald, Margaret Lamb. The Independent Woman in the Restoration Comedy of Manners. Salzburg, Austria: Institut für Englische Sprache und Literatur/Universität Salzburg, 1976.
Mignon, Elisabeth. Crabbed Age and Youth: The Old Men and Women in the Restoration Comedy of Manners. Durham, NC: Duke Univ Press, 1947.
Miles, Dudley Howe. The Influence of Molière on Restoration Comedy. New York, NY: Columbia Univ Press, 1910.
Montgomery, Guy. "The Challenge of Restoration Comedy." University of California Publications, English Studies 1 (1929): 135-151.
Mudrick, Marvin. "Restoration Comedy and Later." English Stage Comedy: English Institute Essays 1954. Ed. W. K. Wimsatt, Jr. New York, NY: Columbia Univ Press, 1955, 98-125.
Muir, Kenneth. The Comedy of Manners. London, England: Hutchinson, 1970.
Myers, William. "Plot and Meaning in Congreve's Comedies." William Congreve. Ed. Brian Morris. London, England: Ernest Benn, 1972.
Nardo, Anna K. The Ludic Self in Seventh-Century English Literature. New York, NY: State Univ of New York Press, 1991.
Neill, Michael. "Heroic Heads and Humble Tails: Sex, Politics, and the Restoration Comic Rake. The Eighteenth Century: Theory and Interpretation 24 (1983): 115-139.
Perkinson, Richard H. "Topographical Comedy in the Seventeenth Century." Journal of English Literary History 3 (1936): 270-290.
Perry, Henry Ten Eyck. The Comic Spirit in Restoration Drama: Studies in the Comedy of Etherege, Wycherley, Congreve, Vanbrugh, and Farquhar. New York, NY: Russell and Russell, 1962.
Persson, Agnes V. Comic Character in Restoration Drama. The Hague, Netherlands: Mouton, 1975.
Peter, John. Complaint and Satire in Early English Literature. Oxford, England: The Clarendon Press, 1956.
Peters, Jan Eden, and Thomas Michael Stein. Scholastic Midwifery: Studien zum Satirischen in der englischen Literatur 16000-1800. Tübingen, Germany: Gunter Narr Verlag, 1959.
Pollin, Burton R. "Verse Satires on William Goodwin in the Anti-Jacobin Period. Satire Newsletter 2.1 (Fall, 1964): 31-40.
Priestley, J. B. "After the Puritans." English Humour. New York, NY: Stein and Day, 1976, 26-38.
Priestley, J. B. "Some Elizabethans and Jacobeans." English Humour. New York, NY: Stein and Day, 1976, 13-17.
Rayner, Alice. Comic Persuasion: Moral Structure in British Comedy from Shakespeare to Stoppard. Berkeley, CA: University of California Press, 1987.
Roberts, Philip. "Mirabel and Restoration Comedy." William Congreve. Ed. Brian Morris. Totowa, NJ: Rowman, 1972, 39-53.
Rothstein, Eric, and Frances M. Kavenik. The Designs of Carolean Comedy. Carbondale, IL: Southern Illinois Univ Press, 1988.
Schneider, Ben Ross, Jr. The Ethos of Restoration Comedy. Urbana, IL: Univ of Illinois Press, 1971.
Scouten, A. H. "Notes toward a History of Restoration Comedy." Philological Quarterly 45

(1966): 62-70.

Sitter, John. Arguments of Augustan Wit. New York, NY: Cambridge University Press, 1991.

Smith, John Harrington. The Gay Couple in Restoration Comedy. Cambridge, MA: Harvard Univ Press, 1948; New York, NY: Octagon, 1971.

Snider, Rose. Satire in the Comedies of Congreve, Sheridan, Wilde, and Coward. New York, NY: Phaeton Press, 1972.

Stubbs, John Heath. "The Jacobeans," and "The Restoration." The Verse Satire. London, England: Oxford University Press, 1969, 22-50.

Suckling, Norman. "Molière and English Restoration Comedy." Restoration Theatre. Eds. John Russell Brown and Bernard Harris. New York, NY: St. Martin's, 1965, 93-107.

Symons, Julian. "Restoration Comedy (Reconsiderations II)." The Kenyon Review 7 (1945): 185-197.

Thorndike, Ashley H. "Manners and Wit, 1680-1700" English Comedy. New York, NY: Macmillan, 1929. 304-341.

Thorndike, Ashley H. "The Restoration, 1660-1680." English Comedy. New York, NY: Macmillan, 1929. 269-303.

Vernon, P. F. "Marriage of Convenience and the Moral Code of Restoration Comedy." Essays in Criticism 12 (1962): 370-387.

Wain, John. "Restoration Comedy and its Modern Critics." Essays in Criticism 6.4 (1956): 367-385.

Walker, Hugh. "Elizabethan and Jacobean Verse Satire." English Satire and Satirists. New York, NY: J. M. Dent, 1925, 57-90.

Walker, Hugh. "Post Restoration Prose Satire." English Satire and Satirists. New York, NY: J. M. Dent, 1925, 180-221.

Wardroper, John. "The Hell-Begotten Jacobins." Kings, Lords, and Wicked Libellers: Satire and Protest, 1760-1837. London, England: John Murray, 1973, 141-166.

Weber, Harold. The Restoration Rake-Hero: Transformations in Sexual Understanding in Seventeenth-Century England. Madison, WI: University of Wisconsin Press, 1986.

Wedgewood, C. V. "Social Comedy in the Reign of Charles I." Truth and Opinion: Historical Essays. New York, NY: Macmillan, 1960, 191-221.

Wells, Susan. "Jacobean City Comedy and the Ideology of the City." Journal of English Literary History 48 (1981): 37-60.

Welsford, Enid. The Fool: His Social and Literary History. New York, NY: jFarrar and Rinehart, 1936.

Wilcox, John. The Relation of Molière to Restoration Comedy. New York, NY: Columbia Univ Press, 1938.

Wilkinson, D. R. M. The Comedy of Habit: An Essay on the Use of Courtesy Literature in a Study of Restoration Comic Drama. Leiden, Netherlands: Universitaire Pers, 1964.

Wolfe, Humbert. "The Elizabethans and Carolines." Notes on English Verse Satire. London, England: Leonard and Virginia Woolf, 1929, 49-74.

Thomas Dekker (c1572-c1632)

Louis Cazamian considers Thomas Dekker to be "a genuine master of humor, with a sure grasp of its method, no less than of its spirit, and a range that took in not only its broad basis of observation, realism, and tolerance, but many, though not all, of the higher and subtler shades" (Cazamian 171). In terms of his humor, which tends to be cordial and kind, Cazamian considers Dekker to be a direct-line precursor to Richard Steele and Charles Dickens, and he feels that when he is at his best, he can even be compared to Chaucer (Cazamian 171, 175).

The Wonderful Year, which is about the death of Queen Elizabeth I and about the plague, is "written with a realism equal to that of Defoe," but this is followed by stories of comic relief told with composure and skill. One such story is that about the Cobbler's wife; another is a story about a red-nosed Innkeeper. Cazamian considers these stories to be "a cross between the Canterbury Tales and Rabelais (Cazamian 175). Cazamian feels that Dekker had a flair for humor of the "finesse" genre, humor which is drier, subtler, and more intellectual than most humor of the day; the "finesse" humor is usually associated with the genre of the fabliaux. Dekker's The Bachelor's Banquet is an imitation of the Quinze Joies de Mariage, but it is uneven in quality. Its best chapters are considered by Cazamian to be delightfully sly and witty. The dire lot of the patient husband is developed with lively zest (Cazamian 175).

The Sun's Darling is a charming masque in which one of the characters is an allegorical personification of "Humour," but only in the pre-Jonson sense of the word. The Honest Whore is a dramatic masterpiece, and again humor is discreetly infused. But Shoemaker's Holiday is the best example of Dekker's humor. Shoemaker's Holiday is cheerful, and pleasant; it is a mixture of the humorous with the humane. In this piece he effectively employed a combination of sly implicit meanings and irony. The humor of this piece is centered around the mirth, high spirits, and good fellowship of the boistrous Simon Eyre. These high spirits are so reflected in the atmosphere of his workshop and in Simon's men that the reader is caught up in the "torrent of picturesque language" (Cazamian 172). But Dekker's humor is more than this. It is a blend of rollicking farce and artistic intuition. Dekker's humor owes its success to Dekker's verve, his comic invention, and his familiarity with concrete experiences. Furthermore, his humor can be satirical and biting, and this is especially true in his Satiromastix (Cazamian 172-173). Alfred Gu L'Estrange feels that the most important quality of Dekker's humor is his power of invective. Dekker's "Gull's Hornbook" says about coxcombs, for example, that their "vinegar railings shall not quench his Alpine resolutions" (L'Estrange 303).

In Blurt, Master Constable (1602), Fontinelle pursues a sexual encounter to the point of trickery, and Mary Bly points out that this is also what Helena does in Shakespeare's All's Well that Ends Well. In both of these comedies there is a maiden who

> obstinately marries the man she chooses, her young husband importunes another woman, a bed-trick is enacted by the deserted wife, and the husband turns abruptly from the woman he desired to the wife now confronting him. Both plays deliberately juxtapose Petrarchan rhetoric, bawdy jokes and a recusant female stubbornness in matters of sexuality; both are laden with sexual language, foregrounding women whose desiring voices are not quelled by repentance. (Bly 37)

Bly concludes by saying that All's Well that Ends Well and Blurt, Master Constable represent the height of a localized experiment in English comedy: that of presenting "lascivious Scenes" as explicitly as possible, while at the same time guarding the desiring woman from wholesale condemnation (Bly 37).

Thomas Dekker Bibliography

Bly, Mary. "Imagining Consummation: Women's Erotic Language in Comedies of Dekker and Shakespeare." Look Who's Laughing: Gender and Comedy. Ed. Gail Finney. New York, NY: Gordon and Breach, 1994, 35-52.
Cazamian, Louis. "Dekker." The Development of English Humor. Durham, NC: Duke

University Press, 1952, 171-175.
Champion, L. S. "From Melodrama to Comedy: A Study of the Dramatic Perspective in
    Dekker's The Honest Whore." Studies in Philology 69 (1972): 192-209.
L'Estrange, Alfred Gu. History of English Humour. New York, NY: Burt Franklin, 1878.

John Donne (1572-1631)

John Donne's humor "works in several senses, almost always contributing to the
moral, thematic, and structural integrity of his poems (Evans 326). Robert Evans says that
the comic touch is pervasive in Donne's poetry, adding that he often uses "paradoxes,
analogies, hyperbole, irony, striking imagery, and unexpected juxtapositions or twists of
thought" (Evans 327). Evans says that it is not uncommon for people to think of John
Donne chiefly as a humorous poet, and he also has a reputation as a wit. In fact such
words as "wit" and "witty" appear frequently in various analyses of Donne's writing.
Donne's poetry is more than just funny, however. In addition, it is challenging,
exhilarating, and delightful. "Recognizing that he often wrote in a voice not his own is
crucial to appreciating many of his poems, and this is especially the case with his
'humorous' poems" (Evans 321). In his poetry, Donne plays with situations, with tones,
and with speakers. Donne's speakers, "can be either self-consciously witty and clever or
implicitly mocked and satirized by the poet himself, and sometimes both possibilities seem
involved. Speakers proud of their own glibness and wit often seem the butts of Donne's
irony." Irony of some sort is a frequent aspect of Donne's writing, as is paradox, and both
irony and paradox contribute to Donne's humor. His poems are often filled with puns and
other types of word play. His imagery can range all the way from the homely and familiar
to the abstract and outlandish (Evans 322). One of the comic moods that can be found in
Donne's poetry is cynicism. Donne's mocking tone can undercut the bitter, disillusioned
"wittiness" of various speakers whose cynicism often reveals more about their own limits
and defects than it reveals about the faults or failings which they attack are attacking.
Donne's humor is gentle and teasing. In poems which celebrate a satisfying mutual love,
there is often a flippant wit that tends to underscore the depth of the affection. Donne uses
humor to cope with pain, and to intensify his "serious" feelings. "By mixing tones, Donne
deepens them" (Evans 323).

Donne considered literature to be a language game designed to question sense and
logic in the order of things. He felt that literature tends to compare disparate or
incongruous objects or situations. In his "A Valediction: Forbidding Mourning," for
example, Donne compares two lovers to the legs of a pair of compasses. Donne's
metaphysical conceits are often so far-fetched that they transcend the limits of the
conventional figures of speech, and this can be seen very easily in his "An Anatomy of the
World. Wherein, By Occasion of the Untimely Death of Mistris Elizabeth Drvry the
Frailty and the Decay of this Whole World is Represented" (Elderhorst 97). This poem is
divided into four sections parallel to the four sections of medical anatomy that were
prevalent in Donne's day. The poem, in comparing the dead world with a corpse, first
dissects the intestines, then the heart, then the head, and finally the limbs. The anatomy
of the poem is intended to serve a didactic purpose, just like many anatomical
demonstrations of Donne's time. The poet-anatomist performs the dissection in order to
show unambiguously the deficiencies-diseases of the world's condition (Elderhorst 99).

The beginning of the poem draws attention to the moribund condition of the world
after Queen Elizabeth's death. Donne viewed her as the "Intrinsique Balme," without
which the natural order of the world would be destroyed. This again was consistent with
the Paracelsian theory of the intrinsic balm contending that every living body contains its

antidote for all poisons, and that when this balm is exhausted the creature must surely die (Elderhorst 98-99). The poem begins by examining the earth's intestines, called by Elderhorst the "microcosm or mankind." The second part of the poem examines the heart, or what Elderhorst calls the "macrocosm, the world's whole frame." The third part of the poem examines the head, or what Elderhorst calls the "loss of colour and proportion, both properties of beauty." And then, following the same sequence of the anatomist performing an autopsy, the poem finally examines the limbs, or what Elderhorst calls "the discord of heaven and earth," and the "loss of the influences of heaven upon earth" (99-100).

In Donne's Elegies, satire is at times the predominant mood. These elegies are written with piquancy, quaintness and drollery, and are filled with enough brilliance of humorous illustration to be comparable to the writings of Sterne and Lamb in their primes. Donne's Songs and Sonnets are even more filled with humor than are the Satires and the Elegies. Here the humor usually hovers in the background, but it occasionally becomes the center and the focus of the conceits (Cazamian 364). Some critics have read Donne's Songs and Sonnets as serious statements about romantic love, but other critics consider them to be comic or ironic.

"The Flea" is one of Donne's most witty poems. It starts out as follows:

> Mark but this flea, and mark in this,
> How little that which thou deny'st me is;
> It sucked me first, and now sucks thee,
> And in this flea, our two bloods mingled be;

This poem illustrates Donne's characteristic use of paradox, hyperbole, and vigorous speech. One of the targets of the poem is the speaker's smugness in developing his outlandish analogy. "Those readers who interpret the poem ironically can point to the religious language embedded in all three stanzas." Donne's speaker is witty, but Donne is nevertheless making fun of the speaker by having him use "language whose full implications may subvert the arguments that they so cleverly attempt to make" (Evans 325).

Donne's "Elegy 6" is entitled "The Perfume" and shows how Donne can exploit humorous situations and humorous language. Here the indignant speaker is complaining about having been caught carrying on a secret affair with the daughter of a rich citizen. It was his potent cologne that gave him away, and caused him to be apprehended. Part of the humor comes from the poem's zestful language and vigorous descriptions, and part of it comes from the speaker's tendency to describe inanimate objects as if they were alive and doing things intentionally. In this poem, he attacks the perfume as if it were a person, complaining that it "me traitorously hath betrayed." Donne's "love of paradox and word play is exemplified when the speaker complains that his perfume 'at once fled unto him [the father], and stayed with me." The final couplet of the poem reads, "All my perfumes, I give most willingly / To embalm thy father's corpse; What? will he die?" This final image is grotesque and repugnant. It is an unattractive picture of a cocky speaker, who is all the better indicted because the portrait which is being drawn is a self-portrait (Evans 325). Robert Evans says, "While "The Perfume" is one of Donne's funniest poems, in some ways it also is one of his most ironic, probing, and disturbing" (Evans 326).

"The Good Morrow" is a poem in Donne's The Songs and Sonnets, in which the speaker uses humor to contrast the total love that his mistress and he now enjoy with their incomplete love before they had met. The Songs and Sonnets begins with the suggestion, "Go, and catch a falling star," and then goes on to give a catalogue of other comic impossibilities (Evans 326). In "The Sun Rising," the speaker is lying in bed with his mistress, as he chastises the sun as a "Busy old fool," and a "Saucy pedantic wretch." He tells the sun to "Go chide / Late schoolboys, and sour prentices," and he threatens to "eclipse and cloud" the sun's rays "in a wink" (Evans 326).

In his "Hymn to God the Father," Donne plays with his own name as he uses such expressions as he contrasts "hast done" with "hast not done," and as he asks God to swear that he will be merciful. "Having done that, thou hast done, / I fear no more." The poem has a playful teasing tone, and "alludes to an earlier, secular love poem (with a similar refrain) by the sixteenth-century wit Sir Thomas Wyatt." In the poem, Donne is also playful in his humorous familiarity with God. The relationship between the speaker in the poem and God "displays the kind of comic affection that one might expect to find between an impetuous child and his sometimes stern but dependably loving parent" (Evans 327).

Alfred Gu L'Estrange suggests that for John Donne, Joseph Hall, and Thomas Fuller, humor was a vehicle of instruction, not one for entertainment (L'Estrange 241). Raymond Alden discusses Donne's five satires which were published posthumously in 1633, and two additional satires that were published in 1635 and 1669 respectively (Alden 75-76). After examining the evidence in some detail, Alden concludes that all seven satires had been written during a ten-year period dating from 1593 to 1603, and he further concludes that if these dates are correct the satires were published during a decade when satire was at its greatest vigor in England. Donne's satires were greeted with a great deal of enthusiasm. Dryden, Jonson, and Drummond admired them; and Freeman called Donne a Persius, and demanded that he write more satires (Alden 82).

Donne's writing style is vigorous, rugged, free, and conversational in tone, but at the same time compact, and sometimes obscure. The vocabulary is concrete, intellectual, and insightful. The development is dramatic. The writing also expresses some coarseness and cynicism (Alden 83). The satirical types range from satirical narrative, to satirical reflection, to direct rebuke. There are both Horatian and Juvenalian elements to the satire. Although the satires vary in tone and target, they are always pessimistic (Alden 85). There is much more of a classical influence on Donne's satires than an English influence. The pessimistic tone can be traced to the Roman satires. The same can be said of the reflective disposition and the emphasis on private morals, fashions, and humors. Donne's allusive, compact, and indirect writing style also has important classical antecedents. Donne also used dialogue in the Latin manner, and his selection of vices to be satirized (flattery of heirs, various forms of lust, luxury and avarice, idleness, wantonness, personal vanity, etc.) are also reminiscent of classical satire (Alden 88-89).

Humor was a positive and significant force in Donne's life, but it is the humor of intensity, not the humor of relaxation, for intensity is probably the dominant feature of Donne's writing style (Cazamian 362). The intensity and the exaggeration of Donne's writing style were used in moments of passionate ardor to create a tone of cynical mockery and lyrical fervor. In the development of the "Conceit of Impertinence," for example, "the comic effect [was] produced by breathtaking frankness and cynical candor in matters where reticence of thought and expression was expected as of right" (Cazamian 366).

Donne effectively used both overstatement and understatement in his writing. Louis Cazamian feels that overstatement is the most salient feature of Donne's humor, and he feels that understatement is merely an inverted form of overstatement: "The systematic exaggeration builds up a fictitious scale of values, which Donne consistently pretends to be the right, normal one; this superimposes seriousness on absurdity, and is the method of his humor" (Cazamian 366).

Donne's humor is usually satirical, and often sardonic. Humor appears not only in his Satires, but is also a feature of much of his other writing, and this humor is filled with scornful and violent denunciation, and with preposterous exaggerations that often become grotesque. It is a picturesque humor filled with verve. It contains a rich mixture of wit and fancy, and not a small amount of moral indignation. It is hyperbolic and intense humor, written tongue in cheek (Cazamian 362-363).

As to the targets of the satires, the first satire deals with various affectations of the period, and it also deals with lust, conceit, and flattery (Alden 85). This first satire is about a "fondling motley humorist;" Cazamian notes that this target would have been called a "fop" one century after Donne's writing, and he would have been called a "snob" today, but the important feature about this person's character is that he is entirely innocent of any humorous intent (Cazamian 363). The second satire is about the sins of lawyers, the third about religion, the fourth about the wretchedness of the court and affectations of dress and speech, the fifth about "officers' rage and suitors' misery," the sixth about a foolish lover, and the seventh about the foolish conversation and conduct of Sir Nicholas Smyth (Alden 84-85).

John Donne Bibliography

Alden, Raymond MacDonald. "John Donne." The Rise of Formal Satire in England under Classical Influence. New York, NY: Archon, 1961, 75-90.
Cazamian, Louis. "Donne." The Development of English Humor. Durham, NC: Duke University Press, 1952, 362-366.
Elderhorst, Constance. "John Donne's First Anniversary as an Anatomical Anamorphosis." Explorations in the Field of Nonsense. Ed. Wim Tigges. Amsterdam, Holland: Rodopi, 1987, 97-102.
Evans, Robert C. "John Donne." Encyclopedia of British Humorists, Volume I. Ed. Steven H. Gale, New York, NY: Garland, 1996, 319-329.
Gardner, Helen, Ed. The Elegies and the Songs and Sonnets [of John Donne]. Oxford, England: Oxford University Press, 1963.
Hester, M. Thomas. Kinde Pitty and Brave Scorn: John Donne's Satyres. Durham, NC: Duke University Press, 1982.
L'Estrange, Alfred Gu. "Donne--Hall--Fuller." History of English Humour. New York, NY: Burt Franklin, 1878, 243-249.
LeComte, Edward, ed. Grace to a Witty Sinner: A Life of Donne. New York, NY: Walker, 1965.
Leishman, J. B. The Monarch of Wit: An Analytical and Comparative Study of the Poetry of John Donne 5th edition. New York, NY: Harper and Row, 1965.
Milgate, Wesley, ed. The Satires, Epigrams, and Verse Letters [of John Donne]. Oxford: Oxford University Press, 1967.
Morris, Brian. "Satire from Donne to Marvell." The Metaphysical Poetry. Eds. Malcolm Bradbury, and David Palmer, Bloomington, IN: Indiana University Press, 1971, 210-235.
Rosten, Murray. The Soul of Wit: A Study of John Donne. Oxford, England: Clarendon Press, 1974.

Ben Jonson (c1572-1637)

Robert Evans says that the fundamental purpose of Ben Jonson's comedies is to teach by pleasing. Jonson encourages virtue by ridiculing and exposing folly and vice. His comedies are often satirical, and they are designed to teach ethics. Jonson's characters are meant to represent particular social classes, types, or vices, and Jonson's plays, therefore, can be placed firmly in the tradition of the great "morality" plays. Jonson mocks all kinds of pretension, obsession, fantasy, and deceit (Evans 601). The names of his characters, names like Manly, Lovewit, Truewit, Subtle, and Justice Overdo are highly suggestive of their emblematic functions (Evans 599). Much of Jonson's writing is based on earlier writing, but his ability to "adopt, adapt, echo, modify, and parody his sources...gives many of his own works much of their interest." Jonson's tone tends to be witty and farcical. In his comedies there are many dupes and dupers, gulls and knaves. Some of his characters are remarkably stupid, and others are too clever for their own good. The most frequent target of Jonson's comedies is pride, or its related qualities, vanity, egotism, self-righteousness, immoderation, willfulness, inflexibility, meanness, greed, hypocrisy, and so forth. "Ironically, much of the energy of Jonsonian drama comes from the impulsive drive and verbal wit of the characters who are most morally repugnant, whereas the characters who are most obviously virtuous can sometimes seem the least interesting and most thin." In Jonson, the visual imagery can be intense, as when the greedy Sir Epicure Mammon imagines how he will dine after he becomes rich. When that time comes, he will eat "oiled mushrooms; and the swelling unctuous paps / Of a fat pregnant sow, newly cut off, / Dressed with an exquisite and poignant sauce" (Evans 600).

Ben Jonson and William Shakespeare were rivals in real life. They would frequently meet at the Mermaid Club on Fleet Street, a place where the wits of the day went to sharpen their abilities in verbal duelling. Alfred Gu L'Estrange describes their relationship as follows. "Here [the Mermaid Club] it was that Shakespeare and Jonson often contended, the former like 'a light English man-of-war' the latter like 'a high-built Spanish galleon' " (L'Estrange 268).

Louis Cazamian feels that only Ben Jonson is a rival to William Shakespeare in his significance as a writer in the development of English humor. And while Shakespeare and Jonson were active as writers, the prevailing view was that Jonson would be the more important of the two dramatists. Although Jonson's development of the "theory of humors" was significant, however, and although his development of the present sense of the word "humor" was significant, "Shakespeare's contribution to the advance of the thing itself was much more substantial" (Cazamian 308). In his plays, Jonson fully developed the concept of humor of manners or decorum. A Jonson character exhibited the predominance of a given feature, and once drawn, this feature became the ruling determinant in the development of that character. For Jonson, the concept of "humor" was equivalent to the whole code and rule of conduct, the standard of manners, of a character. Jonson's "humors" comedy was the climax in a long development of the "humors" comedy in the two genres of storytelling and playwriting lasting from 1550 to 1600 (Cazamian 311). Jonson's characters were controlled by their "humors." It was their "humors" that made them odd, and it was their "humors" that made them vigorous, and powerful, and queer, and paradoxical, and funny. It was their "humors" that made them funny in a very serious way. So "humor" became a feature of the national English mind. It represented not only a consciousness of one's oddity, but even the pleasure and the pride of being odd. Sir William Temple says, "We have more humour, because every man follows his own, and takes a pleasure, perhaps a pride, to show it" (Cazamian 329). Jonson did more than any other English writer to transform the word "humor" to its modern sense. Although "humor" had been used in this sense long before Jonson, it was Jonson's strong authority and dogmatic mind that left a permanent imprint on the word (Cazamian 308). "In no nation was the...extension of meaning which brought the medieval term to its full modern sense so decisive and consequential as in England" (Cazamian 328).

Leigh Hunt compares Ben Jonson's humor to Jonson's own life. Both his humor and his life were pampered, jovial, and dictatorial, and in both, Jonson was in control. "He always gives one the idea of a man sitting at the head of a table and a coterie. He carves up a subject as he would a dish" (Hunt 139). Hugh Walker considers Jonson's satire to be crude but vigorous. He considers Jonson's lyrics to be coarse, but exquisite, and he feels that they portray "the massive strength of his physical frame." Walker feels that Jonson is "the great master in English of satirical comedy," and feels further that he left "by far the completest satirical complementary we possess upon the Elizabethan age." Shakespeare's writings have survived better than Jonson's not because Shakespeare is a better writer, but because the truth in Shakespeare's writings was a more universal kind of truth. Walker considers satire to be "a relatively low form of literature, just because it embodies a relatively small element of truth." What Walker means by this statement is that the truth of most satire is largely bound to the time and place of writing, since it deals with local issues, customs, and personalities (Walker 119).

Ben Jonson was a parodist, but a parodist with a difference. Instead of simply placing on the stage caricatured versions of hackneyed plots and motifs, as an ordinary parodist would do, Jonson placed these plots and motifs in the minds of his foolish characters (Watson 1). In Jonson's plays, each character fights with the others for the privilege of controlling the story, in which he sees himself as the hero (Watson 2). Jonson's satiric plays have two general targets. On the one hand, Jonson is exposing London society in general; on the other hand, Jonson is exposing the London stage in particular, and Jonson's style is synergistically to combine the social satire with the parodic satire into a single unit (Watson 4). Robert Watson compares Ben Jonson to John Milton in terms of how they relate to their characters. Milton hated Satan, but Satan is nevertheless the most vivid inhabitant of Paradise Lost, in spite of Milton's efforts to ironically expose the vividness. In the same way, Jonson clearly despises his gulls and hypocrites, but they are nevertheless his most vivid characters (Watson 17). Watson describes Jonson as a "revolutionary working in a paradoxically conservative medium, courting the audience he needed for his new form of art and the allies he needed for his guerilla campaign against the idolatries of England's theatricalized culture" (Watson 18).

Every Man In His Humour (1598), was Jonson's first great theatrical success, and continued the "humors" comedy tradition which George Chapman had started only one year earlier with his An Humorous Day's Mirth (Harry Levin 8). But Jonson systematically added an important element to the humors-comedy tradition by integrating parodies, and Latin comedy with the humors-comedy of Chapman. In Every Man In His Humour, the wits superseded the fools in controlling the plot, because the satiric comedic style was superseding the fables about prodigal sons, the farces about cuckolding, and the romantic tragedies that were so common on London stages during Jonson's time (Watson 19).

Many scholars have criticized the fact that the plot of Every Man In His Humour is very difficult to follow. Jonson's plays are said to be "jury-rigged in order to facilitate the collisions of humorous types" (Watson 20). T. S. Eliot, however, saw structure in Jonson's writing; in fact he saw an "immense dramatic constructive skill...not so much skill in plot as skill in doing without a plot." What Eliot found in Jonson's writing was an "action" rather than a "plot"--in other words, a simple principle of movement given significance by what he calls "unity of inspiration" (Jagendorf 45). Robert Watson also feels that the difficulty of the plot was intentional, and that it adds to the satiric and parodic power of the play. According to Watson, the "scattershot plotting" gave Jonson an opportunity for "systematic parody that Chapman had failed to exploit" (Watson 20). In his plots (or lack of them), Jonson is playing with his audience; and he is also playing with his audience in ridiculing characters who try to pose as conventional heroes. Jonson is using parody to satirize other playwrights--including Shakespeare--and at the same time he is pleading for a more sophisticated audience, by implying that "those who fail to understand the play's critical argument will, by their unthinking devotion to familiar dramatic modes, necessarily be casting themselves as the play's gulls" (Watson 21). Every Man In His Humour is about liberating the London theatre goers from their bondage to theatrical conventions, and Jonson does this by capturing alive the "melodramatic monsters" that were threatening to take over the Elizabethan stage. About these "monsters" Watson says: "The stage that had once been their home becomes their menagerie, with all their absurdities on display" (Watson 45-46). Watson concludes that Jonson's pockets were "stuffed with shreds from the works of other authors, not because he lacks a voice of his own, but because he can make himself heard most clearly by temporarily mimicking voices more familiar to his audience" (Watson 46).

Jonson owes his literary life to William Shakespeare. As a young poet, Jonson submitted his <u>Every Man In His Humour</u>, a play giving complete directions for the conduct of a gentleman of the time, to one of the leading actors, a comedian, in the company to which Shakespeare belonged. The actor read Jonson's play and was planning to reject it. But Shakespeare asked if he could read the play, and Shakespeare immediately recognized Jonson's talent, and recommended that the play be performed. That was the key point of Jonson's literary career. Harry Levin indicates that it was Jonson who transposed "the category of humor from the plane of physiognomy to the sphere of comedy." In both <u>Every Man In His Humour</u>, and <u>Every Man Out of His Humour</u> Jonson develops characters whose obsessive traits make them appear ridiculous (Evans 601).

Raymond Alden notes that <u>Every Man Out of His Humour</u> (1599) was entered in the Stationers' Register as "a comical satire." Although Jonson did not write what Alden calls "formal satire," he was nevertheless one of the writers most responsible for the development of the special genre of "English satire" (Alden 198). There are three things which make <u>Every Man Out of His Humour</u> a strange play. In the first place, there is no attempt at unity of either plot or tone; rather there are conflicts, discords, and irreverences which control the play. In the second place, the affectations and the delusions of the humorous characters are very bookish in nature and can be associated with the recurring humors of character types throughout literature. Jonson's superior characters are alert both to literature, and to the role-playing nature of literature. In the third place, the affectations and delusions are "strategically arranged to compel the audience to recognize and approve Jonson's new satirical mode of comedy if they are to avoid a degrading identification with the fools on stage" (Watson 47). Jonson was criticizing his fellow Elizabethan playwrights, but by destroying his contemporaries he was also destroying himself.

> What was it that he wished to write on the blank of the stage, once he had erased the works of his rivals? What was he going to sell to an audience he had taught not to buy fool's gold.... How could he end his plots in a way that would be satisfying without being overly pat, happy without being overly romantic, ethical without being overly moralistic? How could he give pleasure without reinforcing unhealthy complacency? These are the questions raised by the strikingly peculiar course of <u>Every Man Out of His Humour</u>, which pursues to their logical extremes the devices and principles established in <u>Every Man In His Humour</u>. Never again would Jonson edge quite so close to the theoretical limits of his satiric method. (Watson 79)

Jonson was so successful with his parodic satires that he frightened himself. The plays which follow his <u>Every Man Out of His Humour</u> all show Jonson's "discomfort with his role as satiric city-comedian" (Watson 81).

Alice Rayner suggests that in <u>Every Man Out of His Humour</u>, Mitis and Cordatus serve as bridges between the play and the audience in

> explaining not only the moral action but the purpose of [the] comedy. These two characters make manifest the generally latent capacity of comic satire to penetrate theatrical barriers so that the audience, told the opinions of the author directly, is implicated in the moral postures of the comic satire. (Rayner 43)

Not only do these characters function as comic theorists, but function as critics and critical respondents as well, for they imagine objections that might be raised, and answer these objections thereby establishing a dialogue between an imaginary critical audience and the author himself (Rayner 43). Shakespeare's plays were ambiguous in presentation and ambivalent in interpretation, but this was not true of Jonson's plays.

Jonson's [plays] have no mitigating circumstances, no qualified errors or character, no degree or proportion in values. Moral structure is absolute in that moral faults are singularly themselves, not aspects of multifaceted characters or situations. The faults, indeed, create the situations. (Rayner 45)

This is because Jonson's plays are produced with a goal of conversion in mind. Jonson sees himself as wielding the "sword of righteousness in a corrupt world." He sees and exaggerates moral problems to make them self-evident, because he is not so interested in the completeness and credibility of his fictional world as he is interested in dealing with the corruption in the real world. Jonson's world is an evil place--a dystopia. And Rayner points out that in Jonsonian dystopian comedy the world is divided between the purely comic on the one hand, and the purely moral on the other. Jonson uses the comedy to ridicule evil, but what he is really doing is seeking justice and judgment against the evil and obsessive characters (Rayner 59). Therefore, Jonson's characters become caricatures of his dystopian comedy. "The corrective motive begins in a moral perspective that generates a contradiction between what is and what ought to be, between the picture of a diseased world and an imagined ideal of perfect health" (Rayner 60). Rayner feels that Jonson's dystopian comedy does not reflect the complexities and contradictions that are to be found in the real world, but rather distorts reality to present a world with only two mentions, good and bad, for that is the world that exists in the mind of the novel's creator, Jonson. (Rayner 60).

Volpone (1606) is one of Jonson's best plays. The basic action of Volpone is summarized in the acrostic that Jonson appended to the first edition:

V olpone, childless, rich, feigns sick, despairs,

O ffers his state to hopes of several heirs,

L ies languishing; his Parasite receives

P resents of all, assures, deludes; then weaves

O ther cross plots, which ope themselves, are told.

N ew tricks for safety are sought; they thrive; when, bold,

E ach tempts th' other again, and all are sold. (Evans 601)

In Volpone, all of the characters are again susceptible to "self-dramatizing disease," and this includes the wits as well as the fools, and the victimizers as well as the victims (Watson 96). The characters are led astray by the flattering scripts which they have written for themselves, and in Volpone the "satiric manipulators delude and injure themselves in the process of deluding and injuring their gulls" (Watson 82). The main criticism of Volpone has to do with its classification. It is a comedy and a satire, but its harsh ending in which severe sentences are given to Mosca and Volpone makes it a tragedy as well. Edward Partridge asks, "Is it satire, burlesque, farce, comedy of humours, or melodrama?" Northrop Frye calls it "a kind of comic imitation of a tragedy." Robert Watson says that Jonson's Volpone is like Jonson's earlier plays, a satire targeting the trite dramatic expectations of Elizabethan authors and Elizabethan audiences (Watson 83). "If his critics demand a moral ending, they will receive it only in the harsh discordant form of the court's official sentences, and they will have to decide whether they really prefer that to the comic spirit that survives in Volpone's Epilogue" (Watson 97).

Diogenes, it will be remembered, travelled the folly-ridden world in search for a single honest man. Epicoene (1609) is a comedy of manners and a farce in which Morose, reminiscent of Diogenes, is in search of a single silent woman. But because there is no such thing according to the play's conventionally sexist point of view, Morose's search is superseded by other plots and subplots, and the play becomes first an energetic and abusive farce, managed by Truewit, one of the characters, and then a witty coup contrived by Dauphine (Watson 98). The audience is intentionally misled in Epicoene in three different ways. First, Truewit's name would suggest that his perspective is also the perspective of Jonson. Second, the "silent woman" that is found becomes a "shrewish clamorous woman" as soon as she is married. And third, Epicoene is not even a woman at all, but rather a boy in disguise. "When the boy Epicoene throws off his disguise as a woman, the play Epicoene throws off its disguise as a play" (Watson 110).

In the beginning of Epicoene there is an extraordinarily quiet young girl that Morose marries. But he later discovers that she is in truth talkative, annoying, and assertive. Dauphine, Morose's nephew, promises to free his uncle from the bondage of this marriage in return for an inheritance, and when Morose agrees to the terms, Dauphine reveals that Epicoene has actually been a young boy all along, and that there was therefore no marriage. It is in interesting that in Jonson's day the roles of young women were played by young men, so for Jonson's theatre public we have here a boy playing a girl playing a boy (Evans 602).

> What initially appears to be another competition of plots finally resolves itself (at least among the gallants) into a sort of commedia dell'arte piece, with the various lazzi decorating a pleasant path to a satisfying destination. It is, in this sense, a preparation for the opening scene of The Alchemist [1610], where Jonson again presents three witty plotters and self-conscious performers--Subtle, Face, and Dol--all working together to take advantage of the gulls' conventional fantasies, and using any spare energy and ingenuity to battle each other for control of the conclusion. (Watson 112)

Jonson's The Alchemist (1610) is about a gentleman who leaves his house in town. The housekeeper, who is now in charge, allows fortune-tellers and vagabonds to live in the house, and this is where they carry on their trade (L'Estrange 258). The character Subtle promises to change lead into gold, but what he does instead is to change human follies into profit (Watson 113). Again, much of the play is concerned with determining which of the characters will control the plot and therefore establish his true identity. And again, Jonson is establishing the distinction between role and reality, as "the conspirators vacillate between playfully ironic role-playing and dangerously proud self dramatizations" (Watson 136-136). The Alchemist ends with an Epilogue in which both Lovewit and Face apologize for any breaches of the rules of drama they may have made. But since the play is about the confusion of drama with life, it is appropriate that there is an ambiguity as to whether they are apologizing as actors or as characters (Watson 137). Jonson's plays were performed in a theatre in the Blackfriars section of London, and Watson notes that, "There is still an alchemist at work in the house in Blackfriars, and he mocks the naive Londoners who gather there, even while he transforms the base dramas they bring to him into his own satiric gold" (Watson 138).

The Alchemist is "so full of shenanigans and inventiveness that its immediate appeal is almost irresistible" (Evans 602). The Alchemist is a work of gritty comic realism, whose linguistic exuberance gives it a real vitality. Some of Jonson's most memorable characters are the aggressive Subtle, the wily Face, and the self-indulgent Sir Epicure Mammon. The play explores such themes as egotism, deception, gullibility, greed, and self-deceit. The main target of the satire is the hypocrisy that Puritanism tends to encourage (Evans 603). Northrop Frye notes that Sir Epicure Mammon has a dream of what he will do with the philosopher's stone when he finds it, and that this fact puts Mammon into Frye's second phase of comedy, the category in which the hero does not transform a humorous society, but rather escapes from it. Frye calls this the "quixotic" phase (Frye 180).

Bartholomew Fair (1614) is again about the distinction between role and reality, but here the distinction is blurred. "By depicting a carnival world that victimizes authority figures, Bartholomew Fair enables Jonson to subvert his own authoritarian attitudes toward literature and to relax his hierarchical construction of the dramatic canon. The ending of the play is an endorsement, rather than a repression, of plays and playfulness" (Watson 139). Zvi Jagendorf notes that Bartholomew Fair is not about a particular character or characters. "It is the fair that controls the action rather than any character, though the wits profit from it while the fools are fleeced and beaten. The fair includes all levels of humanity, indeed, animals and objects as well, and stresses what they have in common" (Jagendorf 77).

There are a number of grotesques in Bartholomew Fair, Ursula is a grotesque "pig woman." Cokes is childish and stupid. Humphrey Waspe is irascible, and Zeal-of-the-Land Busy is a hypocritical puritan fanatic. And the way that these ridiculous characters interact is also "patently ludicrous" (Evans 603). The fools in Bartholomew Fair are more likeable than those in Jonson's earlier comedies, and even the robberies and the physical violence come across as more playful than cruel (Watson 140). Parody and satire are still in evidence in Bartholomew Fair, but there is a difference. When Jonson's satiric parody has progressed to the point where he would usually make his satiric coup de grace, he instead forgives the dramatic transgressions, and "urges that even the silliest and most grotesquely conventional aspects of plays be continued and enjoyed" (Watson 139). There were social forces in Jonson's England that caused him to turn his satiric strategies away from his rivals, and toward the newly empowered censoring puritans that were threatening to close down all Elizabethan theatres. Jonson found his own critical position to be too close to that of the Puritans he detested, so he turned his attack on the Elizabethan prodigal son narratives, Cicero's Orations, Whetstone's Mirror for Magistrates of Cities, and the Bible, which corrupted such Jonsonian characters as Wasp, Overdo, and Busy. In Bartholomew Fair, Jonson seems to be saying, "The fault is not in men's plays, but in themselves, if they are fools" (Watson 140).

The Devil Is an Ass (1616) is neither a didactic story of absolute evil, nor a satiric statement of inevitable human frailties, but is rather written from a sympathetic, even sentimental, perspective. Jonson probably took this stance in order to "reserve a place for himself in the next wave of dramatic practice" (Watson 172). At first, Jonson may have been attempting the traditional morality drama with its "bogeyman devils, its hokey hellmouths, and its ponderous didactic allegories," but he finally positions himself against the unrealistic and simplistic solutions of this tradition (Watson 174). Rather, he saw that the development of sentimental comedy was inevitable in England, and it is probably for this reason that he developed the tone of The Devil Is an Ass to be consistent with this new genre. It would allow him a position from which he could continue writing (Watson 209).

There are 133 epigrams in Ben Jonson His Epigrams, which was published in 1616. These all followed Jonson's concept of epigrams as short poems, each restricted to a single idea, and expressing the various passions of everyday life (Alden 192). Jonson's epigrams employed decasyllabic couplets with special satirical effect (Alden 193). The characters in Jonson's epigrams are the same characters as are to be found in his satires, but in the epigrams they are more individualized, and they are "drawn more rapidly and by a more masterly hand" (Alden 194).

In The New Inn (1629) Jonson has come full cycle. Watson considers this play to be one of the greatest ironies in all of English literary history, because

> the play represents a profound and ceremonious concession to the popular tastes Jonson had resisted for so long. The new inn, for the audience as well as the characters, is a place where their long-cherished fantasies are miraculously fulfilled. The location of the inn in a distant London suburb may reflect the location of the play halfway between the satiric world of city-comedy and the romantic world of pastoral. (Watson 210)

In Jonson's earlier plays there were base puns, schemes, and brawls, but in The New Inn the common people are forgotten, and the play focuses on the sentimental hopes of the "upstairs characters" and indeed of the audience itself (Watson 211). Critics are confused as to whether to call The New Inn a romantic indulgence or a burlesque of the romantic tradition, and Watson suggests that it is both. "It is the work of a man who could neither submit completely to dramatic illusions nor resist completely their seductive appeal" (Watson 212).

> The contradictions can be partly resolved by recognizing that the play offers a running commentary on the struggle between satiric distance and romantic absorption involved in its own composition. The New Inn is Jonson's genial reevaluation of his approach to moral drama, and at its center is a reevaluation of his parodic strategy. The irony is that the spirit of parodic satire Jonson had nurtured for so long, a spirit whose natural prey is conventional romantic melodrama, escaped from the cellar of the new inn into the audience at the first performance and (like Frankenstein's monster) attacked its maker. Jonson would have found himself trapped in a bitter role-reversal, chastised by his audience for his own apparent excursion into melodramatic conventionality. (Watson 212)

Jonson was too good a satirist not to realize the trite and sentimental qualities of The New Inn. But our realizing this makes its truth all the more ironic and poignant (Watson 224).

Like Plautus, Jonson was very fond of coining new words, and of using very long and obscure words, and in fact this was one of his most effective humorous techniques. In The Alchemist, Subtle tells Face to "name the vexations and the martyrizations of metals in the work," and Face responds, "Sir, putrefaction, solution, ablution, sublimation, cohabitation, calcination, ceration, and fixation" (L'Estrange 260-261).

Jonson insists, as Swift would later insist, that "humor is ingrained and not to be achieved by affectation" (Harry Levin 8). The genre which Jonson devised has come to be known as "the comedy of humors" (Harry Levin 9). Raymond Alden eloquently summarizes Jonson's contribution to the field of humor and satire:

> In his treatment of humours; in his unfailing ridicule of the absurdities of the time; in his character-sketches (from the "characters" in the list of dramatis personae at the opening of some of the plays to his most elaborate attempts at characterization); and, not least of all, in his use of sharp personal satire in the conduct of his quarrels--he led the way to much of the satire of the seventeenth and eighteenth centuries. (Alden 198)

Ben Jonson's writing style is in many respects unique. One of his conceits was the stopping of the play and introducing persons who would in turn explain the plays and make remarks about the characters. Such interruptions would give variety and amusement to the audience or the reader (L'Estrange 262). Jonson also liked to indulge in strong language, but although this was true, he seldom employed any really coarse allusions (L'Estrange 263).

Jonson had gone from a working-class environment first, into several terms in prison, and then to become the leading poet of the royal court. When he had a stroke he found himself permanently confined to his room, and banished from royal favor. His children died, and his pension was inadequate. It is in view of these facts that The New Inn takes on its real significance.

> It is both striking and suggestive that, after a career devoted to separating the grim truths of life from the pleasant fantasies of popular literature, and extirpating romantic melodrama from that theater, Jonson could suggest so seductively that life can be like theater after all, and could dismiss realism in favor of a conventional happy ending which brings lost children miraculously back to life and a melancholic old intellectual back into the flow of life. The romantic plot of The New Inn may have been for him, as

it was for Love, a fantasy so badly needed that it overrode the guiding principles of a lifetime. (Watson 225)

Johnson's "masques" contain much vigorous language and vital wit. They are also cleverly satirical and good fun, and they all have happy endings. "The humor can be variously gentle, teasing, rollicking, biting, boisterous, whimsical, parodic, farcical, and so on." There is much playful dialect humor in The Irish Masque (1613), for example, and in For the Hunour of Wales (1618) there is also playful dialect humor. This Welsh masque opens with swaggering and bluster, "Room, room! make room for the bouncing belly, / First father of sauce, and deviser of jelly." News from the New World Discovered in the Moon (1621), and Time Vindicated to Himselfe and to His Honours (1623) both contain both stinging satire. The humor of the masques may be a bit dated, since much of the fun of these pieces depended on the particular ways that they were performed. But even today they have the power to amuse and to instruct, for according to Robert Evans, Jonson "was, and remains, the foremost writer of English masques" (Evans 604).

Jonson's poems also contained much humor, and in Epigrammes the prevailing tone is satire. Here again, Jonson is targeting all kinds of foolishness and pretension. Evans notes that "in the Epigrammes, his satire is often dismissive and contemptuous (Evans). In such memorable poems as his epistle to Edward Sackville, "An Epistle to a Friend," "Speech According to Horace," "Tribe of Ben," and "Epigram on the Court Pucell" Jonson is a ferocious satirist. But Jonson wrote whimsical, cheerful, and playfully foolish poems as well, as can be seen in "A Fit of Rhyme Against Rhyme," or "Execration Upon Vulcan, or his various poems about Thomas Coryate (Evans 605).

In discussing the endings to Jonson's comedies, Zvi Jagendorf notes that it is rarely the judges, lawyers, or officers who bring about discovery at the ends of the plays. Rather, they are part of the cheat (as can be seen by the mock lawyers in Epicoene), or they are the victims (as in The Alchemist), or they are subjected to the exposure themselves (as in Bartholomew Fair), or at best they are just observers of the unmasking (as in Volpone)(Jagendorf 44). Jonson's endings are involved with discovery and unmasking which is strongly ironic in effect. But "denouement" in the traditional, romantic, sense of the word was one of the things which Jonson rejected, and one of the things which he was parodying and satirizing (Jagendorf 45).

Ben Jonson Bibliography

Alden, Raymond MacDonald. The Rise of Formal Satire in England under Classical Influence. New York, NY: Archon, 1961.

Bacon, Wallace A. "The Magnetic Field: The Structure of Jonson's Comedies." Huntington Library Quarterly 19 (1956): 121-153.

Barish, Jonas A. Ben Jonson and the Language of Prose Comedy. Cambridge, MA: Harvard Univ Press, 1960.

Barish, Jonas A. "Feasting and Judging in Jonsonian Comedy." Renaissance Drama NS5 (1972): 3-35

Barton, Anne. "The New Inn and the Problem of Jonson's Later Style." English Literary Renaissance 9 \92979\0; 495-528.

Baskervill, Charles Read. English Elements in Jonson's Early Comedy. New York, NY: Gordian, 1967.

Baum, Helena Watts. The Satiric and the Didactic in Ben Jonson's Comedy. Chapel Hill, NC: Univ of North Carolina Press, 1947.

Beaurline, L. A. "Comic Language in Volpone." Ben Jonson's Volpone, or the Fox. Ed. Harold Bloom. New York, NY: Chelsea, 1988.

Beaurline, L. A. Jonson and Elizabethan Comedy: Essays in Dramatic Rhetoric. San

Marino, CA: Huntington Library, 1978.

Beecher, Don. "The Progress of Trickster in Ben Jonson's Volpone." Cahiers-Elisabethans: Late Medieval and Renaissance Studies. Montpellier, France. Apr, 1985: 43-51.

Bryant, J. A., Jr. The Compassionate Satirist: Ben Jonson and His Imperfect World. Athens, GA: University of Georgia Press, 1972.

Cazamian, Louis. The Development of English Humor. Durham, NC: Duke University Press, 1952.

Champion, L. S. "The Comic Intent of Jonson's The New Inn." Western Humanities Review 18 (1964): 66-74.

Colley, John Scott. "Bartholomew Fair: Jonson's 'A Midsummer Night's Dream.' " Comparative Drama 11 (1977): 63-71.

Corman, Brian. "Thomas Shadwell and the Jonsonian Comedy of the Restoration." From Renaissance to Restoration: Metamorphoses of the Drama. Eds. Robert Markley and Laurie Finke. Cleveland, OH: Bellflower, 1984, 126-152.

Danson, Lawrence. "Jonsonian Comedy and the Discovery of the Social Self." Publications of the Modern Language Association 99 (1984): 179-193.

Davidson, P. H. "Volpone and the Old Comedy." Modern Language Quarterly 24 (1963): 151-157.

Davis, Joe L. The Sons of Ben: Jonsonian Comedy in Caroline England. Detroit, MI: Wayne State Univ Press, 1967.

Dean, Leonard F. "Three Notes on Comic Morality: Celia, Bobadill, and Falstaff." Studies in English Literature 1500-1900 16 (1976): 263-271.

Dessen, Alan C. Jonson's Moral Comedy. Evanston, IL: Northwestern Univ Press, 1971.

Dick, Aliki Lafkidou. Paedeia Through Laughter: Jonson's Aristophanic Appeal to Human Intelligence. The Hague, Netherlands: Mouton, 1974.

Donaldson, Ian. The World Upside-Down: Comedy from Jonson to Fielding. Oxford, England: Clarendon, 1970.

Empson, William. "Comic Language in Volpone." Ben Jonson's Volpone, or the Fox." Ed. Harold Bloom. New York, NY: Chelsea, 1988.

Enck, John J. Jonson and the Comic Truth. Madison, WI: Univ of Wisconsin Press, 1957.

Evans, Robert C. "Ben Jonson." Encyclopedia of British Humorists, Volume I. Ed. Steven H. Gale, New York, NY: Garland, 1996, 594-608.

Felperin, Howard. "Quick Comedy Refined: Towards a Poetics of Jonson's Major Plays." Southern Review: Literary and Interdisciplinary Essays 13 (1980): 153-169.

Flachmann, Michael. "Epicoene: A Comic Hell for a Comic Sinner." Medieval and Renaissance Drama in England 1 (1984): 131-142.

Frye, Northrop. Anatomy of Criticism. Princeton, NJ: Princeton University Press, 1957.

Gendron, Charisse. "The Expanding License of Jonson's Comedies: Volpone, The Alchemist, and Bartholomew Fair." Jacobean Miscellany 3 Salzburg, Austria: Inst. für Anglistik and Amerikanistik, 1983, 5-31.

Gertmenian, Donald. "Comic Experience in Volpone and The Alchemist." Studies in English Literature, 1500-1900 17 (1977): 247-258.

Gibbons, Brian. "Congreve's The Old Bachelour and Jonsonian Comedy." William Congreve. Ed. Brian Morris. Totowa, NJ: Rowman, 1972.

Gibbons, Brian. Jacobean City Comedy: A Study of Satiric Plays by Jonson, Marston and Middleton. 2nd ed. London, England: Methuen, 1980.

Gottwald, Maria. "Ben Jonson's Theory of Comedy." Germanica Wratislaviensia 10 (1966): 31-53.

Graham, C. B. "The Jonsonian Tradition in the Comedies of Thomas D'Urfey." Modern Language Quarterly 8 (1947): 47-52.

Gum, Coburn. The Aristophanic Comedies of Ben Jonson: A Comparative Study of Jonson and Aristophanes. The Hague, Netherlands: Mouton, 1969.

Heffner, Ray L., Jr. "Unifying Symbols in the Comedy of Ben Jonson." English Stage Comedy. Ed. W. K. Wimsatt, Jr. New York, NY: Columbia University Press, 1955, 74-97.

Howarth, Herbert. "The Joycean Comedy: Wilde, Jonson, and Others." A James Joyce Miscellany. Second Series. Ed. Marvin Magalaner. Carbondale, IL: Southern Illinois Univ Press, 1959, 179-194.

Hunt, Leigh. "Ben Jonson." Wit and Humour. New York, NY: Folcroft, 1972, 139-157.

Jagendorf, Zvi. "Perplexing the Catastrophe: Endings in Jonson's Comedy." The Happy End of Comedy: Jonson, Molière, and Shakespeare. Newark, DE: Univ of Delaware Press, 1984, 78-110.

Jensen, Ejner J. Ben Jonson's Comedies on the Modern Stage. Ann Arbor, MI: UMI Research Press, 1985.

Juneja, Renu. "The Unclassical Design of Jonson's Comedy." Renaissance and Reformation NS4 (1980): 74-86.

Kay, W. David. "Bartholomew Fair: Ben Jonson in Praise of Folly." English Literary Renaissance 6 (1976): 299-316.

Kerr, Mina. Influence of Ben Jonson on English Comedy, 1598-1642. New York, NY: Phaeton, 1967.

Kifer, Devra Rowland. "The Staple of News: Jonson's Festive Comedy." Studies in English Literature, 1500-1900 12 (1972): 329-344.

Knights, L. C. Drama and Society in the Age of Jonson. London, England: Chatto, 1937.

L'Estrange, Alfred Gu. "Shakespeare--Ben Jonson--Beaumont and Fletcher--The Wise Men of Gotham." History of English Humour. New York, NY: Burt Franklin, 1878, 250-270.

Leech, Clifford. "The Incredibility of Jonsonian Comedy." A Celebration of Ben Jonson. Eds. William Blissett, Julian Patrick, and R. W. van Fossen. Toronto, Canada: Univ of Toronto Press, 1973, 3-25.

Leonard, Nancy S. "The Persons of the Comic in Shakespeare and Jonson." Research Opportunities in Renaissance Drama 22 (1979): 11-15.

Leonard, Nancy S. "Shakespeare and Jonson Again: The Comic Forms." Renaissance Drama NS10 (1979): 45-69.

Levin, Harry, ed. Veins of Humor. Cambridge, MA: Harvard Univ Press, 1972.

Levin, Lawrence L. "Replication as Dramatic Strategy in the Comedies of Ben Jonson." Renaissance Drama NS5 (1972): 37-74.

Lumley, Eleanor P. The Influence of Plautus on the Comedies of Ben Jonson. New York: NY: Knickerbocker, 1901.

McCanles, Michael. "Festival in Jonsonian Comedy." Renaissance Drama NS8 (1977): 203-219.

McDonald, Russ. "Jonsonian Comedy and the Value of Sejanus." Studies in English Literature, 1500-1900 21 (1981): 287-305.

McDonald, Russ. "Skeptical Visions: Shakespeare's Tragedies and Jonson's Comedies." Shakespeare Studies 34 (1981): 131-147.

McGalliard, John C. "Chaucerian Comedy: The Merchant's Tale, Jonson, and Molière." Philological Quarterly 25 (1946): 343-370.

McPherson, David. "Some Renaissance Sources for Jonson's Early Comic Theory." English Language Notes (1971): 180-182.

Madelaine, R. E. R. "Parasites and 'Politicians': Some Comic Stage Images in Volpone." Journal of the Australasian Universities Language and Literature Association 58 (1982): 170-177.

Manlove, C. N. "The Double View in Volpone." Ben Jonson's Volpone, or the Fox." Ed.

Harold Bloom. New York, NY: Chelsea, 1988.

Marcus, Leah S. The Politics of Mirth: Jonson, Herrick, Milton, Marvell, and the Defense of Old Holiday Pastimes. Chicago, IL: University of Chicago Press, 1986.

Meier, T. "The Naming of Characters in Jonson's Comedies." English Studies in Africa 7 (1964): 88-95.

Mueschke, Paul and Jeannette Fleisher. "Jonsonian Elements in the Comic Underplot of Twelfth Night." Publications of the Modern Language Association 48 (1933): 722-740.

Nash, Ralph. "The Comic Intent of Volpone. Studies in Philology 44 (1947): 26-40.

Neufeld, James E. "The Indigestion of Widow-Hood: Blood, Jonson, and The Way of the World." Modern Philology 81 (1984): 233-243.

Ornstein, Robert. "Shakespearian and Jonsonian Comedy." Shakespeare Survey 22 (1969): 43-46.

Park, B. A. "Volpone and Old Comedy." English Language Notes 19 (1981): 105-109.

Parrott, T. M. "Comedy in the Court Masque: A Study of Ben Jonson's Contribution." Philological Quarterly 20 (1941): 428-441.

Partridge, Edward B. The Broken Compass: A Study of the Major Comedies of Ben Jonson. New York, NY: Columbia University Press, 1958.

Paster, Gail Kern. "Ben Jonson's Comedy of Limitation." Studies in Philology 72 (1975): 51-71.

Philias, Peter G. "Comic Truth in Shakespeare and Jonson." South Atlantic Quarterly 62 (1963): 78-91.

Potter, John M. "Old Comedy in Bartholomew Fair." Criticism 10 (1968): 290-299.

Rayner, Alice. "Jonson's Poesis: Use and Delight in Dystopia." Comic Persuasion: Moral Structure in British Comedy from Shakespeare to Stoppard." Berkeley, CA: University of California Press, 1987. 41-60.

Robinson, James E. "Bartholomew Fair: Comedy of Vapors." Studies in English Literature, 1500-1900 1.2 (1961): 65-80.

Salingar, Leo. "Comic Form in Ben Jonson: Volpone and the Philosopher's Stone." English Drama: Forms and Development: Essays in Honour of Muriel Clara Bradbrook. Eds. Marie Axton and Raymond Williams. Cambridge, England: Cambridge Univ Press, 1977.

Savage, James E. Ben Jonson's Basic Comic Characters and Other Essays. Hattiesburg, MS: Univ and College Press of Mississippi, 1973.

Simpson, Evelyn M. "Jonson and Dickens: A Study in the Comic Genius of London." Essays and Studies 29 (1943): 82-92.

Snuggs, Henry L. "The Comic Humours [of Jonson]: A New Interpretation." Publications of the Modern Language Association 62 (1947): 114-122.

Thorndike, Ashley H. "Ben Jonson." English Comedy. New York, NY: Macmillan, 1929. 167-191.

Townsend, Freda L. Apologie for Batholomew Fayre: The Art of Jonson's Comedies. New York, NY: Modern Language Association, 1947.

Walker, Hugh. English Satire and Satirists. New York, NY: J. M. Dent, 1925.

Watson, Robert N. Ben Jonson's Parodic Strategy: Literary Imperialism in the Comedies. Cambridge, MA: Harvard Univ Press, 1987.

Weld, John S. "Christian Comedy: Volpone." Studies in Philology 51 (1954): 172-193.

Woodbridge, Elisabeth. V Studies in Jonson's Comedy. New York: NY: Gordian Press, 1966.

Joseph Hall (1574-1656)

James Hannay considers Bishop Hall to be "the great opener of our classic and formal satire, i.e. a special satirical poem in the heroic metre." Hall's satires were in the tradition of Juvenal (Hannay 116). Louis Cazamian agrees with Hannay that Hall is clearly a disciple of Juvenal, Persius, and Horace in his satiric approach. The humorous element of Hall's work should be considered under the "humanist" influence. Hall does not write the "humor of conceits;" rather, he uses "humor of realism," stressing those aspects of life which show shocking injustice, rankness, or indecency. Hall had a concrete imagination which he combined with a pithy, concise writing style to result in vigorous, humorous, and sometimes cynical stretches of prosè (Cazamian 367).

Alfred Gu L'Estrange points out that some of our earliest humorists were ecclesiastics, and this includes John Donne, Joseph Hall, and Thomas Fuller. "Pleasantry was with them little more than a vehicle of instruction; the object was not to entertain, but to enforce and illustrate their moral sentiments" (L'Estrange 243). In 1597 Joseph Hall published the first three books of his Virgidemairum. These first three books dealt with things poetic, things academic, and things moral. In 1597 he published the three last books of his Virgidemairum. The first three books were his "toothless satires," as he attacks bad writers, astologers, drunkards, gallants, and others (L'Estrang 244). The last three books were his "biting satires." Here Hall attacks the effeminacy of his times such as strange dress and high heels. He also severely attacks the Pope. So far as we know, these six satires are Hall's earliest literary work, and they were an immediate success. Indeed, in 1599 they were condemned, along with some other satires, by order of the ecclesiastical authorities of the time (Alden 98). When Hall's satires were criticized for not being sufficiently "riddle-like," Hall responded that his satires are milder than the classical satires in the same way that the classical satires are milder than are their predecessors (Alden 106).

In Virgidemiarum the satires are preceded by A Defiance to Envy. This is followed by Book I, which contains Hall's famous pretension of being the first English satirist. There are nine satires in Book I, which deals with poetry. The first contrasts satire with other forms of poetry; the second discusses the Muses; the third deals with theatrical critics, the fourth with bad heroic poetry, the fifth with elegiac verse, the sixth with pseudo-classical versification, the seventh with extravagant love poetry, the eighth with religious poetry in pseudo-classical style, and the ninth with licentious poetry of the passions. There are seven satires in Book II, which deals with academic issues. The first deals with the abundance of bad poetry, the second with the folly of writing for money, the third with the follies of the law, the fourth with the follies of medicine, the fifth with the buying of indulgences, the sixth with the follies of the clergy, and the seventh with the follies of astrology. Book III deals with moral issues. The first satire contrasts the ancient golden age with the luxury and greed of modern times, the second with the folly of desiring a great monument, the third with an ostentatious but miserly host, the fourth with the love of personal display, the fifth with the loss of a courtier's wig, the sixth with the extraordinary thirst of a Gallion, and the seventh with a gallant named Ruffio. Book IV has satires dealing with the obscurity of being a satirist, a son made rich by his father's work, the vanity that comes from inherited fortune, a young gallant named Gallio, the gaining of fortune through the misfortunes of others, the vanity of human desires, and the Papacy. Book V deals with the oppression of landlords, the decline of oldtime hospitality, the abuse of real-estate people, and the spendthrift son of a thrifty farmer. Finally, Book VI describes Labeo's reception of Hall's satires, and it also discusses contemporary poetry at some length, especially that of Labeo (Alden 109-110). The satire in Virgidemiarum is typically that of direct rebuke; there is little satire here that is purely reflective. The model of Juvenal is clearly prevalent here, and the attitude toward life is generally pessimistic. Sometimes the satires are intended to be corrective rather than just educational (Alden 111).

Joseph Hall implies that he is the first English satirist by saying the following:

"I first adventure; follow me who list,
And be the second English satirist." (Alden 113)

Alden remarks that "One may be sure that had the author realized how many pages would have been written in comment of these lines, he would have omitted them or have added a footnote" (Alden 113-114).   John Milton was probably the first critic to have made objection to Hall's claim, but Milton's voice was followed by the voice of many other critics who have responded. After citing a number of these reactions, Alden concludes, "In all these places it is pointed out that, whatever interpretation of the term 'satirist' be accepted, Hall was not the first of that line in England" (Alden 114).   Hall might have contended that such English satirists as William Langland and Sir Thomas Wyatt did not write satires in the classical tradition. However, he must have known of the satires of John Donne and of Thomas Lodge, both of whom wrote satires not only in the classical manner, but in the decasyllabic couplet as well (Alden 114).   Alden continues, "Lodge's Fig for Momus was published only two years before Hall's satires, and contained such obvious imitation of classical satire that it is difficult to see how it could have been explained away" (Alden 116).

But Alden goes on to explain why Hall may have made such a claim, by noting that when Hall published Virgidemiarum he was very young, and was only slightly acquainted with English writers, since his college training was basically limited to a study of the classics.

Brinsley Nicholson takes an even more sympathetic view to Hall's statement: "As to Hall's assertion that he was the first English satirist, I would lay some but not much stress on his being the first to publish, believing he would rest his chief claim on this, that his were the first English satires which by being written in a rugged rustic and archaic style answered to the old Roman satires" (Alden 102).   In calling himself the earliest English satirist, Hall is considering the "first satire" to be the first satire of the fourth book, which is the book beginning the series of "biting" satires.   This satire is "the most perfect imitation of Juvenal in the entire work, being also the most difficult to understand.... Hall's explicit statement [is] that this satire is intentionally obscure, the others intentionally clear" (Alden 107).

Raymond Alden indicates that Joseph Hall was the first satirist to adopt the compact satirical couplet which became traditional by later satirists.   Hall's satiric writing style combines the qualities of smoothness, regular scansion, and vigor to a greater degree than had any of the satirists who preceded him (Alden 101, 104).   The obscurity of Hall's vocabulary arises from his "remote phraseology [archaisms], constrained combinations, unfamiliar allusions, elliptical apostrophes, and abruptness of expression" (Alden 104). Alden notes that Hall's obscurity, whether intentional or not, comes from the fact that the satires were written on classical models (Alden 105).   In support of this contention, Alden notes that Persius's writing was "wilfully rugged and obscure."   According to Alden, Persius "lacked the gift of Horace and Juvenal to be at once concise and clear..., and Elizabethans found him hard reading, though strangely attractive" (Alden 106).

Alden also feels that Joseph Hall had an important influence on his successors:

It was undoubtedly the satires of Hall...which had most influence on all his successors; and if we could but know whether he was familiar with those of Donne, of Lodge, or of both, or whence he derived the measure which he used so skillfully, we should know something of no little importance for the history of satirical verse. (Alden 92)

Joseph Hall Bibliography

Alden, Raymond MacDonald. The Rise of Formal Satire in England under Classical

Influence. New York, NY: Archon, 1961.

Beller, Martin. "Joseph Hall." _Encyclopedia of British Humorists, Volume I_. Ed. Steven H. Gale, New York, NY: Garland, 1996, 503-511.

Cazamian, Louis. "Joseph Hall." _The Development of English Humor_. Durham, NC: Duke University Press, 1952, 366-368.

Hannay, James. _Satire and Satirists_. Folcroft, PA: Folcroft Press, 1969; originally published in 1854.

L'Estrange, Alfred Gu. "Donne--Hall--Fuller." _History of English Humour_. New York, NY: Burt Franklin, 1878, 243-249.

Cyril Tourneur (c1575-1626) IRELAND

See, Nilsen, Don L. F. _Humor in Irish Literature_ (Greenwood, 1996).

John Webster (c1575-c1634)

Louis Cazamian feels that beneath John Webster's grim and tragic world of bitterness there is an imaginative realism that contains "the germ of a scathing dramatic irony and of a sardonic humor, which one may compare either to that of _Hamlet_ or to the Swiftian manner" (340). In his _Horrid Laughter in Jacobean Tragedy_, Nicholas Brooke explains how laughter is achieved in John Webster's works by saying that there is an affinity between tears and laughter, in that "either in extremity tends to turn into the other."

> This is certainly one point at which the subject [of laughter] relates importantly to tragedy. Tragedy deals in extreme emotions, not all of the same kind: death, suffering, heroism, torture, cruelty, nobility, horror, and so on. And because they are extreme, they are all _liable_ to turn over into laughter. (Brooke 3)

Webster's _The Devil's Law Case_ (date unknown) is classed by Nicholas Brookes as a "tragi-comedy" (Brooke 31). _The White Devil_ (c1612) is classed as a "tragedy," and although it is not properly amusing, it nevertheless contains a subdued irony that often mixes with the most tragic aspects of the play. There is a paradox in the title, "White Devil." This is an oxymoron relating to the ambiguity of Vittoria's nature. "We are continually prompted to wonder what she is--innocent or devil" (Brooke 32). Vittoria is both vicious and virtuous, both bold and coy, both magnificent and cheap. She is understood in "the peculiar laughter that establishes her splendour, whatever her morals" (Brooke 47). The play also contains much macabre humor:

> There is, as Flaminco says, some goodness in his death, and in his sister's; its definition is far too subtle to be contained in a term such as "stoicism." It depends essentially on the relation here of laughter to tears, and that is superbly controlled; by establishing the parody first, Webster releases the superb mocking courage for its full effect. We laugh and weep at nearly identical language, distinguished by only the slightest shift of tone. On that, its unique power to move depends. (Brooke 47)

In an important passage at the beginning of _The Duchess of Malfi_ (c1613), Webster "shows himself aware of the policy of repression and reserve in laughter, as an aspect of moral and social fastidiousness" (Cazamian 341). According to Nicholas Brooke, it is grotesque laughter which firmly establishes the tone of _The Duchess of Malfi_. The play is defined by the grotesque figures which move about in the dark, executing plots which misfire, and by mistaken deaths. The play is "grotesquely ludicrous, horribly funny"

(Brooke 67).

> Julia's curt stoicism, the Cardinal's heavy guilt, Ferdinand's obscurely pertinent savagery, Bosola's desperate irony--those give the play its weight, and make the countertone a necessarily, and intelligibly, horrid laughter. Allowed its place, the laughter is by no means a rejection of the play, but an integral part of it. (Brooke 67-68)

John Webster Bibliography

Brooke, Nicholas. Horrid Laughter in Jacobean Tragedy. New York, NY: Barnes and Noble, 1979.

Cazamian, Louis. "Webster." The Development of English Humor. Durham, NC: Duke University Press, 1952, 340-341.

John Marston (c1576-1634)

The kind of satire that emerged in England during Marston's prime was a popular bawdy verse with a sort of Rabelaisian gusto and robustness. In contrast, Marston's satire was far more sophisticated, though admittedly a bit neurotic and self indulgent (Peter 157). Marston says that his "Metamorphosis" was a parody, written to ridicule the tendency of the day to write erotic, improper, even pornographic verses; however, "If the poem was meant to be a parody then it is a ludicrously bad one, an endorsement instead of a travesty of all that it was supposed to criticize" (Peter 159). "Metamorphosis" is written in an Ovidian style, as Marston assures the reader that the poem will "tickle vp our leud Priapians." Marston praises the poem profusely, but he also condemns it as worthless froth, and even as a "maggot-tainted lewd corruption." In saying this, Marston takes this ammunition away from other people who might criticize the poem, but not nearly so well as the author himself had done (Peter 159).   Marston's satires tended to be filled with obscenity, and this obscenity strained the "ethical pretensions of the context where it figured." The tension in Marston's satires is not so much a result of the strain between morality and immorality as such, but rather the strain between "satire" and "complaint."

John Marston's work may be weak in plot structure, and his fools, fops, buffoons, and clowns may be one-dimensional characters. Marston's work is nevertheless very comically innovative. Marston uses a wide range of comic devices, but his disguise and stereotyping are especially effective (Cooperman 730). In John Marston: Satirist Anthony Caputi, Anthony writes mainly about the parody and the burlesque to be found in Marston's writings (Cooperman 732-733). Robert Cooperman says that Marston is a playwright who is best remembered for his biting satires on the foolishness of his day, and for his festive plays. His plays ranged from joyous comedies to tragicomedies to revenge tragedies (Cooperman 731). Marston is comfortable with many styles, ranging from high comedy, to low comedy to light comedy, and even to black comedy (Cooperman 732).

In 1598, John Marston published a great deal of satiric poetry. Marston's The Metamorphosis of Pigmalions Image, And Certaine Satyres (1598), and his The Scourge of Villanie. Three Books of Satyres (1598) Marston writes both serious and comical satires. Raymond Alden states that both Pigmalion's Image and The Scourge of Villanie were popular in their day. In fact, these satires were popular enough to be included in the 1599 list of publications that were condemned and ordered to be burned (Alden 130). Marston's style was "crabbed and distorted." He was intentionally careless about poetic niceties, and said, "My liberty scorns rhyming laws," and "I crave no sirens of our halcyon times, / To grace the accents of my rough-hew'd rhymes" (Alden 131).

Robert Cooperman feels that Metamorphosis of Pigmalions Image demonstrates Marston's propensity for parodying the rhetorical practices of his day. His favorite target was the Petrarchan sonnet (Cooperman 729). The narrator in Metamorphosis takes an ironic stance, which R. C. Horne says can be seen in "the sheer silliness" of the situation in which Pigmalion is not able to see the absurdity of worshiping the statue (Horne 18). "Satire XI" of The Scourge of Villanie, is about a narrator who says he has a "jocund Muse," thereby setting himself up as a humorist (Cooperman 729).

Marston's Histriomastrix, or the Player Whipt (ca 1599) is a parody of the theater in general, and acting companies in particular (Cooperman 729). Marston's Histrio Mastix is written in the form of a "complaint" and is in effect a satiric attack on the English poet Anthony Munday. Marston was distancing himself from authors like Munday, Jonson, and Shakespeare, who wrote primarily for money. Marston "felt that he was entering the camp of learned and 'free-borne' dramatists, who wrote for the plaudits of a good and gentle audience rather than the camp of ex-actors and professionals who wrote for monetary reward (Peter 221).

In The History of Antonio and Mellida (1600), Marston makes fun of Marlowe's rhetoric, especially the rhetoric of Tamburlaine (1587). He is also making fun of all types of love poetry and the lovers it portrays. Antonio's Revenge (1600) is considered by many critics to be a satire of the revenge tragedy, especially as it is presented in a popular and influential play by Thomas Kyd entitled The Spanish Tragedy (ca. 1587). Antonio and Mellido contains a subplot that involves buffoonish Italian characters with such attributive names as Balurdo (meaning "fool"), and Dildo (Cooperman 731). According to Nicholas Brooke, Marston's Antonio plays vascilate "between tragic rhetoric and blatant farce, moral sententiae and apparent self parody" (Brooke 6).

Marston wrote a comic play, entitled, Jacke Drums Entertainment: Or, The Comedie of Pasquill and Katherine (1601) in which he lampoons the exaggerated language of young talents. Pasquil, one of his characters, says, "When I turne fickle, vertue shall be vice," and Katherine responds, "When I prove false, Hell shall be Paradise." This exchange of rhymed couplets servs to parody the bloated rhetoric of the day (Cooperman 729). The humor of Marston's Jacke Drum's Entertainment, and his What You Will is usually associated with the words and actions of the unprincipled jesters, and tends, therefore, to be less offensive than is the humor of his formal satires. The humor becomes more offensive, however, when it is attributed to respectable characters like Quadratus, in whose mouth the humor seems "quite out of place" (Peter 252-253). Jacke Drums Entertainment and What You Will are both primarily festive comedies, and only secondarily satires. Both plays involve singing, dancing, pantomime, puns, mistaken identity, farcical characters, and practical jokes Both plays lampoon the absurdities of inflated language, foppery, and pretentiousness. In both plays, Marston's sense of fun and festivity operate as a very powerful force (Cooperman 730).

Cooperman compares the character Quadratus in What You Will (1601) to Shakespeare's Falstaff. Like Falstaff, Quadratus is a self-centered clown who is both the perpetrator and the victim of practical jokes. He is also the wise fool whose judgments about his friends and acquaintances are very astute (Cooperman 730). Cooperman says that Lampatho in What You Will is meant to be a mockery of Ben Jonson, Marston's rival and friend. Philip Finkelpearl, however, feels that Lampatho is a mockery of Marston himself (Finkelpearl 164). The complete title of this play is What You Will, a slight toye, lightly composed, to swiftly finisht, ill plotted, worse written, I feare me worst acted, and indeed What You Will (Cooperman 730).

In both Malcontent (1604), and The Fawn (1604), the heroes have to disguise themselves in order to observe and ridicule the "fashionable pretentiousness of their respective courts." The Fawn is also given the name of Parasitaster in order to show that it is a lampoon of Ben Jonson's Poetaster (1601). This is ironic, since Jonson's Poetaster contains a lampoon of Marston in the character of Crispinus. The characters in The Fawn have very revealing names, like Sir Amoroso Debile-Dosso, whose names means, "lover with a weak back" (Cooperman 731).

Marston labels his The Dutch Courtezan (1605) as a "city comedy." This is a genre in which "tradesmen, merchants, and other urban inhabitants are lampooned" (Cooperman 729). The Dutch Courtezan is a play about Franceschina, and some critics consider Franceschina to be a parody of Thomas Dekker's Bellafront in The Honest Whore (1604). Mrs. Faugh is a good example of a humorous figure in Marston's Dutch Courtesan. She is the procuress who says that she may well eat of the forbidden fruit, but she will not lower herself to eating fish on Fridays. Cockledemoy is a prank player who says in Act 2, Scene 2, "I have an odd jest to trim Master Mulligrub, for a wager; a jest, boy; a humour," associating the older meaning of "humour" with the new meaning developed by Ben Jonson where "humour" in the old sense "has the quality of making us laugh; but the jest is only in us" (Cazamian 343).

John Marston Bibliography

Alden, Raymond MacDonald. "John Marston." The Rise of Formal Satire in England under Classical Influence. New York, NY: Archon, 1961, 129-148.
Brooke, Nicholas. Horrid Laughter in Jacobean Tragedy. New York, NY: Harper and Row, 1979.
Caputi, Anthony. John Marston: Satirist. Ithaca, NY: Cornell University Press, 1960.
Cazamian, Louis. The Development of English Humor. Durham, NC: Duke University Press, 1952.
Cooperman, Robert. "John Marston." Encyclopedia of British Humorists, Volume II. Ed. Steven H. Gale, New York, NY: Garland, 1996, 728-733.
Finkelpearl, Philip J. John Marston of the Middle Temple: An Elizabethan Dramatist in His Social Setting. Cambridge, MA: Harvard University Press, 1969.
Gibbons, Brian. Jacobean City Comedy: A Study of Satiric Plays by Jonson, Marston and Middleton. 2nd ed. London, England: Methuen, 1980.
Horne, R. C. "Voices of Alienation: The Moral Significance of Marston's Satiric Strategy." Modern Language Review 81.1 (1986): 18.
Hunter, G. K. "English Folly and Italian Vice: The Moral Landscape of John Marston." Jacobean Theatre. New York, NY: St. Martin's, 1960.
Peter, John. "Marston and the Metamorphosis in Satire." Complaint and Satire in Early English Literature. Oxford, England: Clarendon Press, 1956, 157-186.
Peter, John. "Marston's Plays." Complaint and Satire in Early English Literature. Oxford, England: Clarendon Press, 1956, 219-254.

Robert Burton (Democritus Junior) (1577-1640)

The first half of the seventeenth century is considered by many critics to be the age of the eccentrics, and Louis Cazamian feels that Robert Burton and Thomas Coryate both fall into this tradition. Cazamian feels that literary eccentricity overlaps humor, and frequently shades into it. "The eccentric is so to say a potential humorist, one who having the gift, has reached only an incomplete awareness of its possible exploitation" (Cazamian 377). Cazamian feels that Burton ranks highest as a humorist of all of the prose-writers of his age. Burton's writing shows a mixture of characters with queer idiosyncrasies with a strategy of deliberate quaintness (Cazamian 378). He himself said that his purpose was to amuse as much as it was to instruct (Cazamian 379).

Robert Burton Bibliography

Cazamian, Louis. "Burton." The Development of English Humor. Durham, NC: Duke University Press, 1952, 378-384.

Thomas Coryate (c1577-1617)

Louis Cazamian considers the eccentricities of Coryate, Burton, and Browne, and concludes that Thomas Coryate is "far and away the queerest figure of the three." Cazamian sees Coryate as the butt of the court of James I, with his comically shaped head, and the rough verbal and physical handling he received. Coryate somehow was able to save face and maintain some dignity through the use of his wit as both a defensive and an offensive tool. Coryate had developed theatrical gestures to go with his poetry readings, and most of his poems were ironical or mock-heroic in nature. His Coryate's Crudities, Hastily Gobbled up in Five Moneths Travells in France, Savoy, Italy, Rhetia commonly called the Grisons country took on special significance when he hung up in Odcombe church the shoes in which he had walked back from Venice. "Coryate enjoyed playing practical jokes under the cloak of grave behavior" (Cazamian 377-378). Coryate had the humorist's power of realistic perception. Coryate was an eccentric, and his work was odd. He was a humorist in the Elizabethan sense of the word, but the eccentrics that appear in his work are humorous both in the Elizabethan sense and in the modern sense of the word (Cazamian 378).

Thomas Coryate Bibliography

Cazamian, Louis. "Coryate." The Development of English Humor. Durham, NC: Duke University Press, 1952, 377-378.

John Taylor (1578-1653)

John Taylor, the "Water Poet," wrote The Scullers Travels from Tyber to Thames with His Boat Laden with a Hotch-Potch, or Gallimawfry of Sonnets, Satyres, and Epigrams in 1612. After a number of epigrams targeting the "Romish Church," this book contains two satires, the first showing the evils that befall all types of sinners, and the second showing the evil-doers themselves. In 1614 Taylor published The Nipping or Snipping of Abuses: or, The Wool-gathering of Wit. This book is an imitation of George Wither's Abuses Stript and Whipt (1613) in both style and versification. The anagrams and sonnets in this book are followed by a satire which, according to Taylor, is "composed and compacted of sundry simples, as salt, vinegar, wormwood, and a little gall, very profitable to cure the impostumes of vice" (Alden 176). Nearly forty years later, in 1651, Taylor published a book of epigrams, with two new satires. The first satire is on the hypocrisy of Puritans, the second is against "swearing, equivocation, mental reservation, and detestable dissimulation" (Alden 176).

Edmund Miller says that John Taylor was the "first popular journalist to earn his living through writing" (Miller 1111). In his playful moments as a writer, it was John Taylor who in essence founded the English tradition of nonsense poetry (Miller 1109), and Edmund Miller considers this to be Taylor's chief claim to a place in the history of British humor. Such pieces as Sir Gregory Nonsense His Newes from No Place (1622) specializes in oxymorons like "scalding ice", contradictions like "a Crimson Robe, as blacke as jet", and incongruities such as "aged Ganymede. Taylor's Nonsense upon Sence (1651), which was later expanded and given the new title of The Essence, Quintessence, Insense, Innocence, Lye-Sense, and Magnificence of Nonsense upon Sense (1654) is a continuation of this tradition, and is described by Miller as a "general social satire." Taylor also wrote Mad Verse, Sad Verse, Glad Verse, and Bad Verse (1644), which Miller considers to be "conscious nonsense," and Wit and Mirth (1626) which is a complication of jests described by Miller as "prose nonsense." (Miller 1110).

John Taylor developed the Gargantua myth in England even though he did not know French, and even though the works of Rabelais had not yet been translated into English (Brown 86). Edmund Miller considers Taylors Feast (1638) to be "a sort of Rabelaisian cookbook, and he considers Jack-a-Lent (1620) to be similar in this respect. In this book some of the descriptions of the dishes degenerate into shaggy dog stories. As can be seen by the titles of some of his works, Taylor clearly specializes in humours characters. Consider, for example, A Bawd, a Virtuous Bawd, a Modest Bawd (1635), A Common Whore (1622), An Arrant Thief (1622), The Great Eater of Kent (1630), and The Olde, Old, Very Olde Man (1635), which is his elegy to Thomas Parr (Miller 1108).

Edmund Miller says that John Taylor may have had two wives, both of them named Alice (Miller 1106). Although John Taylor was a poet, he had a reputation for having a tin ear. In his elegy for Thomas Parr, Taylor wrote the line "Day found him work and night allowed him rest," and Wallace Notestein said of this line that it was "probably the nearest to poetry of anything Taylor ever wrote" (Notestein 184). Miller, however, feels that this assessment is a bit harsh, suggesting that the poetry in Taylor's A Very Merry Wherry-Ferry-Voyager (1622), and his Yorke for my Money (1622), and The Certain Travailes of an Uncertain Journey (1654) flows very smoothly. Nevertheless, Taylor follows the tradition of criticism by criticizing his own poetry, as he considers his The Scoller...; or, Gallimaufry of Sonnets, Satyres, and Epigrams (1612) "the first-born issue of my Worthless wit" (Miller 1108).

Taylor's works in praise of the old values, and the traditional ways of life include Taylors Pastorell (1624), which praises the sheep industry. He also wrote pamphlets in praise of clean linen, and in praise of jails (Miller 1108). Eugene Kirk feels that many of Taylor's works fall into the category of Menippean satire, saying that in his works can be found the ludicrous rhymes that undermine the dignity of their targets, and the frequent mixture of prose and verse, and most important, the biting wit (Kirk 179-182). John Taylor was an important combatant in the "pamphlet wars" of the seventeenth century. He satirically attacks Thomas Coryate in his Laugh and Be Fat (1612), and in his A Reply as True as Steele (1641), it is William Fennor who is his target. Aqua-Musae (1645) and Taylor's Motto (1621) are both satirical attacks of George Wither, and Edmund Miller says that Aqua-Musae is a "short lashing satire on Wither with occasional parody of that poet" (Miller 1109).

Taylor wrote such political satires as A Plea for Prerogative (1642), The Kings Most Excellent Majesties Wellcome to His Owne House (1647), and Rebells Anathematized, and Anatomized (1645), all of them royalist polemics. His The Fooles of Fate (1648) is a satiric attack of Parliamentary newspapers (Miller 1109). Taylor also wrote satires to expose the foibles of Roman Catholicism, such as Pedlar and a Romish Priest (1641), and his A Delicate Dainty, Damnable Dialogue, Between the Devil and a Jesuite (1642). When the Parliament arrested a number of Catholic bishops for treason, Taylor wrote a satire entitled The Apprentices Advice to the XII Bishops (Miller 1109). Taylor's A Juniper Lecture; With the Description of All Sorts of Women (1669), is a satire in which Taylor gives a conservative view of the place of women in society. In his The Women's Sharp Revenge; or, an Answer to Sir Seldon Sober (1640), Taylor takes on the role of two spinsters named Mary Tattle-well, and Joan Hit-Him-Home, in a fake and intentionally unconvincing response to his Juniper Lecture (Miller 1109).

John Taylor wrote many satires on the religious and political topics of his day. About his writing, Robert Southey says, "There is nothing in John Taylor which deserves preservation for its intrinsic merit alone; but...there is a great deal to illustrate the manners of his age." Southey says that some critics dismiss Taylor's poetry as doggerel, but many of his poems are in truth imaginative and are good mirrors of popular taste during Taylor's time. Furthermore, Southey feels that much of Taylor's Hudibrastic verse is both witty and facile (Southey 86).

John Taylor Bibliography

Alden, Raymond MacDonald. "John Taylor." The Rise of Formal Satire in England under Classical Influence. New York, NY: Archon, 1961, 175-176.

Brown, Huntington. Rabelais in English Literature. Cambridge, MA: Harvard University Press, 1933.

Kirk, Eugene P. Menippean Satire: An Annotated Catalogue of Texts and Criticism. New York, NY: Garland, 1980.

Miller, Edmund. "John Taylor." Encyclopedia of British Humorists, Volume II. Ed. Steven H. Gale, New York, NY: Garland, 1996, 1106-1113.

Notestein, Wallace. Four Worthies: John Chamberlain, Anne Clifford, John Taylor, Oliver Heywood. New Haven, CT: Yale University Press, 1957.

Phelps, Wayne H. "John Edwards and the Date of the Lost [play by Taylor] 'Saturnalia.'" Notes and Queries 30 (1983): 435-437.

Southey, Robert. "John Taylor." The Lives and Works of the Uneducated Poets. Ed. J. S. Childers. London, England: Humphrey Mitford, 1925 15-88.

John Fletcher (1579-1625)

Louis Cazamian is impressed with Fletcher's comic talent. He feels that Fletcher had "a ready fund of sprightliness and wit, a faculty of comic invention, a swift, and a supple style." He also feels that Fletcher handled dialogue cleverly and that racy episodes and a humorous flavor emerge frequently in Fletcher's long series of comedies.   In Fletcher's The Wild Goose Chase, Mirabel is a humorous character, and Rosalura and Lillia Blanca are also humorous characters as they criticize their tutor for not teaching them well enough the proper way to attract husbands (Cazamian 346). In Little French Lawyer, La-Writ is a character torn between crankiness and humor.   At first it is the humor that predominates, but the play quickly degenerates, and at the end La-Writ is crestfallen and humorless.   Spanish Curate is a happy play that goes merrily along providing the audience with quite a bit of humor, but Cazamian feels that the humor here is not of the highest quality.   The Humorous Lieutenant is about a lieutenant who is amusing because he is paradoxical. In this character, "the Elizabethan sense of 'humor' and the modern one seem to be caught in the transitional stage that was leading from one to the other" (Cazamian 347). The lieutenant is an extension of the comic tradition that contains both Shakespeare's Falstaff, and Cervantes's Sancho Panza (Cazamian 347-348).   Leon, the servant in Fletcher's Rule a Wife and Have a Wife answers Juan de Castro's questioning with a mixture of slyness and silliness. Juan describes Leon as follows: "This fellow has some doubts in's talk that strike me; he cannot be all fool" (Cazamian 348).

John Fletcher and Francis Beaumont are the co-authors of The Knight of the Burning Pestle (1613), which is a spirited parody of the chivalric romance. The irony in this farcical comedy is double edged, mocking not only chivalric conventions, but also mocking the middle-class that aspires to high-class taste and manners (Chapman 373). John Fletcher and Francis Beaumont are also the co-authors of The Woman Hater (ca 1607), a satire filled with extravagant humor and sympathetic parody of theatrical conventions. The Woman Hater mocks romantic conventions, and its satirical tone mirrors the increasingly cynical and pessimistic mood of the Jacobean era.

The Woman's Prize, or The Tamer Tamed was written by Fletcher alone. It contains much broad slapstick, and also much genial and ribald humor. In this farce, Petruchio, who is an overbearing bridegroom, is based on Shakespeare's earlier farce, The Taming of the Shrew. In Fletcher's play, Maria witholds her sexual pleasures from her arrogant husband in an attempt to battle for women's rights and dignity (Chapman 373). This play is reminiscent of Aristophanes's Lysistrata which is also based on this same type of female power. The tone of The Woman's Prize is earthy and ribald, and humorous metaphors with sexual innuendo are frequent. Chapman considers Fletcher's Petruchio to be more of a Jacobean rake than is the clever and worldly rogue which Shakespeare developed (Chapman 374).

It was in the Preface to his The Faithful Shepherdess (ca 1608) that Fletcher wrote his famous definition of "tragicomedy." "A tragicomedy is not so called in respect of mirth and killing, but in respect it wants deaths, which is enough to make it no tragedy, yet brings some near it, which is enough to make it no comedy." Fletcher collaborated with Shakespeare in the writing of a tragicomedy to match this definition, The Two Noble Kinsmen (Chapman 374).

In Wit Without Money (1614), Fletcher demonstrates his command of comic imagery, and his control of the vigorous London colloquial speech of his day. In this play, Valentine is an eccentric, a pedant who ignores the counsels of prudence that he receives. As a pedant, he must defend his conduct and must display his "ferocious verbal exuberance." Valentine's speech is filled with comic metaphors and allusions, and his language and behavior contrasts starkly with the language and behavior of his brother who lives a Spartan life and speaks in a terse and laconic prose style. Valentine is clearly a humours character (Chapman 376). Celia, in The Humorous Lieutenant (1619) is a charmer who enjoys her whimsical schemes as much as the audience does. In Monsieur Thomas (ca 1622) there is a gallery of humors characters, including lecherous old men, egotistical gentlewomen, absent-minded family chaperons, befuddled pedants, brash young heirs, and rascally servants (Chapman 377).

Fletcher collaborated with Beaumont in the writing of The Scornful Lady (1616), which is filled with scenes of comic embarrassments to an arrogant heiress. The action is based on comic intrigue, and the central figure is described as a humours character. Edgar Chapman says that this play shows Fletcher to be an urbane ironist (Chapman 374). Rule a Wife and Have a Wife (1624) is a more spirited comedy than is The Scornful Lady. In this play there is a series of plans to establish male dominance over a wife. The Chances (1624) is also about male-female relationships. The womanizer Don John is one of the lead characters. He claims to be an expert in matters of love, and he complains bitterly if things don't go right for him. The development of the character Don John illustrates one of Fletcher's strongest qualities as a humorist, "the ability to deal with a foolish character's sense of comic exasperation" (Chapman 375). Don John's escapades are ludicrous, and it is also humorous in this play when Fletcher reverses the male-female roles by having a charming and wily woman pursue Don John, whom Chapman describes as "a rascally young gallant (Chapman 375). This same type of male-female role reversal can be seen in The Wild-Goose Chase (1621) where the hero is constantly trying to escape from a marriage that a very determined young woman wants to take place. The Wild-Goose Chase is a precursor to George Bernard Shaw's Man and Superman. In Fletcher's comedy,

Mirabel is a rebellious young man, and Oriana is a virtuous woman, and much of the amusement of the play results from the audience's growing admiration for Oriana's craftiness, and from Mirabel's constant complaints about the evils of matrimony (Chapman 375).

In The Elder Brother (1624), which was co-authored by Fletcher and Phillip Massinger, Charles is the older "bookish milksop" brother. Because of his non-assertive personality, Charles is about to lose both his inheritance and his fiancee to his jealous and amoral younger brother. But then Charles undergoes a metamorphosis. He changes from a retiring and tiresome pedant into a decisive man of action (Chapman 376).

John Fletcher's works are filled with comic imagery and invention. His sharp eyes were always searching social behavior for things he could satirize, and he had an impressive command of the "comic possibilities in numerous variations on the theme of the war between the sexes (Chapman 373). Fletcher lived his life as a comedy of manners, and he died in the same way. While he was in London, waiting for a new suit of clothes, he suddenly and unexpectedly died of cholera (L'Estrange 264).

John Fletcher Bibliography

Cazamian, Louis. "Beaumont and Fletcher." The Development of English Humor. Durham, NC: Duke University Press, 1952, 344-348.

Chapman, Edgar L. "John Fletcher." Encyclopedia of British Humorists, Volume I. Ed. Steven H. Gale, New York, NY: Garland, 1996, 371-378.

Hoy, Cyrus. "Fletcherian Romantic Comedy." Research Opportunities in Renaissance Drama. 27 (1984): 3-11.

L'Estrange, Alfred Gu. "Shakespeare--Ben Jonson--Beaumont and Fletcher--The Wise Men of Gatham." History of English Humour. New York, NY: Burt Franklin, 1878, 250-270.

Shirley, James, ed. Comedies and Tragedies: Written by Frances Beaumont and John Fletcher, Gentlemen. London, England: Humphrey Robinson and Humphrey Moseley, 1647.

Thorndike, Ashley H. "Beaumont and Fletcher." English Comedy. New York, NY: Macmillan, 1929. 192-217.

Thomas Middleton (1580-1627)

Although some of Thomas Middleton's humor is coarse, it is at the same time racy and is thus somewhat reminiscent of Rabelais. With both Middleton and Rabelais, there is a lighthearted innocence that is diffused through a great deal of gross realism (Cazamian 338). Thomas Middleton wrote some of the funniest comic plays of the Jacobean period. Middleton believed in poetic justice, as his characters are usually punished by the forces of their own particular vices (Brunning 758). Middleton rejected romantic comedy in order to devote his talents to social comedy, where the humor is to be found in the portrayal of the disorder and breakdown of society (Brunning 759).

Your Five Gallants was Middleton's first play that can be considered a "city comedy." In this play, the characters seem to "embody every vice possible," and the play is "set against a background of depravity" (Brunning 759). Quomodo in Michaelmas Term (1607) feigns death in order to test his family's true opinion of him. But instead of hearing himself praised, he is cheated by his employees, and his daughter gets married to the wrong man, and his wife marries Easy, the person whom Quomodo has tricked out of his estate (Brunning 759).

The three plays which are considered Middleton's most successful city comedies are A Tricke to Catch the Old One (1608), A Mad World, My Masters (1608), and A Chast Mayd in Cheapside (1630). In these three plays, Middleton makes social wry observations with ironic detachment. He uses his sharp wit to produce these three fast-moving drams that expose the trickery, the vice, and the corruption of Middleton's day (Brunning 759).

Alizon Brunning considers A Tricke to Catch the Old One (1608) to be Middleton's best City Comedy. Witgood is swindled out of his estate by his uncle, Pecunious Lucre. The moral of the play is probably best described by the two meanings of the word "cozen," a pun used in the play. "Cozen" can mean "to swindle," or it can mean "cousin." This appropriate pun is reinforced by another appropriate pun, the word "aunt" which can either refer to a particular relative, or to a prostitute. The point of these two puns, and the point of the play itself is that "kinship counts for very little in this corrupt society" which is so filled with usury, trickery, and the equation of sex with money (Brunning 761). Middleton's characters think up schemes that fail, or backfire, and the last words of A Tricke to Catch the Old One (1608) appears to be the controlling metaphor of Middleton's plays: "Who seem most crafty prove oft-times most fools" (Brunning 759). Middleton's humor is simple, realistic, and cynical. For Middleton, "that atmosphere of subdued cynicism harmonizes very well with the detachment which is a major trait of humor" (Cazamian 337). Louis Cazamian feels that Middleton's tendency toward exaggeration and farce defines his humor without effacing it. Although A Tricke to Catch the Old One is written early in Middleton's career, it already demonstrates his "cool mastery in the treatment of comic themes." In the last scene of Act III, for example, the audience watches Dampit, a drunkard, being put to bed by his servant Audrey. The humor of this episode comes from their trying to preserve Dampit's dignity in a basically undignified situation (Cazamian 338).

A Mad World, My Masters (1608) contains the comedy of characterization and the comedy of frank burlesque in the development of Sir Bounteous Progress. The main plot of A Mad World, My Masters (1608) is about the tricking of an old, rich man by the name of Sir Bounteous Progress by his ingenious grandson, Follywit. Follywit devises a series of tricks to get money from his grandfather. He disguises himself as Lord Owemuch. He and his men rob the house and tie themselves up to make it appear that they are victims, leaving one of the number to escape with the booth. He disguises himself as his grandfather's mistress, Frank Gullman, and perplexes Sir Bounteous, who says, "I gave her a kiss at bottom o'th'stairs, and by th' mass, methought her breath had much ado to be sweet, like a think compounded methought of wine, beer, and tobacco." Follywit in this disguise succeeds in stealing jewelry from the house. For his final trick, Follywell disguises himself as an actor, and he requests that certain articles, such as a watch, be provided to help him put on a dramatic presentation. When these items are brought to the actor, they are passed backstage and Follywit's accomplices carry them away. They are apprehended in the act by a constable who brings them all back to the house, but in a stroke of genius, Follywell makes the constable a part of the play, and tells him that the script says that he must be tied up. Follywit plays the sympathetic character of a boyish rogue in this play. Another character in this particular play is named "Penitent Brothel," and as this oxymoronic name would suggest, this character is both lecherous and repentant (Brunning 760). The secondary plot of A Mad World, My Masters is about the possessive jealousy of Harebrain for his wife, as he treats her as if she were a piece of property. It is the brilliant and cunning plots which provide much of the comic element of the play (Brunning 760).

In A Chast Mayd in Cheapside (1630), the scenes are often parodies of the romantic comedies of Middleton's day (Brunning 259). A Chast Mayd ("A Chaste Maid") is filled with depravity and corruption. Alizon Brunning thinks that one of the funniest scenes in the play is the christening of Allwit's/Sir Walter's latest child. At this christening there are several gossips and two Puritans who gather round the bed. Allwit is depressed because he suspects that they have come only for the food and drink, and he discovers that his suspicions the Puritans become more and more drunk and eventually say to the nurse, "Bring hither the same cup, nurse, I would fain drive away this (hup!) anti-christian grief." It is ironic that Middleton seems to be satirizing the Puritans while Middleton himself is a Puritan. What Middleton was satirizing, however, was not the Puritan beliefs, but rather the false beliefs and irreligious behaviors of these particular Puritans (Brunning 760).

Cazamian considers the third act of Middleton and Dekker's The Roaring Girl (1611) to contain a number of very amusing scenes (Cazamian 339). There is so much of the comic in Women Beware Women (1657) that Cazamian would call it a tragicomedy if it were not for its very tragic ending (Cazamian 339).

Thomas Middleton Bibliography

Bains, Yashdip. "Thomas Middleton's Blurt, Master Constable as a Burlesque on Love." Essays Presented to Amy G. Stock. Ed. R. K. Kaul. Jaipur, India: Rajasthan University Press, 1965, 41-57.

Bald, R. C. "The Sources of Middleton's City Comedies." Journal of English and Germanic Philology 33 (1934): 373-387.

Brooke, Nicholas. "The Changeling (Middleton and Rowley), 1622." Horrid Laughter in Jacobean Tragedy. New York, NY: Barnes and Noble, 1979, 70-88.

Brooke, Nicholas. "Women Beware Women (Middleton), c1920-25." Horrid Laughter in Jacobean Tragedy. New York, NY: Barnes and Noble, 1979, 89-110.

Brunning, Alizon. "Thomas Middleton." Encyclopedia of British Humorists, Volume II. Ed. Steven H. Gale, New York, NY: Garland, 1996, 757-763.

Cazamian, Louis. "Middleton." The Development of English Humor. Durham, NC: Duke University Press, 1952, 337-340.

Charney, Maurice. "Comic Villainy in Shakespeare and Middleton." Shakespearean Comedy. Ed. Maurice Charney. New York, NY: Literary Forum, 1980, 165-173.

Covatta, Anthony. Thomas Middleton's City Comedies. Lewisburg, PA: Bucknell Univ Press, 1973.

Davidson, Clifford. "The Phoenix: Middleton's Didactic Comedy." Papers in Language and Literature 4 (1968): 121-130.

Gibbons, Brian. Jacobean City Comedy: A Study of Satiric Plays by Jonson, Marston and Middleton. 2nd ed. London, England: Methuen, 1980.

Marotti, Arthur F. "Fertility and Comic Form in A Chaste Maid in Cheapside." Comparative Drama 3 (1969): 65-74.

Parker, R. B. "Middleton's Experiments with Comedy and Judgment." Jacobean Theatre. Ed. John Russell Brown and Bernard Harris. New York, NY: St. Martin's, 1960.

Pujante, Angel Luis. "Satira, Comicad y Juegos de Palabras en A Game at Chess, de Thomas Middleton." Literary and Linguistic Aspects of Humour. Barcelona, Spain: Univ of Barcelona Dept of Languages, 1984, 211-216.

Rowe, George E., Jr. Thomas Middleton and the New Comedy Tradition. Lincoln, NE: Univ of Nebraska Press, 1979.

Williams, Robert I. "Machiavelli's Mandragola, Touchwood Senior, and the Comedy of Middleton's A Chaste Maid in Cheapside." Studies in English Literature, 1500-1900 10 (1970): 385-396.

Philip Massinger (1583-1640)

Louis Cazamian considers Massinger to be serious, staid, and not very optimistic in his outlook. Furthermore, there is a moral or religious tone that permeates his works. In short, he feels that Massinger was "not endowed by nature with a gift of comedy" (Cazamian 350). Nevertheless, Massinger realized that comic relief was desirable, and he attempted to create it in his works, though his attempts were for the most part disappointing. In the play A New Way to Pay Old Debts, for example, Justice Greedy is designed for comic relief and is therefore portrayed as having a voracious and impatient appetite. The egregious oaf, Sylli in The Maid of Honor is also designed for comic relief, and so are Calandrino and Petzonella of The Great Duke of Florence. Calandrino and Petzonella do their best --or worst--to make us laugh, but for Cazamian, the best he can manage is a smile, and even this is merely because "we must be tolerant to an author who has given us charming scenes" (Cazamian 351). Cazamian feels that all of the successful dramatists of Massinger's age had a sense of humor, even Massinger himself. His writing was spontaneous and showed a shrewd knowledge of life. His humor is to be found not only in the plays already mentioned, but also in The City Madam which contains the humorous pranks of Lady Frugal's daughters, and the humorous scenes in Secret's house, and the humorous display of Luke's fortune and greatness, and the humorous retrospective survey of the Frugal family's rise to wealth, but in all of these cases, the humor is merely to provide realistic detail, and is therefore more insightful than merry (Cazamian 351).

Philip Massinger Bibliography

Cazamian, Louis. "Massinger." The Development of English Humor. Durham, NC: Duke
    University Press, 1952, 350-352.

Francis Beaumont (c1584-1616)

Francis Beaumont and John Fletcher's first comedy was the wittily erotic piece entitled Salmacis and Hermaphroditus. Beaumont and Fletcher's first two plays were comedies, and they later wrote tragicomedies that used stock comic characters and situations. Both Beaumont and Fletcher were known for their wit, their sparking expressions, and their lively fancy. Their plots were teasingly convoluted but at the same time carefully modulated. John Dryden noted the gaiety of Beaumont and Fletcher's plays, he also noted an "easy, gentlemanly fluency of their language..., and a wittiness surpassing Jonson" (Bliss 94). Beaumont specialized in romantic tragicomedy, tragedy, and comedy that were based on love, and they were not afraid to borrow from other authors:
> Specific borrowings and allusions appear in Beaumont's first dramas: parodies of speeches from Hamlet, Othello, and Antony and Cleopatra in The Woman Hater; a comic use of Hotspur's paean on honor in The Knight of the Burning Pestle. Later in the joint plays and continuing in Fletcher's work after 1613, Shakespearean speeches, characters, situations--even whole plays--get recycled in the works of the "Beaumont and Fletcher" canon. (Bliss 95).

Louis Cazamian considers Beaumont's writing to be vigorous, self-possessed, and virile. Some of the scenes in Philaster have a sustained force and beauty which have frequently been compared to scenes in Shakespeare's writing. "A Shakespearean note indeed is to be heard as well in his humor" (Cazamian 344).

In The Woman Hater (1607), Beaumont and Fletcher develop a clever, out-spoken heroine reminiscent of Marston, but even more reminiscent of Beatrice in Shakespeare's Much Ado About Nothing. There are many witty exchanges in The Woman Hater, but they take place between Oriana and Gondarino, the title's misogynist, rather than between Oriana and the Duke she will later marry. Gondarino is an obsessed anti-feminist, and Oriana punishes his foul-mouthed slander by taking his own stereotype of women and turning this stereotype against him. Thus, she becomes talkative, lustful, and aggressive, thereby reversing the conventions of masculine seduction, and she chases Gondarino around his own house, peppering him with compliments and threatening him with her eternal devotion. Oriana's intentional violations of decorum provide a number of very funny scenes, but they do not shock Gondarino out of his obsessive hatred of women. At the very end of the play, Oriana is allowed to choose Gondarino's punishment, and she has him bound to a chair, and publicly "wooed" and fondled by a bevy of ladies (Bliss 95).

Beaumont and Fletcher's Knight of the Burning Pestle (1613) is a highly spirited burlesque of dramatic literary conventions of Beaumont and Fletcher's day (Bliss 96). Knight of the Burning Pestle is a play which owes a great debt to Cervantes's Don Quixote (1605) which had a great effect on English writing, especially when the English translation came out in 1612. Beaumont's debt to Cervantes is not only in the subject, but also in the tone and the manner of the comedy. In Knight of the Burning Pestle there is a "mixture of sense and wit, amusement and seriousness which gives the humor of the play its gentleness, as it inspired the grave reflective banter of Cervantes's novel" (Cazamian 345). Lee Bliss says that Knight of the Burning Pestle is now regarded as a minor comic masterpiece. It is also important because it was the first great English dramatic burlesque (Bliss 97).

Both The Coxcomb, and The Scornful Lady (1616) contain a wit that is both urbane and scurrilous. There are often sarcastic asides and set speeches on standard satiric topics. Finally, there are prickly interchanges, "wit duels" between the romantic couple whose courtship is the play's primary focus. These "wit duels" provide an important model for Restoration Comedy. The Scornful Lady "deftly updates the witty exuberance of Elizabethan romantic comedy with topical satire, stylish double entendre, and a new style of wooing to complement the 'new' woman" (Bliss 96).

In The London Merchant, two members of the audience, a grocer and his wife, climb on stage to sit with the actors.

> They object to the theater's intended offering, a city comedy called The London Merchant, and demand that the actors perform--if not instead of, at least in alternating scenes--a citizen-adventure story to be dictated by them and to star their own apprentice, Rafe. Initially, the play's focus seems wholly satiric, aimed at the boorish, egoistic citizens--their demand that the theater conform to their wishes and flatter their class; their out-moded taste in literature; their failure as audience and as playwrights--and against public theaters like the Red Bull and Curtain, where exactly the named plays they prefer could be found. (Bliss 96)

Alfred Gu L'Estrange points out that Francis Beaumont's name is often linked with that of John Fletcher, since as young men these two authors lived together in the same house and even wore each others clothes (L'Estrange 264). L'Estrange suggests that the "prurient coarseness" of Fletcher's writing was due to the licentiousness of the period during which he wrote (L'Estrange 265). Fletcher and Beaumont had the reputation of being great conversationalists. Their "racy raillery" is said to have been as good in person as in their plays, and they were members of a group of wits named the "Mermaid Club" in Fleet Street. This is where "the wits of the day sharpened their humour in friendly conflict." In a letter to Ben Jonson, Beaumont writes:

> What things have we seen done at the "Mermaid!" [We've] heard words that

have been so nimble and so full of subtle flame, as if that every one from whom they came had meant to put his whole wit in a jest, and had resolved to live a fool the rest of his dull life. (L'Estrange 268)

In talking about Beaumont and Fletcher, Leigh Hunt notes that their confidence, their wit, and their enjoyment was unbounded. Everyone listened acutely to hear what these two gay authors had to say (Hunt 158). Hunt contrasts the fierce weight of the satire of Ben Jonson's Volpone, where poison and suffocation enter the play as techniques of aggravation, with the lighter and happier caricatures of Beaumont and Fletcher. The latter treatment is equally founded in truth, and equally serious in its depiction of this truth, but it is clear that Beaumont and Fletcher had a more enjoyable relationship with reality than did Jonson (Hunt 159). Beaumont and Fletcher helped in determining the shape of Restoration comedy in general, and also helped in the emergence of Comedy of Manners in particular (Bliss 97).

Francis Beaumont Bibliography

Bliss, Lee. "Don Quixote in England: The Case for The Knight of the Burning Pestle. Viator 18 (1987): 361-380.

Bliss, Lee. "Francis Beaumont." Encyclopedia of British Humorists, Volume I. Ed. Steven H. Gale, New York, NY: Garland, 1996, 92-99.

Cazamian, Louis. "Beaumont and Fletcher." The Development of English Humor. Durham, NC: Duke University Press, 1952, 344-348.

Finkelpearl, Philip J. "'Wit' in Francis Beaumont's Poems." Modern Language Quarterly 28 (1967): 33-44.

Gale, Steven H. "The Relationship between Beaumont's Knight of the Burning Pestle and Cervantes' Don Quixote." Anales Cervantinos 12 (1972): 87-96.

Hunt, Leigh. "Beaumont and Fletcher." Wit and Humour. New York, NY: Folcroft, 1972, 158-183.

L'Estrange, Alfred Gu. "Shakespeare--Ben Jonson--Beaumont and Fletcher--The Wise Men of Gatham." History of English Humour. New York, NY: Burt Franklin, 1878, 250-270.

Shirley, James, ed. Comedies and Tragedies: Written by Frances Beaumont and John Fletcher, Gentlemen. London, England: Humphrey Robinson and Humphrey Moseley, 1647.

Thorndike, Ashley H. "Beaumont and Fletcher." English Comedy. New York, NY: Macmillan, 1929, 192-217.

Waith, Eugene M. The Pattern of Tragicomedy in Beaumont and Fletcher. New Haven, CT: Yale University Press, 1952.

Willis, Lawrence B. Fletcher, Beaumont and Company: Entertainers to the Jacobean Gentry. New York, NY: King's Crown Press, 1947.

Richard Brome (c1585-1652)

Richard Brome wrote a number of successful comedies, one of which was the Jovial Crew, or Merry Beggars. Brome's laughable "Old Men Going to School" was placed by Charles Lamb into his Dramatic Specimens. According to Leigh Hunt, the description of the old man's second childhood is very ludicrous (Hunt 211). Brome's The Holy Pedlar is written in swinging verse, and Hugh Walker suggests that this poem "must have been roared out at many a Cavalier drinking-bout" (Walker 123).

Brome wrote with spirit and effect, he was capable of learning from adversity, and he had a power which few of the political satirists show, of detecting the vices and weaknesses of his own side. One of his best pieces, On Sir G. B. his Defeat, is full of a sad acid wisdom taught by the Civil War. (Walker 123)

Richard Brome Bibliography

Hunt, Leigh. "Brome." Wit and Humour. New York, NY: Folcroft, 1972, 211-213.
Walker, Hugh. English Satire and Satirists. New York, NY: J. M. Dent, 1925.

John Ford (c1586-c1638)

John Ford was like Philip Massinger in going out of his way to provide comic relief, but not being very successful in the attempt. Borgetto, the "dolt" in 'Tis a Pitty She's a Whore is considered by Cazamian to be an unsuccessful attempt at comic relief. There is also a humorous dialogue between Putana and Annabella in Act 1, Scene 2 of 'Tis a Pity. The farce of Perkin Warbeck is another unsuccessful attempt. The Prologue to The Broken Heart warns the audience not to expect "apish laughter," or "some lame jeer at place or person," and indeed these are not to be found here. Cazamian considers the best humor of The Broken Heart to be at the end of Act 1, Scene 2, where the two maids of honor banty with the courtiers turned soldiers. Although Ford's humor is not always hilarious, he nevertheless writes with a "modicum of realistic zest," and he also relies on the ironies that are produced by a melancholy mind (Cazamian 352-353).

John Ford Bibliography

Bhattacharya, Jibesh. "The Comic Plays of John Ford: An Appraisal." Literary Half-Yearly 23.2 (1982): 48-57.
Brooke, Nicholas. "'Tis Pity She's a Whore (Ford), c. 1625." Horrid Laughter in Jacobean Tragedy. New York, NY: Barnes and Noble, 1979, 111-130.
Cazamian, Louis. "Ford." The Development of English Humor. Durham, NC: Duke University Press, 1952, 352-353.

Richard Brathwaite (1588-1673)

In 1621 Richard Brathwaite published Natures Embassie: or the Wilde-Mans Measures: Danced Naked by Twelve Satyres, with Sundry Others Continued in the Next Section. Raymond Alden notes that the "satires" in this volume are not satires in the modern sense of the word. They are written in six-line stanzas, with a rhyme scheme of a, b, a, b, c, c. The poetry is classical or medieval in style, with many classical allusions. Alden feels that the poetry is lacking both in satirical strength and poetic sweetness. He furthermore feels that the tone is serious and dull (Alden 216). Alden feels that Brathwaite's satire shows a lack of logic and order, and that the moral, and the rhetorical figures as well, are quite strained (Alden 219). Despite these criticisms, Brathwaite's satire was original, and can be said to be in the general form of "satire of abstract qualities" (Alden 218).

> Brathwaite used the classics...as the medieval writers did, only as a storehouse of allegorical and ethical material. For him the Renaissance had never come. His general idea of satire as a rebuke of the vices of a

degenerate age he of course derived from the imitators of classical satire.
(Alden 219)

Richard Brathwaite Bibliography

Alden, Raymond MacDonald. "Richard Brathwaite." The Rise of Formal Satire in England
under Classical Influence. New York, NY: Archon, 1961, 216-222.

George Wither (1588-1667)

In 1613 George Wither published Abuses Stript and Whipt: or Satyricall Essayes.
This work was so popular that it got the author imprisoned in the Marshalsea, where he was
not released until he had written his Satire Dedicated to the King's Majesty in 1614.
Wither wrote his satires in a conversational style, and they exhibited freedom and fluency.
Many of his couplets had feminine endings. Although Wither's satire tends to be very
abstract, he also had the ability to be concrete when he wished to be (Alden 176-177). In
1617 Wither published The Scourge, a book which contained a picture of a shaggy and
naked Satyr, holding a scourge in his right hand, and a shepherd's pipe in his left hand
(Alden 179). Hugh Walker feels that Wither's satires are extraordinarily comprehensive,
treating such diverse subjects as vices, manners, customs, classes, institutions, literature,
education, and religion.

George Wither Bibliography

Alden, Raymond MacDonald. "George Wither." The Rise of Formal Satire in England
under Classical Influence. New York, NY: Archon, 1961, 176-190.
Walker, Hugh. English Satire and Satirists. New York, NY: E. P. Dutton, 1925.

Robert Herrick (1591-1674)

Robert Herrick was known as "Jolly Herrick" because of his love of pleasure, his
liveliness, and his charming lyrical gift. Herrick was especially enthusiastic for sack, roses,
daffodils, and mistresses. His humor is Chaucerian in nature with its hints, innuendoes and
slyness, and with its racy realism, as it depicts Devonshire life in the fourth and fifth
decades of the seventeenth century. Herrick is able to write humor with realistic verve, and
sometimes writes a mixture of humor with love poetry. But Herrick's humor can also be
bitingly satirical, as can be seen in his "Another," "To Criticks," "Upon Blanch," "Upon
Bunce," and "Upon Pink" (Cazamian 372).

Robert Herrick Bibliography

Cazamian, Louis. "Suckling, Herrick." The Development of English Humor. Durham, NC:
Duke University Press, 1952, 370-372.
Marcus, Leah S. The Politics of Mirth: Jonson, Herrick, Milton, Marvell, and the Defense
of Old Holiday Pastimes. Chicago, IL: University of Chicago Press, 1986.

George Herbert (1593-1633)

Thomas Merrill shows how Herbert relates the language of love, the language of religion and the language of parody in his poem entitled "A Parodie." In "The Ironing of George Herbert's 'Collar,'" and in "Herbert's 'Easter Wings,'" Dale Randall and John Ray discuss George Herbert's many puns, and they also discuss the relationship between figurative language and punning for Herbert (Rosen 525). George Herbert's early Greek and Latin poetry and his early epistles both testify to his acquaintance with the classical forms of humor. Herbert wrote a series of Latin verses in response to Andrew Melville's Anti-Tami-Cami-Categoria, and in this series is to be found a number of satirical pieces, including one that mocks Melville's vocabulary. Indeed, Herbert had a reputation among his contemporaries for his wittiness and his humor. He enjoyed mirth, and his contemporaries enjoyed his practice of mixing quaint quirks and pranks with twisted and extended metaphors known as "conceits." Herbert enjoyed displaying "metaphysical wit." This type of wit employs strange distortions of language. It also employs surprise and paradox, and its images tend to be novel and far-fetched. Metaphysical Wit also tends to blend a simple and direct speaking voice with compelling emotions and mind-stretching ideas (Rosen 523).

There is a harmonic tension in The Temple (1633) that produces an effect in the reader which David Rosen calls "surprising fitness." The individual poems in this volume show the symbolic relationship between a human body and a temple, elaborating on the architecture of a church building (Rosen 523). The title of this collection is playfully ambiguous, and throughout the volume, Herbert shows how mirth and play are important tools for developing his message. This is very appropriate for Herbert because "from the standpoint of salvation, he considers life a comedy" (Rosen 524). One of the poems in The Temple is named "The Church Porch." Here Herbert tells worldly people not to give up their humor, but to purify it: "When thou dost tell another's jest, therein / Omit the oaths, which true wit cannot need." Consistent with this is Herbert's statement "Laugh not too much; the witty man laughs least." Much of the wit of "The Church Porch" comes follows from the interplay of the language with the tight structure of the poem. There are seventy-seven interlocking but independent verses all of which show the impact of the epigrammatic forms of humor. There are three sections in each verse. The first two lines state the general proposition. These are followed by a witty comparison, and then finally there is a pointed aphorism (Rosen 524).

The titles of some of the poems in The Temple show Herbert's leanings in the direction of humor. Such titles include "Parodie," "Paradox," "Quidditie," "Quip," "Charms and Knots." Even when the poems have unhumorous titles they nevertheless develop humorous or paradoxical ideas. In the poem "Time," for example, Herbert develops the idea that Time is not a good thing, for it allows people to live too long and get into trouble. As Herbert notes in this poem, a good Christian should wish for an early death because that will bring a speedier resurrection. Herbert uses many humorous poetic devices, one of which is shaped poetry. His "Easter Wings" for example, is patterned in the shape of a bird with wings. In "Paradise," Herbert "dices up the endings in each stanza, taking off the first letter of the previous rhyme to create the next--"start," "tart," "art." Rosen notes that there is a range of satire in The Temple. The satire in "The Church Porch has "a sharpness of satire that Herbert could have found in Juvenal." In contrast, the satire in "Affliction" "employs a Horatian tone to mock Herbert's own previous view" (Rosen 524).

George Herbert Bibliography

Merrill, Thomas F. "Sacred Parody and the Grammar of Devotion." Criticism 23.3 (1981): 195-210.

Randall, Dale B. J. "The Ironing of George Herbert's 'Collar.'" Studies in Philology 81.4 (1984): 473-495.

Ray, Joan Klingel. "Herbert's 'Easter Wings.'" Explicator 49.3 (1991): 140-142.
Rosen, David. "George Herbert." Encyclopedia of British Humorists, Volume I. Ed. Steven
    H. Gale, New York, NY: Garland, 1996, 522-525.

James Howell (c1594-1666)

Many of James Howell's letters contain a vein of satire, and toward the end of his
writing career he wrote A Perfect Description of the Country of Scotland, which is an
unrestrained satire of the Scotts, and A Brief Character in the Low Countries under the
States, which, in contrast to the Scottish satire, effectively creates distance and uses restraint
in satirizing the Dutch (Walker 181).

James Howell Bibliography

Walker, Hugh. English Satire and Satirists. London, England: J. M. Dent, 1925.

James Shirley (1596-1666)

Edgar Chapman says that James Shirley was "the most prolific playwright of the
1630s (Chapman 978). Louis Cazamian considers the comic elements of Shirley's plays
to have been quite explicit and often farcical. His writing is facile, elegant, and cynical,
and is filled with sprightliness, quaintness, contrast, absurdity, and paradoxical invention
(Cazamian 353). Love Tricks is Shirley's first comedy. It ridicules the affected social
behavior of the period, such as the exaggerated compliments, and the hyperbolic polite
forms of address. There is also a comic Welshman in the play whose dialect humor
contributes to the amusement (Chapman 975). Cazamian would consider Shirley's The
Grateful Servant and his The Witty Fair One to be "conscious humor." The scene between
Sir Nicholas Treedle and his tutor in Act 2, Scene 2 is an example of "conscious humor,"
as is Act 5, Scene 3, where Penelope and Fowler are engaged in conversation. Fowler
coolly and ironically moralizes upon his "supposed decease" (Cazamian 353). In The Witty
Fair One there is a clever but chaste ingenue who pursues and tames a rebellious would-be
rake of the same class (Chapman 975). Shirley's The Humorous Courtier is not as strongly
humorous or satirical as the title might suggest. Cazamian considers Oncolo, the woman
hater to be a totally humorless character. The words "humor" and "humorist" are used
throughout this play "in a way that betokens not the slightest change of meaning from the
time of Jonson" (Cazamian 354).

In Changes, or Love in a Maze (1632) there is a group of lovers lost in a comic
labyrinth (Chapman 977). Lucina is the charming "merry Widow" in The Ball (1632).
Lucina is witty and urbane in her various exchanges with her suitor, a gruff and
inexperienced Colonel (Chapman 975). "Conscious humor" can be found in Hyde Park
(1632), where the animated and picturesque episodes of Act 4, Scene 1 are fresh, novel,
and filled with a spirit of sober amusement (Cazamian 353). Edgar Chapman describes
Hyde Park as "a cheerful and sometimes romantic comedy (Chapman 975). As the title
suggests, Hyde Park takes place on the opening day of Hyde Park, and the wedding
celebration that is going on makes Hyde Park a festive comedy. This day is also the
wedding day of another "merry widow" by the name of Mrs. Bonavent, and what emerges
from this double wedding are two duels of wits between two pairs of lovers--Lord Bonvile
and Julietta on the one hand, and Fairfield and Mistress Carol on the other. Mistress Carol
is a scornful lady who likes to mock social constraints, and who values her own

independence, and who professes to hate both men and the institution of marriage. And even though she falls in love with Fairfield, Fairfield trickers her into swearing an oath that she will "never fall in love with Fairfield."   Caught in this paradoxical trap, she is nevertheless able to pursue Fairfield in order to entrap him, while at the same time pretending to stick to the letter of her oath never to love him.   Thus, the normal expectations about the courtship ritual are reversed, as Carol pursues Fairfield, a person she does not love. "She escapes her oath to reject his love finally by forging his name to a lame Petrarchan sonnet written by another lover and pretending to take the trite Petrarchan hyperbole seriously. Thus, in a bold move, she agrees to marry him to "save his life," offering in the process an amusing parody of Petrarchan love conventions" (Chapman 976). Hyde Park has three plots. The first plot is a satirical parody of Petrarchan courtship; the second plot is based on a farcical misunderstanding; and the third plot is based on intrigue. Much of the humor of this play is based on Shirley's skilled portrayal of the London colloquial idiom. The play is a blend of farce and high comedy. It is a blend of festivity with light romance. And it is a gentle satire on the manners of Shirley's day (Chapman 977).

The Gamester (1633) is a comedy of intrigue whose humor comes from the ability of a clever heroine to avoid the unwanted advances of her lady-friend's husband. This clever ingenue named Penelope, and her lover, Will Hazzard ensnare the would-be philanderer, Wilding, in a situation of embarrassment that was well known to the Elizabethan stage and was called "the bed trick." They humiliate Wilding by arranging a rendezvous between Penelope and Wilding, but the rendezvous is kept instead by Wilding's wife (Chapman 975).

The Lady of Pleasure (1635) contains a number of hilarious scenes, and Aretina's elaborate affair with Kickshaw is close to being grotesque satire. In this play, there is an effective combining of caricature, farce, biting wit, and satirical realism, and Edgar Chapman says that this combination of humorous rhetorical devices serves to make this comedy Shirley's "most convincing moral statement" (Chapman 978). Cazamian feels that it is The Lady of Pleasure that provides the "best tenor of subdued pleasantry," since this work contains light and pleasant satire of the affectations imported from France, and is done so well as to be considered by Cazamian to be an "early sketch of Molière's Précieuses Ridicules (Cazamian 353-354). In fact, Edgar Chapman says that Lady of Pleasure is a satirical work that can be viewed as a forerunner of the more cynical Restoration comedies (Chapman 975-976). Edgar Chapman considers Lady of Pleasure to be one of Shirley's two major comic plays, along with Hyde Park, but of these two major comedies, Lady of Pleasure has more of a satirical edge. Here there is an ironic contrast between the young Celestina, who is clever but innocent, and Aretina, who is a foolish wife from the country who has vowed to become better acquainted with "London's gamier amusements and night life." Aretina is trying to break away from provincial sobriety, as she wants to experiment with the latest London fashions. These desires lead her into a number of different amusing episodes. Aretina's husband, Sir Thomas Bornwell, feels that he must abandon his responsible conduct and plunge into gambling in order to teach his wife a lesson, and to "shock her into restraint." Chapman notes that "their competition in fashionable folly is often hilarious." Aretina, for example, enters into a disguise and has an affair with a worthless person named Kickshaw, but later Aretina is sobered by Kickshaw's account of her sexual performance. He calls her "a demon," "a devil," and "a hellcat." "Aretina's discovery of how her conduct appears to her lover is one of Shirley's harshest comic epiphanies and leads her to a fresh awareness of social responsibility. This comic embarrassment also prompts her to return to her husband in a chastened state" (Chapman 977).

James Shirley Bibliography

Cazamian, Louis. "Shirley." The Development of English Humor. Durham, NC: Duke
    University Press, 1952, 353-354.
Chapman, Edgar L. "James Shirley." Encyclopedia of British Humorists, Volume II. Ed.
    Steven H. Gale, New York, NY: Garland, 1996, 974-980.
Wertheim, Albert. "Games and Courtship in James Shirley's Hyde Park." Anglia 90 (1972):
    71-91.

Sir Thomas Browne (1605-1682)

Marylynn Layman notes that Sir Thomas Browne, like William Shakespeare, was
linguistically very creative. "Browne acts as a pioneer and a champion of the English
language in writing Pseudodoxia in the early 1640s, deliberately choosing the vernacular
and introducing new vocabulary to express his meanings." Layman notes that Browne is
quoted 3,467 times in the Oxford English Dictionary, and that 2,257 of these quotes come
from his Pseudodoxia. Of that number, Browne coined 657 new words, of which only
about 210 are now obsolete. "Thus two thirds of the words Browne introduced into English
are still in use" (Layman 26-27).

A. C. Patrides writes that in Thomas Browne's Hydriotaphia, The Garden of Cyrus,
"delight, exhilaration, and joy are the unmistakable effects" (Patrides 38). Joan Webber,
and Anna Nardo have noted Browne's use of humorous devices in his Religio Medici.
Webber has commented on Browne's witty persona, and Nardo has discussed Browne's
playful language. "Many have defended Browne's wit in Religio Medici against Stanley
Fish's attack on it as "indecorous," pointing to Browne's intentions to delight and instruct
and his use of humanistic playful language" (Layman 8). The persona in Browne's
Pseudodoxia Epidemica also often uses humor and wit to form a relationship with his
readers. He uses rhetorical devices ranging from dry irony, to puns, to paradoxes, to black
humor to achieve his purposes (Layman 5).

Joan Bennett notes that Browne "loves to accumulate evidence, making a vulgar
error seem more and more absurd, and then to conclude with a pretended uncertainty,
leaving the reader to deduce that the belief is ridiculous" (Bennett 179). For example,
Browne addresses the seventeenth-century belief that man is erect in order to allow him to
look toward Heaven. Browne humorously argues against this claim by discussing the
postures and positions of various animals and then he notes that if man's erectness is
designed to allow him to see Heaven more clearly, then God would not have given man
such a huge upper eyelid and overhanging eye lashes. Browne noted that birds do not have
such an upper eyelid and therefore have an advantage over man in their ability to have an
unobstructed view of Heaven. Browne further notes ironically that the animals lower on
the evolutionary scale seem to have the best view of Heaven. The cartilagineous fish have
eyes on the sides of their head which makes a Heavenward glance very easy for them.
Furthermore, the position of a frog's eyes--bulging out of the top of his head--provides this
animal with the clearest view of Heaven possible (Layman 13).

Sir Thomas Browne Bibliography

Bennett, Joan. Sir Thomas Browne: A Man of Achievement in Literature. Cambridge,
    England: Cambridge University Press, 1962.
Layman, Marylynn T. " 'A Language Best Conceived': The Cultural and Linguistic Impact
    of Sir Thomas Browne's Pseudodoxia Epidemica." Unpublished MA Thesis. Tempe,

AZ: Arizona State University, 1994.

Patrides, C. A. " 'The Best Part of Nothing': Sir Thomas Browne and the Strategy of
Indirection." Approaches to Sir Thomas Browne: The Ann Arbor Tercentenary
Lectures and Essays. Ed. C. A. Patrides. Columbia, MO: University of Missouri
Press, 1982, 31-48.

Thomas Randolph (1605-1634)

Randolph was a disciple of Ben Jonson, and wrote gay and amiable comedies like
Muse's Looking-Glass (his best-known play), and the pastoral Amyntas, or the Impossible
Dowry; both plays are filled with what Hunt calls "animal spirit." Muse's Looking-Glass
is an allegory in which Deilus, Aphobus, and Colax are caricatures of Rashness, Fear, and
Flattery respectively. The extravagances of Fear, and the excessive double-dealing of
Flattery, with his asides to the two others, is quite ludicrous, and have a foundation in
reality. The Impossible Dowry is a pastoral fairy investiture that is filled with gaiety and
graceful fancy. Randolph died at the age of 29, while still a Fellow of Trinity College,
Cambridge. He had earlier lost a finger while trying to separate two combatants, and he
turned this event into his own epitaph, saying of the finger that he hoped to "shake hands
with it in heaven" (Hunt 184-185).

Thomas Randolph Bibliography

Hunt, Leigh. "Randolph." Wit and Humour. New York, NY: Folcroft Library, 1972, 184-
197.

Sir William Davenant (1606-1668)

It was Sir William Davenant who introduced "opera" into England, and it was Sir
William Davenant who developed what was later to become known as "heroic drama." It
was also Sir William Davenant who tried to aggrandize himself by circulating the story that
Shakespeare was his father. Howard Collins notes that Davenant is the only important
playwright to span the Stuart, Caroline, Interregnum, and Restoration periods, a time during
which remarkable changes came about in the treatment of dramatic comedy (Collins 7).
Collins says that Davenant helped to develop various forms of dramatic comedy, humors
comedy, satiric comedy, and comedy of manners, and he adds that it was Davenant who
actually introduced burlesque to the Restoration stage (Collins 8).

Sir William Davenant's first comedy, The Wits, brought him to the attention of
King Charles I because there was a debate about whether or not it should be licensed. The
play was licensed, was well liked in court, and Davenant was commissioned by the Queen,
who was "determined to bring Platonic Love to her husband's somewhat wayward court."
The Wits was to present "a masque celebrating an unconsummated relationship between the
sexes." The Temple of Love also pleased the Queen, so much in fact that she honored
Davenant with her livery. The works which followed included Love and Honour, a tragicomedy, and The Platonick Lovers, which was again a tragi-comedy, but which could also
be classified as a satire. Davenant's News from Plymouth was described by Collins as "a
roistering comedy." This was Davenant's only early work not written for an aristocratic
private audience. It was presented at the Globe, a plebeian theatre, and of course it catered
to the more basic tastes in comedy. Thus, it had more right than his earlier pieces to be
termed "comic" (Collins 16).

Davenant had an uncanny ability to dazzle his benefactors at their request, and his Britannia Triumphans and Luminalia were masques of magnificent splendor which sometimes contained "soporific rhetoric." Davenant's Salmacida Spolia was written in such a way that the Queen herself, pregnant at the time, could take part in the role of being hoisted by a machine so that she could make an entrance as if she were descending from a cloud. This scene was both dangerous and ridiculous. Although Davenant never officially became Poet Laureate of England, he was nevertheless honored in 1638 with a financial grant from the king that was "sufficiently significant," and at the siege of Gloucester, Charles I dubbed William Davenant a knight (Collins 17). Only eleven years later, in 1649, the Cavalier cause was lost, and Charles I was beheaded at Whitehall. For Davenant, this meant a tedious exile during which he returned to his own writing--the epic Gondibert (Collins 18). When Charles II came into power at the beginning of the Restoration, William Davenant was back in favor. It is true that in age and temperament Davenant was not very compatible with Charles II's rowdy court; nevertheless, out of respect for his past services, he was given the managership of the Duke's Playhouse, one of the two licensed theatres in England at the time (Collins 19).

Davenant's most original play during this period was entitled A Playhouse to Be Let. This play compounded some Commonwealth pieces, at the same time adapting from the French, in broad burlesque fashion. Since Davenant considered Shakespeare to be his father--or at least his godfather--he also borrowed heavily from that source. His The Law Against Lovers is a combination of Shakespeare's Measure for Measure and Much Ado About Nothing. Davenant's The Rivals was based on Shakespeare's The Two Noble Kinsmen, and also contained elements from Macbeth and The Tempest (Collins 20).

Sir William Davenant Bibliography

Collins, Howard S. The Comedy of Sir William Davenant, Berlin, Germany: Mouton, 1967.

Edmund Waller (1606-1687)

In The Proper Wit of Poetry, George Williamson demonstrates how important Edmund Waller was in the development of eighteenth-century verse satire (Beller and Miller 1173). In Andrew Marvell, and Edmund Waller: Seventeenth-Century Praise and Restoration Satire Alexander Chambers suggests that Waller should have been given more credit than he has been given for influencing Marvell's satiric poetry (Beller and Miller 1172). About Edmund Waller, John Dryden said, "unless he had written, none of us could write." Waller "changed the heroic couplet from the medium for continuous narrative that it is in Geoffrey Chaucer's writing into a stanza form, a way of making a single complete point. This is exactly how the heroic couplet comes to be used by Dryden and Pope." About his love lyrics, Martin Beller and Edmund Miller say, "His finest effects tend to grow out of moments of anxiety, hesitancy, regret, resignation, and renunciation rather than anguish, aggression, or possessive desire" (Beller and Miller 1169). Waller's intentional humor was most obvious in his humorous epigrams, but Beller and Miller says that for the modern audience, the humor there is "rather thin, forced, and unconvincing." A more important testament to Waller's humor was in the wit with which he conducted his long public life. "His wit is indeed perhaps less at home in verse than in prose--as in his Parliamentary speeches. Since these speeches are topical, they are, however, now even less read than the poems" (Beller and Miller 1171).

Waller's main claim to history is that he was an informer and a turncoat, but it is often forgotten that he was true to his principles. He sacrificed his fortune and nearly sacrificed his life in the pursuit of his political principles. But Waller was an enigma to his contemporaries, because he adhered neither to person nor to party. Rather he maintained a passionate commitment to the politics of moderation and stability as long as he lived. It is ironic that Waller's love poems appear to the modern eye as studied and cool, while it is his political poems that are written in praise of virtue, and which "carry with them an appealing air of hopefulness" (Beller and Miller 1170).

The reader feels somewhat finished after reading the title of Waller's "Instructions to a Painter, for the Drawing of the Posture and Progress of his Majesty's Forces at Sea, under the Command of his Highness-Royal: together with the Battle and Victory obtained over the Dutch, June 3, 1665." By using the process of "ut pictura poesis" which in English means "as with a picture, so with a poem," Waller vividly portrays a "painterly" image of battle scenes in order to praise the conduct of the English as they go into battle (Beller and Miller 1170). These poems were very popular during Waller's day, and Beller and Miller feel that some of them have "earned an important place in the history of English satire." Douglas Bush considers Waller "notorious" for having been the "progenitor of a race of parodies, since his "Instructions to a Painter" was frequently and unrestrainedly parodied. "Waller's "Instructions" not only inaugurated a genre but also provided a powerful impetus toward the development of mock-heroic verse in the half-century after his death. It might be argued that Waller's single most enduring contribution to the development of English literary humor was, in fact, the writing of this serious poem" (Beller and Miller 1171).

Edmund Waller Bibliography

Beller, Martin, and Edmund Miller. "Edmund Waller." Encyclopedia of British Humorists, Volume II. Ed. Steven H. Gale, New York, NY: Garland, 1996, 1168-1173.
Chambers, Alexander B. Andrew Marvell, and Edmund Waller: Seventeenth-Century Praise and Restoration Satire. University Park, PA: Pennsylvania State University Press, 1991.
Williamson, George. The Proper Wit of Poetry. Chicago, IL: University of Chicago Press, 1961.

Thomas Fuller (1608-1661)

In Worthies of England, Thomas Fuller enumerates the distinguished and eminent men of England, and also gives an account of England's products and proverbs. Fuller says that a proverb should be short, plain, common, figurative, ancient, and true. An example of a proverb which exhibits these characteristics is "He knows little, who will tell his wife all he knows." According to Alfred Gu L'Estrange, "Fuller abounds with figures and illustrations in which learning and humour are excellently intermingled" (L'Estrange 247). Fuller is also famous for his observations. He notes about seamen, for example, that "If a single meteor or fire-ball falls on their mast, it portends ill-luck, but if two come together (which they count Castor and Pollux) they presage good success" (L'Estrange 249). In the Bedfordshire section of Worthies of England, Fuller defines the "Lark," as follows: "A harmless bird while living, not trespassing on grain, and wholesome when dead, then filling the stomach with meat, as formerly the ear with music" (L'Estrange 246).

Thomas Fuller Bibliography

L'Estrange, Alfred Gu. History of English Humour. New York, NY: Burt Franklin, 1878.

John Milton (1608-1674)

Louis Cazamian considers Milton to be humorless, because in both his personal life and in his writing he is totally devoted to "truth, beauty, and single-mindedness." Milton does not have the divided mind that is necessary for humor to flourish. In Milton's writing, there is never any "suspicion of double meaning" (Cazamian 388). Charles Ross suggests that current critics typically find Milton "decidedly unfunny in his patriarchal depiction of Eve, and a current quip has it that all of God's jokes in Paradise Lost have to be so identified" (Ross 153). Paradise Lost is not so much to be read, as it is to be taken like medicine. Samuel Johnson says, "Paradise Lost is one of the books which the reader admires and lays down, and forgets to take up again. None ever wished it longer than it is. Its perusal is a duty rather than a pleasure" (Kantra 76-77). Randall Jarrell says, "Paradise Lost is what it was; but the ordinary reader no longer makes the mistake of trying to read it--instead he glances at it, weighs it in his hand, shudders, and his eyes shining, puts it on his list of the ten dullest books he has ever read" (Kantra 78-79). But despite this criticism, such literary critics as T. S. Eliot, William Empson, and Isaac Asimov have read Milton extensively, and they find in Satan a laughable, entertaining, and dramatic persona (Kantra 79).

John Evans points out that the best villains must be attractive and clever, and he gives many examples of humor in Paradise Lost to support this view. In the debate in Hell at the beginning of Book II, for example, the debaters sequentially make light of one another, using what they believe to be witty put-down humor in the process. There is also Satan's triumphal humor, what Evans calls "epic scorn" in Book VI, the book describing the battle in heaven where the loyal angels are bombed over by the rebel cannon fire. Evans also points out the delightfully humorous section in Book VII of Paradise Lost where Adam goes to God and asks for a mate, and God teases Adam as he playfully asks him why he is not content, being the master of all he surveys. In Book IX, Satan makes fun of God during the temptation, all the time realizing that the joke will be on Eve if she is foolish enough to fall for his line. Evans also refers to Satan's humor in Book IV when he sees Adam and Eve for the first time and muses that "Hell will open wide its doors" to entertain them.

In an article entitled "Heavenly High Jinx," Barbara Steward points out that scholars have tended to interpret the heavenly battle in Milton's Paradise Lost as pure satire, or as mock heroic satire, or as burlesque, or as folly--the folly of war, or the folly of not having the right hero. But there are many purely comic elements in this heavenly battle as well, as "Titanic mountains are heaped upon the rebels by loyal angels in response to blasts from cannon fortuitously invented by Satan." Furthermore, Satan and his company are "hurled to Hell, like a 'herd of goats' " (Steward 56). Steward considers the battle to be a mixture of the comic, the bawdy, and the profane. But there is also the serious and the didactic, as Milton was writing in the well-established Christian literary tradition, where this would be expected. Steward points out that this blending of the comic with the serious already had a long and respected tradition even during Milton's time, a tradition that dates back not only to the morality plays, but to the mysteries as well (Steward 56).

Carolyn O'Hearn would probably agree with Steward's position, as she discusses the ironies in Paradise Lost. John Milton was very brilliant, and he was also very Christian. Yet it appears to many critics that he made Satan the hero of Paradise Lost. It is clear that the portrait of Satan is artistically superior to the portraits of God or Christ in Paradise Lost.

> It is usually said that Milton makes Satan to be a very magnificent creature in the first two books of Paradise Lost, [and] that through the rest of the

> poem Satan degenerates, and that the misreading of Satan's role results from the fact that Milton made his creation so magnificent in the first two books that no subsequent degeneration can remove the earlier images from our minds. (O'Hearn 61)

There are three ways in which the Satan of the first two books is impressive. He is huge in stature. He is a military leader and a monarch to the devils. And he makes magnificent speeches. Satan is described in terms of a Leviathan, a tower, and a fleet of ships. He is a commander and an emperor. Satan's armies are disciplined and united, and he was an eloquent speaker. But O'Hearn believes that these facts do not demonstrate that Milton was on Satan's side. Rather, Milton was deliberately drawing attention to the fact that vanity and public adoration can trap a person into believing that he is more than he is. To support her contention that Milton was not identifying with Satan, O'Hearn points to the negative references Milton uses to describe Satan. He is called the "fiend," and the "author of all ill," and the "antagonist of heaven," and the "adversary of God and Man."

> The symmetry of Paradise Lost is so balanced that both the first reference, Book I, line 34, and the last, Book X, line 580, are to Satan as the serpent.... Milton finishes up Satan in Book X with such references as the "Prince of the Air," the "Prince of Darkness," and the "great adventurer." (O'Hearn 62)

According to O'Hearn, the figure of Satan is painted so very well because before Paradise Lost, no satisfactory portrait of Satan had existed. Rather, there was the hump backed, cloven-hoofed creature found in earlier descriptions, which were simply too tawdry and insignificant to be a worthy adversary to God. It is interesting to note that since Milton's time, the Satan in the Sunday sermons and in the literature throughout the world have been derived from Milton's Satan rather than from the numerous other religious sources (O'Hearn 62).

In a Chapter of his All Things Vain: Religious Satirists and Their Art entitled, "Miltonic and Other Utopias," Robert Kantra contrasts Milton's utopia with the utopias of science-fiction or futuristic writers. Although the depiction of both types of utopias can appear to be satiric, only the Miltonic satire is truly satiric, because only the Miltonic satire is based on a clear conception of the good and bad qualities of utopia. "Milton's distinction between 'grave and noble invention' and 'this world of evil' blurs and is lost in their kind of expository artistry. Therefore, some unintentional satire--utopias that look like satires-- gets written" (Kantra 76). Kantra criticizes the "unintentional satire" of these futurists "which reads like jokes, or at least word-games," and then he quotes a typical passage, "There is no real difference between a hammer and a spaceship, no real difference either between the invention of fire and that of the steam engine" (Kantra 90), and then says about this that "machinery has always had uses in utopia that border on hilarity, in the sense that physics and metaphysics have contradictory referents and different languages" (Kantra 90). But Miltonian satire is true satire. Milton knew what utopia was, and what it was not.

F. McD. C. Turner considers Milton to have been at first one of the gentlest and most melodious of the lyrical poets. Yet he became one of the fiercest and most bitter of the English pamphleteers. He further feels that Milton is merely a caricature of what happened in England as a whole. During Milton's time the Puritan tragedy was enacted in miniature; the rule of saints was destined to fail because they were in a perpetual minority and weakened by dissensions among themselves (Turner 21). Milton's Paradise Lost was true to Milton's time and place.

> It is, on the whole, incomplete and unrestrained, because it lacks the sure foundation of an adequate casus belli; and the wrath behind it, being an unreasonable wrath, is always overflowing and disturbing the outward suavity that is essential to successful irony.... It is very effective and very

vigorous, but spoilt in places by an excess of rage.... The personal indignation of the author is, as nearly always with Milton, far too apparent. (Turner 22-23)

Turner feels that only in <u>Areopagetica</u> are Milton's powers of irony fully displayed, for only here are the subjects significant and dignified enough to support the grandeur of his prose. Usually, Milton is so grave and logical that his irony "has the double effect of being both ludicrous and very sensible" (Turner 24). Turner concludes his article on "Milton and the Dawn of the Age of Irony" by saying that Milton was a gigantic figure in an age of feeble and irritable ironists. Milton alone is worth our consideration.

His worst irony can compete with any of his contemporaries' maledictions.... His best irony, on the other hand, stands by itself in attaining to a dignity, and almost to a grandeur, very rarely associated with ironical utterance, and as an appeal to common-sense and a wide and sane toleration it has not been surpassed. The pity is that there is so little of it. (Turner 25-26)

John Milton Bibliography

Anselment, Raymond A. <u>Betwixt Jest and Earnest: Marprelate, Milton, Marvell, Swift and the Decorum of Religious Ridicule</u>. Toronto, Canada: Univ of Toronto Press, 1979.
Cazamian, Louis. <u>The Development of English Humor</u>. Durham, NC: Duke University Press, 1952.
Flannagan, Roy. "Milton's Sense of Humor." <u>Paradise Lost</u>. New York, NY: Macmillan, 1993.
Kantra, Robert A. "Miltonic and Other Utopians." <u>All Things Vain: Religious Satirists and Their Art</u>. University Park, PA: Penn State University Press, 1984, 75-92.
Marcus, Leah S. <u>The Politics of Mirth: Jonson, Herrick, Milton, Marvell, and the Defense of Old Holiday Pastimes</u>. Chicago, IL: University of Chicago Press, 1986.
Nilsen, Don L. F. "A Warm-Up Act for John Milton." <u>Alabama English</u> 6 (1994): 25-29.
O'Hearn, Carolyn. "Milton's Satan: Metaphor Misunderstood." <u>WHIMSY</u> 2 (1984): 61-62.
Ross, Charles. "The Grim Humor of Spenser's <u>Faerie Queene</u>: Women and Laughter in a Renaissance Epic." <u>Humor: International Journal of Humor Research</u> 2.2 (1980): 153-164.
Steward, Barbara. "Heavenly High Jinx." <u>WHIMSY</u> 7 (1989): 56-57.
Turner, F. McD. C. "Milton and the Dawn of the Age of Irony." <u>The Element of Irony in English Literature</u>. Cambridge, England: University Press, 1926, 13-26.

Sir John Suckling (1609-1642)

Sir John Suckling was an important author in the development of literary "wit." His writings expose the affectations of court life, especially those of the Neoplatonists, the Petrarchanists, and the Euphuists. His new style of writing was free from conventions, and had an easy grace, but David Rosen points out that "the easy grace and freedom of this style was itself a new affectation." Rosen further notes that this new affectation became the model for the Restoration comedy that would follow, a comedy that features the paradoxical mixing of bawdiness and polish, a poetry that poses at being disinterested, but nevertheless contains a "never-ending stream of easy-flowing witticisms" which clearly take a particular stance. Suckling's plays had a powerful influence on the plays of Richard Brinsley Sheridan in particular, and on the genres of comedy of manners and satirical drama aimed at social affectation in general. Suckling's plays are filled with characters of "gentility, verbal wit, and licentiousness." "Suckling's "wit," in its dizzying multiplicity, shaped a new and powerful entity, a gentlemanly persona that combined highly mannered ease, artificial grace, and melodic smoothness, with licentious, profane, and withal coolly urbane realism bordering on cynicism." This can be seen in his poem, "Out upon It," which develops a character who is both seductively coy and affectedly nonchalant. This speaker seems to be winking to the audience as he addresses the woman:

> Out upon it! I have lov'd
> Three whole days together;
> And am like to love three more,
> If it prove fair weather. (Rosen 1081)

Suckling's humor reflects a paradoxical, quick-witted, cynical attitude of superiority, but the wit is always shifting and always dynamic. It has the type of liveliness that is parodied by William Congreve, the Restoration playwright in his "witless witty-would-be, Witwoud." Suckling was part of Jonson's circle, though he disapproved of Jonson's "pretentious classicism," and in fact lampooned it in his unfinished play, The Sad One (ca 1633) The Sessions of Poets (1637), and in and in The Goblins (1638). He also parodies Jonson's style in such poems as "Upon the first sight of my Lady Seimor," which is a parody of Jonson's "A Song to a Lute" (Rosen 1082).

Suckling was the first writer to record the so-called "Sessions," during which the poets of his day such as Rochester and Sheffield got together each to claim his superiority. Suckling's account of these encounters is entitled The Sessions of the Poets (1637), and Leigh Hunt suggests that he wrote the book in a single setting, which accounts for its spirit and impulsiveness but which also accounts for some of its "negligence" (Hunt 201). According to Hunt, Suckling's poetry is light and witty, but it is at the same time substantial (Hunt 200). In The Sessions of the Poets, Suckling said, "A Laureats Muse should be easie and free" (Rosen 1081).

The satire and the structure of The Sessions of the Poets is very often imitated and parodied. Suckling's work develops caricatures of poets of his day, as they competed for "Apollo's laurel." The Sessions became the model for many other satiric and poetic tournaments, such as "The Trial of the Poets for the Bays" by John Wilmot, "The Election of a Laureat" by John Sheffield, "The Feast of the Poets" by James Henry Leigh Hunt, and "The Sessions of the Poets" by Robert Buchanan. Suckling's satire "exhibits a characteristic aristocratic disdain over vulgar judgment," and in fact Suckling's "chummy mockery of his friends" includes a "mild raillery, through learning, and graceful manner." This entire group of poets seems to appreciate irony, and some eighteenth-century authors feel that it is this appreciation of irony that separated the civilized from the uncivilized (Rosen 1082).

Aglaura (ca 1637) is a lavish court comedy of intrigue about brothers, mistresses, lovers, and virtuous men and women. It was written first as a tragedy of misunderstandings, but was later revised and given an alternate fifth act to make it into a comedy of errors (Rosen 1084). The Goblins (1638) is the play which contains the most sustained humor of all of Suckling's plays. Here Suckling uses the device of urbane characters who are masked as bumpkins. This play is filled with excellent verbal wit and much good burlesque and buffoonery, though it is topical in its subjects. The play is a "confusing series of improbable and interlocking stories of lost brothers, virtuous maidens, and court intrigues" (Rosen 1083). The Goblins is very lively. It has breakneck action, complicated schemes, gay songs, and witty characters (Rosen 1084). Suckling's Brennoralt, or the Discontented Colonel (1639) also contains some humor, as when he says that the prince of Darkness is a Gentleman (Cazamian 371).

Suckling's poetry is frequently hilarious. His "If When Don Cupid's Dart" compares love to flatulence. In both cases, it pains the speaker "when 'tis kept close," and yet in both cases it "doth offend when 'tis let loose." Suckling's "The Deformed Mistress,"

"His Dream," "Upon T. C. Having the Pox," and "A Candle" all show how Suckling took delight in grotesque and obscene humor (Rosen 1083). Suckling's masterpiece poem is "Ballad upon a Wedding." Louis Cazamian considers this book to be charmingly roguish, and to be filled with raciness, happy naïvité, and rustic manners (Cazamian 371). "Ballad upon a Wedding" has a distinctive style that has been often imitated and parodied. It is about the marriage of John, Lord Lovelace with Lady Anne Wentworth, and it exhibits Suckling's use of "rustic perspective":

> Her feet beneath her petticoat
> Like little mice, stole in and out,
> As if they feared the light.

David Rosen says of these lines that the vivid image of the delicate movement of the dainty feet is in fact a "light, humorous criticism of the bride's mincing steps." Furthermore, the "mice" in the poem were symbols of sexual activity, and thus the poem becomes ribald. "The lines, then, are simultaneously delicate, sensual, ribald, bestial, sophisticated, and laugh-provoking" (Rosen 1083).

Suckling is said to have lived life to the hilt. Once he gave a supper to a number of ladies of his acquaintance, and the last course consisted of millinery items and other trinkets (Hunt 199). Louis Cazamian considers Suckling to have been one of the wittiest of the Cavalier poets. Suckling's brilliance in repartée, and his ability to create perfect witty epigrams displaying reserve and self-control qualify him to be considered a "humorist." Suckling's letters were also filled with "thoughtful sprightliness." Suckling was elegant and polished. He poked fun with slyness and grace, and he targeted himself as much as he targeted other people. When Suckling died, his brother stated that he was a man of "grave deportment" (Cazamian 370).

Sir John Suckling Bibliography

Cazamian, Louis. "Suckling, Herrick." The Development of English Humor. Durham, NC: Duke University Press, 1952, 370-372.

Hunt, Leigh. "Suckling." Wit and Humour. New York, NY: Folcroft Library, 1972, 198-210.

Rosen, David. "John Suckling." Encyclopedia of British Humorists, Volume II. Ed. Steven H. Gale, New York, NY: Garland, 1996, 1080-1084.

Samuel Butler (c1613-1680)

Although the modern reader might find much that is indelicate in his writing, and although there is too much of "bear-fighting" of both the literal and metaphorical kind, Alfred Gu L'Estrange feels that Samuel Butler possessed a real gift of humour, and an "astonishing fertility of invention" (L'Estrange 297-298). The name of "humorist" was at first applied to an eccentric rather than to a writer who pointed out the eccentricity. Gradually, however, it shifted from the objective to the subjective mood, and from the passive to the active sense. Samuel Butler is said to have been instrumental in marking the change. Leigh Hunt considers Butler to have been the wittiest of English poets of his day. He was at the same time one of the most learned, and one of the wisest (Hunt 22).

Butler published his Hudibras in 1662, and when it first appeared Samuel Pepys bought a copy for 2s. 6d, but he thought that the book was so silly that he immediately sold it to a Mr. Townsend for 1s. 6d. Less than two months later, Pepys had to buy a second copy because everybody was talking about the book, "it being certainly some ill-humour to be so against that which all the world cried up to the example of wit" (Bruce 13).

Samuel Johnson didn't feel that Hudibras worked (Browning 1). In the 1880s, W. E. Henley spoke of Hudibras as "tedious, trivial, spiteful," and "ignoble" but then he adds that "these are the qualities which we praise in him [Butler]" (Browning 3).

Butler's main design in creating his Hudibras was to produce an English Don Quixote. There is much detail supporting the contention that Butler had Cervantes's hero in mind as he created Sir Hudibras. There is a long and detailed account of his arms, his Squire, and his horse. In addition, he targeted several well-known rogues of his day, especially those pretending to necromancy and prophetic powers, who seem to have been quite numerous (L'Estrange 298). Butler's Hudibras is filled with witty excess (Hunt 222). But although Hudibras is filled with wit, it contains little humor. The two protagonists are Hudibras and Ralph, and they are pedants rather than humorists. They are based on Cervantes's Don Quixote and Sancho Panza. They are dull people, but witty characters, though their wit is not their own. Rather it is the wit of their author, Butler. Hudibras is a ludicrous figure who displays a combination of wit, learning, and felicity. His wit is pure and constant. His learning is quaint and esoteric. And the rhymes of Hudibras are incongruous, laughable, and admired by critics. Butler's satire targeted the follies and vices of the court. Butler also provided a balance for Marvel's satire, since Marvel was the wit of one political party, while Butler was the wit for the opposing party (Hunt 224).

L'Estrange points out that Hudibras is written in the mock heroic style, and that the structure of the verse is "burlesque." Butler's rhymes are one of the features of his wit, as he tended to terminate lines in strange ways. He rhymed "perpendiculars" with "bricklayers;" "wince" with "sense," "fabric" with "a brick," and "thistle" with "his tail" (L'Estrange 301). L'estrange points out that in the seventeenth century, the humor of Butler was more popular than was the sentiment of Milton, though he was not paid well for his writing (L'Estrange 302).

Laurel Brodsley says that in seventeenth-century England there was an enormous expansion in scientific achievements and discoveries, but added that many Englishmen, including Samuel Butler, were skeptical of these scientific advances. One such scientific experiment involved some glass drops which, when hit with a hammer would not break, but which when their tails were snapped off, the glass bubble exploded with a shattering bang. The King of England sent these glass drops to the Royal Scientific Society, and they were amazed. Many public demonstrations were also made, which pleased and astonished many audiences. The glass drops were the delight of London. Butler's Knight, Sir Hudibras, anachronistically describes "honor" by alluding to this scientific experiment which had been so popular a few years before the poem was published (Brodsley 64). The poem went as follows:

> Honor is like that glassy Bubble
> That finds Philosophers such trouble,
> Whose least part crackt, the whole does fly
> And Wits are crack'd, to find out why. (Brodsley 63)

Butler's The Elephant in the Moone is also a criticism of scientific exploration and discovery. Butler feels that scientists prefer to invent truth rather than discover it.

> That 'twas more noble to create
> Things like Truth, out of strong Conceit,
> Than, with vexations Pains and Doubt,
> To find, or think t'have found her out. (Brodsley 65).

The Elephant in the Moone is one of Butler's minor poems, but it is effective satire. It targets the Royal Society, which had the reputation in Butler's day of concentrating on minutiae. The poem derives its title from Butler's suggestion that "some learned astronomers think they have made a great discovery, but it is really owing to a mouse and some gnats having got into their telescope" (L'Estrange 300-301).

In Repartées between Cat and Puss at a Caterwaling, Butler ridiculed the "swelling style of the modern heroic way" (Walker 151).

Hugh Walker considers Samuel Butler to have been the last and greatest of those English satirists who shared the medieval spirit (Walker 152).

> The light of a classical type of satire had glimmered and gone out and glimmered again. It was about to gleam yet once more, and this time it was destined to shine permanently. Dryden's Absalom and Architophel appeared only three years after the third part of Hudibras. Yet Hudibras rarely shows any trace of the classical influence. In spirit and effect, Butler is wholly medieval. His whimsical and grotesque yet highly effective rhymes are medieval. So are all his irregularities. That looseness of plan which enabled him to find a place in Hudibras for almost anything that occurred to his mind--this, which is the very antithesis of the classical, is of the essence of the medieval mind.... Butler is the last as well as the greatest of the medieval satirists. (Walker 143)

It was John Wesley's father who wrote Butler's epitaph--in unforgettable sarcasm:
> See him when starved to death and turned to dust,
> Presented with a monumental bust;
> The poet's fate is here in emblem shown,
> He asked for bread, and received--a stone. (L'Estrange 302)

Samuel Butler Bibliography

Brodsley, Laurel. "The Glass Bubble Cracked: An Analysis of Samuel Butler's Elaborate Scientific Joke in Hudibras." WHIMSY 2 (1984): 63-65.
Browning, J. D. ed. Satire in the 18th Century. New York, NY: Garland, 1983.
Bruce, Donald. Topics of Restoration Comedy. New York, NY: St. Martin's, 1974.
Hunt, Leigh. Wit and Humour. New York, NY: Folcroft Library, 1972, 222-240.
L'Estrange, Alfred Gu. "Rochester--Buckingham--Dryden--Butler." History of English Humour. New York, NY: Burt Franklin, 1878, 271-302.
Levin, Harry, ed. Veins of Humor. Cambridge, MA: Harvard Univ Press, 1972.
Walker, Hugh. "From the Eclipse of Satire to Butler." English Satire and Satirists. New York, NY: J. M. Dent, 1925, 120-144.

John Cleveland (1613-1658)

John Cleveland's conceits were often burlesque in style, as can be seen in his "Mark Antony," and "The Author's Mock Song to Mark Antony." Even his political poems, such as "Dialogue between Two Zealots," or his "The Rebel Scot" are filled with verve, humor, and stinging satire. Cleveland secretly and silently enjoyed the comic exaggeration in which he indulged. His "To the State of Love" is filled with wit, and is described by Louis Cazamian as "the metaphysical method run mad" (Cazamian 373-374). Most critics agree that Cleveland "did out-conceit the makers of conceits." Because of his exaggerations and his parodies, Cleveland was "the most popular poet of his time." He was, in Cazamian's words, "the last and most characteristic poet of the metaphysical school" (Cazamian 373).

Edward Paolella says that Lee Jacobus's John Cleveland competently discusses Cleveland's prose satire as well as the satire in his love poems, and concludes that in Jacobus, "all the articles on Cleveland's satires are very good," but then he goes on to say, "Jacobus on the love poems is appreciative but limits that appreciativeness by seeing the love poems as nifty comic rhetorical exercises when, in fact, they are that but much, much more." Papella notes "the depth and breadth of the love lyric traditions, conventions, and styles in the long line of wit of Western love poetry." Paolella also says that Morris and Withington's The Poems of John Cleveland is "right on target about the satires, but, in my opinion, about half right about the love poems.

John Cleveland Bibliography

Cazamian, Louis. "Cleveland." The Development of English Humor. Durham, NC: Duke University Press, 1952, 372-375.
Jacobus, Lee. John Cleveland. New York, NY: Twayne,
Morris, and Withington. The Poems of John Cleveland. New York, NY: Oxford University Press, 1967.
Paolella, Edward C. "Personal Letter" dated April 29, 1996.

Richard Lovelace (1618-1657)

Richard Lovelace, like John Donne, is most humorous when he assuming the pose of a womanizing rogue attempting to satisfy his libidinous appetite, or when his exuberant praises for his mistress oversteps the bonds of modesty and becomes either erotic or frivolous (Keller 705).

Lovelace's "The Scrutinie" develops a witty argument against monogamy among lovers. First, he asserts that his lady friend is unreasonable to hold him to a pledge of loyalty he had made a full twelve hours earlier (Keller 705). Since he made the pledge, he had been working very hard to please her, and he now feels that these twelve hours of sincere labor should suffice in fulfilling his promise of eternal love. He argues furthermore that if he honored his pledge he would be depriving other women of his company, and that it is his responsibility to seek out beauty, just as it is the duty of a mineralist to seek out precious minerals. Nevertheless, he offers to return to his lady friend after he has completed his study of the region's beauties, and suggests that after that study he will be much better able to recognize his lady friend's admirable qualities, since he would then have used his amorous embraces of other ladies to develop a standard of comparison. James Keller says "the young rake's desperation coupled with the young woman's clinging devotion and expectations constitutes a comic tension capable of delighting audiences of any time" (Keller 706).

Lovelace also wrote "The Apostasy of One, and but One Lady" a poem in which the speaker satirizes his mistress's passions. He describes his unfaithful lady friend with oxymoronic metaphors. Her love is as hard as "Ice in the Sun's Eye," and as permanent as a reflection in the mirror after the subject has passed by. He says that she remains as calm as lightning, and as constant as the wind. She is as certain as the journeys of the blind, and as gentle as chains (Keller 706). "Depose Your Finger" is a bawdy seductive poem filled with playful and entertaining wickedness. In this poem, Lovelace's speaker argues that his lady friend's "chaste treasure" will become much more valuable through its being leant, both because of the pleasure it has caused, and by the child that has resulted from the union. The speaker humbly contends that her own joys will be much greater than his own (Keller 706). "The Faire Begger" is amusing because it is a reversal of expectations. Here, the mistress is the lascivious partner, and the speaker is the person who wants love and commitment (Keller 706). The speaker in "You Are Deceiv'd" is a rascal who mistreats women. "The poem is quite unkind at the same time that it is hysterically funny." Much of the humor of "You Are Deceiv'd" comes from the fact that the speaker draws more attention to negative qualities than is polite or expected in a love poem. He describes his mistress as "a wicked owl in cloth of gold." He also compares her to "the ridiculous ape, in sacred Vesta's shape. "The roguishness of this abusive verse is the source of its humor." Furthermore, this poem is a parody of Petrarchan prose in general, and the tedious sentimentality of sixteenth and seventeenth-century love lyric in particular (Keller 707).

"A Black Patch on Lucasta's Face" is another parody of the love poem. Here, the speaker explains how a mole came to Lucasta's face, by suggesting that a fly flew too near her eyes and was scorched by their brightness. This "black patch" then, " is a monument, honoring the insect's suicidal devotion to beauty." James Keller says that despite this tribute to Lucasta's devastating beauty, she would probably not be very flattered by his vulgar accounting. "It is also doubtful that true praise was the purpose behind the work. Instead, the poet clearly hoped to advance a clever joke" (Keller 707). Still another parody of the love lyric is "Elinda's Glove." While picking some flowers, Elinda has discarded her glove, and the speaker retrieves this glove and for him it becomes an object of devotion. He lavishes praise on it as if it were a holy relic (Keller 707). "The exaggerated devotion and desperation of the amorist become the object of considerable mirth" (Keller 708).

Erna Kelly points out that Richard Lovelace is not considered to be a writer of humorous poetry by literary scholars, nor by seventeenth-century scholars, nor by poetry scholars, nor by the general public. In fact, he generally had no intention of writing humorous poetry. Nevertheless, his poetry is humorous--in retrospect. It was Richard Lovelace who wrote To Althea, from Prison (1642), which contains the couplet

> Stone walls do not a prison make,
> Nor iron bars a cage.

He also wrote "To Lucasta, Going to the Warres" a poem which places patriotism in front of romantic love--war above women:

> I could not love the deare so much,
> Lov'd I not honor more. (Kelly 157)

Arthur Guiterman wrote a parody of Lovelace's "To Lucasta" as follows:

> Blame me not, Sweet, if here and there
>   My wayward self inclines
> To note that others, too, are fair,
>   To bow at lesser shrines.
>
> What though with eye or tongue I praise
>   Iona's gentle wile,
> Camilla's happy turn of phrase,
>   Or Celia's winning smile?
>
> My constancy shall be thy boast
>   From now to Kingdom Come.
> How could I love thee, Dear, the most,
>   Loved I not others, some? (Zaranka 87)

Guiterman's parody demonstrates how the sentimentality of Lovelace's poetry is humorous--though the humor is unintentional. But some Lovelace's poetry is humorous--on purpose. His "To Ellinda, That lately I have not written" is written in the mock heroic genre. The poem treats a minor offense as a very serious matter. The narrator is silent because of his inability to praise Ellinda sufficiently. It is not negligence, but zeal that keeps him from writing:

> Children and Fooles the words repeate,
> But Anch'rites pray in teares and sweate. (Kelly 158)

The mocking tone of the poem can be seen in the placement of "That lately I have not written" immediately after "To Ellinda." "By exaggerating the seriousness of the issue, by treating her complaint 'so very seriously,' Lovelace is telling Ellinda it is, in fact, trivial. They should both see it as such and laugh at her mistake" (Kelly 158). The mocking of the poem can be further seen in the bouncing meter and weak rhyme. The weak rhyming of "Sickness" with "quickness," "hovered" with "recover'd," "languish" with "anguish" adds to the poem's humor, as does the consideration of the lover's "flames" as symptoms of a physical, not a spiritual disease. There is also a juxtaposition of the very colloquial ("beat out of dore") with the very formal ("for love compell'd to wander."

The narrator gives thanks for being "treated to Ellinda," and also gives thanks for a "rollicking, riotous, sumptuous feast, and warm visit." It should be noted that Lovelace first notes all of the particulars of the meal, then makes an excuse for not writing from Holland, and finally requests to be remembered to particular members of the family--"with certane promise (to your Brother)." "Of the Virginity of another" appears to refer to an uncut pie, but it also refers to Ellinda herself, "Freest, freshest, Faire Ellinda" (Kelly 158). Lovelace is not merely writing a verse letter to Ellinda for having been treated so well by Ellinda and her family in the past, it is in addition some wishful thinking about "Being treated to Ellinda" in the future. Lovelace's poem may show some slight resentment at being rejected by Ellinda, but this resentment is obscured by Lovelace's paradox, irony, and humor (Kelly 158). Kelly concludes by saying that "Behind the 'distressed' speaker, we find a confident poet sharing his wit with an intelligent woman" (Kelly 159).

Richard Lovelace Bibliography

Evans, Willa McClung. "Richard Lovelace's 'Mock Song.'" Philological Quarterly 24 (1945): 317-328.

Keller, James R. "Richard Lovelace." Encyclopedia of British Humorists, Volume II. Ed. Steven H. Gale, New York, NY: Garland, 1996, 704-709.

Kelly, Erna. "Lovelace's Ellinda Poems: 'Primarily the Property of Men.' " WHIMSY 1 (1983): 157-159.

Zaranka, William, ed. The Brand-X Anthology of Poetry. New York, NY: Apple Wood, 1981.

Andrew Marvell (1621-1678)

Andrew Marvell wrote in many genres, ranging from the lyrical to the occasional, and from satirical verses to controversial prose. Humor be seen in all of these genres, but it is especially evident in his satires which in he wrote both in verse and in prose. "His humor ranges from the highly intellectual wit of the lyrics to the burlesque, bawdy and sometimes savage humor of his satires. There is often a blend of humor and satire in his writings. This is especially true of "Fleckno, an English Priest at Rome" (ca 1648), "Tom May's Death" (1650), and "The Character of Holland" (1653). "In these three poems, Marvell combines the conceited wit of the metaphysical school with stylistic features that are closer to the Augustan, such as experimentation with the couplet form." According to Denise Cuthbert, Marvell's work "represents an important stage in the development of English satirical humor" (Cuthbert 734). Marvell was one of the drollest wits of his time, and he was so popular among booksellers that many of them placed his names on pieces he had not written (Cuthbert 735). Marvell's humor in enhanced by his acute observations of social and political details, and by his play with these observations. His humor is both highly visual and very concrete. His reductive and parodic humor is especially effective with personalities, character traits, manners, and physical descriptions (Cuthbert 736).

"Fleckno, an English Priest at Rome" (ca 1648) is a study in burlesque and comic exaggeration. It is also a parody of the literary pretensions the "expatriate priest living in Rome" (Cuthbert 735). The ghost of Ben Jonson is resurrected in "Tom May's Death" (1650), to provide a bitingly humorous attack on May, who is reported to have died after a night of drinking. This poem provides an open attack on the excesses of his life. May was the historian of the Long Parliament, and he is attacked by Marvell for his "veniality and mediocrity as a writer (Cuthbert 735).

Hugh Walker feels that Marvell is responsible for creating "perhaps the worst pun ever made" in ridiculing the Dutch Hollanders by calling them "Half-anders" in his "The Character of Holland" (1653). Walker says that this pun "has none of the sort of merit which might turn it into the best" (Walker 146). "The Character of Holland" is an energetic burlesque and exaggeration that caters to the anti-Dutch sentiment during Marvell's time. As in other anti-Dutch literature, the main targets are the Dutch language, the inundation of their land by water, their religious toleration, and their quest for trade. Two other targets are their drunkenness and their boorishness. About the inundation, for example, Marvell plays on the last half of the name "Holland," saying that it is not a "land" at all. For Marvell, the inhabitants of Holland are more fish than men. They are "absurd amphibians whose pretensions on land and sea are lampooned without mercy" (Cuthbert 735). Marvell's writing contains many rich allusions, and they draw on his knowledge of history, and his familiarity with classical and modern languages. Puns and other witty wordplay are special features of his work. He also likes to take metaphors literally. He sees the Dutch as water-logged fish, that are distinguishable neither from the other fish in the sea, nor from the fish which are an important part of their diet. Marvell's puns tend to be epiphinal, as when in "The Character of Holland" he compares the "pickled herring" to the "pickled Heeren" (Cuthbert 737).

In both The Rehearsal Transpos'd (1672), and in The Rehearsal Transpos'd, the Second Part (1673), there is a substantial amount of ecclesiastical satire; however, Hugh Walker considers this novel to be "intolerably dreary." Walker further feels that for the modern reader, the contorted wit of the novel "serves only to obscure the meaning" (Walker 182). Nevertheless, it is in these two works especially, and also in a third work, Mr. Smirke, or The Divine in Mode (1676) to a lesser extent, that Marvell establishes his reputation as a writer of humorous prose (Cuthbert 736). The title of The Rehearsal Transpos'd alludes to George Villiers's The Rehearsal, which is a satirical farce. Marvell takes advantage of the great success of Villiers's play as he refutes Martin Parker's attacks on religious freedom of conscience, "using Parker's own words to condemn him, pulling him up for verbosity, reductively summarizing his arguments in absurd aphorisms, using the structure and argument of Parker's work as the basis for his attack." The Rehearsal Transpos'd, the Second Part is a reaction to Parker's Reproof, and Marvell discredits Parker by his unrelenting and often lampooning attack, as he seizes every opportunity to "fire broadsides" at Parker (Cuthbert 736). Marvell's "His Majesty's Most Gracious Speech to Both Houses of Parliament" (1675) was written on the occasion of Charles II's opening of the thirteenth session of the Cavalier Parliament in 1675 (Cuthbert 736).

"The Last Instructions to a Painter" (1677) is a satire that uses an Italian genre termed by Cuthbert as the "advice-to-a-painter genre." In this genre, the author takes on the role of an art instructor informing an artist on how to paint the Stuart court. In this guise, "Marvell provides a rambling and in parts very funny satirical expose of courtly manners and vice, political corruption, and ineptitude" (Cuthbert 735). "The Loyall Scott" is a satire that attacks the government's "vicious ineptitude" in the handling of the Second Dutch War. It is a mock-heroic poem, and Captain Douglas is the loyal Scot of the title. Captain Douglas is the "hero" who must defend the Royal Oak (Cuthbert 736).

Leigh Hunt feels that Marvell is a "wit of the first water," so effective in his wit, in fact that he played an important role in putting an end to the Stuart dynasty. "His wit helped to render them ridiculous, and his integrity added weight to the sting" (Hunt 214). Hunt feels that the wit of Marvell's prose was much better than that of his verse, which exhibited a strange ruggedness in its versification (Hunt 221). Marvell was true to his convictions, and there is a story told that he refused a carte blanche from the king's treasurer, and then had to send out to borrow a guinea; Hunt feels that this story illustrate's Marvell's "practical wit" (Hunt 214).

Andrew Marvell Bibliography

Chambers, Alexander B. Andrew Marvell, and Edmund Waller: Seventeenth-Century Praise
    and Restoration Satire. University Park, PA: Pennsylvania State University Press,
    1991.
Coolidge, John S. "Martin Marprelate, Marvell, and Decorum Personae as a Satirical
    Theme." Publications of the Modern Language Association 74 (1959): 526-532).
Cuthbert, Denise. "Andrew Marvell." Encyclopedia of British Humorists, Volume II. Ed.
    Steven H. Gale, New York, NY: Garland, 1996, 733-738.
Hunt, Leigh. "Marvel." Wit and Humour. New York, NY: Folcroft Library, 1972, 214-221.
Marcus, Leah S. The Politics of Mirth: Jonson, Herrick, Milton, Marvell, and the Defense
    of Old Holiday Pastimes. Chicago, IL: University of Chicago Press, 1986.
Morris, Brian. "Satire from Donne to Marvell." The Metaphysical Poetry. Eds. Malcolm
    Bradbury, and David Palmer, Bloomington, IN: Indiana University Press, 1971,
    210-235.
Walker, Hugh. English Satire and Satirists. London, England: J. M. Dent, 1925.

John Hall (1627-1656)

Henry More praises Hall as a "Young monster! born with teeth" (Miller 501). In his Rabelais in English Literature, Huntington Brown suggests that John Hall was one of the first English writers to appreciate the satire of Rabelais (Miller 502). John Hall was not a very good poet. George Saintsbury says that Hall caught the "poetic measles" which were epidemic during his time, and which produced a multitude of poets--good, bad, and indifferent. But even though Hall was not an especially good poet, his poetry does demonstrate the full development of Hudibrastic rhyming, including two words rhymed with one, as in "press" and "ne'ertheless", and surprising off-rhymes the develop a strange type of sameness, as in "prescription" and "confusion." Hall was influential in the development of verse satire. His writing "shows not only the aesthetic of rhyming and a general taste of mockery but also gives an early indication of eighteenth-century philosophical ideas of the hierarchy of intellectual values" (Miller 502).

John Hall did much to support a genre which could be called "List Literature." "Upon the King's Great Porter," is an example of Hall's simple observations presented in the form of a witty list. "Upon the King's Great Porter" is "a series of hyperbolic exclamations noting how small all other things seem in comparison to Evans the Porter: he must use the Rhine River for a looking glass; he wears his wife's bracelet as a thumb ring; his breath is a whirlwind" (Miller 501).

"Upon T. R., A Very Little Man, but Excellently Learned" is another witty list developing a humours character. Here, Hall provides a list of surprising conjunctions of big things with little things, calling T.R. "this giant and this dwarf in one" (Miller 501). "An Eunich" is a list of exclamations about the ambiguities of androgyny: "How doth

Nature quibble, either He, or she, boy, girl, or neither." Edmund Miller notes that John Hall writes "occasional verse," such as "T. R., a Very Little Man," "Deformed X. R., and "M. W. the Great Eater" that would be a great deal more meaningful to the audience if it did not concern such local matters. Such pieces have lost much of their effect through the passage of time (Miller 501).

John Hall Bibliography

Brown, Huntington. Rabelais in English Literature. Cambridge, MA: Harvard University Press, 1993.
Miller, Edmund. "John Hall." Encyclopedia of British Humorists, Volume I. Ed. Steven H. Gale, New York, NY: Garland, 1996, 499-502.

Sir William Temple (1628-1699)

Sir William Temple paid special attention to the word "humor" in his "On Poetry" (1690). where he traced the special senses of the word not back to Jonson, but to Shakespeare, pointing to the "essential Englishness of both the word and the vein."
> Temple attributes this favorable outgrowth to the native soil, the changeable climate, and above all a government which tolerates free opinion and speech. The environment fosters an individualism which brings out eccentricities to a degree not paralleled elsewhere. Where conformities of the Continent are expressed through the same old typical characters, England glories in its Originals, whose variety is mirrored in the theater. (Levin 11-12)

For Temple, as for almost all writers and critics of his time, "humor remains indissolubly connected with temperament, in the physical sense" (Cazamian 397). For Temple, humor depicts particular life in the same way that comedy depicts general life. "No nation outside England can show anything like it; the very word is peculiar to our language too, and hard to be expressed in any other" (Cazamian 398). Humor for Temple represented the racy originality of the English character: "We have more humour, because every man follows his own, and takes a pleasure, perhaps a pride, to shew it.... We are not only more unlike one another than any nation I know, but we are more unlike ourselves too at several times" (Cazamian 398). Louis Cazamian notes that when Temple claimed that the English have a special privilege of humor, he started a fallacy which would pass on to our very day.
> Of French, Italian, German humor, he seems to be ignorant; of dramatic humor before Shakespeare he apparently has no inkling. Of the fact that humor is not a native English word, and that the French and Italian languages notably, had equivalents, he is not aware. (Cazamian 399)

Louis Cazamian feels that Temple's major contribution is that he raised humor to the level of being approved as an inventive art form, and made it a creative activity among the elite. When Temple bluntly declared that nowhere in the world is there "so much true genius as among the English..., more sharpness of wit, more pleasantness of humour, more range of fancy, more penetration of thought, or depth of reflection among the better sort," he was merely voicing his legitimate pride in his native country (Cazamian 399).

Sir William Temple Bibliography

Cazamian, Louis. The Development of English Humor. Durham, NC: Duke University Press, 1952.
Levin, Harry, ed. Veins of Humor. Cambridge, MA: Harvard University Press, 1972.

George Villiers (2nd Duke of Buckingham)(1628-1687)

Villiers's The Rehearsal is a burlesque of the heroic rhyming couplet that was prevalent in plays of the Restoration period. The author targets contrived plots, bombastic speeches, and artificial characters in this parody. He also targets the creations of such contemporary playwrights as John Dryden, Sir William Davenant, Thomas Killigrew, and Aphra (Johnson) Behn. Bayes, the protagonist in The Rehearsal, is a poet who is "not only the epitome of the bad writer, but also a vicious personal caricature" (Persson 37). In The Rehearsal John Dryden was clearly the target of the satire.

> Like Dryden, Bayes prefers to dress in black and is fond of snuff and stewed prunes. His mistress, who takes the part of Amaryllis in the play that he is rehearsing, is an allusion to Dryden's mistress, Anne Reeves, a pretty actress of small talent. Also, Bayes's appearance, his gestures, his dry and hesitant manner of delivery, as they were represented by John Lacy who originally played the role, were all modeled closely on Dryden's. (Persson 37)

George Villiers (2nd Duke of Buckingham) Bibliography

L'Estrange, Alfred Gu. "Rochester--Buckingham--Dryden--Butler." History of English Humour. New York, NY: Burt Franklin, 1878, 271-302.
Persson, Agnes V. Comic Character in Restoration Drama. The Hague, Netherlands: Mouton, 1975.

John Dryden (1631-1700)

John Dryden developed a new kind of comedy that was a blend of humor and wit. He describes this new genre in the "Preface" to An Evening's Love as follows:

> I will not deny but that I approve most the mixed way of comedy, that which is neither all wit, nor all humour, but the result of both. Neither so little of humour as Fletcher shows, nor so little love of wit as Jonson, neither all cheat, with which the best plays of the one are filled, nor all adventure, which is the common practice of the other. I would have the characters well chosen, and kept distant from interfering with each other, which is more than Fletcher or Shakespeare did, but I would have more of the urbana, venusta, salsa, faceta, and the rest which Quintillian reckons as the ornaments of wit, and these are extremely wanting in Ben Jonson. (Watson 149)

Brian Corman points out, however, that Dryden did not always practice what he preached, since his comedies certainly don't contain equal amounts of wit and humor. According to Corman, Dryden, and most of the other good writers of his day, preferred "wit" to "humor" (Corman 356).

Hugh Walker feels that John Dryden was the first of the modern satirists. It was Dryden who first demonstrated that it was possible to write satiric poetry which was neither inflated nor harsh. Dryden

> once [and] for all banishes the conceit which had so recently dominated verse through the example of Cowley, and he puts behind him (if he ever felt it) the temptation to torture language.... He produces his effects through a wit too incisive to be called urbane, yet in which there is often an element of urbanity. (Walker 152)

Dryden differed from the earlier satirists, who knew only the superlative degree. "Their instruments were the biggest drum and the loudest trumpet (Walker 157). Dryden was just the opposite.

> He never tries to include everything; on the contrary, the inmost secret of his art is careful selection of that which is most effective. Not to tire the reader, but just to give enough to stimulate imagination--that is his aim. His satires are comparatively short, not merely because his style is condensed, but also because of this principle of selection. Herein he is the precise opposite of Butler; it is what most of all distinguishes the classical way from the medieval. (Walker 156)

Another subtlety of Dryden's satire resides in his spirit of justice, and in his ability to see both good and bad in a target. He does not withhold praise when he feels that praise is due. While denouncing Anthony Ashley Cooper, third Earl of Shaftesbury, as a politician, he ungrudgingly praises Shaftesbury as a judge, and this balance is unprecedented in earlier satires except, perhaps in those of Brome. This recognition of the good along with the bad gives Dryden's satire more credibility, and also gives his satire "the added grace of variety" (Walker 157). Dryden's verse was smooth; his style was lucid; his manner was urbane; and these qualities made Dryden's satire strikingly original. Walker points out that in England there had been nothing comparable to it (Walker 152-153).

Harry Levin suggests that historically, the contrast between wit and humor seems to have emerged from the hard-hitting controversy between John Dryden and Thomas Shadwell. Shadwell was Jonson's most faithful disciple, and he was trying to revive the older comedy of humors, while Dryden inclined toward a newer, French-inspired and more elegant comedy of manners (Levin 11). For Dryden, humor is "not a passive bent of character, but an active faculty of mind" (Cazamian 397). Leigh Hunt feels that Dryden's wit was masculine and eloquent when roused. Dryden's satire was aimed at the individual and at his public standing.

The Rival Ladies (1663) is a tragicomedy utilizing the rhymed couplet (Neilson 442). Marriage-a-la-mode (1673) is Dryden's best comedy (Neilson 442). In Dryden's Secret Love (1667), Dryden creates a witty, irreverent comic couple named Celadon and Florimell, who became famous in Restoration comedy manners because of their railings with each other. When this play was first performed, the roles of Celadon and Florimell were played by the famous actor Charles Hart, and his mistress Nell Gwynn. This is one of the first parts in English drama to be played by a woman, since women's parts had always been played by men or boys before the Restoration (McDonald 3). Donald Bloom says that in Secret Love, Dryden reworked the idea of witty heroines presented earlier by Fletcher and others, but Dryden's witty heroines were equivalent to the rakish heros they were in competition with both in wit and wildness. Dryden's witty heroine, Florimell, talks gaily about having many lovers and servants, but she is also militantly virginal. Nevertheless, the Hero (Celadon) and the Heroine (Florimell) eventually marry. Throughout most of the play, Floramell finds herself in the tricky position of wanting something that cannot exist, for she is not interested in "one of those solemn Fops; they are good for nothing but to make Cuckolds: Give me a servant who is an high Flier at all games, that is bounteous of himself to many women; and yet whenever I pleas'd to throw out the lure of Matrimony, should come down with a swing, and fly the better at his own quarry" (3.1.296-302)(Bloom 62-63).

Secret Love ends where Marriage à la Mode (1671) begins, continuing the theme that it is impossible for love to last far into marriage. In Marriage à la Mode, Doralice wonders why people should make a foolish marriage vow, because love wears out, and the married state thus becomes a waste. Later Rhodophil echoes these sentiments, viewing marriage with a mixture of cynicism and regret. He claims to have "lov'd her a whole half year, double the natural term of any Mistress," and admits that he "could have held out another quarter; but then the World began to laugh at him" (Bloom 64-65). Marriage à la Mode captures the wit and the gaiety of the Restoration theater (Ritchie 334). The Conquest of Granada (1672) was probably Dryden's greatest commercial success (Ritchie 334). All for Love (1678) is regarded by many critics as the best example of Restoration Comedy written by any author (Ritchie 334).

Partly in retaliation for George Villiers's ridicule of heroic drama in The Rehearsal, Dryden wrote Absalom and Architophel (1681). This is a crushing satire on James Scott, Duke of Monmouth, Anthony Ashley Cooper, Earl of Shaftesbury, George Villiers, Second Duke of Buckingham, Charles II, Titus Oates and others who were involved in the conspiracy to exclude the Duke of York in favor of Monmouth (Neilson 442). Dryden's Absalom and Architophel is a blending of the genre of satire with the genre of epic poetry, but Paul Ramsey suggests that it is a blending of even more genres, "Hence we can say that the poem is an occasional, polemical, historical, satirical, panegyrical, truncated, narrative, allegorical poem" (Guilhamet 80). But Guilhamet suggests that even Ramsey "has not included all the possibilities" (Guilhamet 80). Absalom and Architophel is a political satire written on behalf of the Tories, and is a classic example of the mock-heroic genre (Ritchie 334). It parodies the principles of the Whig party, and is especially harsh in its treatment of George Villiers, Duke of Buckingham, who had targeted Dryden ten years earlier in his satiric play The Rehearsal (Ritchie 335).

The magnificent character of Achetophel represents Ashley Shaftesbury in Dryden's poem which Earl Miner says has moved from "partisan history" to a "quasi-judicial setting." Earlier, Achitophel had upheld the law, but now (in the poem) he violates and abuses the law. Leon Guilhamet suggests that Achitophel (Shaftesbury) represents Milton's grandly-drawn Satan, and he further feels that the elaborate temptation also contains Miltonic diction:

> Him he attempts, with studied Arts to please,
> And sheds his Venom, in such words as these. (Guilhamet 83)

For Guilhamet, "Satanic evil on the grand scale is evoked...; the Miltonic effects set off Achitophel's rhetorical speech from the rest of the poem in a particularly striking way" (Guilhamet 83).

One of Dryden's most well known satires is entitled MacFlecknoe (1682), a poem named after an inferior Irish poet who would have no important place in history were it not for Dryden's poem (L'Estrange 295). One purpose of the poem is the comic ridicule of Thomas Shadwell; a second purpose is to assess the impact of Shadwell and his kind on culture and art. Leon Guilhamet points out that the mock-heroic nature of the poem has a double significance. "MacFlecknoe (Shadwell) is reduced in stature by implied comparison with the heroes of the epic. But also the maintenance of the heroic style and manner imparts, paradoxically, some significance to MacFlecknoe and thus to what he represents" (Guilhamet 71). The poem MacFlecknoe states that all things must decay, and this is as true of empires as of anything else. So MacFlecknoe finds himself to be the ruler, "without dispute / Through all the Realms of Non-sense, absolute" (Guilhamet 72). Guilhamet feels that the word "Non-sense" is the turning point of the poem. It changes the poem from the genre of "Heroic Poetry" into its countergenre, "Mock-Heroic Poetry" (Guilhamet 72). Following the word "Non-sense," the words are in the heightened language of panegyric, "but, of course, only MacFlecknoe and his attendants can regard them as words of praise" (Guilhamet 72).

There are a number allusions in the poem, for the writings of MacFlecknoe (Shadwell) must be compared with those of other poets:

> Heywood and Shirley were but Types of thee
> Thou last great Prophet of Tautology:
> Even I, a dunce of more renown than they

Was sent before but to prepare thy way. (Dryden lines 29-32; Guilhamet 73)
Here Dryden takes MacFlecknoe (Shadwell) away from the tradition of Ben Jonson, with
whom he would align himself, and places him among such lightly regarded poets as John
Heywood and James Shirley (Guilhamet 73).

MacFlecknoe was written in response to Shadwell's The Medal of John Bayes. It
is rather coarse, and it targets Shadwell, who had been made poet laureate. King William
had ousted King James the Second, and by ousting King James, King William had also
ousted Dryden, who had been King James's poet laureate. Hugh Walker considers
MacFlecknoe to be the most severe of all personal satires in seventeenth-century England,
with the possible exception of Holy Willie's Prayer or The Vision of Judgment. Walker
adds that "in this almost miraculously witty piece, Dryden breaks what is for him fresh
ground: it is no longer political but literary satire" (Walker 160). Jeffrey Ritchie notes that
Thomas Shadwell's satiric attack of Dryden in "The Medal of John Bayes" (1682) is "little
more than a diatribe." Dryden's response in Mac Flecknoe (1682) however was "both swift
and crushing. It remains one of the best verse satires in the English language." Ritchie
continues that the satire is "at once sharp, rollicking, and slightly vulgar." Dryden's use
of the expression Sh____ to represent Shadwell is ingenious. "A close reading of the poem
reveals that in many cases "Shadwell" would not fit the rhyme scheme of the heroic
couplet--the common word for excrement, however, would fit" (Ritchie 336).

On a number of occasions Shadwell had intimated his own superiority compared
with Dryden, so that Dryden was provoked both politically and poetically to write
MacFlecknoe, a satirical attack on Shadwell's writing. Hunt points out the irony that in
this particular satire, all of the best wit comes out of the mouth of MacFlecknoe, who
represents Shadwell in the poem.

In John Dryden and His World, James Anderson Winn does an excellent job of
describing the time and the place and the events which resulted in the writing of
MacFlecknoe. John Wilmot, Earl of Rochester, had publicly insulted Dryden by calling
him a "Poet Squab," but Dryden was not able to respond to Rochester's insult directly not
only because of Rochester's elegant shape, but also because Rochester was an Earl.

> The obese Shadwell, however, provided a perfect substitute target for his
> resentment. If Rochester had called him "Poet Squab," Dryden could refer
> to Shadwell's "mountain belly." But that phrase, like so much else in this
> poem, is an allusion as well as an insult: Ben Jonson, Shadwell's hero, had
> referred to his own "mountaine belly" in a poem to his friend Drummond;
> for those who caught it, Dryden's echo implied that Shadwell's girth was his
> only resemblance to Jonson. (Winn 290)

In this way, Dryden not only keeps his rival, Shadwell, from becoming the poetic successor
to Ben Jonson, but in addition, he "anoints him as the son and successor to Flecknoe, a
self-styled but laughably incompetent imitator of Jonson's epigrammatic style" (Winn 290).

The poem MacFlecknoe makes enough allusions to Virgil, Horace, Spenser, Milton,
Cowley, Waller, and Augustus to prompt James Winn to claim that "no previous English
satire is so relentlessly literary" (Winn 292). This is part of the parody, which is signalled
in part by the juxtaposition of such significant names as these next to the funny sounding
name of MacFlecknoe. Dryden writes,

> All humane things are subject to decay,
> And, when Fate summons, Monarchs must obey:
> This Flecknoe found, who, like Augustus, young
> Was call'd to Empire, and had govern'd long:
> In Porse and Verse, was own'd, without dispute
> Through all the Realms of Non-sense, absolute.

Here we see language that is usually associated with grand occasions being invaded by indecorous words like <u>Flecknoe</u>, and by dislocations where a word like "<u>Non-sense</u>" appears in a place where the reader is expecting a word like "England" or "Learning" depending on whether we are talking about literal or metaphorical realms. The praise of Shadwell is also filled with oxymorons, as he is described as "Mature in dullness," and "confirm'd in full stupidity," and it is further confirmed that he "never deviates into sense" (Winn 292-293). Years later, when he wrote "Discourse Concerning the Original and Progress of Satire," Dryden describes the satiric process he had used in writing "MacFlecknoe," by proclaiming that "there is...a vast difference between the slovenly butchering of a man, and the fineness of a stroke that separates the head from the body, and leaves it standing in its place" (Winn 293).

In Dryden's <u>Satires of Persius</u>, published in 1693, he notes that he remembers translating these pieces while still a king's scholar at Westminster. By 1679, his satires had become so powerful that his farcical play, <u>The Kind Keeper, or Mr. Limberham</u>, had to be withdrawn because it was felt to have been libelous to Lauderdale. Dryden therefore, had some practice in writing satire before he wrote <u>Absalom and Achitophel</u>. In 1680 a prose tract appeared entitled, <u>Absalom's Conspiracy: or, the Tragedy of Treason</u>. It was this tract that stimulated Dryden to write <u>Absalom and Achitophel</u> and to publish it in 1681. This is a satire in which King Charles is criticized by having his virtues listed. Charles is positively described as being mild, and as being lavishly generous to his subjects. Some of King Charles's vices are also mentioned, but they are the vices he was proud of, not ashamed of, such as his various love intrigues. Dryden was skilled in framing his criticism in the form of a panegyric so that it would be more acceptable to the Court (Walker 153).

The subject of Dryden's satire entitled, <u>The Medal: A Satire against Sedition</u> (1682) was Anthony Ashley Cooper, Earl of Shaftesbury, in whose honor a medal had been struck to celebrate his escape from a charge of treason (Walker 158). Dryden was like many of the great literary men from Shakespeare to Carlyle in having a profound distrust of the multitude. In Shaftesbury Dryden saw an unprincipled politician who had tried in vain to seduce Charles to "arbitrary government," and who had joined the roundheads to "drive down the current with a popular gale" (Walker 155). Dryden exposes the fickleness of the English by saying, "We loathe our manna, and we long for quails." And he links the fickleness of the English to the fickleness of the israelites, and the fickleness of the Athenians in earlier times, saying,

> Athens no doubt did righteously decide
> When Phocion and when Socrates were tried. (Walker 155)

<u>The Medal</u> is a satire written against the Whits and their leader, and "although the poem is somewhat lacking in the variety of its satire, in many places it is equal of <u>Absalom and Architophel</u> in its vigor and wit," as when he says it took the craftsman five days to create the medal, adding that this was four more days than it took for God to create Adam (Ritchie 335).

In his <u>Religio Laici</u> (1682) Dryden argued in defense of the Anglican Church and against the one extreme coming from Rome, Italy, and the opposite extreme coming from Geneva. <u>Religio Laici</u> begins with a satire targeting the schools of philosophy, which Dryden feels exhibit irreconcilable differences. One school finds the <u>summum bonum</u> in Content, another in Virtue, and a third in Pleasure (Walker 164). In <u>Religio Laici</u>, Dryden attacks both the Papists, and the Dissenters, but while he believes that both are threatening, Dryden clearly favors Catholicism (Ritchie 336).

<u>The Hind and the Panther</u> (1687) is a satire in the form of a beast fable. <u>The Hind and the Panther</u> was later ridiculed and parodied in <u>The Country Mouse and the City Mouse</u>, written by Charles Montague and Matthew Prior. In <u>The Hind and the Panther</u>, Dryden satirizes the various sects, mainly because of their greed. Dryden "detests the Independent bear and the Baptist boar, but more than either he hates the Presbyterian wolf"

(Walker 163). The Hind and the Panther differs from Religio Luici (1682) in that in The Hind, Dryden finds pure Christianity in Rome, but in Rome only (Walker 164).

Don Sebastian (1690) is a tragicomedy (Neilson 442). Amphitrion (1690) is a comedy (Neilson 442). Love Triumphant (1694) is a tragicomedy (Neilson 442). In Alexander's Feast (1697), and Fables, Ancient and Modern (1699), Dryden wrote adaptations of Geoffrey Chaucer's Canterbury Tales, and Giovanni Boccaccio's Decamaron (Neilson 442). Dryden's Virgil (1697) is not a literal translation, since "it bears an unmistakable mark of its translator, including some sly satires on current political leaders" (Ritchie 337).

John Wilmot says that Dryden's writing does not have the graceful humour of Tassoni, or the exquisite power of Boileau. Wilmot considers Dryden's wit to have more weight than edge--"it beat in armour, but could not cut gause" (L'Estrange 296). L'Estrange adds that Dryden wrote an essay on Satire, in which he "shows a much better knowledge of history than of humour" (L'Estrange 297). But other critics are much kinder in evaluating Dryden's contribution. Hugh Walker says,

> The work of Dryden fixed for several generations the course of English satire. After its masterly handling in Absalom and Achitophel there could be no doubt as to the fitness of the heroic couplet as the vehicle, and the consummate sketches of character set an example which could not fail to be useful as long as political controversy endured. (Walker 165)

John Dryden wrote eight comedies and several tragicomedies with comic plots over a period of thirty years. None of them showed the excellence of his best non-comic writing; nevertheless, Dryden's comedies were far from negligible. "Perhaps his loud contempt for comedy as a literary genre was the cause of his relative mediocrity in the type" (Wilcox 116).

John Dryden Bibliography

Allen, Ned Bliss. The Sources of John Dryden's Comedies. Ann Arbor, MI: University of Michigan Press, 1935.

Bloom, Donald A. "Dwindling into Wifehood: The Romantic Power of the Witty Heroine in Shakespeare, Dryden, Congreve, and Austen." Look Who's Laughing: Gender and Comedy. Ed. Gail Finney. New York, NY: Gordon and Breach, 1994. 53-80.

Cazamian, Louis. "Dryden, Sir William Temple." The Development of English Humor. Durham, NC: Duke University Press, 1952, 396-400.

Corman, Brian. " 'The Mixed Way of Comedy': Congreve's The Double-Dealer. Modern Philology 71.4 (May, 1974): 356-365.

Guilhamet, Leon. "Dryden." Satire and the Transformation of Genre. Philadelphia, PA: University of Pennsylvania Press, 1987, 71-99.

Hume, Robert D. "Marital Discord in English Comedy from Dryden to Fielding." The Rakish Stage: Studies in English Drama 1660-1800. Carbondale, IL: Southern Illinois Univ. Press, 1983, 176-213.

Hunt, Leigh. "Dryden." Wit and Humour. New York, NY: Folcroft Library, 1972, 241-254.

L'Estrange, Alfred Gu. "Rochester--Buckingham--Dryden--Butler." History of English Humour. New York, NY: Burt Franklin, 1878, 271-302.

Levin, Harry, ed. Veins of Humor. Cambridge, MA: Harvard University Press, 1972.

Loftis, John. "Dryden's Comedies." John Dryden. Ed. Earl Miner. Athens, OH: Ohio Univ Press, 1972, 27-57.

McDonald, Margaret Lamb. The Independent Woman in the Restoration Comedy of Manners. Salzburg, Austria: Institut für Englische Sprache und Literatur/Universität Salzburg, 1976.

Moore, Frank Harper. The Nobler Pleasure: Dryden's Comedy in Theory and Practice. Chapel Hill, NC: Univ of North Carolina Press, 1963.

Neilson, William Allan. Webster's Biographical Dictionary Springfield, MA: G. and C. Merriam, 1971.

Ritchie, Jeffrey. "John Dryden." Encyclopedia of British Humorists, Volume I. Ed. Steven H. Gale, New York, NY: Garland, 1996, 333-337.

Walker, Hugh. "Classical Satire from Denham to Dryden." English Satire and Satirists. New York, NY: J. M. Dent, 1925, 145-165.

Watson, George, ed. "Of Dramatic Poesy" and Other Critical Essays. London, England: Oxford University Press, 1962.

Wilcox, John. The Relation of Molière to Restoration Comedy. New York, NY: Columbia Univ Press, 1938.

Winn, James Anderson. John Dryden and His World. New Haven, CT: Yale University Press, 1987.

John Locke (1632-1704)

John Locke evaluated the distinction between "Wit" and "Judgment," and he clearly came down on the side of "Judgment." For Locke, wit was an assemblage of ideas, while judgment was a discrimination of ideas; wit was done quickly, while judgment was done with care; wit demonstrated variety, while judgment demonstrated clarity; wit was for entertainment and pleasantry, while judgment was for truth and reason; wit showed the immediate picture, while judgment required a labor of thought; wit contained metaphors and allusions, and gaiety of fancy, while judgment contained empirical evidence, distinction, and severity of truth and good reason (Sitter 52).

> Locke's opposition of wit and judgment entails three major claims: (1) we can know and speak of things as they are; (2) we can (and should) speak naturally and literally; (3) we can (and should) speak without allusion. (Sitter 54-55)

Locke regrets that wit requires no "labour of thought," that it is not responsive to the rigor of "truth and reason," and that it is therefore so "accessible Duchesto all people" (Sitter 63).

John Locke Bibliography

Sitter, John. Arguments of Augustan Wit. New York, NY: Cambridge University Press, 1991.

Sir George Etherege (c1635-c1691)

Alfred Gu L'Estrange feels that the two courtiers Sir George Etherege and William Wycherly "ushered in the comic drama of the Restoration" (L'Estrange 303). There is very little humor in Etherege's principle plays; nevertheless, he does give some amusing sketches of the affectations of city life of his day. George Etherege was known as "Gentle George" or "Easy Etherege," and he is said to have been a "fop." In fact, he probably "painted the character of Dorimant in Sir Fopling Flutter from himself" (L'Estrange 303-304).

Thomas Fujimura suggests that the salient features of Etherege's comic writing include witty dialogue, a naturalistic view of man, and realistic technique. Although Fujimura feels that Etherege excelled as a writer, many critics disapproved of his realism and naturalism (Fujimura 86). Captain Alexander Radcliffe censured Etherege for a realism which he considered to be too "photographic." Fujimura feels that Etherege does not excel in the comedy-of-manners genre; but he does excel in his witty dialogue, his naturalistic content, and his realistic technique. His writings also contained a "malicious laughter" at fools, and a generally skeptical and libertine philosophy (Fujimura 87).

Etherege's first comedy was entitled, The Comical Revenge, or Love in a Tub (1664). This is a comedy of manners, whose principal character, Sir Frederick Frollick, has been compared to Congreve's Mirabell. "Sir Frederick is a gay gentleman, accomplished in the fashionable arts of Restoration society. His wit is revealed in epigrammatic prose, frivolity á la mode, and airy nothings said with incomparable grace" (Wilcox 73). Much of the comedy revolves around Sir Frederick's friends and servants, such as his ridiculous French valet, Dufoy. At times the stage is crowded with "low rogues intent on ill-gotten gain and ugly debauchery." In this way, The Comical Revenge conforms to English structure with multiple plots, a constant clamor onstage, and a mixture of genres--comedy of manners, heroic romance, and low comedy incidents (Wilcox 73). In The Comical Revenge the witty Lord Buckhurst helped Etherege gain the respect of the aristocratic Wits of his day. In this play, there are three comic plots: Wheadle and Palmer set plots against Sir Nicholas Cully, only to be outwitted themselves by the Truewit; Betty exposes Dufoy; and Sir Frederick and the Widow try to outwit each other in a series of "comical revenges" (Fujimura 87-88). Having vivacity, perspicacity, and malice, Sir Frederick can be defined as the "Truewit," but Sir Frederick does not always display refinement, and in fact he can be gross in his double-entendres (Fujimura 89). In contrast to Sir Frederick, the Widow is too warm and too generous to be a "Truewit." She lacks the perspicacity and the malice of a Truewit, so in truth, she is no real match for Sir Frederick. The combats between these two characters often degenerate into tricks ("comical revenges"); nevertheless, these verbal encounters are the best repartée the play has to offer, for although there is not much wit, there is a great deal of humor and spirit (Fujimura 91).

The Comical Revenge has three plots, high, middle, and low. The high plot is written in couplets and is based on love, honor, and confidants, as it tells about both Lord Beaufort's and Colonel Bruce's love for Graciana, and about the unrequited love that Graciana's sister, Aurelia, has for Bruce. The middle plot deals with Sir Frederick Frollick, Beaufort's cousin, who pursues the Widow Rich with very little conviction. The low plot deals with a rogue named Wheadle who is a friend of Sir Frederick's and Palmer. Wheadle is a card-sharp, who swindles a Cromwellian knight named Sir Nicholas Cully. The title of The Comical Revenge is based on an incident in which Betty, the widow's maid, lures Sir Frederick's valet, Dufoy, into a sweating tub because he has what was called in the seventh century "French disease" (Holland 21).

Many critics have assumed that Etherege was significantly indebted to Molière because The Comical Revenge was in the comedy-of-manners tradition; however, Wilcox points out that Etherege's play was written before most of Molière's plays. It is true that Etherege spent much of his early life in France, and that from 1658 to 1663 he was principally in Paris. It is also true that Etherege's French was as fluent as his English (Wilcox 74). It is also true that Etherege's plays have many allusions that show him to have been intimately acquainted with Parisian matters, and with the new school of French comedy. But one critic went so far as to suggest that what gave Etherege's The Comical Revenge its peculiar value and novelty was Etherege's having seen Molière's L'Etourdi, Le Depit Amoureux, and Les Précieuses Ridicules. However Wilcox suggests that the details of The Comical Revenge shows only general, and not specific, influences from the French (Wilcox 75).

Robert Markley suggests that in The Comical Revenge, Etherege was concerned with such mechanics of play writing as the character, structure, exits, entrances, farcical aspects of stage business such as getting Dufoy locked up into a tub, and convincing Davenant to accept this play for his performance. But Etherege was also concerned with four different aspects of comic style:

> As a means of individual expression; as his rewriting or adaptation of systems of theatrical signification that he could find in the comedies of Fletcher, Jonson, Shakespeare, and other predecessors; as the reflection--or refraction--of particular cultural codes of speech and behaviour that would be accessible to his audience; and as a comment upon the culture of which he and his audience were a part. (Markley 1)

Etherege's The Man of Mode was published in 1676. The cynicism of the author (Etherege) through his protagonist (Dorimant) is overshadowed in this play by the relationship of cleverness to fulfillment, so the evaluation of folly and vice is an intrinsically open question in this play, and can be resolved only by the details of the events themselves (Myers 76).

It is interesting to note that in discussing the subtitle of his book "Studies in the Comedy of Etherege, Wycherley, Congreve, Vanbrugh, and Farquhar," Henry Perry considers Etherege and Wycherley to be the only two writers of Restoration comedy, for Congreve, Vanbrugh, and Farquhar wrote chiefly during the reign of William III, and should more accurately, therefore, be termed "Orange Dramatists" (Perry x).

Sir George Etherege Bibliography

Brown, Harold Clifford, Jr. "Etherege and Comic Shallowness." Texas Studies in Literature and Language 16 (1975): 675-689.

Fujimura, Thomas H. The Restoration Comedy of Wit. Princeton, NJ: Princeton University Press, 1952.

Hayman, John G. "Dormimant and the Comedy of a Man of Mode." Modern Language Quarterly 30 (1969): 183-197.

Holland, Norman N. The First Modern Comedies: The Significance of Etherege, Wycherley, and Congreve. Bloomington, IN: Indiana Univ Press, 1959.

L'Estrange, Alfred Gu. "Comic Drama of the Restoration--Etheridge--Wycherly." History of English Humour. New York, NY: Burt Franklin, 1878, 303-311.

Markley, Robert. Two-Edg'd Weapons: Style and Ideology in the Comedies of Etherege, Wycherley, and Congreve. Oxford, England: Clarendon Press, 1988.

Myers, William. "Plot and Meaning in Congreve's Comedies." William Congreve. Ed. Brian Morris. London, England: Ernest Benn, 1972, 73-92.

Perry, Henry Ten Eyck. The Comic Spirit in Restoration Drama: Studies in the Comedy of Etherege, Wycherley, Congreve, Vanbrugh, and Farquhar. New York, NY: Russell and Russell, 1962.

Powell, Jocelyn. "George Etherege and the Form of a Comedy." Restoration Theatre. Eds. John Russell Brown, and Bernard Harris. New York, NY: St. Martin's, 1965, 43-69.

Underwood, Dale. Etherege and the Seventeenth-Century Comedy of Manners. Hamden, CT: Archon, 1969.

Wilcox, John. The Relation of Molière to Restoration Comedy. New York, NY: Benjamin Blom, 1938.

Zimbardo, Rose A. "Of Women, Comic Imitation of Nature, and Etherege's The Man of Mode." Studies in English Literature, 1500-1900 21 (1981): 373-387.

Thomas Traherne (c1637-1674)

Wilson Baroody feels that Thomas Traherne was the most optimistic of the metaphysical poets. Baroody can think of no poet who equals Traherne in the proclamation of joy, especially of the joys of heaven and earth. For Traherne, "every spire of grass is mine." Another person's clothes, even his colorful ribbon "is my joy by another worn." Traherne's attitude was that it is nice that other people wear beautiful clothing for his enjoyment since he would not be able to wear all of this clothing at the same time (Baroody 65-66).

Thomas Traherne Bibliography

Baroody, Wilson G. "Thomas Traherne and the Joys of a Child-Son-Heir." WHIMSY 2 (1984): 65-67.

Earl of Dorset (Charles Sackville)(1638-1706)

Charles Sackville was the Earl of Dorset, and was very much in the favor of Charles II, James II, and William. He was in fact one of the most accomplished courtiers of his day (L'Estrange 358). Most of his poems depict pastoral settings, and some of them, such as the following, are humorous:

> Dorinda's sparkling wit and eyes
> United, cast two fierce a light,
> Which blazes high, but quickly dies,
> Pains not the heart, but hurts the sight. (L'Estrange 359)

Earl of Dorset (Charles Sackville) Bibliography

L'Estrange, Alfred Gu. "Congreve--Lord Dorset." History of English Humour. New York, NY: Burt Franklin, 1878, 355-360.
Nelson, Timothy G. A. "The Rotten Orange: Fears of Marriage in Comedy from Shakespeare to Congreve." Southern Review--Australia 8 (1975): 205-226.
Snider, Rose. Satire in the Comedies of Congreve, Sheridan, Wilde, and Coward. New York, NY: Phaeton, 1972.

Aphra (Johnson) Behn (1640-1689)

In A Room of One's Own, Virginia Woolf considers Aphra Behn's career to have been a turning point for women authors.

> We leave behind, shut up in their parks among their folios, those solitary great ladies who wrote without audience or criticism, for their own delight alone. We come to town and rub shoulders with ordinary people in the streets. Mrs. Behn was...forced...to make her living by her wits.... She made, by working very hard, enough to live on. The importance of that fact outweighs anything that she actually wrote..., for here begins the freedom of the mind, or rather the possibility that in the course of time the mind will be free to write what it likes. For now that Aphra Behn had done it, girls could go to their parents and say, You need not give me an allowance; I can make money with my pen. (Woolf 66-67)

Catherine Gallagher considers Aphra Behn to have been England's "first professional female author" (Gallagher 23). Behn's writing was a combination of the commercial, the sexual, and the linguistic; because of her place in history, she presented herself to the world of English letters as "the professional woman writer as a new-fangled whore," a persona which Catherine Gallagher sees as having many functions in Behn's work: "It titillates, scandalizes, arouses pity, and indicates the vicissitudes of authorship and identity in general" (Gallagher 24). Angeline Goreau, one of Aphra Behn's biographers has pointed out that the seventeenth-century ear "heard the word 'public' in 'publication' very distinctly" (Gallagher 27). Aphra Behn became problematic for later women writers, because they had to overcome not only the bawdiness in Behn's real life, but they also had to overcome the author-whore metaphor she celebrated in her works, and her playful challenges to the possibility that women could write about their own lives and observations interestingly (Gallagher 41).

In the prologue to Behn's first play, The Forc'd Marriage; or, the Jealous Bridegroom (1671), Behn warns the audience that playwriting now requires the writer to add a new weapon (her wit) to her old weapon (her beauty) and that this "has become a means of extending and exerting female power" (Kinney 86). In making such statements as this, Aphra Behn is linking herself with contemporary feminist comedy in the following way:

> Despite the qualified nature of her comic rebellion, in her controversial women and their unorthodox behavior Behn still manages to sketch the outlines of what I would like to call a "countertradition" of comedy. In her shaping of women characters and especially in her frank portrayal of women's sexuality, she prefigures contemporary British comedy by women, a comedy that still more clearly asserts a tradition of its own. (Carlson 128)

In a gambling scene of Behn's The Lucky Chance (1686), Gayman has won 300 pounds from Sir Cautious, and is willing to stake this money against something that Sir Cautious owns:

SIR CAUTIOUS: I wish I had anything but ready money to stake; three
         hundred pound, a fine sum!
GAYMAN: You have moveables Sir, goods, commodities.
SIR CAUTIOUS: That's all one, Sir. That's money's worth, Sir, but if I
         had anything that were worth nothing.
GAYMAN: You would venture it. I thank you, Sir. I would your lady
         were worth nothing.
SIR CAUTIOUS: Why so, Sir?
GAYMAN: Then I would set all 'gainst that nothing. (Gallagher 39)

Gallagher notes that in seventeenth-century slang, the word "nothing" was a word for female genitals. Then Gallagher adds that "one's wife is this nothing because in the normal course of things she is not a commodity" (Gallagher 39).

Florinda and Hellena are the "virtuous" women in The Rover (1709). They are both under the control of their father, who has planned their futures in advance. Hellena is to take her vows and enter into a nunnery. Florinda is to be married to an unattractive aristocrat. In the course of the play, however, Hellena and Florinda both extricaste themselves from the control of their father and assert their love and sexual attractions to their respective lovers and prospective husbands. The audience approves of their victories (Kinney 88).

Aphra (Johnson) Behn Bibliography

Carlson, Susan. Women and Comedy. Ann Arbor, MI: University of Michigan Press, 1991.
Gallagher, Catherine. "Who Was that Masked Woman? The Prostitute and the Playwright
    in the Comedies of Aphra Behn." Last Laughs: Perspectives on Women and

Comedy. Ed. Regina Barreca. New York, NY: Gordon and Breach, 1988. 23-42.
Kinney, Suz-Anne. "Confinement Sharpens the Invention: Aphra Behn's The Rover and
    Susanna Centlivre's The Busie Body." Look Who's Laughing: Gender and Comedy.
    Ed. Gail Finney. New York, NY: Gordon and Breach, 1994. 81-98.
Woolf, Virginia. A Room of One's Own. New York, NY: Harvest-Harcourt, 1929.

William Wycherley (1641-1716)

William Wycherley's father sent William to France at the age of fifteen to study
with the Marquise de Rambouillet, the forty-year-old leader of a group of French
aristocratic women known as "Les Précieuses." The marquise was a friend of Vincent
Voiture, of Pierre Corneille, and of Armand Richelieu, and the marquise and her group
were constantly getting together for amateur theatricals, colloquia, and ballets. This group
of "précieux" encouraged young writers, promoted many research programs, and in general
fostered intellectual excellence; however, they had an exaggerated sense of their own
accomplishments, and they fell into habits of affectation. This is the group that Molière
was describing both in his Les Précieuses Ridicules, and in his Les Femmes Savantes, and
this is the group which had a profound influence on William Wycherley's formative years
(Bruce 36-37). Wycherley's shrill tone was very similar to that of the Elizabethan satirists
(Clark 1229).
        Wycherley was a libertine; however, there are some critics who feel that he loathed
the life that he led; however, such critics must overlook the constant libertinism of
Wycherley's life and his works. In the 1704 and 1728 editions of his poetry there are
many libertine verses, and it appears that at no time does he appear to disapprove of these
values. Furthermore, Wycherley calls various Christian dogmas into question in The Plain
Dealer (ca 1674), and the clergy are frequently the target of Wycherley's satire.
> The only standard that Wycherley accepted was the naturalistic one,
> according to which the one great sin is the sin against nature. Thus, his
> "satire" was directed against "preciseness" (a punctilious insistence on
> honor), false wit, and coxcombry, rather than against violations of morality.
> (Fujimura 119)
William Wycherley is very interested in skeptical and sexual wit, in comic wit or raillery,
and he is also very interested in his own reputation as a Wit. A close examination of
Wycherley's life and work reveals that he has the qualities of a "Truewit," since he is
libertine, skeptical, naturalistic (Fujimura 119). Widow Blackacre in The Plain Dealer is
a good example of a false wit. She is very litigious, as she forges her life out of the cruel
business of claims, writs, briefs, subpoenas, and lawsuits (Clark 1229).
        Since Wycherley was a Truewit, he chose Truewits as his friends as well--John
Dryden, Sir George Etherege, the Earl of Dorset, the 2nd Duke of Buckingham, the Earl
of Rochester, Samuel Butler, John Dennis, and Alexander Pope. In his "Upon the
Impertinence of Knowledge, the Unreasonableness of Reason, and the Brutality of
Humanity; proving the Animal Life the most Reasonable Life, since the most Natural, and
most Innocent," Wycherly questioned the superiority of mankind over the animal kingdom.
Wycherley felt that the reasonable life was the natural life, and he advised men to follow
nature. Because of his naturalistic bias, Wycherley was skeptical of the supernatural;
nevertheless, religion was a compelling subject to Wycherley even though he was not
devout. Wycherley was not an atheist, but he didn't know what type of religion he wanted
to espouse. As a child he was a Protestant, but he converted to Catholicism as a youth;
then he reconverted to Protestantism, and finally died a Catholic. Wycherley said that
Churchmen "believe that they believe, and so make others believe what they themselves do

not; since their actions contradict their faith, and the flesh is generally observed to get the better of the spirit" (Fujimura 123).

Wycherley's first play was entitled Love in a Wood, or St. James's Park (1671). It is here that Wycherley's love of maxims becomes well known, maxims like "The jealous, like the Drunkard, has his Punishment with his Offence" (Bruce 38). The Duchess of Cleveland and the Duke of Buckingham both liked Love in a Wood (Neilson 1603). Love in a Wood is a play filled with wits and fops, and much of the humor comes from their various ploys and complications (Clark 1229).

Because of his appearance, Wycherley was called "Brawny Wycherley." The Duchess of Cleveland was so captivated by Wycherley's appearance that she went out of her way to make his acquaintance by passing by him in her carriage. Their carriages actually collided in Hyde Park, and the duchess jocosely called out that Wycherley was the "son of a whore," a witty allusion to a song the Duchess had just heard in Wycherley's play (Fujimura 120; L'Estrange 304). Being always civil, Wycherley made a gallant reply, and continued by getting permission to call on her the next morning (Bruce 39). After this incident, the Duchess of Cleveland was said to have visited Wycherley quite often at a Temple. During these rendezvous, she is said to have worn a straw hat on her head, patterns on her feet, to have carried a basket on her arm, and to have been in general disguised as a country girl (L'Estrange 305). It is interesting that for a time William Wycherley and Charles II were sharing the same mistress (Bruce 39).

T. W. Craik feels that Wycherley was primarily a satirist.

> His satire is not intended to be more than a source of amusement for his fashionable audience, and does not spring from a consistently moral view as does that of Jonson and Molière in their best plays.... These moral flaws reveal that his real interest was theatrical effectiveness for which he was content to lose the greater world of the truly senior comedians. (Craik 179; Lara 155)

Wycherley's writing contains much sprightly dialogue. He also entertained his readers with tricks, deceptions, and misadventures of lovers. In his "Gentleman Dancing Master" (1672), a comedy of intrigue, a young lover visits a rich man's daughter by pretending to be teaching the daughter how to dance. However, there is a rival lover, described by Alfred Gu L'Estrange as "a Frenchified puppy," who is made unconsciously to support the dancing master's cause at his own expense, while the duped father jokes with the dancing master, and goes so far as to ask him whether or not he is engaged to one of his rich pupils. Saying this, the father laughs heartily at the word-picture he is painting about the other father's indignation if this is the case.

In The Country Wife (1675), Wycherley describes a jealous husband (Jack Pinchwife, the husband of Margery) who locks up his wife to keep her a close prisoner, and who obligates his wife to write a disdainful letter to another gentleman who is after her affections. The lady, however, slyly substitutes a letter of quite a different character, which the husband pompously delivers to the lover. Alfred Gu L'Estrange notes that most of Wycherley's humor is of this nature.

> Here are no verbal quips, no sallies of professed fools, no stupidities of country boobies. These have passed away from good comedy. Speaking of the change, he says that formerly they were content to make servingmen fools on stage, "but now you shall scarcely see a fool on the stage who is not a knight." (L'Estrange 306)

But although The Country Wife does not contain verbal quips, it does contain verbal insights, and these are discussed in detail in Alice Rayner's "Wycherley's Aphorism: Delight in Dystopia." Margery Pinchwife, for example, says "I did not care for going; but when you forbid me, you make me, as 'twere, desire it" (Rayner 61). Rayner suggests that this statement might provide a lesson not only to critics, but to jealous husbands as well, but the real importance of this statement is the insight it gives into Restoration thinking. "As an indifferent object collects special interest once it becomes a forbidden object, so Restoration comedies collect special critical questions by exploiting special moral taboos" (Rayner 61). The character Horner illustrates this principle. It is ironic that Horner, a self-proclaimed eunuch, would have his way with other husbands' wives. The Restoration audience delights in the play's rupturing of the conventions of sexual morality and punishment, but the play's indulgence against restriction leaves the audience in a quandry of guilt and satisfaction. The debauched characters are attractive to the audience; their satiric punishments are slight, ambiguous, and incomplete, and that is just what the Restoration audience requires (Rayner 61). Aesthetically, the audience admires Horner, as The Country Wife continually jostles it between moral disapproval and astonished admiration. The play "dares the audience to take it seriously, but repels all attempts to do so" (Rayner 79). The significance of Quack in the play is basically to help "spread the rumor of Horner's impotence and to confirm it to the husbands at the end of the play." It is ironic that "the saddest eunuch is the greatest rogue" (Rayner 79-80).

> The collapse of seeming and being into one image is both morally offensive and formally wonderful. And because no justice is finally imposed on Horner, because he will continue the deception, there seems no end to the collapse; the game will continue, breaking all the rules of the real world. (Rayner 80)

Rayner goes on to say that the humor The Country Wife depends on our sense of these rules. "We must know that deception, hypocrisy, rampant lust are essentially antisocial or we will not laugh at their rupture" (Rayner 80).

One of the funniest scenes in The Country Wife is an episode regarding "china." Horner is a philanderer who aspires to have sexual relations with any and every woman he can "lay his hands upon." Horner's main ploy in the seduction of women is his collection of china which he keeps concealed behind a screen. Women flock to see and to ogle over his enviable and desirable collection of chinaware and he allows them to handle the pieces, and even to own a piece of it for themselves. In this way, Wycherley manages to satirize not only Horner, but the entire Restoration comic mode of which he is a part (Clark 1229). It is ironic that Wycherley was not only a master of the Restoration comic mode, but he was also a master of savage parody of that same mode (Clark 1230).

Wycherley is a master at aphorism, as can be seen in the following examples from The Country Wife: "Good Wives and private soldiers should be ignorant;" or "'Tis my maxim, he's a fool that marries, but he's a greater that does not marry a fool;" or "Mistresses are like books. If you pore upon them too much, they doze you, and make you unfit for company, but if used discreetly, you are the fitter for conversation by 'em;" "Women and fortune are truest still to those that trust 'em;" and "Any wild thing grows but the more fierce and hungry for being kept up, and more dangerous to the keeper" (Rayner 67). All of these aphorisms are spiced with irony; for Wycherley and for other writers of Restoration comedies, irony was an attitude, not a content.

> Although these speeches gain some grace from apt comparisons and witty turns, they are absolute and nonnegotiable nonetheless. They are assertive speeches, expressing no doubt, rarely qualifying themselves, often not moving the action forward.... The aphorism, as its etymology suggests, "divides a territory" and puts "boundaries on the horizon...." The aphorism, moreover, is the linguistic version of the Restoration acting style of self-display. Taking a position down front and center, the actor makes a leg, strikes the pose, and delivers. (Rayner 68)

Erich Segal gives an example of Schadenfreude in Wycherley's Plain Dealer (1674)

"I wonder...that young fellows should be so dull, as to say there's no humor in making a noise, and breaking windows! I tell you there's wit and humor too in both." (V.ii)
Segal points out that in Restoration comedy "wit" very often referred to cruelty and cynicism. He considered the word "wit" to have been unrefined during the time of Wycherley. In fact, during that time, "wit" was used to describe almost any antisocial act (Segal 78). In 1704 Wycherly published his Miscellany Poems: As Satyrs, Epistles, Love-Verses, Songs, Sonnets, Etc. in London (Clark 1230).

Wycherley distinguishes between many different kinds of wit, all of which are endowed with a certain cunning:

> Your court wit is a fashionable, insinuating, flattering, cringing, grimacing fellow, and has wit enough to solicit a suit of love; and if he fail he has malice enough to ruin the woman with a dull lampoon; but he rails still at the man that is absent, for all wits rail. (L'Estrange 306-307)

He considers all wits to be rakes, and therefore he is not at all certain that a woman can be both witty and virtuous. He goes on to describe the "scribble wit," and the "judge wit or critic" (L'Estrange 307).

Wycherley was a master of hyperbole. His best characters are the ones that are the grossest and the most excessive. His characters include holier-than-thou gossips, scandal-mongers, doltish fops, empty-headed beaux, fortune hunters, slanderous jades, gruff and surly misanthropes, and self-proclaimed whoremasters, and many of them exhibit French or Spanish manners in their flirtations, jilts, and money-grubbing. John Clark says that these strong archetypes pushes the comedy into the realm of biting satire (Clark 1230).

William Wycherley Bibliography

Bruce, Donald. Topics of Restoration Comedy. New York, NY: St. Martin's Press, 1974.

Clark, John R. "William Wycherley." Encyclopedia of British Humorists, Volume II. Ed. Steven H. Gale, New York, NY: Garland, 1996, 1227-1231.

Cohen, Derek. "The Revenger's Comedy: Female Hegemony in The Country Wife." Atlantis 5 (1980): 120-130.

Connely, Willard. Brawny Wycherley: First Master in English Modern Comedy. London, England: Kennikat Press, 1969.

Craik, T. W. "Some Aspects of Satire in The Country Wife." English Studies 41 (1960), 179.

Fujimura, Thomas H. The Restoration Comedy of Wit. Princeton, NJ: Princeton University Press, 1952.

Holland, Norman N. The First Modern Comedies: The Significance of Etherege, Wycherley, and Congreve. Bloomington, IN: Indiana Univ Press, 1959.

L'Estrange, Alfred Gu. "Comic Drama of the Restoration--Etheridge--Wycherley." History of English Humour. New York, NY: Burt Franklin, 1878, 303-311.

Lara, Manuel José Gómez. "Discurso Ironico en The Country Wife." Literary and Linguistic Aspects of Humour. Barcelona, Spain: Univ of Barcelona, 1984, 155-161.

Markley, Robert. Two-Edg'd Weapons: Style and Ideology in the Comedies of Etherege, Wycherley, and Congreve. Oxford, England: Clarendon, 1988.

Neilson, William Allan. Webster's Biographical Dictionary. Springfield, MA: G. & C. Merriam, 1971.

Perry, Henry Ten Eyck. The Comic Spirit in Restoration Drama: Studies in the Comedy of Etherege, Wycherley, Congreve, Vanbrugh, and Farquhar. New Haven, CT: Yale Univ Press, 1925.

Rayner, Alice. "Wycherley's Aphorism: Delight in Dystopia." Comic Persuasion: Moral Structure in British Comedy from Shakespeare to Stoppard. Berkeley, CA:

University of California Press, 1987, 61-80.

Segal, Erich. "Marlowe's Schadenfreude: Barabas as Comic Hero." Veins of Humor. Ed. Harry Levin. Cambridge, MA: Harvard Univ Press, 1972, 69-92.

Terry, Sam G. "The Comic Standard in Wycherley's The Gentleman Dancing-Master." Enlightenment Essays 6 (1975): 3-11.

Vernon, P. F. "Wycherley's First Comedy and Its Spanish Source." Comparative Literature 18 (1966): 132-144.

Zimbardo, Rose A. Wycherley's Drama: A Link in the Development of English Satire. New Haven, CT: Yale University Press, 1965.

Thomas Shadwell (c1642-1692)

The arrogant Thomas Shadwell was an imitator and worshiper of Ben Jonson; Shadwell was also John Dryden's enemy and satirical target. But the fact that Shadwell's plays remain to the present time challenge Dryden's charge that they were dull (Wilcox 117).

Shadwell's realistic comedy was an imitation not only of Jonson, but of Molière as well (Wilcox 117). The plot of Molière's comedy-ballet entitled Les Fâcheux involved Eraste, the lover of Orphise, who, in his attempts to see her, is constantly interrupted by a dozen different types of bores, each representing a particular stereotype in French society. Shadwell's The Sullen Lovers (1668) has basically the same plot, but with fewer bores, and therefore more character development. Furthermore, Shadwell's bores are based on English stereotypes rather than French. Shadwell's Stanford is a morose and melancholy man who is tormented so much by the bores that he resolves to leave the world in order to be rid of them. A friend of Stanford's, is Love, "who gets recreation by laughing at these same impertinents and at Stanford's misanthropic hatred of them" (Wilcox 118). Emilia and Carolina are the female counterparts of Stanford and Love respectively.

> The play centers in the same situation as Molière's, the manners are vulgarized, the speeches are occasionally obscene, but the deft imagination of Molière is missing; on the whole, however, it contains the same social criticism and develops it by the same method. (Wilcox 118)

Wilcox concludes the comparison by saying that "it ranks fairly high as an adaption of Molière" (Wilcox 119).

Shadwell's second comedy, The Humorists, was published in 1670, and is based on the Duke of Newcastle's The Humorous Lovers, published in 1667. Shadwell's character named Crazy is a lover of all women. His other characters include a witty coxcomb, a vain fop, a verbose parson, a French surgeon, an amorous old lady, a silly city woman, a vain Wench, and a busy bawd. Contrasted to these there are a gentleman of wit and honor, and a witty young lady both alluded to in the play's title (Wilcox 119).

As the name suggests, Shadwell's The Miser (January of 1672) is based on Molière's L'Avare. After The Miser came Epsom Wells (December of 1672). Here, Shadwell shifted in the direction of wit (Wilcox 119). John Wilcox feels that Shadwell was justified in rating Epsom Wells high among his plays. The social attitudes in this play were characteristic of the best comedies of the time, and the play exhibits the "humors" of Jonson's time. The characters and the action both follow English traditions. In the play, Raines and Bevil are matched with Carolina and Lucia to provide the social norm of Restoration wits of both sexes. Kick and Cuff are what Wilcox calls "cowardly pretenders to the rank of gentlemanly rakes" (Wilcox 120). In this play, as in most English comedy after Jonson, the shams of social pretenders are contrasted with the elegant manners of people who are more socially secure (Wilcox 120).

Shadwell's comic opera <u>Psyche</u> was published in 1675. In the prologue, Shadwell says that he wrote the opera in only five weeks, and that it was therefore a very bad opera, then adding about his critics,

But none of them yet so severe can be,

As to condemn this Trifle more than [me]. (Wilcox 121)

In 1675 Shadwell published <u>The Libertine</u> which had a fatal ending even though the treatment was essentially comic. This play was based on Molière's <u>Le Festin de Pierre</u>, which was itself based on the Don Juan legend (Wilcox 121). During the next eighteen years of his life, Shadwell published nine more comedies. His <u>The Squire of Alsatia</u> (1688) is as original as any plays of that period; however, "the fact that he did borrow previously seems to have led critics to assume a wholesale plagiarism where none existed" (Wilcox 122). In <u>Bury Fair</u> (1689) Shadwell develops the characters of Mr. Oldwit, a truly witty gentleman, and his friend Sir Humphrey Noddy, a perpetrator of practical jokes and absurd puns (Wilcox 122). Shadwell's last play to contain a convincing parallel to Molière is <u>The Amorous Bigot, with the Second Part of Tegue O'Divelly</u> (1690). This play is a "potboiler of little merit." It contains "a great many tested dramatic devices from Shadwell's own works and from others" (Wilcox 125). Talking about the alleged borrowings of Shadwell, Wilcox concludes:

> Shadwell produced fourteen comedies in all. Two of these, <u>The Miser</u>, and <u>The Libertine</u>, are successful adaptations of French plays, the first of which is.Molière's. <u>The Sullen Lovers</u>, <u>Bury Fair</u>, and <u>The Amorous Bigot</u> show positive use of his work. The other nine cannot be placed on the list of proved borrowings, although they contain vague resemblances called positive reminiscences by the credulous. (Wilcox 126)

Wilcox goes on to suggest that even Shadwell's borrowings made a contribution to the development of English humor. "Apparently under the inspiration of Molière, he set forth social ideas contrary to the Restoration notions. Despite these influences Shadwell was sturdily British, and his best work is, viewed largely, a continuation of pre-Restoration English comedy" (Wilcox 126). Wilcox would therefore not agree with Alfred Gu L'Estrange's assessment of Shadwell's written contribution when he said, "If Shadwell had burnt all he wrote, and printed all he spoke, he would have had more wit and humour than any poet" (L'Estrange 295).

Thomas Shadwell Bibliography

Corman, Brian. "Thomas Shadwell and the Jonsonian Comedy of the Restoration." <u>From Renaissance to Restoration: Metamorphoses of the Drama</u>. Eds. Robert Markley and Laurie Finke. Cleveland, OH: Bellflower, 1984, 126-152.

L'Estrange, Alfred Gu. <u>History of English Humour</u>. New York, NY: Burt Franklin, 1878.

Wilcox, John. "Thomas Shadwell." <u>The Relation of Molière to Restoration Comedy</u>. New York, NY: Columbia Univ Press, 1938, 117-126.

Earl of Rochester (John Wilmot)(1647-1680)

The Reverend Alfred Gu L'Estrange may be damning with faint praise when he indicates that John Wilmot, Earl of Rochester "might have produced something good." L'Estrange continues by saying, "His verses have more traces of poetry and humour than we should expect from a man who out of the thirty-four years of his life, was for five of them continually drunk" (L'Estrange 292). John Wilmot and his friend Sir George Etherege preferred hackney coaches to rooms of state, and their writing clearly shows that they preferred the "harmless lusts of the town" to the "ambitious designs of Princes." In a 1676 letter to his friend George Savile, Wilmot wrote, "They who would be great in our little government seem as ridiculous to me as schoolboys who with much endeavor and some danger climb a crab-tree, venturing their necks for fruit which solid pigs would disdain if they were not starving" (Weber 49).

Hugh Walker considers John Wilmot and John Oldham to be more noteworthy than were other satirists of their time. Although he was a genius, Wilmot wasted his talents in a licentious Court. The truth about Wilmot may not have been as bad as his reputation, but his life was nevertheless filled with shame and disgrace that were typical in the circles to which he belonged. His most notable piece of writing is entitled A Satire against Mankind, and it illustrates his excellent, but profoundly skeptical Roman and perverted writing abilities (Walker 147). This Satyr against Mankind is a poem in which the author defines "wit" or "right reason." In this poem, Wilmot uses subtle imagery, faulty logic, and juxtaposition to trick the reader into identifying with a persona who is guilty of the very hypocritical "wit" he condemns.

> Inherent in this irony is Rochester's real point: that the reader is also hypocritical, believing himself to be the only rational human being. The parson is more clearly revealed to be an irrational religious fanatic, but the major persona's argument is just as extreme. The two speakers, then, represent two extremes, both confident, one an ascetic parson, the other a Hobbesian cynic. For the poet, the answer lies in the moderate position that implicitly lies between the two extremes, and ironically, in much of the persona's speech. (Thompson 67)

Donald Bruce suggests that Rochester's descent from his society in his late satires was "outright and clamorous," even though his earlier satires had been relatively mild. A Letter from the Town to the Country is a satire about the prostitution of love by promiscuity.

> Here Rochester militates against himself and his own earlier standards. In the character of Corinna, Rochester represents the self-betrayals of a woman who followed the libertine mode as he had followed it himself. The poem, On Charles II, which shades over into the ferocious moral satires, has a gloss of bonhomie upon it which does not really conceal its contempt. There are three intensely felt moral satires by Rochester: A Satire on Mankind, A Ramble in St. James's Park (which Professor Sola Pinto rightly calls a powerful and indecent poem), and the unfinished poem generally known as Rochester's Farewell. (Bruce 26)

About these satires, Donald Bruce says, "They have the force of Jeremiah inveighing against Jerusalem, of Juvenal pounding at the city of Rome with piled-up loathing, of Dante prowling the lurid cinders of the Inferno. Rochester was a Pharisee who had chosen to live in Babylon" (Bruce 27). Bruce continues, "Rochester has often been compared, in his failed idealism, to Milton's Satan; and certainly the devil was, after all, a fallen angel" (Bruce 28).

Earl of Rochester (John Wilmot) Bibliography

Bruce, Donald. Topics of Restoration Comedy. New York, NY: St. Martin's, 1974.
L'Estrange, Alfred Gu. "Rochester--Buckingham--Dryden--Butler." History of English Humour. New York, NY: Burt Franklin, 1878, 271-302.
Thompson, Lou. "The Joke's on Us: Rochester's Exploitation of Reader and Persona in 'A Satyr against Mankind'." WHIMSY 2 (1984), 67.
Walker, Hugh. English Satire and Satirists. New York, NY: J. M. Dent, 1925.

Weber, Harold. The Restoration Rake-Hero: Transformations in Sexual Understanding in Seventeenth-Century England. Madison, WI: University of Wisconsin Press, 1986.

Index

About the Author

DON L. F. NILSEN is Professor of English Linguistics at Arizona State University and Executive Secretary of the International Society for Humor Studies. His previous books include *Humor Scholarship: A Research Bibliography* (Greenwood, 1993) and *Humor in Irish Literature: A Research Guide* (Greenwood, 1996).

ISBN 0-313-29706-1

90000>

EAN

9 780313 297069

HARDCOVER BAR CODE